ON POETRY:
Collected Talks and Essays

ON POETRY:
Collected Talks and Essays

by Robert Graves

Doubleday & Company, Inc., Garden City, New York

1969

Foreword

The first six of these pieces were given as the Clark Lectures at Cambridge University in the year 1954.

The next four, beginning with *Dr. Syntax and Mr. Pound,* were essays published in *Punch, The Hudson Review, Encounter* and *The New Statesman.*

The next four were talks: *Legitimate Criticism of Poetry* given at Mount Holyoke College; *The White Goddess* at the YM-YWHA Poetry Center, New York; *Sweeney Among the Blackbirds* at the University of Texas; *Pulling a Poem Apart* at the Chicago Arts Center.

The last sixteen, beginning with *The Dedicated Poet* were mostly lectures given at Oxford University where I held the Chair of Poetry from 1961–66. The three exceptions are *Poetic Gold,* a talk to the Oxford University Philological Society; *The Word "Báraka",* an address to the American Academy and Institute of Arts; and *The Poet's Paradise,* a talk to the Oxford University Humanist Society.

If occasionally I repeat myself, this is only natural: when enlarging on a discovery made way before, a lecturer cannot expect his audience to have read and remembered the book in which it first appeared.

Earlier talks and essays on poetry will be found in *The Common Asphodel* (1949). To include them would have made this bulky book even bulkier.

Deyá, Mallorca, Spain   R.G.

Contents

ON POETRY:
Collected Talks and Essays

The Crowning Privilege

Unlike stockbrokers, soldiers, sailors, doctors, lawyers, and parsons, English poets do not form a closely integrated guild. A poet may put up his brass plate, so to speak, without the tedious preliminaries of attending a university, reading the required books and satisfying examiners. A poet, also, being responsible to no General Council, and acknowledging no personal superior, can never be unfrocked, cashiered, disbarred, struck off the register, hammered on 'Change, or flogged round the fleet, if he is judged guilty of unpoetic conduct. The only limits legally set on his activities are the acts relating to libel, pornography, treason, and the endangerment of public order. And if he earns the scorn of his colleagues, what effective sanctions can they take against him? None at all.

This difference between the poetic profession and others may seem platitudinous, but I shall insist on it all the more strongly; because what English poets have always been free to enjoy, if they please, is the privilege of not being formally enrolled as such. Where is there any official roll of poets, analogous to the Army and Navy Lists, the Medical Register, or *Crockford*? This general privilege, as I understand it, implies individual responsibility: the desire to deserve well of the Muse, their divine patroness, from whom they receive their unwritten commissions, to whom they eat their solitary dinners, who confers her silent benediction on them, to whom they swear their secret Hippocratic oath, to whose moods they are as attentive as the stockbroker is to his market.

I do not, of course, suggest that every English poet has always been sensible of this crowning privilege, or even aware that the Muse has a real existence—as real, for her devotees, as Karl Marx's existence, or Freud's, or Aquinas's, to theirs.

And it may be asked what right I have to formulate the principles governing the professional conduct of poetry. I have no prescriptive right at all; and it must be clearly understood that I am not speaking *ex cathedra*. The function of a guest lecturer, as I understand it, is merely provocative. Besides, gratitude for not being enrolled in any organized society of poets prevents me from suggesting that I may voice the opinion of even a minority of my fellows. What I have to offer for your scrutiny are personal principles, deduced for my own guidance from a long study of poems and poets. Whoever finds them too subjective may correct them or formulate others.

First, then, to consider the economics of the poetic profession: an interesting theme, because it should not really arise and yet has become a stock subject of debate in Bloomsbury pubs, the more cultured weeklies, and certain philo-philanthropic cultural uplift organizations. When I was twelve or thirteen years old my father asked me: "What are you going to be, my boy?" I answered: "A poet." His inevitable reaction was: "Splendid, but what will you do for your bread and butter?" Fresh from my history class on the French Revolution, I found myself answering improvidently: "I shall eat cake." "Oatcake?" asked my father in a kindly voice.

Yes: I ate oatcake for some years, and liked it—I had a Scottish grandmother.

A soldier or sailor draws his pay; a parson draws his stipend, eked out with Sunday collections "for church expenses"; a doctor or lawyer draws his fees; and I who was once young and am now old have never seen a stockbroker forsaken, or his seed begging bread. But, as my father pointed out, one well-known peculiarity of the poetic profession is that the poet cannot expect to support himself by it. My father, himself a poet, earned his bread and butter as one of Her Majesty's Inspectors of Schools.

In most professions the size of a man's income is a fairly reliable criterion of worth: no inefficient soldier or sailor can hope to draw the pay of a Field-Marshal or Admiral of the Fleet. It is seldom either by chance or by favour that a particular Q.C. or Harley Street surgeon earns a thousand guineas a year more than his fellows. And, as for parsons, such high intellectual and executive qualifications are demanded nowadays from Bishops, Deans, and Canons, however saintly, that the extra loaves and fishes accruing to them need no apology. Among poets, however, the income test works in reverse: make a comfortable living by writing poems and you risk being treated with derision. The argument runs: "Poetry does not pay, consequently what you sell is not poetry." And I agree that there seem to be few exceptions to this rule.

The terms of the Clark bequest forbid me to deal with English literature before Chaucer; yet a few flash-backs would probably be in order, to provide the necessary historical data for the post-Chaucerian scene. In Anglo-Saxon times, grants of land, or money-presents in lieu of land, were given to poets by kings and princelings. These gifts were made, it seems, because the presence of a poet at Court was an ancient tradition of royalty (like the healing of diseases by the laying on of hands) that had lasted over from earlier times. And although no written records survive, anthropologists will, I think, allow me to assume an original situation, back in the neolithic age, when the king enjoyed no executive power, being merely a sacred consort of the queen and under her magic tutelage. The queen appointed druids, or oak-men, skilled in magical charms, to stand constantly by the king's side and ensure that no accidental breach of royal taboo on his part—by eating beans, touching a dog, wearing a knot in his clothes, and so on—could endanger the safety or fertility of the realm. King and druid owed allegiance to the sovereign goddess incarnate in the queen—the goddess who was still nostalgically invoked in Classical Greece by the *Homeridae*, as the Muse—meaning the Mountain-goddess.

The revolutionary usurpation by the All-Father Wotan, or Odin, or Gwydion, of the throne occupied by the variously-named Northern All-Mother, parallels the triumph of All-Father Zeus over the variously-named Mediterranean All-Mother. In the course of the second millennium B.C. the sacred king, after first being occasionally permitted to deputize for the queen and wear her robes, broke the shackles of taboos—how strong they were can be judged from ancient Welsh, Irish, Roman, and more recent African analogies— and instituted armed patriarchalism. He became the most powerful individual of his tribe rather than the sacred ritual leader; and, thereafter, instead of persuading his people to the right behaviour which his own sacrificial example exemplified, he sustained the social order by giving summary commands to his henchmen. Thus the druids became court bards, whose function was no longer to guide, protect, and cherish the king, but merely to celebrate his temporal power.

The earlier system continued in Ireland until historical times, having there been modified rather than superseded when the king turned warrior. His *ollamhs*, or druids, continued to enjoy a prolonged and intense training in the magical and poetic arts at a forest college. The *arch-ollamh* ranked in dignity next to the queen and acted as a vizier; his profession was endowed, his person was sacrosanct, and a gift for killing by satire made him the terror of the warrior class and even of the king. If the Church was slow to undermine his power, this was because Christianity had been introduced by eloquent and tactful missionaries, not (as elsewhere) at the point of the sword; and because the colleges of *ollamhs* accepted Jesus and his Mother as completing, rather than discrediting, their ancient theology. The Irish bishops, appointed at first by the kings, not by the Pope, were expected to sing low, and did sing low. They Christianized the Triple-goddess Brigit, patroness of poets, as St. Bridget, and her immemorial altar-fire at Kinsale was still alight under Henry VIII.

In Wales, where the Goddess was called Cerridwen, the change from paganism to Christianity came suddenly and violently: the North British Brythons, who entered North Wales with the fifth-century King Cunedda, were Christians. The pagan Goidelic *ollamhs* whom they turned out, and who seem to have been educated and organized in the Irish style, became wandering minstrels. At the Welsh Courts they were superseded by their own apprentices, young men who had not yet been initiated into the supreme religious mysteries. These low-grade bards (*bard* was a word of contempt in Ireland) were willing to embrace Christianity and accept the restrictions imposed on their art by the bishops; so that the Chief Bard eventually won a respectable place at the king's board— though below that of the royal chaplain, the chief falconer, and the steward of the table. A bard's task now was to honour God, praise the king, refrain from untruth (meaning any poetic reference to Cerridwen) and from hurtful satire.

The Anglo-Saxon invaders of England, on the other hand, had no organized colleges of *ollamhs*, nor even (so far as is known) any guild of saga-singers, like the Greek *Homeridae* who claimed the sole right of performing in public. Anyone might compose poems to the harp, if he could; and (this is the point that I want to make) it has fortunately been the same ever since among the English-speaking peoples. An Anglo-Saxon *scop* might inherit his father's stool and harp and repertoire; but his position at Court depended on the king's indisputable pleasure, and should he fail to hold it, he must turn wandering gleeman, to combine recitation with tumbling and mime in the country market places. His standing was far from high: *scop* (versifier) being a polite synonym for the pejorative word *scald*, which meant a "scold"—one who talks too loud and long. The *Deor*, an Early English fragment of about the year 600, preserved in the *Exeter Book*, witnesses to his social insecurity. It is a coda, attached to the Geatish saga-cycle (of which *Beowulf* also formed part) and summarizing the sufferings of the principal characters in the cycle. The refrain runs:

> Thaes ofereōde, thisses swā maeg.
> [That overpassing, this also may.]

The last verse, suddenly becoming personal, runs:

> Then I of myself/will this make known:
> That awhile I was held/the Heodenings' scop.
> To my duke most dear;/and Deor was my name,
> I performed many winters,/a worthy office
> For a handsome lord,/until Heorrenda,
> Being skilled in lays,/my land-right usurped
> Which the kingdom's strength/of old assigned me.
> That overpassing,/this also may.

Deor attempts no harmful satire on the handsome lord who had preferred another *scop* to himself. He merely registers disappointment and hopes that one day the loss will be remedied.

The Norman Conquest scotched the Anglo-Saxon tradition of the court-*scop*, and though Richard Coeur de Lion and Henry III employed a *Versificator Regis*—I suppose for rhymed chronicles, epitaphs and suchlike—at their Norman-French Courts, the office lapsed about a century before Chaucer's day. Chaucer did not revive it, nor did he even make poetry a wholetime profession. He was a valuable public servant with an entrée at Court secured by his marriage into the family of John of Gaunt, Richard II's uncle. Slavish commendations of royalty had not yet become fashionable. The *envoys* to Chaucer's shorter poems are dignified; he even dares lecture Richard II on what kingly conduct should be. Nor did he sue for royal bounty until late in life; and even then the humorous *Compleint to his Empty Purse* pays a most restrained court to Henry IV. He simply recognizes Henry as the rightful sovereign of the realm:

> To you, my purse, and to non other wight
> Compleyne I, for ye be my lady dere!
> I am so sory, now that ye be light;
> For certës, but ye make me hevy chere,
> Me were as leef be leyd up on my bere;
> For whiche un-to your mercy thus I crye:
> Beth hevy ageyn, or ellës mot I dye!

Now voucheth sauf this day, or hit be night,
That I of you the blisful soun may here,
Or see your colour lyk the sonnë bright,
That of yelównesse haddë never pere.
Ye be my lyf, ye be myn hertës stere,
Quene of comfort and of good companye:
Beth hevy ageyn, or ellës mot I dye!

Now purs, that be to me my lyvës light,
And saveour, as doun in this worlde here,
Out of this tounë help me through your might,
Sin that ye wole nat been my tresorere;
For I am shave as nye as any frere.
But yit I pray un-to your curtesye:
Beth hevy ageyn, or ellës mot I dye!

Lenvoy de Chaucer
O conquerour of Brutës Albioun!
Which that by lyne and free eleccioun
Ben verray king, this song to you I sende;
And ye, that mowen al our harm amende,
Have minde up-on my supplicacioun!

Henry filled the purse at once, but in recognition of Chaucer's non-poetical services: as Clerk of Works, Comptroller of the Wool and Petty Customs, diplomat, and secret-service agent.

Gower, Chaucer's contemporary, also had close relations with the King, and did not depend on him for money; he seems to have preferred Court pleasures and honours to the dull routine of a Kentish landowner's life. But, his social position being perhaps less secure than Chaucer's, he wrote courtly praises of Richard II in his *Confessio Amantis* (the subject of which was set him by Richard himself); and, his spirit being less noble than Chaucer's, recast these in Henry IV's favour when Richard abdicated.

Lydgate's case is instructive and exceptional. Though Chaucer wrote solely for his own pleasure, and Gower had been glad to adopt Richard's suggestion of a poetic theme, Lydgate was forced (apparently against his will) to become a sort of scholarly *Versificator*

Regis. The rules of his Order compelled every monk to unthinking obedience; so Henry V commissioned Lydgate, through his superior, to translate Giovanni delle Colonne's 30,000-line *Historia Trojana,* which took eight years; then the Earl of Warwick called him to Paris in 1426 to turn into English a French poetical pedigree proving Henry VI to be the rightful King of France. In the same year the Earl of Salisbury set him another translating task: the 20,000-line *Pélérinage de la Vie Humaine*—an allegory by de Guileville. Next, the Duke of Gloucester commanded him to translate Boccaccio's 36,000-line *De Casibus Illustrium Virorum,* an even more formidable commission. Lydgate records how unwelcome it was:

> Thus my self remembyring on this boke
> It to translate how I had undertake,
> Ful pale of chere, astonied in my loke,
> Myn hand gan tremble, my penne I feltë quake.
>
> I stode chekmate for feare when I gan see
> In my way how littel I had runne.

But he could not refuse the task, though it obliged him to resign his position at Hatfield Priory, where he had been educating young noblemen in the humane arts. A small yearly stipend was then granted him, by way of compensation, and he carried on with his hack duties until he died, pen in hand; though seven years earlier he had complained that his wits were long "fore-dulled."

John Skelton, a horse of a very different colour, tutored Prince Henry, afterwards Henry VIII, and they continued on friendly and even joking terms for many years. Henry's mother had given Skelton the cure of Diss in Norfolk to reward his conscientious tutorship and good influence on the unruly boy, and protected him while she lived. Skelton consented, as "Royal Orator," to write a Latin epitaph for her husband, Henry VII, ending this with a loyal address to her son. One of his earliest poems, the elegy *On the Death of the Noble Prince Edward the Fourth,* her father, is sincerely felt, extremely moving, and contains no single word of flattery:

Miseremini mei, ye that be my frendis!
This world hath forméd me downe to fall:
How may I endure, when that eueri thyng endis?
What creature is borne to be eternall?
Now there is no more but pray for me all:
Thus say I Edward, that late was youre kynge,
And twenty two yeres ruled this imperyall,
Some vnto pleasure, and some to no lykynge:
Mercy I askë of my mysdoynge;
What auayleth it, frendes, to be my foo,
Sith I can not resyst, nor amend your complaining?
Quia, ecce, nunc in pulvere dormio! . . .

Where was in my lyfe such one as I,
Whyle lady Fortune with me had continuaunce?
Graunted not she me to haue victory,
In England to rayne, and to contribute Fraunce?
She took me by the hand and led me a daunce,
And with her sugred lyppës on me she smyled;
But, what for her dissembled countenaunce,
I could not beware tyl I was begyled:
Now from this world she hath me excyled,
When I was lothyst hens for to go,
And I am in age but, as who sayth, a chylde,
Et, ecce, nunc in pulvere dormio! . . .

Skelton, despite the contempt of Pope and Milton, showed a stronger sense of poetic calling than almost any of his successors. It was as a poet, not as a priest, that he dared openly defy Cardinal Wolsey, Henry's right-hand man; for which bravado he spent the last six years of his life in confinement. The following *Merrie Tale of Skelton* reads authentically enough. He had ridiculed Wolsey for his lack of learning and presumption, and called him "cur and butcher's dog":

On a tyme Skelton did meete with certain frendes of hys at Charyng crosse, after that he was in prison at my lord cardynals commaundment: & his frende sayd, I am glad you bee abrode

amonge your frendes, for you haue ben long pent in. Skelton sayd,
By the masse, I am glad I am out indeede, for I haue been pent
in, like a roche or fissh, at Westminster in prison. The cardinal,
hearing of those words, sent for him agayne. Skelton, kneeling of
hys knees before hym, after long communication to Skelton had,
desyred the cardinall to graunte hym a boun. Thou shalt haue
none, sayd the cardynall. Thassistence desirid that he might haue
it graunted, for they thought it should be some merye pastime that
he wyll shewe your grace. Say on, thou hore head, sayd the cardynall
to Skelton. I pray your grace to let me lye doune and wallow, for
I can kneele no longer.

The medieval English court-poet, then, was not engaged as such
by the king; but just as there is a fat boy in every school (even if
he is not really very fat), and a funny man in every barrack-room
(even if he is not really very funny), so there was always a Court-
poet at Court, even if he was not much of a poet. Between
Gower and Skelton came the undistinguished John Kay and Andrew
Bernard. But not until the reign of Elizabeth could a talent for
verse-writing support an application for a place of trust. Then
Spenser—through Leicester's influence—secured a secretaryship in
Ireland, a country which he hated, hoping that if he could please
Elizabeth by his praises of her in the *Faerie Queene*, he would be
called to London. Unfortunately, before he had finished his task,
the rebellious O'Neils, unaware that he was a poet, turned Spenser
out of his castle. He returned, broken in health and purse, and
died soon after.

James I, who regarded himself as a critic of poetry, and wrote
an elementary handbook of prosody, recognized Samuel Daniel's
talent for verse by appointing him gentleman-in-ordinary. This encouraged Michael Drayton to panegyrize James, and even write a
sonnet commending his Royal Muse—a breach of professional dignity; but, as it happened, room could not be found for Drayton at
Court, so he crossly revoked the sonnet. In the next reign, pique
at being denied positions in the King's gift turned at least two
poets into the Puritan camp: Milton, because of the Royal Fellowship at Christ's which he thought should be his but which

was conferred on the original of "Lycidas"; and May, who was vexed at not being appointed Jonson's successor as Poet Laureate.

Since poets still had no guild, nor any traditional economic status, nothing—let me repeat—prevented noblemen or royalty itself from writing poetry. James IV of Scotland would be remembered as author of *The Gaberlunzie man,* even if Flodden had never been fought. And Henry VIII would be remembered for his love song *As the Holly Groweth Green,* even if there had been no breach with Rome. Wyatt, Surrey, Sidney, Oxford, Raleigh, and Queen Elizabeth herself were all poets.

It is an ancient tradition of the European feudal system that the lord does not demean himself by taking wages, under any circumstances; or by going into trade. He may march to war, sack towns, and hold fellow-knights to ransom, or he may stay at home and live on his rents; but he must never openly infringe the function of the merchant or artisan. In Greece, the poet ranked as an artisan, which is (I suppose) why Agamemnon, Odysseus, and Achilles never sang in public to a lyre; and why Peisistratus, the tyrant of Athens, contented himself with patronizing the *Homeridae* rather than being adopted a member of their guild. In England, until the invention of printing, the poet—if we except the wandering minstrel, who went round the country ale-houses with his store of ballads and an orphan (*vide* Sir Walter Scott) to carry the harp—did not expect to earn a living by his poems. There was as yet no publishing system to make this possible, and when finally the stationer (a publisher-cum-bookseller) set up shop, no copyright law at first protected the author. A poem was not a physical object of agreed value, liable to be stolen in the usual sense. Unless the author could prove theft of a manuscript book of poems (an obvious felony, because vellum had value, and copyists' fees were high), he had no cause for complaint if someone memorized and printed his poems.

Thus, to be a poet agreed with the code of nobility. When Tottell set the fashion of poetic anthologies, it was the stationer, not the poet, who profited; and after the Charter given in 1566 to the Stationers' Company (as a means for facilitating censorship) it was the stationer, not the poet, who held the copyright. Stationers, by the way, were so called because, unlike the book-peddlers, they kept stationary. Once Thomas Thorp had secured copies of Shakespeare's sonnets from the enigmatic Mr. W. H., and entered them at Stationers' Hall, Shakespeare was powerless in law either to prevent, or to profit from, their sale. It is possible that Shakespeare (shrewd businessman though he was in malt, hides, and real-estate) had sold the copyright of *Venus and Adonis* to the publisher who entered the volume at Stationers' Hall; but if so, he would not have advertised the fact. He was bound to keep his distance from the professional ballad-writers: low-born scoundrels who supplied the great public with the brief equivalent of Sunday newspapers, who seldom signed even their initials to what they wrote, and who did not dare claim poet's rank. Shakespeare satirized their patter in a well-known passage of his *Winter's Tale*.

If small poets of the day starved in garrets, that was because they had no patron and tried to live on hack-writing jobs at the playhouse, or among the stationers of St. Paul's Churchyard. Davenant in his *Long Vacation* records:

> Now man that trusts, with weary thighs,
> Seeks garret where small poet lies:
> He comes to Lane, finds garret shut;
> Then, not with knuckle, but with foot,
> He rudely thrusts, would enter dores;
> Though poet sleeps not, yet he snores:
> Cit chafes like beast of Libia; then
> Sweares, he'l not come or send agen.
> From little lump triangular
> Poor poet's sighs are heard afar.
> Quoth he, "Do noble numbers chuse
> To walk on feet, that have no shoose?"
> Then he does wish with fervent breath,
> And as his last request ere death,
> Each ode a bond, each madrigal,
> A lease from Haberdashers Hall,
> Or that he had protected bin
> At court, in list of chamberlain;
> For wights near thrones care not an ace
> For Woodstreet friend, that wieldeth mace. . . .

> In stockings blew who marcheth on,
> With velvet cape his cloack upon;
> In girdle, scrowles, where names of some,
> Are written down, whom touch of thumbe,
> On shoulder left must safe convoy,
> Anoying wights with name of roy.
>
> Courts pay no scores but when they list,
> And treasurer still has cramp in fist. . . .

Davenant concludes with:

> But stay, my frighted pen is fled;
> My self through fear creep under bed;
> For just as Muse would scribble more,
> Fierce City dunne did rap at door.

This is a joke on himself. Davenant was comfortably off, though he may have been overspending his income. And poetry as a gainful profession was not yet respectable. . . . Why did Elizabethan and Jacobean noblemen leave drama alone, apart from Masques and Interludes written for Court use, or for performance in their own courtly mansions? Because a peer might not engage in trade: and the Elizabethan theatre was a money-making concern.

This brings me to the subject of dedications. When Shakespeare, Drayton, Daniel, Donne, Chapman, and Jonson published their poems—though not their plays, which did not count as poetry, even if they were—the stationer expected them to supply a formal dedication, sanctioned by some person of honour and influence, as a means of selling the book. The buyer would read the dedication and say: "Hm! This is no bookseller's hack writing for profit. This is a true poet, a gentleman of breeding and substance, and on easy terms of friendship with the Earl of So-and-so." (Or with the Lord Chamberlain; or with the Countess of Such-and-such.) "The Queen herself would not disdain to cast her eyes on it. Here's my shilling." The buyer was satisfied, the bookseller delighted, the dedicatee flattered, and the dedicator did not think ill of himself.

Similarly, in Elizabethan times, when the feudal system still went creaking on, a poet who happened to be *sine nobilitate* (a phrase which, shortened to *s.nob* has, some say, given English the valuable word "snob") was obliged to secure a patron: much as a private soldier today cannot address an officer unless escorted by an N.C.O. Moreover, to gain recognition by the right people—unless he were a *nob*, without the preliminary *s*—the poet had to be either in holy orders or a gentleman. The courtesy of gentlemanly rank (eventually stabilized by the title *Esquire*) was accorded to all masters of art at Oxford and Cambridge, or members of the Inns of Court; which helped several leading dramatists in their social climb, though not Shakespeare. Shakespeare's position was equivocal, despite his eminence on the stage and his friendship with Southampton, Pembroke, and Essex. But he managed to secure a coat-of-arms for his father— which drew derisive hoots from the rival theatre—and thus became presentable at Court and even (as appears in a sonnet) eligible as a canopy-bearer on some State occasion.

One great difference between now and then is that to rank as a poet in the Elizabethan or Jacobean sense, a man must have published a longish work—such as *Venus and Adonis* and *The Rape of Lucrece*. With a few dozen sonnets he could also qualify. But a verse play, even one containing so many detachable poems as *The Tempest*, or *Hamlet*, or *Anthony and Cleopatra*, was considered irrelevant. And, whereas the poetry written today consists almost wholly of "lyrics"—lyrics without music—in Elizabethan times, every lyric had its music, but lyrics did not count as poems. Shakespeare wrote the lyrics for his plays; probably also the incidental songs required while properties were being shifted and the change of scene announced. (In my *Common Asphodel* I give evidence for supposing that the strange and beautiful poem *Loving Mad Tom* was Shakespeare's adaptation of a Bedlamite ballad, sung by Edgar in *King Lear* after his "Edgar I nothing am.") No dramatist felt obliged to be his own lyricist; any more than the matador at a Spanish bull-fight feels obliged to plant his own *banderillas;* though a few of the better matadors do so, and thereby improve the afternoon's performance. Shakespeare would have disdained to advertise: "*King Lear,* a tragedy by Mr. Wm. Shakespeare, with lyrics by the same hand." Nearly all the lyrics from the Elizabethan song books, among them some of the truest poems written in English, are anonymous. The musicians who arranged with the stationers to have their songs published gave the author of the words no printed credit. It is unknown who supplied Captain Tobias Hume with his:

> Fain would I change this note,
> To which false love hath charmed me.

Or Thomas Ford with:

> There is a lady sweet and kind,
> Was never face so pleased my mind.

Or Robert Jones with:

> And is it night? Are they thine eyes that shine?
> Are we alone, and here? And here, alone?

Or John Dowland with:

> Deare if you change, I'll never choose again;
> Sweet if you shrink, I'll never think of love.

—though it now seems likely that Dowland, like Campion, wrote his own lyrics. Even Henry Vaughan's authorship of *Yet if His Majesty, our Sovereign Lord,* in the manuscript collection of early music books at Christ Church, Oxford, must remain a surmise. Yet these poems were the work of highly educated men, not stationers' hacks. One of them, written for Thomas Weelkes:

> A sparrow hawk proud did hold in wicked jail
> Music's sweet chorister, the nightingale. . . .

is a literal translation from Hesiod; and the language of the Song Books never fails to be courtly. We may be certain that the lyricist asked no money for such "idle toys and trifles"; though the musician may have invited him to a venison pasty and a bottle of good wine, which would not compromise his amateur status. It had been the same with the medieval carols—a form originally introduced by Franciscan friars: to find an author's name attached to them is rare.

I have mentioned the laureateship. Skelton had been appointed "Royal Orator"; and he was also "Laureate" in the sense that he had won distinction for his Classical scholarship at Oxford, Cambridge, and Louvain. Ben Jonson had been similarly laureated: and the Crown did not venture to award its own laurel garland to a poet until 1638, when Charles I bestowed it on Davenant. Jonson's pension was a charitable one. Hearing that he had lost his library by fire, had suffered two paralytic strokes, and had seen his *New Inn* hissed off the stage, Charles increased the pension awarded by James I: in recognition not of Jonson's general poetic fame, but of his services to the Crown in the writing of Court Masques. It is noteworthy that Jonson refused the honour of knighthood offered him as a reward for his Masque *Gipsies Metamorphosed;* presumably because he thought that though a knight might become a poet, poetry was not honoured by the irrelevant accolade. He dismissed titles as "birdlime for fools"; and called poetry "The Queen of Arts, which had her original from Heaven."

Indeed, the only rewards in which a poet is properly entitled to rejoice are three. First, the sense that what he has written not only stands on all four feet, but has sufficient animation to walk away by itself, and perhaps go on walking long years after his death. Second, he rejoices if his worthy poetic contemporaries acknowledge this creative event—though the Elizabethan practice of writing "commendations" to the works of a fellow-poet, and even dropping them into his grave, has now lapsed. Last, and above all, he rejoices in the approval shown by the personal Muse for whom he has written the poem, however grudgingly her praise may be couched.

Ben Jonson, the first poet who lectured to his fellows on the subject of professional standards, died in 1637, just before the Puritan Revolution. The vacating of his chair in the *Apollo* room at the Old Devil's Tavern, the closing of the theatres, and the extinction of Merry England on the field of Naseby make a sharp break in this story. As an anonymous Cavalier wrote in a ballad called *The World Turned Upside Down:*

> To conclude, I'll tell you news that's right:
> Christmas was kil'd at *Nasebie* fight,
> Charity was slain at that same time,
> *Jack Tell-troth,* too, a friend of mine.

Poetry, also, had received a deep wound, from which the recovery was long delayed. 1645 is a convenient date for me to call a halt; but I trust I have made my point, which is that professional tradition, since Chaucer, prevents the English poet from letting any hopes of gain or of social advancement influence his work. This is not to say that he should refrain from offering his poems for sale as a means of circulating them, or that he should refuse assistance offered him for that purpose by friends or acquaintances. Only, he must not allow a private patron, or a publisher, the right to call the tune: by which I mean the right to decide how he shall write or what he shall write. To call the tune is the function of the Muse alone. Her demands are unforeseeable and ungainsayable; and her hand cannot be forced.

Let me enlarge on this. The legitimacy of accepting official honours for poetry may seem a moot point, but in my opinion, as in Ben Jonson's, they should be politely declined. It is not as though the Sovereign personally chose beneficiaries of Birthday or New Years honours. Both lists are prepared, under orders of the Cabinet, by a committee of political officials; and these have no more right to decide who is a true poet than the poet has to intervene in Cabinet meetings. The situation is made worse by the invidious sliding-scale of official honours conferred. Just as the Distinguished Conduct Medal was devised to enhance the dignity of the Victoria Cross (and, incidentally, to save the Crown the 6d. a day pension which went with it), and the Military Medal to enhance the dignity of the Distinguished Conduct Medal, so the Companionship of Honour was first devised to enhance the dignity of the Order of Merit; and inferior awards now enhance the dignity of the Companionship of Honour. Bestowal of a greater or lesser Order on a man for his supposed services to poetry—as opposed to scientific, military, or political services, which are more easily assessable and in the public domain—that is an act of criticism which no politician nor permanent civil servant has any right to make. Granted, Thomas Hardy, one of the most moral of poets, accepted the Order of Merit. But he knew that the award was conferred on him for his novels, which the Cabinet's advisers had read, rather than for his poems, which they had not; and, on the whole, Civil Servants are as likely to know a good novel from a bad as are professional reviewers or publishers' readers.

Thomas Hardy told me himself, when I stayed with him in August 1920, that he was not interested in the fate of his poems once he had written them.

(By the way, an amusing example of social distinction in the painting world is the certificate of merit awarded to an Associate of the Royal Academy: it is made out to, say, Timothy Dauber, Gent. When Dauber is elected a Member he goes up in rank: he is Timothy Dauber, Esq. I inquired into this, and was told that the "Gentleman" was originally a certificate of good conduct: that, if commissioned to paint a portrait, he could at any rate be trusted not to steal the silver or insult the chambermaids. The "Esquire," a certificate of elegant manners, gave him access to the drawing room.)

Professional standards in poetry, then, are founded upon the sense enjoyed by every English poet since the time of Chaucer, that he forms part of a long and honourable tradition. Usually he has contemporaries whom he can love and respect; thus it has meant a great deal to me that I once lived on terms of friendship with my elders Thomas Hardy and William Davies, and with men of my own age like Wilfred Owen and Norman Cameron—to name only the dead. It meant much to Keats and Darley that Coleridge had been kind to them, and to Swinburne that Landor had given him the poetic blessing he demanded. A sense of kinship with poets of an earlier age can be as strong as any contemporary bond; and I realize now how deep a professional influence my favourites have had upon me. Not only by the opinions they expressed, but by their behaviour and character; for who has ever successfully disguised his character in what he wrote?

I have never been able to understand the contention that a poet's life is irrelevant to his work—unless this means merely, as it did in the 1870's, that acceptance of the Thirty-Nine Articles, or membership of a reputable club, or an orthodox love-life, are not a *sine qua non* of literary eminence. If it means that a poet may be heartless or insincere or grasping in his personal relations and yet write true poems, I disagree wholeheartedly.

Nearly all poets make out a critical list of their favourites, convinced that they alone represent the authentic English tradition. Skelton's list occurs in *Philip Sparow*, fathered on Jane Scroop (the pretended authoress):

> Gowers Englysh is olde,
> And of no value told;
> His mater is worth gold,
> And worthy to be enrold.
>   In Chauser I am sped,
> His tales I haue red:
> His mater is delectable,
> Solacious and commendable,
> His Englysh well alowed,
> So as it is enprowed . . .
> At those days moch commended,
> And now men wold haue amended
> His Englysh, whereat they barke,
> And mar all they warke:
> Chaucer, that famous clerke,
> His termes were not darke,
> But pleasaunt, easy, and playne;
> No worde he wrote in vayne.
>   Also John Lydgate
> Wryteth after an hyer rate;
> It is dyffuse to fynde
> The sentence of his mynde,
> Yet wryteth he in his kind . . .
> But some men fynde a faute,
> And say he wryteth to haute. . . .

And in his *Garland of Laurel* these three poets, in beautiful apparel adorned with diamonds and rubies, lead Skelton to the Goddess's Temple. His only criticism of their works is that they all lacked sound Classical learning.

Ben Jonson's preferences occur in *The Return from Parnassus* (1601), and in his undated *Discoveries*. He lists:

> *Chaucer,*
> *Wyatt,*
> *Surrey,*
> *Spenser,*
> *Raleigh,*
> *Daniel,*
> *Drayton,*
> *Davies,*
> *Marlowe,*
> *Shakespeare,*

and, of course, Jonson himself. But he had changed his mind about some of these by 1619, when Drummond of Hawthornden records of him:

> . . . His Censure of English Poets was this, that Sidney did not keep a Decorum in making every one speak as well as himself.
> Spencer's stanzaes pleased him not, nor his matter, the meaning of which Allegorie he had delivered in Papers to Sir Walter Raughlie.
> Samuel Daniel was a good honest man, had no children, bot no poet.
> that Michael Drayton's Polyolbion (if had performed what he promised to writte the deeds of all ye worthies) had been excellent. His long verses pleased him not.
> that Silvesters translation of Du Bartas was not well done. . . .

William Browne, Jonson's contemporary, but rather more of a modernist, praises Sidney, Drayton, Ben Jonson, Daniel, Brook, Davies, and Wither. Milton as a young man wrote marginal comments on *The Pastorals*, apparently approving Browne's choice. He might have added to the list, with a certain disdain: "Sweetest

Shakespeare, fancy's child, warbling his native wood notes wild."
But probably not Chaucer, and certainly not Skelton, whom he
later mentioned in his *Areopagitica* among the authors who deserved total suppression:

> I name him not for posterity sake, whom Henry the 8th named
> in merriment his vicar of hell.

Milton called Skelton:

> One of the worst of men, who are both most able and most diligent
> to instil the poison they suck into the courts of princes, acquainting
> them with the choicest delights and criticisms of sin;

and refused to see the point of Henry's boyish joke: namely that
Skelton was Rector of Diss in Norfolk and that "Dis" is the Latin
for Hell.

Pope persuaded his contemporaries that nothing of consequence
had happened in English poetry until Denham and Waller introduced the French style—all before was rusty, rude, and low, or at
the best, quaint in the Spenserian style; just as (according to the
contemporary French theory) all French poetry, including Villon's,
had been until Malherbe. This apostasy caused a serious break in
English poetic education. The threads were eventually gathered up
again by Hazlitt and Coleridge, when it once more became possible
to read Chaucer, Skelton, and Shakespeare in the original, without
condescension, and realize that "Chauser, that famous clerke, His
terms were not darke, But pleasant, easy and playne, No worde he
wrote in vayne."

Today we are threatened by a new apostasy from tradition; which
has been my main reason for accepting the College's generous
invitation. I am not a born lecturer, nor even a very willing one;
but it seems to me that someone has to speak out, and nobody else
seems prepared to do so. My own preferences among the poets,
and my reasons for making them, will be clearly given.

If, in the course of this lecture, I have said anything out of order,
pray forgive me. I am a stranger here.

The Age of Obsequiousness

To resume my rambling commentary from 1645, when the English world got turned upside down at Naseby: four years later, King Charles was beheaded. This monstrous event silenced some honest poets for ever, among them Herrick, though he lived another quarter of a century and at the Restoration won back the benefice from which his Royalism had excluded him during the Commowealth. For when the Restoration came, no poet could follow the central English tradition of Chaucer, Skelton, and Ben Jonson. Hitherto professional standards had been approved at Court, and on the Court's return it was found to have gone all French. Charles and his boon-companions ruled that the age of poetical independence was over ("independence" having secured an evil name in the politico-religious context); and that the age of correctness, which in practice meant the Age of Obsequiousness, had begun.

Usually the European power with the strongest army sets the fashion in literary forms, as in clothes and domestic furniture. Spain had done so throughout the sixteenth century, and the Spanish *alto estilo* (advertised by Lyly and his colleagues as "Euphuistic wit") persisted in English prose until the early seventeenth century, when the Spanish Empire began to crack from overstrain. Then came the turn of the French. A brief intermediate phase of so-called "Metaphysical" poetry took Euphuistic wit one degree farther into nonsense, and so prepared the way for clean-cut French Classicism, which any commonsensical gentleman could understand and imitate. The metaphysicals were led by Abraham Cowley, a literary careerist who specialized in what Dr. Johnson afterwards called "enormous and disgusting hyperboles":

> By every wind that comes this way,
>   Send me at least a sigh or two:
> Such and so many I'll repay
>   As shall themselves make winds to get to you.

It had all been very well for Ovid, Cowley's mentor, to cut Latin poodle-fashion and put it through the circus hoops. Ovid cultivated a Hellenistic modernism, acceptable in Imperial Rome only because the dignified republican tradition had long lapsed. "Rome had now become a jack-daw's nest of promiscuousness and imprudent spoliation,"—Gibbon might have written, but didn't—"strange rites were celebrated in temples raised to enigmatic Eastern deities, and barbarian chieftains paraded Romulus's Forum equivocally wrapped in snowy togas." Cowley had no such excuse for his frivolities: London was not yet a metropolis of Empire. Despite Cromwell's military and naval successes, England remained a cool, green island off the north-western coast of Europe, frequented by few strutting Continentals, and with a vigorous native tradition of honour, decency, and straight speaking. Why then *meta*physicality? Why this rejection of the physical? Had Marlow, Shakespeare, Ben Jonson, and Webster written in vain? Far-fetched rhetorical tropes are not acceptable among the English, except for purposes of burlesque, or to overawe the simple—as Touchstone used them on clownish William in the Forest of Arden (quoting that "most capricious poet, honest Ovid"); or as, more recently, Dylan Thomas used them on gaping listeners to the Third Programme. Cowley's excuse was that he modelled himself on Donne, whom Ben Jonson had called "the first poet in

the World in some things," and who had written the oddly tortured *Elegy on the Untimely Death of Prince Henry*. Cowley was
perhaps unaware that Donne (according to Ben Jonson) confessed
to having written it as a jest: "to match Sir Edward Herbert in
obscureness."

Cowley's successor, Dryden, who consolidated Denham and Waller's so-called reforms in the simplifying of metres and diction, was
a vigorous time-server, the first of a gifted line of poets who made
Israel to sin. He earned the doubtful glory of having found English
poetry brick and left it marble—native brick, imported marble. Dryden
had begun his literary career as a metaphysical. His *Collected Poems*
start with the *Epitaph on Lord Hastings*, which he had not troubled,
in later life, either to suppress or to smuggle in among his *facetiae*:

> Must noble Hastings immaturely die,
> The honour of his ancient family,
> Beauty and learning thus together meet,
> To bring a winding for a wedding sheet?
>
> Was there no milder way but the small-pox,
> The very filthiness of Pandora's box?
> So many spots, like naeves o'er Venus' soil,
> One jewel set off with so many a foil;
> Blisters with pride swell'd, which through's flesh
>   did sprout
> Like rose-buds, stuck i' th' lily-skin about.
> Each little pimple had a tear in it,
> To wail the fault its rising did commit:
> Which, rebel-like, with its own lord at strife,
> Thus made an insurrection 'gainst his life.
> Or were these gems sent to adorn his skin,
> The cab'net of a richer soul within?

This is so well-known that I quote it only to fix attention on one
particular couplet, which is less grotesque than downright shocking:

> So many spots, like naeves o'er Venus' soil,
> One jewel set off with so many a foil. . . .

The filthy pustules rising on the peer's diseased body are compared to the halo, or ring of rosy dots, which enhanced the fresh beauty of Venus' breast.

Can a man who has once sinned so grossly against the Muse hope to redeem himself in her eyes by however spectacular a conversion? Mr. T. S. Eliot has recently published his *Homage to Dryden*. "Homage to Dryden" indeed! And Dryden's conversion from metaphysicality was not to the poetic faith of his English predecessors, but to current French theory—an axiom of which was that English poetry reflected confusion and barbarity. Louis XIV's consolidation of power made this theory almost irresistible, because Charles, who trusted in a French alliance, favoured only those English writers who looked to France for their salvation. Paris, in the imagination of the French Court poets (and therefore of Dryden's), was ancient Rome renewed; and London consequently became a Trans-Tiberine extension of Rome. Charles's leading courtiers modelled their licentious behaviour on the heroes of Petronius's *Satyricon* (first published in Padua and Paris, 1664) and on hints found in Suetonius's *Twelve Caesars*. Sedley, Buckingham, Rochester, and the rest cultivated a cynical, sycophantic, most un-English elegance, mocked at religion, faith, virtue, and humanity, as outmoded relics of Puritanism, and became adepts in the "mannerly obscene."

Charles rewarded Cowley with friendship for his long, grovelling *Ode upon His Majesty's Restoration and Return*. He also forgave Dryden, Waller, and Denham their panegyrics on his father's murderer. But it was the egregious Sedley whom he held up as a literary model. Charles's only dealings with Milton (whom I shall discuss later) were indirect: royal emissaries came secretly to Milton's modest house in Bunhill Fields, asking for legal information that would help them to steer the Lord Roos Divorce Bill safely through Parliament—for Charles wanted to divorce his barren Queen, as Milton had wanted to divorce poor Marie Powell.

There remains, of course, Andrew Marvell. Though finding it impossible at the Restoration to continue a poet in the romantic, sheltered, Appleton House vein, Marvell did not go French. He rejected Court fashions, made the still English city of Hull his spiritual home, not London, and thereafter confined himself to satire.

His wit, as in the *Coy Mistress,* was sometimes fantastical, but always robustly humorous. Though Marvell bore no grudge against kings as such, he regarded Charles II as a disaster, and his nostalgia for the Commonwealth derived principally from the great name that England had enjoyed in Europe while it lasted. His parody of a Speech from the Throne (1675—two years before he died) shows by its very moderation, and its closeness to the original, that he was still poetically sound in heart and head. This is Charles himself speaking, not a character of mock-heroic fiction:

> . . . My Lords and Gentlemen,
>
> . . . I can beare my own straits with Patience, but my Ld. Treasurer protests that the Revenue, as it now stands, is too little for us both; one of us must pinch for it, if you do not help us out. I must speak freely to you: I am under Incumbrances, for besides my Harlots in service my Reformado ones lye hard upon me. I have a pretty good Estate I confess, but Godfish, I have a great Charge upon it. Here is my Ld. Treasurer can tell you that all the Mony designed for the Summer Guards must of necessity be employed to the next Yeare's Cradles and Swaddling-Clothes. What then shall we do for ships?
>
> I only hint this to you, it is Your Business, not mine. I know by Experience I can live without them, I lived ten years without them abroad and was never in better health in my life. But how will you live without them you had best say; and therefor I do not intend to insist upon it. There is another thing which I must press more earnestly, which is, it seems a good part of my Revenue will fail in two or three Yeares, except you will be pleased to continue it. Now I have this to say for it, Pray why did you give me as much except you resolved to go on? The Nation hates you already, for giving me so much, and I will hate you now if you doe not give me more. So that now your interest obliges you to stick to me or you will not have a friend left in England.

The severance of poetry from the Court, emphasized by the sorry farce of the eighteenth-century Laureateship with its obligatory Birthday and New Year Odes, soon tempted noblemen to expect even more fulsome praise from their protégés than the Sovereign had once earned. Dryden's *Dedicatory Address to the Duke of Ormonde*

(1699) is remarkable only because it was written by so firm a hand
as his:

> My Lord,
> God Almighty has endued you with a softness, a beneficence, an
> attractive behaviour, winning on the hearts of others, and so sensible
> of their misery, that the wounds of fortune seem not inflicted on
> them, but on yourself. You are so ready to redress, that you almost
> prevent their wishes, and always exceed their expectations: as if what
> was yours, was not your own, and not given you to possess, but to
> bestow on wanting merit. But this is a topic which I must cast in
> shades, lest I offend your modesty, which is so far from being ostenta-
> tious of the good you do, that it blushes even to have it known: and
> therefore I must leave you to the satisfaction and testimony of your
> own conscience, which, though it be a silent panegyric, is yet the
> best. . . .

There are pages more of this. Dr. Johnson explains Dryden's case as
follows:

> The inevitable consequence of poverty is dependence. Dryden had
> probably no recourse in his exigencies but to his bookseller [Ton-
> son]. The particular character of Tonson I do not know; but the
> general conduct of traders was much less liberal in those times than in
> our own; their views were narrower, and their manners grosser. To
> the mercantile ruggedness of that race, the delicacy of the poet was
> sometimes exposed. Lord Bolingbroke, who in his youth had culti-
> vated poetry, related to Dr. King of Oxford, that one day, when he
> visited Dryden, they heard as they were conversing, another person
> entering the house. "This," said Dryden, "is Tonson. You will take
> care not to depart before he goes away: for I have not completed
> the sheet which I promised him; and if you leave me unprotected,
> I must suffer all the rudeness to which his resentment can prompt
> his tongue."
> What rewards Dryden obtained for his poems, besides the payment
> of the bookseller, cannot be known. Mr. Derrick, who consulted
> some of his relations, was informed that his Fables obtained five
> hundred pounds from the duchess of Ormond; a present not unsuit-
> able to the magnificence of that splendid family. . . .

"The inevitable consequence of poverty is dependence." Perhaps. But is the inevitable consequence of poverty, obsequiousness? That seems to have been the general theory in Dryden's day. A poet, to secure support and preferment from a nobleman, had to be both a gentleman and a party-man, responsive to the whip. And whether he chose to be Whig or Tory, it was presently ruled that he might not write anything "low"—as Chaucer had done in his *Miller's Tale,* Skelton in his *Elinor Rumming,* and Ben Jonson in his *Bartholomew Fair*—or offend against *decorum,* a magical word meaning any thought or expression unacceptable to contemporary French taste. What the reformed poets lacked was not exactly a schoolmaster (for Ben Jonson, from his chair in the *Apollo* room at the Old Devil's Tavern, had put his scholars through the poetic rudiments); it was a posture master. Dryden, who now assumed this office, gave his classes at Will's, a fashionable coffee-house. He acted as referee in all literary matters, deciding what might (or might not) be considered graceful, elegant, sublime, smooth, just, correct, or modeish. He rehabilitated Chaucer by tricking him up in buckled shoes, silk stockings, and a wig. Yet Dryden had learned his critical trade too late, and could himself be accused of inelegancies by the posture-masters of a later generation.

Thus Dr. Johnson again:

He had a vanity, unworthy of his abilities, to show, as may be suspected, the rank of the company with whom he lived, by the use of French words, which had then crept into conversation. . . .

His faults of negligence are beyond recital. Such is the unevenness of his composition, that ten lines are seldom found together without something of which the reader is ashamed. Dryden was no rigid judge of his own pages; he seldom struggled after supreme excellence, but snatched in haste what was within his reach; and when he could content others, was himself contented. He had more music than Waller, more vigour than Denham, and more nature than Cowley; and from his contemporaries he was in no danger. Standing therefore in the highest place, he had no care to rise by contending with himself; but while there was no name above his own, was willing to enjoy fame on the easiest terms.

At the turn of the century, a delicate and precocious boy, named Alexander Pope, persuaded some friends to take him to Will's and introduce him to Dryden. Pope seems to have decided at once that Dryden's position would suit him well and that he would gain it by hook or crook. He had escaped regular schooling since early childhood, and now set himself a course in modern English literature, paying special attention to Dryden and to translations from Italian, French, Greek, and Latin poetry. William Walsh, a critic of repute, told young Pope:

> . . . that there was one way left of excelling: for though we had several great poets, we never had one great poet that was correct, and desired me to make that my study and aim.

A neighbour then introduced Pope to the French critics, René le Bossu, René Rapin, and Boileau, whom he mugged up in the original. At the age of seventeen, being prevented by his Catholicism from conquering either of the Universities, he set out to conquer Town, and headed straight for Will's.

When I read English Literature at Oxford, my moral tutor reproached me for a report sent in by one of his colleagues: "It is suggested, Mr. Graves, that you prefer some authors to others." Well, I still hold that the whole period between, say, Marvell and Blake was poetically barren, except for a few resolute blades of green grass showing up here and there between the marble paving stones. By all means let historians of English literature consider *The Age of Dryden* and *The Age of Pope*. As Nature abhors a vacuum, so does literary history; and Dryden and Pope were certainly the dominant figures of their days. But (and this *but* is introduced by a great A, little a, bouncing B), English poets do not wear wigs; they wear their own hair—while it lasts. And the force inspiring them is love, controlled by reason; not rhetoric controlled by timidity; not correctness controlled by cynicism.

My father gave me a strictly Classical education, which meant that for several years I composed Latin verses once a week throughout term-time. Latin being a dead language, I could dissociate this classroom activity from the private writing of poems in my cubicle by the light of a pocket torch. I came of a large Victorian family and, at home, excelled in parlour games. This game of Latin Verse Composition challenged my wits. I had to be meticulous about quantity— I well remember the big *Male* I won, when I first started, for carelessly ending a hexameter composition on the diving-bell with the words *Bona Machina*.* And I had to make Virgil or Ovid my exemplars in metrical correctness. But more important still was the poetic vocabulary. If asked to versify: "Aeneas's fleet sailed north-east from Mt. Eryx to Italy," I learned to wrap it up like this, with the help of Smith's Classical dictionary: "Daedalus's tasteless honey-offering to the Dardanian leader's smiling grandmother having been left behind on the heathered couch of the Argonaut, the prows of destiny cleft the caerulean plain of Cronos's trident-armed son, slantingly impelled to the Ausonian shore by kindly bulging Favonian cheeks." The *Gradus ad Parnassum* suggested minor evasions of the difficulties provoked by an originally foreign metre—the natural Latin metre was the Saturnian; and if I doubted whether a word might be legitimate in poetry of the ironically named *Golden Age*, I could consult my *Lewis and Short*. So I learned exactly in what a *Gradus ad Parnassum* spirit eighteenth-century odes and pastorals were written; and how easy it was to compose mock-heroic satires on my Charterhouse Masters, from sheer boredom with the literary epic.

Here is Dr. Johnson on Pope:

> Alexander Pope was born in London, May 22, 1688, of parents whose rank or station was never ascertained: we are informed that they were of "gentle blood"; that his father was of a family of which the Earl of Downe was the head; and that his mother was the daughter of William Turner, Esquire, of York, who had likewise three sons, one of whom had the honour of being killed, and the other of dying, in the service of Charles the First; the third was made a general officer in Spain, from whom the sister inherited what sequestrations and forfeitures had left in the family. This, and this

* When I gave this lecture, my audience looked puzzled, and I had to explain that the proper scansion of these words was not *bŏnă măchĭnă*, but *bŏnă măchĭnă*.

only, is told by Pope; who is more willing, as I have heard observed, to show what his father was not, than what he was. It is allowed that he grew rich by trade; but whether in a shop or on the Exchange was never discovered, till Mr. Tyers told, on the authority of Mrs. Racket, that he was a linen-draper in the Strand. Both parents were Papists.

Dr. Johnson then mentions Pope's deformed body, his rigorous self-education and his megalomania: "as he confesses, he thought himself the greatest genius that ever was." The schemes and shifts by which Pope made himself not merely a posture-master, but a dictator, are common knowledge. He began by disclaiming any originality—his *Windsor Forest* was an avowed imitation of Denham's *Cooper's Hill;* and by inspiring pity and making full use of his one physical asset, a beautifully modulated voice, to secure introductions to the nobility and the chief literary figures in London: Wycherley, Congreve, Addison, and the rest. As Dr. Johnson notes: "Pope was through his whole life ambitious of splendid acquaintance." And the more splendid it became, the cooler grew his relations with the less splendid.

Up the ladder went this sedulous ape, continually turning about to bite and scratch those below him. He reached the top triumphantly with the *Dunciad,* which he flattered Sir Robert Walpole into laying before the King and Queen—though he later changed the hero-victim from Lewis Theobald to the King's own Laureate, Colley Cibber. A new departure: hitherto poets had felt themselves bound by a sacred tie, despite occasional "flyting" matches, staged as a tournament of wit. Ben Jonson had voluntarily jailed himself in the company of colleagues who expected to be docked of their ears for treason; and showed himself as generous in his praise of contemporaries as just in his censure. Nobody had ever thought of securing the Prime Minister's support for a general libel on humbler colleagues.

Pope, not having a University degree, solved his social problems by claiming gentle birth, on however doubtful grounds, and then bestowing his patrician praise on men like "low-born Allen" of Bath, who had achieved fame despite their plebeian origins. He solved his economic problems by the subscription list—persuading friends to rope in subscribers for a translation of the *Iliad* (though he knew practically no Greek), and later for a translation of the *Odyssey* (which he used ill-paid hacks to help him complete). With the large sums of money that accrued he bought annuities, representing a high rate of interest on the capital, and could thereafter afford to despise the "unabashed Defoe" and other low hand-to-mouth writers. To set a good moral example he complained:

> Chaucer's worst ribaldries are learned by rote
> And beastly Skelton Heads of Houses quote . . .

But to show that he himself was beyond criticism, he published a smutty—"smutty" is the exact word—*Imitation of Chaucer*, "done by the author in his youth." And the extraordinary thing is that, as a technician even in the limited field to which he confined himself, Pope was an extremely poor one.

If I had time, I should be charmed to take you line by line through any long poem of Pope's you pleased, demonstrating its technical incompetency when judged by the standards of his predecessors and successors. Pope has no control of his *s*'s, he does not sufficiently vary his vowel sounds, his antitheses are forced, his poetic vocabulary inexact, his inversions of syntax are not only un-English but misleading. As a test of my opinion, while preparing this lecture, I opened *Pope's Works* at random, and came across this six-line passage from his *Imitations of Horace*. It should have been carried through three more drafts at least.

> Let Envy howl, while Heaven's whole chorus sings,
> And bark at honour not conferred by Kings . . .

Envy and *Heaven*, like *howl, while,* and *whole,* are too close in sound to occur decently in the same line. *Howl, Heaven,* and *whole* are over-alliterative. *Chorus sings* is not as tuneful as the sense requires. The suggested antithesis between the Heavenly Chorus and royal honours can hardly be intended.

> Let Flattery sickening see the incense rise
> Sweet to the world and grateful to the skies. . . .

Pope's s's are quite out of hand here. And does he mean that Flattery sickens others, or that Flattery itself falls sick? And if the latter, was this sickness antecedent to the sight of rising incense, or due to it?

Do "the skies" mean merely the sky, to which the fumes ascend, as opposed to earth; or do they mean God's Heaven, as opposed to this world of men? And is the incense a flattering incense, or is it an incense which all devout Catholics, like Pope, are required to burn?

> Truth guards the poet, sanctifies the line
> And makes immortal, verse so mean as mine.

The incense, *the* world, *the* skies, *the* poet, *the* line! Five *the's* in nineteen words. Pope could never control his definite article. And does "the line" stand for the lines of a poet's verse, or the line of succession—as he uses it three couplets later. *-fies the line* is ugly. *Makes immortal, verse so mean as mine* is over-alliterative again, and the inversion of "makes verse so mean as mine immortal" calls for an awkward comma to separate *immortal* from *verse*—otherwise the sense would be: "And makes even immortal verse as mean as mine."

The Dunciad (its revision provoked by a fancied slight from Cibber in the matter of a stage-crocodile) was supposedly aimed at dullness. But is anything duller in the world than the ideal of correctness, even if not seriously framed?

One result of Pope's largely successful attempt to put contemporary verse into a straight-jacket of which he held the key (and buried this in his coffin at Twickenham), was the virtual disappearance of personal Muses. Skelton had honoured his Jane Scroop; Donne his Anne More—though he never mentioned her by name, and laid a curse on anyone who thought he knew it; Ben Jonson his Lady Venetia Digby, of whom he wrote at her death:

> 'Twere time that I dy'd too, now she is dead,
> Who was my Muse, and life of all I sey'd.
> The spirit that I wrote with, and conceiv'd,
> All that was good, or great in me she weav'd,

> And set it forth; the rest were cobwebs fine,
> Spun out in name of some of the old Nine,
> To hang a window or make darke the roome,
> Till swept away, th' were cancell'd with a broome!

By the rules of Ben Jonson's *Apollo Room*, "chosen women" (*lectae feminae*) might not be debarred from entry; but what woman of reputation would have been admitted to Will's Coffee House sixty years later? Romantic love, forbidden by the Puritans as a seduction and snare, was disavowed at the Restoration in favour of a rakish carnality. It is a long way from Dowland's—if it was Dowland's—*"Deare, if you change, I'll never choose again,"* to Rochester's modeish lines:

> All my past life is mine no more,
>   The flying hours are gone,
> Like transitory dreams given o'er,
> Whose images are kept in store
>   By memory alone.
>
> The time that is to come, is not;
>   How can it then be mine?
> The present moment's all my lot,
> And that, as fast as it is got,
>   Phillis, is only thine.
>
> Then talk not of inconstancy,
>   False hearts, and broken vows:
> If I by miracle can be
> This live-long minute true to thee,
>   'Tis all that heaven allows.

The true lover was unmasked, as he has been unmasked again today by Doctors Freud and Kinsey; and Pope's rider, that

> Every woman is at heart a rake . . .

was tacitly accepted for the next hundred years to excuse men for treating women as, at best, an amusing, if irksome, sexual convenience. Martha Blount may have been Pope's mistress, or even his wife (though this is only a surmise), and became his residuary legatee; but she does not figure in his poems and is not even implied by them, however shadowily.

So, although the age abounded in impersonal Chloes, Amandas, and Belindas, the only personal Muse I can recall was Swift's Stella. Swift may seem to be joking to his *To Stella Visiting Me in My Sickness* (1720), when he writes:

> Pallas, observing Stella's wit
> Was more than for her sex was fit,
> And that her beauty, soon or late,
> Might breed confusion in the state,
> In high concern for human-kind,
> Fix'd *honour* in her infant mind. . . .
>
> And lest we should for honour take
> The drunken quarrels of a rake;
> Or think it seated in a scar,
> Or on a proud triumphal car,
> Or in the payment of a debt
> We lose with sharpers at picquet;
> Or when a whore in her vocation
> Keeps punctual to an assignation . . .
> Let Stella's fair example preach
> A lesson she alone can teach . . .
> Ten thousand oaths upon record
> Are not so sacred as her word:
> The world shall in its atoms end,
> Ere Stella can deceive a friend.

But Swift is earnest. My old friend Richard Ashe King once remarked:

> I do not envy the man who is untouched by the infantile prattle of Swift's *Journal to Stella*—written in the intervals of his dictating the policy of England at home and abroad—or who is unmoved by the white-hot agony of his anxiety during her illness, or of his anguish after her death.

Dryden had told Swift at Will's: "Cousin Jonathan, you will never be a poet!" And indeed, Swift never did become a poet of the Age of Obsequiousness. Like Defoe, Fielding, Dr. Johnson and other writers known for their generous hearts and incorruptible character,* he renounced poetry in favour of prose: except for the composition of trifles. But these trifles, though darkened by a morbid horror of man's physical circumstances, demonstrate the proper use of English: they are clear, simple, inventive, pungent, unaffected, original, generous, utterly outspoken.

A plea can be made on Pope's behalf that Swift counted him in the first rank of his friends. But even this plea, I think, fails. Pope seems to have exerted all his charm on Swift; knowing how cruelly Swift's pen would have scorched him up if it had come to a quarrel, but how readily he could be won over as a loyal and industrious ally by a pretence of sincere friendship. It was only when Swift's wits began to fail that Pope showed the true quality of his friendship. He routed out Swift's early letters to himself and amended them in his own favour, as he had done with Wycherley's.

No, I am not altogether ungrateful to the eighteenth century. I pay the tribute of a sentimental sigh to such pleasant simplicities as John Newton's:

> There is a land of pure delight
> Where saints immortal reign;
> Infinite day excludes the night
> And pleasures banish pain.
>
> There everlasting Spring abides
> And never-withering flowers.
> Death like a narrow stream divides
> That heavenly land from ours.

* Defoe's intelligence work first for the Tories, then for the Whigs (after 1714) while the Tories thought him still their man, proves a sense of humour rather than a failure in integrity.

and Richard Graves's:

> Upon the bridge's coping-stone
> The loitering boy doth lean alone,
> And watches with a steadfast look
> The falling waters of the brook. . . .

as I remember certain pleasant eighteenth-century wallpapers, and formal gardens, and silk handkerchiefs, and magnificent chairs and sets of table silver. Also, one would have to be hard-hearted indeed to dislike either Gray or Collins. But for any sense of personal poetry (except in Swift who was, of course, educated at Kilkenny School and Trinity College, Dublin; and Goldsmith, another Irishman) one must adventure among scribblers and dunces. Goldsmith is exceptional because he had roved about in low company through several countries, rambling and gambling his money away, and would no sooner have thought of buying an annuity than of committing murder. Besides, *The Deserted Village,* despite its air of formality, is a true poem; because, like Swift, Goldsmith was in earnest. He was offering, disguised as an essay on the break-up of English village society, a lament for the ills of Ireland, modelled on contemporary Irish minstrel songs —walk, description, meditation, moral vision, invocation of the Goddess; even the distressful crone is there, and the damsel who tears out her hair in handfuls. Auburn really lies in County Roscommon; the poem is full of personal recollections, and glows with sorrowful anger.

Eighteenth-century scribblers and dunces wrote such splendid drinking-songs as:

> Here's a health to the King and a lasting peace,
> To faction an end and to wealth increase,
> O come let us drink it while we have breath,
> For there's no drinking after Death;
> And he who will this health deny
> Down among the dead men let him lie!

And there were low-life ballads, such as *Wednesbury Cocking,* to set your hair on end; I should like to recite the whole of the

Cocking, because I have it by heart, but have time only for the serene opening verses:

> At Wednesbury there was a cocking,
>   A match between Newton and Scroggins;
> The colliers and nailers left work,
>   And all to old Spittle's went jogging.
> To see this noble sport,
>   Many noblemen resorted;
> And though they had but little money,
>   Yet that little they freely sported.
>
> There was Jeffery and Colborn from Hampton,
>   And Dusty from Bilston was there;
> Flummery he came from Darlaston,
>   And he was as rude as a bear.
> There was old Will from Walsall,
>   And Smacker from Westbromwich come;
> Blind Robin he came from Rowley,
>   And staggering he went home.

And there was Defoe's *True Born Englishman:*

> The *Royal Refugee* our Breed restores,
> With *Foreign Courtiers,* and with *Foreign Whores:*
> And carefully repeoples us again,
> Throughout his Lazy, Long, Lascivious Reign;
> With such a blest and True-born *English* Fry,
> As much Illustrates our Nobility . . .
> *French* Cooks, *Scotch* Pedlars, and *Italian* Whores,
> Were all made Lords, or Lords' progenitors.
> Beggars and Bastards by his new Creation,
> Much multiply'd the Peerage of the Nation;
> Who will be all, e'er one short Age runs o'er,
> As *True-Born* Lords as those we had before.

This brings me to the problem of satire. Poetry has always had two hands, the left and the right; the left for cursing and the right for blessing, as there is a right-handed and a left-handed wor-

ship of the Goddess Khali in India; and as, among the Moham-
medans, the left hand undertakes certain tasks from which the right
shrinks. Yet it is axiomatic that the right hand must be used to
bless only what deserves blessing, and that the left may curse only
what deserves cursing. Marvell's satire was legitimate, because generous. Samuel Butler's satire in *Hudibras* was legitimate, because he
had served under the Puritan colonel whom he ridicules, and been
forced for years to swallow back his Royalist spittle. Defoe's satire
was legitimate: he had been abused as a foreigner by "True-Born
Englishmen." And though he may be blamed for indicting a whole
nation with:

> . . . France,
> Where mankind lives in haste, and thrives by chance,
> A dancing nation fickle and untrue
> Have oft undone themselves and others too. . . .

the times required that this should be jokingly said. But Pope's satire
was patently illegitimate, because neither provoked nor generous.
Professional standards in English, as opposed to Continental, poetry,
have for centuries insisted that satire should not reflect private rancour
or hope of personal gain. Swift understood this well enough, perhaps because the principle was first formulated in Ireland.

I shall now leave Twickenham and Grub Street—eventually dis-
infected of its associations by being renamed "Milton Street"—
and take you over to ancient Connaught. My excuse will be the
elucidation of Rosalind's phrase in *As You Like It*: "I have never been
so berhymed since I was an Irish rat." Rosalind was referring to a
seventh-century satire, *The Proceedings of the Grand Bardic Academy*, which was not translated into English until some ninety years
ago. I have no notion by what chance she, or Shakespeare, came to
hear of it.

The satire describes how three hundred professors and students
of the Grand Bardic Academy, led by the Chief Bard Seanchan, son
of Torpest, abused the munificent hospitality of Guaire, King of
Connaught, with the threat of satire if he refused them anything;
until one Marvan, the Royal Swineherd, took vengeance on them

for this blackmail, and for their murder of his own gifted white pig. Marvan's pig was no ordinary pig, but had been at once his physician, his music-maker and his messenger; and the murder lay at the door of the professor's greedy old foster-mother, who would not be satisfied until Guaire presented her with a great collar of its lard.

Eumaeus the swineherd of the *Odyssey* is addressed as "godlike," an adjective which Classical scholars ignorantly translate either "honest" or "worthy." In Odysseus's Ithaca, as in ancient Ireland and Wales, the swineherd served the sow-headed Phorcis, Goddess of Death and Poetic Inspiration; Eumaeus might therefore be called "Chief Prophet of Heaven and Earth," like his colleague Marvan. The death of Marvan's pig is a mythographic way of recording the murder of inspired poetry by a new-fangled academicism. At first, the bards despised Marvan as an interloper, and asked him to prove his right to converse with them on equal terms. But his poetic passport was a mantle of prophetic wind; and though these professors were skilled in astronomy, mathematics, cosmology, law, cyphers, counterpoint, and all the latest prosodic fashions, they could not stand up against a Royal Swineherd when it came to a battle of wits.

Seanchan asked Marvan pompously: "Tell me, peasant, what was the antecedent of the First Cause?" Marvan did not cite the metaphysical arguments of the Early Fathers, or Aristotle, or Epicurus, or Heraclitus, but answered simply and accurately: "Blind nuts!"—which, for me, remains the only possible answer to such a stupid question, though it might not go down very well nowadays in a D.Phil. *viva*. The hazel was the ancient Irish and Welsh symbol of Divine Wisdom, and the First Cause must therefore be the nut from whose kernel grew the Sacred Hazel which, according to tradition, overshadowed the Salmon-pool of Enlightenment. So what, in poetical terms, could the antecedent of the First Cause be, but a blind nut —a nut without a kernel?

Marvan answered magisterially every one of the professors' questions, and in return humbled them with problems beyond their power to solve—for instance, they could not even guess at the true origin of the poet's harp, or of poetic metre. Incidentally, he treated them to inspired but sorry revelations of what their wives were doing at home. When the three hundred had failed on all counts, he put a bond on them, which debarred them from ever again abusing a patron's hospitality, or from interfering with the affairs of others—"thenceforth to the womb of Judgement."

Seanchan's end came when, after rhyming ten rats to death for stealing his dinner scraps, he turned his petulant rage on the united cats of Ireland. He announced that they had neglected their job, and satirized Irusan, their King, by calling him "Otter's leavings, clumsy claws, with a dandyish drooping tail like a cow's."

The storyteller continues:

> It was told to Seanchan that Irusan was on his way coming to kill him; and he requested Guaire to come with the nobility of Connaught to protect him against Irusan. They all came around him, and had not been long there when they heard a vibrating, impetuous and impressive sound, similar to that produced by a tremendously raging fiery furnace in full blaze; and it appeared to them that there was not in Connaught a plough bullock larger than Irusan.
>
> His appearance was as follows: blunt-snouted, rapacious, panting, determined, jagged-eared, broad-breasted, prominent-jointed, sharp and smooth-clawed, split-nosed, sharp and rough-toothed, thick-snouted, nimble, powerful, deep-flanked, terror-striking, angry, extremely vindictive, quick, purring, glare-eyed; and he came towards them in that similitude. He passed amongst them generally, but did not stop till he reached to the place where Seanchan was. He took hold of him by one arm, jerked him on his back, and returned with him by the same way as he had come, for he had no other object in view but to fetch away Seanchan. Seanchan now had recourse to flattery of Irusan, praising his leap, his progress in his running, his power, strength and activity. . . .

But it was too late. The rats were avenged.

The professional moral of all this is that when a natural urge in poets to resort and debate together—as Shakespeare, Ben Jonson, Drayton, and the rest did at the *Mermaid*—is exploited by literary politicians, and cabals are formed, poetry is in danger. And that arch-poets who petulantly rhyme a few rats to death—meaning the ignorant poetasters—should take care not to satirize the King Cat, the emissary of the Cat-goddess. They must remember that the source of all poetry is not reason, but the wind of inspiration. Only swine can see the wind. And, since I must not hold anything back from you, the origin of the poet's harp was the wind which blew on the sinews of a whale's skeleton in the days of Macuel son of Miduel; and metre originated in the days of Lamiach from the sound of two hammers of different weight beaten alternately on an anvil.* However, the kennings of these riddles—like the kennings of Seanchan's satire on Irusan—are not to be found in Boileau. I reserve them for my fifth lecture, when I shall deal with the technical side of poetry.

* In October 1968 at Santa Clara, Mexico, I listened to eight hammers of different weights beating at a great lump of red-hot copper. It was the same team of Tarascon smiths that, directed by one Don Feliz and in pure pre-Columbian tradition, had forged the great copper receptacle designed by James Metcalfe for the Olympic Fire. The hammers beat out the metre of a *copla* without pause or change for several minutes.

The Road to Rydal Mount

The Seven Years' War shook the absolutist régime set up by Louis XIV, inherited by Louis XV, and either copied or envied by their royal contemporaries throughout Europe. Eventually the revolt of the American colonies, brought to a successful finish by French intervention, touched off the French Revolution. Since absolutism had been extended from the political field to that of philosophy, the arts, and literature, this general collapse in France, which now threatened England too, sent the more inquisitive English poets searching back in history to find out where a false step had been taken. They decided that Dryden, Pope, Addison, and other poets of the Age of Obsequiousness were mistaken: that poetry had not always been a drawing-room product, but had at one time implied a warm relationship between all classes—the early English kings, for instance, had "dear comrades" not subjects. From which they deduced that a man was a man for a' that, and for a' that, and for a' that; and that the current poetic technique was artificial and constrictive. As Romantic Revivalists they dismounted from what Keats irreverently called "the rocking horse" of the heroic couplet; they cultivated the Elizabethans, ceased to court the peerage, avoided public life, and did not feel obliged to live in Town. Most of them were avowed, if ineffective, revolutionaries. Blake walked the streets of London in a red cap of Liberty; Wordsworth carried the British flag in a Jacobin procession and attracted the notice of Pitt's secret police; Shelley sealed a letter to the Duke of Norfolk with a revolutionary wafer. As Hazlitt wrote, they scorned "degrees, priority, place, and the distinctions of birth," and "were surrounded, in company with the Muses, by a rabble of idle apprentices and Botany Bay convicts, female vagrants, gipsies, meek daughters in the family of Christ, of idiot boys and mad mothers, and after them 'owls and night-ravens flew.'"

Others, of course, like Keats, loved the Gothic past more than they welcomed the democratic or the pantisocratic future. "O Chatterton, how very sad thy fate!" wrote Keats. For Chatterton's failure to secure Horace Walpole's patronage by means of his Rowley forgeries had reduced him to writing shilling-a-line satires on the Duke of Grafton, the Earl of Bute, and the Princess of Wales, until he expired in poverty. Keats himself felt the lack of a patron; his lure for publishers, *Cap and Bells,* if not his diploma pieces, *Hyperion* and *Endymion,* prove that he would have attempted any poetical subject within reason suggested to him by a coroneted patron. But fate had attached him to Leigh Hunt's party; and to court the Tories would have have been disloyal. Moreover, as a result of the wonderful profits made by Moore and Byron, who gave the large romantically inclined public what it wanted, individual patronage waned. "Why shouldn't other poets do the same?" the peers began to ask. This was all very well for Samuel Rogers, a rich banker; and for Crabbe, a country parson; and for Shelley, who had private means; and for Lamb, with his not very demanding clerkship in the India Office. But it seemed mighty hard on John Clare.

I can best explain my feelings about professional standards by contrasting the careers of two early nineteenth-century poets: Clare and Wordsworth—Clare, who began as a servant of the public, but ended as a devotee of the Goddess; Wordsworth, who reversed the process—Clare, with his growing sense of what poetry demanded; Wordsworth, with his growing sense of what the public demanded.

Clare, a labourer's son, was mouse-poor, and quite without influence or connexions. Though his first book of poems (1820) proved
immediately successful, it sold well only because poetry happened
to come all at once into fashion, for dubious reasons. Since Taylor,
his publisher, who had seen his work by accident, was billing him
truthfully enough as an "English peasant poet," Clare became a
nine days' wonder. He had clay on his boots, hay-seed in his hair,
genius in his eye, spoke as charmingly odd a dialect as Burns, yet was
able to forge a neat, melodious pastoral rhyme that would not have
disgraced Robert Bloomfield, William Cowper, or even the self-
elected High Priest of Nature, Wordsworth. Visitors came in coaches
from London to the remote village of Helpstone, where they gaped at
this miraculous son of toil, a rival sideshow to his contemporary, the
legless and armless Miss Biffin, who threaded needles and worked
samplers with her lips and teeth alone (poor creature!). Clare (poor
creature!) similarly transcended the disadvantages of birth, environment and education, and though his biographers suggest that he disliked the label of "Peasant Poet," this is not altogether true. He
wrote an autobiographical poem under that title, and in his *Village
Minstrel* romanticized himself as a Spenserian "Lubin":

> Young Lubin was a peasant from his birth;
> His sire a hind born to the flail and plough,
> To thump the corn out and to till the earth,
> The coarsest chance which nature's laws allow—
> To earn his living by a sweating brow;
> Thus Lubin's early days did rugged roll,
> And mixt in timely toil—but e'en as now,
> Ambitious prospects fired his little soul,
> And fancy soared and sung, 'bove poverty's control.

The Village Minstrel appeared in his second volume, which sold
badly. The third and fourth volumes (1827 and 1835) were dismal
failures, but not because Clare refused to cater for popular taste.
He pleased the large "Keepsake" public by imitations of elder poets
and, oddly enough, these are far closer to the originals than Pope's,
as can be seen by comparing their rival imitations of Sir John Haring-

ton. And here Clare is making obeisance to the aristocratic Augustan tradition, which had reasserted its sway after the defeat of Revolutionary France:

To My Oaten Reed

Thou warble wild, of rough, rude melody,
   How oft I've woo'd thee, often thrown thee by!
In many a doubtful rapture touching thee,
   Waking thy rural notes in many a sigh:
Fearing the wise, the wealthy, proud and high,
   Would scorn as vain thy lowly ecstasy,
Deeming presumptuous thy uncultur'd themes.
Thus vainly courting Taste's unblemish'd eye,
   To list a simple labourer's artless dreams. . . .

In the 1820's, unless a poet could take his place naturally and gracefully at a gentleman's table, cut or keep out of sight his plebeian connexions, and move to Town, he still might not hope for advancement. Then what was to be done with Clare, however untainted by Jacobinism and however obligingly he tuned his oaten reed? He had married Patty Turner, a poor illiterate fellow-villager, merely to make an honest woman of her; now lived in an insanitary cottage full of ragged, ailing brats; worked as a day labourer; and never hankered for city life. The fashionable sightseers who visited Helpstone paid no shilling entrance-fee for the privilege of wasting Clare's time; they scattered a few compliments, wrinkled their noses at the sour smell of poverty, and drove away again. Their visits, like his week-long rhyming fits, merely discouraged the local farmers from giving him steady employment. A general slump occurred in the sales of poetry, and Clare slowly went to pieces under the strain.

A fund was, indeed, raised to keep him afloat, but this proved insufficient to feed and clothe his family of seven children. And though it is true that an adequate income might have kept him from sinking so deep into the trough of melancholy, it would not have assuaged his loneliness. The only cure for his disease would have been the society of his fellow-poets. Yet it was not until about the year 1830, when he grew weary of courting "Taste's unblemish'd eye," that he graduated as a true poet. He had by now been favoured with a dream vision of the White Goddess of Poetry, and henceforth his companions should have been those who bore her seal on their brows. He wrote:

> These dreams of a beautiful presence, a woman deity, gave the sublimest conceptions of beauty to my imagination; and being last night with the same presence, the lady divinity left such a vivid picture of her visits in my sleep, dreaming of dreams, that I could no longer doubt her existence. So I wrote them down to prolong the happiness of my faith in believing her my guardian genius.

But where, then, were his fellow-poets? In 1820 there had been talk of a friendly exchange of poetic opinions between Clare and Keats, who knew the Goddess as La Belle Dame Sans Merci, and such a meeting might have done both of them a deal of good. Keats, born a Cockney, criticized an early nature poem of Clare's by saying that "the Description too much prevailed over the sentiment"; whereas Clare wrote of Keats: "He often described Nature as she appeared to his fancies and not as he would have described her had he witnessed the things he described." However, this meeting had never come off; and now Keats was dead, and so was Shelley; and Clare's friendships with Darley, Lamb, and Cary, limited to letters and very occasional visits, died away.

Clare seems to have stumbled accidentally upon the solution to his dilemma; perhaps he found it in the *Book of Samuel*, where David escaped from the Philistines by feigning madness. The best way to discourage unwelcome visitors was casually to identify himself with Lord Byron or with Tom Cribb, the prize-fighter; such deceitful fictions soon scattered them. But being already cut off from village society by presuming above his station, he found that the loneliness increased. He wrote in a letter:

> I live here among the ignorant like a lost man in fact like one whom the rest seems careless of having anything to do with—they hardly

dare talk in my company for fear I should mention them in my writings & I find more pleasure in wandering the fields than in mixing among my silent neighbours who are insensible of everything but toiling & talking of it & that to no purpose.

The distressed Patty was not his equal, either in intellect or sensibility, and as an anodyne he took to deceiving himself with another sort of fiction. He contrived to believe that he was really married to Mary Joyce, a farmer's daughter four years younger than himself, with whom he had been passionately in love as a boy, but whom he had never aspired to marry. She became his pastoral Muse, the perpetual Other Woman. After the failure of his fourth book of poems in 1835, he turned his back on reality and lived more and more in the lost world of his boyhood, peopled only by beasts, birds, and Mary. In 1837, his London friends sent him to a private mental home in Epping Forest, from which he ran away in 1841; but six months later, by order of the local gentry whom he had libellously lampooned in *The Parish,* was confined to Northampton General Lunatic Asylum, where he remained until his death in 1864. The charge was: "years addicted to poetical prosings." Clare's lunacy, being self-inflicted, was only partial—as when recruits shoot off their trigger fingers rather than put bullets through their heads. It did not affect his poetic capacity—if, as it seems, he wrote and talked certifiable nonsense merely to discourage visitors. Though he ceased from satire or such low-life ballads as *The Helpstone Statutes,* he broke quite new ground in *The Dying Child:*

> He could not die when trees were green,
>   For he loved the time too well.
> His little hands, when flowers were seen,
>   Were held for the bluebell,
>   As he was carried o'er the green.
>
> His eye glanced at the white-nosed bee;
>   He knew those children of the Spring:
> When he was well and on the lea
>   He held one in his hands to sing
>   Which filled his heart with glee.

Infants, the children of the Spring!
How can an infant die
When butterflies are on the wing,
Green grass, and such a sky?
How can they die at Spring?

And his "I am, but what I am who cares or knows?" and "I lost
the love of Heaven" are already among the recognized glories of
English poetry. Since in those days warders had officially stopped
flogging lunatics, and doctors had not yet developed drastic thera-
peutic training or shock treatment, he had a less unhappy time
than might be supposed—at any rate, until the governors decided
to deny even harmless inmates leave to wander freely about the
town, and so turned an asylum into a prison.

How good was Clare? At his best he was very good indeed,
with a natural simplicity supported by a remarkable sense of language; he meant what he said, considered it well before he wrote it
down and wrote with love. Most of his poems were about Nature
because, after all, he had never been anything but a countryman
and described only what he knew. By comparison, Wordsworth had
a very cursory knowledge of wild life; he did not get up early
enough in the morning. (Wordsworth on Nature is like Virgil on
boxing; I prefer Theocritus, who had obviously been a bit of a
bruiser himself, as his account of the Amycus-Pollux match shows.)
Clare wrote a great deal of descriptive verse on the nesting habits of
particular birds, and the queer ways of wild animals and insects,
and on country people as part of the landscape. But Clare never
bores, being always precise and economical and relying on patient
observation; besides, he had somehow acquired the rare faculty of
knowing how and when to end a poem. His obsession with Nature
made him think of a poem as a living thing, rather than a slice cut
from the cake of literature, and his poems are still alive. I find myself repeating some of them without having made a conscious effort
at memorization. And though it was taken as a symptom of madness
that he one day confided in a visitor: "I know Gray—I know him
well," I shall risk saying here, with equal affection: "I know Clare;
I know him well. We have often wept together."

There was no Age of Clare, as there was no Age of Smart, the magnificence of whose *Song to David* (1763) makes all other poems of the day look sick and sorry. Smart had also vainly and too long courted Taste's unblemish'd eye—going so far as to translate Pope's *Ode on St. Cecilia's Day,* an imitation of Dryden's on the same subject, into Latin! He wrote *A Song to David* in a lunatic asylum, and when his collected poems were published in 1791, it was omitted as "not acceptable to the reader." This poem is formally addressed to David—Smart knew that he was no madder than King David had been, and a tradition survives that he scrabbled the verses with a key on the walls of his cell; but the deity whom he really celebrated was the central figure of the Muse Triad, the *Lady of Wild Things:*

> Strong is the horse upon his speed;
> Strong in pursuit the rapid glede,
> Which makes at once his game;
> Strong the tall ostrich on the ground;
> Strong through the turbulent profound
> Shoots xiphias to his aim.

> Strong is the lion—like a coal
> His eyeball—like a bastion's mole
> His chest against the foes:
> Strong the gier-eagle on his sail,
> Strong against tide, th' enormous whale
> Emerges, as he goes.

But even Dr. Johnson, who liked Smart personally and did all he could to help him, had no use at all for *A Song to David,* and once ended an argument as to who was the better poet—Smart or a dullard called Derrick—by saying: "Sir, there is no settling the point of precedency between a louse and a flea."

So, as I was saying, there was no Age of Clare, and no Age of Smart, but there was an Age of Wordsworth. You will find it in all the literary histories. "The Age of" is a political term. One may legitimately talk of the Age of Pericles, because Pericles was the most energetic and gifted statesman of fifth-century Athens; and

Athens was the most energetic and gifted city-state in Greece, as Greece was the most energetic and gifted country in Europe or Asia. One can similarly talk of the Age of Augustus, or the Age of Louis XIV. But the "Age of" is a non-poetic concept, and when applied to English poets is either a misnomer—for instance *The Age of Shakespeare* wrongly suggests that Shakespeare was the most influential and esteemed poet of his day—or it means that the poet selected to name the age was a politician rather than a poet.

Wordsworth came of comfortable family and got stung, during an adventurous visit to France in 1791-2, by the gadfly of Republicanism. His intention of presenting himself as a leader of the Girondists was thwarted when an uncle shook the family purse-strings at him; whereupon he came to his senses, and deserted not only his revolutionary friends but his Muse, "Julia"—Annette Vallon—whom he had got with child. And when the "stings of viperous remorse" no longer pricked him, and he could even congratulate himself on his providential escape, that was the end of Wordsworth the poet. He virtuously led his companions back in to the eighteenth-century ecclesiastical Tory fold from which he had strayed. Byron, who also came home, though on his own initiative, wrote to Murray the publisher in 1820:

> *All* of us—Scott, Southey, Wordsworth, Moore, Campbell, I—are all in the wrong . . . that we are upon a wrong revolutionary poetical system, or systems, not worth a damn in itself . . . and that the present and next generations will finally be of this opinion. . . . I took Moore's poems and my own, and some others, and went over them side by side with Pope's, and I was really astonished (I ought not to have been) and mortified at the ineffable distance in point of sense, harmony, effect, and even *Imagination*, passion and *Invention*, between the little Queen Anne's Man, and us of the Lower Empire.

Though Wordsworth (as Matthew Arnold records) did not earn enough money by poetry to keep him in shoestrings, he managed to live frugally on a £900 legacy bequeathed him in 1795, which saved him from going to London and undertaking journalism. Seven years later the then Lord Lonsdale died, and his successor paid the

Wordsworths a long-standing debt owed to their father. After another ten years Wordsworth wheedled his stamp-distributorship out of Lord Lonsdale—soon worth an annual £1,000. De Quincy commented enviously: "Money always fell in" to Wordsworth, enabling him to pursue his poetic career without distraction. In 1842 he gave up the post, and Sir Robert Peel rewarded him for having done so with a £300 Civil List pension, and the Laureateship, which Wordsworth stipulated must be a sinecure. "All for a handful of silver he left us . . . !"

As a birthday present, when I was young, my father sent me without explanation a letter in an old man's hand, undated and signed with the initials W.W. The paper and ink looked ancient, but since the addressee was plainly "Robert Graves, Esq.," I began reading what seemed a personal message rather than a historical document. It began abruptly:

> Mr. Graves will bear in mind what I said against the phrase of making a Tour in Switzerland as generally understood to relate to Alpine Switzerland—the best thing to be done is to cross the Alps by as many passes as you conveniently can; descending into Italy and back again—to and fro.

On turning to the end of the letter again, I discovered the words "Rydal Mt." in the margin. The writer was none other than William Wordsworth, a "sincere friend" of my grand uncle Robert Graves, the physician. I had not yet read Wordsworth with attention, and was prepared to modify my unfavourable first impressions, for my father's sake, if this letter gave me honest cause. A hasty perusal showed that it referred mostly to a tour of the Continent which he had made twenty years previously, in 1820, with his wife and his sister Dorothy. So I reached for my Oxford edition of the *Poems*, borrowed a *Wordsworth Concordance*, and settled down to study him in earnest.

> Taking you up at Berne is in some respects inconvenient—as it leaves the Lakes of Zurich and Wallenstadt and the noble pass of

the Via-Mala, and over the Splugen, and so down upon Chiavenna and the Lake of Como etc., upon your left hand. But as you must start from Berne it would probably be best as *we* did in 1820, to go to Thun—at T. (if you have an hour to spare) is a pleasant walk in the grounds of . . .

Here it seems, Wordsworth, unable to recall the name of the place, consulted his *Memorials of a Tour on the Continent;* but the relevant poem, *Memorial Near the Outlet of the Lake of Thun,* gave him no information. So he wrote:

. . . near the outlet of the lake

but then scratched the words out, and abandoned the problem.

where is a small Tablet to the memory of Alois Reding. The views from the Ch:yd and Castle are also very interesting—up the Lake to Unterbeer and Interlacken.

I found that he had immortalized Reding's tablet as follows:

> Around a wild and woody hill
> A gravelled pathway treading,
> We reached a votive Stone that bears
> The name of Aloys Reding.
>
> Well judged the friend who placed it there
> For silence and protection;
> And haply with a finer care
> Of dutiful affection.
>
> The Sun regards it from the West
> And, while in summer glory
> He sets, his sinking yields a type
> Of that pathetic story. . . .

Raising my eyebrows a little, I read on:

The Lake of Brientz—the falls near it which we did not visit—are worth seeing, if you have time, but we preferred going to Lauterbrunnen.

What poetic harvest had Wordsworth brought back from Brienz? He watched certain "harvest-damsels float, Homeward in their rugged boat. . . . The rustic maidens, every hand, Upon a Sister's shoulder laid": and heard them "chant as glides the boat along, A simple, but a touching song; To chant as Angels do above, The melodies of Peace in love."

And over the Wengern Alp to Grindelwald—thence over the Schidec to Meyringham— Observe on your descent upon M. look for the celebrated fall of Reichenbach. From M. we gave a day to the Oberhasli Vall, and the famous falls of Handec—whence we *might* have proceeded over the Grimsel Pass to Unteren etc.,—but we preferred returning to M.—thence by side of the Lake of Lungern and Sarnan on to Lucerne.

At Lucerne the Wordsworths had met a twenty-year-old Bostonian, Frederick Goddard, and were delighted to hear English spoken again, "while festive mirth ran wild." Three days later, Goddard was drowned in the lake near Zurich and Wordsworth mourned his fate:

> Beloved by every gentle muse
> He left his Transatlantic home.
> Europe, a realised romance,
> Had opened on his eager glance.
> What present bliss! what golden views!
> What stores for years to come!
>
> Fetch, sympathising Powers of air,
> Fetch, ye that post o'er seas and lands,
> Herbs moistened by Virginian dew
> A most untimely grave to strew
> Whose turf may never know the care
> Of *kindred* human hands!

Since Goddard hailed from Massachusetts, "herbs moistened by Virginian dew" is perhaps a festive synonym for tobacco; though this seems a little out of key in an elegiac context.

From Lucerne to the top of Riga—

He means the Rigi. The Rigi ascent he celebrated in *Our Lady of the Snows,* from which a short passage may be quoted for the eighteenth-century ingenuity of the second line:

> Even for the Man who stops not here
> But down the irriguous valley hies,
> Thy very name, O Lady! flings,
> O'er blooming fields and gushing springs,
> A tender sense of shadowy fears
> And chastening sympathies.

Coleridge, by the way, held that love of mountain scenery was a purely literary emotion, found among mountaineers only when they had enjoyed a liberal education. "Where this is not the case, as among the peasantry of North Wales, the ancient mountains, with all their terrors and all their glories, are pictures to the blind, and music to the deaf."

So on to the Rigi and:

> . . . thence, by the Town of Switz to Brunnen on the Uri branch of the Lake of the 4 Cantons. So on, by Boat to Tell's Chapel and Fluellen. Then to Altorf, Amstag, to the valley of Urseren. Here let me observe you might cross over the Difenti, on one of the branches of the Rhine and thence up the Viamala to Splugen and over to Chiavenna, and so down the Lake of Como. This I did 50 years ago, only reversing it.

By "50 years ago" he means 1790 when, as an undergraduate at the end of his third year, he and Robert Jones went on a Long Vacation walking tour. Their itinerary is recorded in his *Descriptive Sketches taken during a pedestrian tour among the Alps.* Tell's Chapel had then greatly impressed him:

> But lo! the boatman overawed, before
> The pictured fane of Tell suspends his oar. . . .

It remains a nice question whether rowing was merely suspended when the chapel hove into view, or whether the boatman disembarked and hung up his oar as a votive offering. The passage ends heroically:

> Where bleeding Sidney from the cup retired
> And glad Dundee in "faint huzzas" expired.

While I appreciated Wordsworth's delicacy in disclaiming the authorship of "faint huzzas," it seemed a pity that metrical exigency had changed "Bonnie" to "Glad."

—or from Urseren as we did in 1820 over the St. Gotard down by *Airola, Bellingzonn, Locarna,* where embark to Luvina and thence by Ponte Tresa to Lugana. Here ascend San Salvador—for the views.

In 1821 he had apostrophized the Church of San Salvador in a few well-turned verses beginning:

> Thou sacred Pile . . .

This contained a stanza which my father occasionally quoted:

> Glory and patriotic Love
> And all the Pomps of this frail "spot
> Which men call Earth" have yearned to seek,
> Associate with the simply meek,
> Religion in the sainted grove
> And in the hallowed grot.

Then take boat for *Porlezza* and over the hill to *Managgio*—thence to *Cannabbia* thence across the lake to the promontory of *Bellagio* and from the Alcove in the Duke's grounds you see parts of the 3 reaches of the Lake of Como—magnificent prospect—here if you find our names, pray refresh them—[he was that sort of traveller].

It was at Cannabbia (or Cadenabbia) that Wordsworth had fallen in with an "Italian Itinerant" who was planning to hawk clay busts of Shakespeare and Milton round the English country-side, and penned the following affectionate lines:

> What stirring wonders wilt thou see
> In the proud Isle of Liberty!
> Yet will the Wanderer sometimes pine
> With thoughts which no delights can chase,
> Recall a Sister's last embrace,
> His mother's neck-entwine;
> Nor shall forget the Maiden coy
> That *would* have loved the bright-haired boy.

And therefore wished him "safe return. To Como's steeps—his happy bourne!, In garden glade to prop the twig, That ill supports the luscious fig." I have seen the branches of apricot, apple, and plum propped to support the weight of fruit; but never the twigs of figs. "Twig," however, undoubtedly rhymes with "fig."

Here you must determine whether you will go to Como and Milan —and so by Varesa, Bavann, the Borromean Islands, and over the Simplon back into Switzerland—or, if time allows on by the Lesca branch to Bergamo a fine situation—Town and Lake of Issea.

His first memories of the Simplon I found in *The Prelude*, Book VI (1850 text): there he was trying to show that poetry can be distilled from the most literally pedestrian experiences, if one *clomb* rather than *climbed*:

> we clomb
> Along the Simplon's steep and rugged road . . .
> The only track now visible was one
> That from the torrent's further brink held forth
> Conspicuous invitation to ascend
> A lofty mountain. After brief delay
> Crossing the unbridged stream, that road we took

> And clomb with eagerness, till anxious fears
> Intruded, for we failed to overtake
> Our comrades gone before. By fortunate chance,
> While every moment added doubt to doubt,
> A peasant met us, from whose mouth we learned
> That to the spot which had perplexed us first
> We must descend, and there should find the road
> Which in the stony channel of the stream
> Lay a few steps, and then along its banks. . . .

Wordsworth was thoroughly scared and it looks as if the mistake was his, not Robert Jones's.

. . . to Louvera at its head and by Brescia, where are Roman Antiquities, to the Lago di Garda, up to Riva at its head where is magnificent scenery. Hence you might cross over into the Tyrol, but all this would carry you a long way from Switzerland.—So I will suppose you to go by the Lake from Cadenabbia to Como—there, if time allows, to Milan for the sake of the Cathedral.

At Milan, in 1820, he had faithfully recorded an Eclipse of the Sun, in a tribute to Science beginning:

> High in her speculative tower
> Stood Science waiting for the hour
> When Sol was destined to endure
> That darkening of his radiant face
> Which Superstition strove to chase
> Erstwhile with rites impure.

He was being broad-minded. Science, despite Erasmus Darwin, was as yet hardly respectable in English poetry, and this is one of the earliest friendly advances made her by a recognized poet.

. . . from Milan to *Varesa* to the Borromean Islands and over the Senplin. But I regret much that we did not turn aside for Banen so to take in the Lago di Orta in our way to Domo d'Ossolo—near

Domo d'Ossolo, (as also near Varesi, I believe) is one of those shrines to which you ascend by different stations, as they are called, which Chantrey told me was altogether striking. From *Brig*, in the Vallais downwards, we turned up to the Baths of Leuk—so up the noble ascent of the Gemmi returning, after we had looked down into the vale which leads to Thun, to Leuk—thence by *Sion* to *Martigny*.

At Gemmi he heard a dog barking and the sound echoing from the mountain. It made so deep an impression on him that he resorted to a Keatsian use of Classical mythology:

> As multitudinous a harmony
> Of sounds as rang the heights of Latmos over
> When from the soft couch of her sleeping lover
> Upstarting, Cynthia skimmed the mountain-dew . . .

Wordsworth was one of the very first Englishmen to explore the Alps, and did so mainly, I think, because of his admiration for Jean Jacques Rousseau, whom George Sand called "the Christopher Columbus of Alpine poetry" and whom Chateaubriand called "the Father of French Romanticism." When Wordsworth's revolutionary enthusiasm cooled and he reverted to eighteenth-century normal verse-technique, he continued to admire Swiss scenery and was proud of his pioneering fame: had he not "discovered" the valley of Chamonix and the Mer de Glace for future generations of British tourists?

He continues:

From this place you might re-cross into Italy by the Grand St. Bernard and here you need directions which I cannot give for coming back from behind Mt. Blanc, somewhere into Savoy or Switzerland. *We* went from Martigny over the Col d'Balin into Chamony from which you explore the Mer d'Glace and as much of Mont Blanc as time and strength will allow.

In 1790 he had been disappointed in Mont Blanc (which is, indeed, a smug wedding-cake of a mountain) and:

> . . . grieved
> To have a soulless image on the eye
> That had usurped upon a living thought
> That never more could be . . .

but consoled himself with the reflection that:

> . . . with such a book
> Before our eyes, we could not choose but read
> Lessons of genuine brotherhood, the plain
> And universal reason of mankind,
> The truths of young and old.

"Nobody must mistake *me* for a North Welsh peasant," he is saying.

> Thence down the vallies to Geneva, on Geneva are steam boats (as
> are also upon the Lago d'Gardo—and a public boat from Iseo to
> Riva)—and now supposing you to bear the General direction in mind
> I have done and will only observe that of the minor Passes, by which
> I mean from one part of Switzerland to another, that of the Gemmi
> and above all that from Meynringham to Sarnan—

Here he crossed out the words "and above all," and also the phrase:
"the one for grandeur and the other for beauty," which followed.

> —are far the most interesting—see them all if possible.

I could find no reference in the *Poems* to these particular steam
boats, though he probably immortalized them somewhere. He had,
as a matter of fact, written a piece about "a steam boat seen off St.
Bees Head" in 1833, and though "depressed," as he admits, by its
steady progress "indifferent to breeze or gale," he made amends for
this emotional lapse in his sonnet *Steamboats, Viaducts and Railways*,
written the same year:

> Motions and Means, on land and sea at war
> With old poetic feeling, not for this,

Shall ye, by Poets even, be judged amiss!
Nor shall your presence, howsoe'er it mar
The loveliness of Nature, prove a bar
To the Mind's gaining that prophetic sense
Of future change, that point of vision, whence
May be discovered what in soul ye are.
In spite of all that beauty may disown
In your harsh features, Nature doth embrace
Her lawful offspring in Man's art; and Time,
Pleased with your Triumphs o'er his brother Space,
Accepts from your bold hands the proffered crown
Of hope, and smiles on you with cheer sublime.

This was quoted with telling effect in Court (1950) by my brother-in-law E. J. Neep, Q.C., when Wordsworth lovers brought an injunction against the Electricity Board for threatening to destroy Lakeland amenities with a line of pylons. The case collapsed at once.

Wordsworth had persuaded himself that no subjects were so novel, so mean, or so prosaic but that a lofty style could extract poetry from them. To seal his Tory convictions, he wrote a spirited protest against the Secret Ballot, beginning:

Forth rushed from Envy sprung and self-conceit
A power misnamed the Spirit of Reform
. . . now stoops she to entreat
Licence to hide at intervals her head
Where she may work, safe, undisquieted
In a close box!

He even deigned to apostrophize a spade. He had been lending a hand in a neighbour's potato patch; but though he called a spade a spade he could not bring himself to call a labourer a labourer, or a potato patch a potato patch. The title is: *To the Spade of a Friend (an agriculturist). Composed while we were labouring together in his Pleasure Ground.*

Well, the Wordsworths felt greatly relieved to get home safely from their Swiss tour (as who does not?); yet it is one thing to be able to feel and another to be able to express in graceful verse the sentiments that are common to all returned travellers. Wordsworth, whom my father had once described to me as a "shrewd philosopher of the natural emotions," managed this very creditably in two Thomas Mooreish stanzas, designed for singing to a tall, gilt drawing-room harp:

> Though the toil of the way with dear Friends we divide,
> Though by the same zephyr our temples be fanned
> As we rest in the cool orange-bower side by side,
> A yearning survives which few hearts shall withstand:
>
> Each step hath its value while homeward we move;—
> O joy when the girdle of England appears!
> What moment in life is so conscious of love,
> Of love in the heart made more happy by tears?

The letter ended:

. . . One word more by way of correction—[in 1837] Mr. [Crabbe] Robinson and I were encumbered with a carriage, so that we were obliged to go back from Louvera to the Town of Isean whereas pedestrians no doubt might cross from Louvera to Resa—and so save space and time. With the best of good wishes

I remain faithfully yours

W.W.

Rydal Mt.

N.B. Every foot of ground spoken of that I have seen myself is interesting.

Wordsworth never visited Clare at Northampton, of course; but throngs of Wordsworthians visited Rydal Mount to be entertained by his sportive sister Dorothy—until she went feeble-minded about 1833—and to be able to say that they had seen the great man. My father was only ten years old when Wordsworth died, but his Uncle Robert took him to the auction of surplus Wordsworthiana at Rydal

Mount, an experience which set him up for the rest of his life.

The moral of all this is, perhaps, that poets should not be "encumbered with a carriage," especially if they owe this luxury to a political patron. And I haven't the heart to take you on a conducted tour into the Age of Tennyson, which ended (as they say in Spain) only yesterday morning. Tennyson's career resembled Wordsworth's: the early escapade in 1830, when he lived and loved in the Pyrenees as a Spanish revolutionary under Torrijos; the romantic poems—*Lady of Shalott, Lotos Eaters, Mariana, Oenone,* and so on; the parsimonious and retired life; rescue from indigence and melancholy by Sir Robert Peel's bounty; the Laureateship; a tour in Switzerland; the rise to fame and respectability; the suitably unromantic marriage; the urge to write major works; self-dedication and post-graduate self-improvement as the mouthpiece of his fellow-citizens; poems dictated by popular patriotism; the increasing sweetness and purity of his style.

But no Muse! Wordsworth had disowned and betrayed his Muse. Tennyson never had one, except Arthur Hallam, and a Muse does not wear whiskers. The Lady of Shalott floating down to Camelot, Oenone deserted by Paris, Mariana among her caked flower pots in the moated grange—"he cometh not" she said—are all Tennyson's pathetic self-inversions. And the *Princess* is his good-humoured, patronizing admission that woman is capable of a certain intellectual and artistic advancement on male lines—a view as repellent in its way as Dr. Johnson's downright view of her general inferiority to man. W. H. Auden recently tried to rehabilitate Tennyson in a modern edition; I cannot say why.

Edmund Gosse wrote:

> Between the years 1866–1870 the heightened reputation of Browning and still more the sudden vogue of Swinburne, Morris and Rossetti considerably disturbed the minds of Tennyson's most ardent readers. He went on quite calmly, however, sure of his mission and his music. In 1889 the death of Browning left him a solitary figure indeed in poetic literature. He soon wonderfully recovered the high spirits of youth, and even a remarkable portion of physical strength.

Gosse notes:

> No living poet has ever held England quite so long under his
> unbroken sway as Tennyson.

This may be true, because Pope died fairly young, and until his
declining years Wordsworth had rivals in Byron, Moore, Rogers,
Southey, and Mrs. Hemans. But for a living poet to hold England
under his sway, even for a brief period, runs counter to English
poetical morality. Pope had won his supremacy by blackmail; Wordsworth had won his by climbing on the band-wagon at exactly the
right moment and sitting tight; Tennyson won his by industry,
sweet persuasiveness, and much the same gearing of his poetic intelligence to national progress, or aspirations of progress, as are
nowadays so roundly condemned in poets and artists of the Com-
munist *bloc*. Pope had suffered agonies of spleen (according to Dr.
Johnson) when he read Cibber's vigorous reply to his *Dunciad*
libels; Wordsworth's surly defiance of Jeffrey and other adverse
critics who ridiculed what he thought his best work "did not" (the
text-books say) "prevent a premature depression and a consequent
deadening of his powers." Tennyson's breakfast (according to my
father, who knew him personally and persuaded him to versify *The
Voyage of Maeldune*) was ruined if the Aldworth postman did not
bring him at least two or three fan-letters from impressionable
young ladies. Tennyson continued to wear his black cape, but in the
same style as those that he and Hallam had worn during the
Torrijos campaign, and in the high spirits of his renewed youth
devoted his leisure to a different sort of literary composition. It is
on record that his family physician, an ardent Tennysonian, coming
to call on the great man one mellow rose-scented August afternoon,
found him drowsing, pencil in hand, on his chair under the great
cedar. A paper of verses fluttered to the ground and the physician
stole forward reverently and picked it up, anxious to be the first to
eye those immortal lines.

It was a limerick, beginning: "There once was a Chinaman,
drunk. . . ."

I should not refrain from discussing the sad case of Blake, who avoided the pauper asylum by being so skilful a painter and engraver that at the worst he could always become a print-seller's hack. Blake began as a poet; later he lost heart and turned prophet. As Laura Riding has written: "To each is given what defeat he will." The prophetic robe with its woof of meekness and its warp of wrath was forced on him by loneliness and his modest station in life: to be a mechanic was even more of a handicap for a late eighteenth-century poet than to be a peasant. Since he had no friends with whom he could converse on equal terms, he went in search of disciples. And though it has hitherto been thought that Blake's prophetic books are original and unprecedented (if only because he claimed angelic inspiration for them, as Milton had done for his *Paradise Lost*), it now appears that the angels tricked him. Instead of a live coal from the altar, they offered a digest of the numerous odd religious and pseudo-historical works current in his day, and he trustfully accepted it. So, despite the magnificence of his language and the splendour of his illustrations, we need not apologize if we find the Prophecies dated, tedious, and perverse.

Blake built up his prophetic corpus as a gigantic compensation for the neglect of his shorter, truer poems. His early *Island in the Moon*—1784, when he was twenty-seven years old—a satire on the dismal literary circle into which he had been drawn, is worth a thousand prophetic books. It contains songs such as:

> Lo, the Bat on leathern wing,
> Winking and blinking,
> Winking and blinking,
> Winking and blinking,
> Like Dr. Johnson.

and:

> When Old Corruption first began,
> Adorned in yellow vest,
> He committed on flesh a whoredom—
> O what a wicked beast!

and:

> I say, you Joe,
> Throw us the ball!
> We've a good mind to go
> And leave you all.
>
> I never saw such a bowler
> To bowl the ball in a turd
> And to clean it with my handkercher
> Without saying a word.

and:

> Little Phoebus came strutting in
> With his fat belly and his round chin.

and:

> When the tongues of children are heard on the green
> And laughing is heard on the hill,
> My heart is at rest within my breast
> And everything else is still.

Most of this playfulness and true inspiration had deserted him by 1804. Blake then wrote in his introduction to *Jerusalem*:

> After my three years slumber on the banks of the ocean, I again display my Giant Forms to the Public. . . . I hope the Reader will be with me, wholly One in Jesus our Lord, who is the God *of Fire* and Lord *of Love* to whom the Ancients look'd and saw his day afar off, with trembling & amazement. . . . When this Verse was first dictated to me, I consider'd a Monotonous Cadence, like that used by Milton & Shakespeare & all writers of English Blank Verse, delivered from the modern bondage of Rhyming, to be a necessary and indispensable part of Verse. But I soon found that in the mouth of a true Orator such monotony was not only awkward, but as much a bondage as rhyme itself. I therefore have produc'd a variety in every line, both of cadences & number of syllables. Every word and

every letter is studied and put into its fit place; the terrific numbers
are reserved for the terrific parts, the mild & gentle for the mild &
gentle parts, and the prosaic for inferior parts; all are necessary to
each other. Poetry Fetter'd Fetters the Human Race. Nations are
Destroy'd or Flourish in proportion as Their Poetry, Painting and
Music are Destroy'd or Flourish! The Primeval State of Man was
Wisdom, Art and Science.

The last sentence is anthropologically indefensible; and the criticism of Shakespeare's blank verse is wilfully obtuse; and Blake
has confused the orator with the poet. An orator might well be
"fettered" if forced to dress his legal arguments in metre and
rhyme; but "fetter" implies slavery. Shakespeare, like every true
poet, accepted the Muse's yoke in the spirit of *Ecclesiasticus:*

> An ornament of gold is her yoke,
> And her traces a ribband of purple silk.

It is not as though anyone had ever been fettered by Blake's
own rhymes—by his *Tyger, Tyger, Burning Bright,* or by his:

> I wonder whether the girls are mad
> And I wonder whether they mean to kill?
> And I wonder if William Bond will die?
> For assuredly he is very ill.

No: poetry and prophecy make ill-assorted bedfellows; prophecy,
especially the evangelical sort, will claim sheet, blankets, and both
pillows in God's name, and let poetry die of exposure.

The truth was that Blake had rallied to Milton's standard in
a deliberate revolt against the Muse, repudiating her as the evil
"Female Will" which seduced Adam, caused the Trojan War, and
was responsible for the idolatrous concepts of Chivalry. He correctly
identified her with Rahab—the Palestinian Love- and Sea-goddess—
but saw her, with the baleful eyes of Isaiah and the Author of
the Apocalypse, as the Great Whore, enemy of spiritual man. Like
Milton, he had apparently been encouraged in this revolt by his

wife's stubborn refusal to accept as gospel whatever he said and decided. His account of the Giant Albion's fall and surrender to Vala—another name for Rahab—parallels Milton's account of Adam's fall and surrender to Eve, and of Samson's to Delilah. In *Milton*, Blake has bloated a local and personal quarrel into monstrous epic proportions. A drunken private soldier named Schofield had accidentally broken into his garden at Felpham; Blake had ejected him; and Schofield, who then charged him with the capital crime of High Treason, appeared to Blake's disordered imagination as a villain in the pay of William Hayley, the poet.

Hayley was Blake's patron, a rich and amiable dilettante who had been trying to help him by directing his genius into socially acceptable channels, securing him commissions for painting miniatures and hand-screens. Blake had at first found Hayley's friendship providential, but soon saw his personal integrity threatened by Hayley's well-meaning approach to Mrs. Blake, who was ill: Hayley had convinced her that Blake ought to postpone his great projected Epic (which would not serve any practical purpose, either religious or poetic), and execute these valuable commissions as a means of earning his bread and butter. Blake now came to the crazy conclusion that Hayley (though Hayley's evidence at the treason trial was instrumental in securing his acquittal) had not only "acted on my wife," but "hired a villain"—Schofield—"to bereave my life." "Skofeld" duly appears among the "Gigantic Forms" of Blake's *Milton* beside Satan (who is Hayley), Palamabron (who is Blake), Elynittria, described as "Palamabron's Emanation" (who is Mrs. Blake), and various unidentifiable friends or relatives of Hayley's. Blake wrote: "The manner in which I have routed out the nest of villains will be seen in a Poem concerning my Three years' Herculean Labours at Felpham, which I will soon Publish." He continued to regard Hayley as a member of an organized conspiracy to swindle him, to spread the rumour of his insanity—unfortunately Hayley had also been patron to Cowper, who was later certified as insane—and to exclude his pictures from the Royal Academy.

It is dangerous to fight the Muse. Milton's end should have been a warning to Blake. Richardson had written of Milton's last years:

Besides what affliction he must have had from his disappointment on the change of times and from his own private losses, he was in perpetual terror of being assassinated. Though he had escaped the talons of the Law, he knew he had made himself enemies in abundance. He was so dejected he would lie awake whole nights . . . and was tormented with headaches, gout, blindness.

These horrors Blake escaped, perhaps because he had a sweeter nature and no frauds or cruelties on his conscience. But despite the nobility of the engravings, which excuse their re-publication, his prophetic books lie under the Muse's curse of permanent unreadability.

Harp, Anvil, Oar

Last week I spoke about Marvan, the seventh-century poet of Connaught who revealed to the professors of the Great Bardic Academy how the poet's harp originated: namely when the wind played on the dried tendons of a stranded whale's skeleton in the time of Macuel son of Miduel. And how metre originated: namely in the alternate beat of two hammers on the anvil, while Lamiach was still alive. The three hundred professors could not follow Marvan here, having long ceased to think poetically. As historic or scientific statements his revelations are, of course, challengeable: not a grain of evidence can be cited for the existence of the whale, or even for that of Macuel son of Miduel. Nevertheless, as poetic statements they are exact. What is the whale? An emblem of the White Love-goddess Rahab, Ruler of the Sea, who used yearly to destroy her sacred kings in numerous cities from Connaught to the Persian Gulf; until at last the god Enlil, or Marduk (or Jehovah, according to the prophet Isaiah) killed her with the new-fangled weapon called a sword—the Babylonians claimed in a hymn that he sliced her like a flatfish. But the King of Babylon still had to do ritual battle with her every year, be swallowed, and spewed up again on the third day, as Jonah was. And though Jehovah's prophets chanted: "O ye whales, bless ye Adonai, praise Him and magnify Him for ever!" they knew that Leviathan was unregenerate, uncontrollable and not to be fished up with any hook let down. Hence the author of the Apocalypse prophesied that one day "there shall be no more sea"; by this he meant "no more Rahab, and no more whales."

The emblems of the Muse Trinity are a white dove in the sky, a white hind in the forest, a whale taking his pastime in the depth of the sea. Where, then, could one find a better figure of death than the white skeleton of a stranded whale? And wind, North Wind, the wind that (proverbially) pigs alone can see, the wind that, as I told you, Marvan carried in his mantle, the wind that fertilized the windswift sacred mares of Trojan Erichthonius and the prophetic vultures of Roman augury—wind (*spiritus, pneuma*) is the emblem of inspiration. The bones of Rahab the Whale may lie stranded on the shore; but, for a poet, there is more truth in her dead sinews than in Marduk's living mouth. When Macuel son of Miduel heard the wind howling tunefully in the Æolian harp of the whale's skeleton, he bethought himself and built a smaller, more manageable one for the same materials. And when he struck his harp and cried: "Sing to me, Muse!" this was no formal invitation—Rahab herself sang at his plea.

A close parallel, by the bye, may be found in English popular poetry. The ballad of the *Twa Sisters of Binnorie* tells of a drowned woman whose hair was used for harp-strings:

> And by there came a harper fine
> *Edinbro', Edinbro'*
> Such as harp to nobles when they dine.
> *Stirling for aye*
> He's ta'en twa strands of her yellow hair
> And with it strung a harp sae rare
> *Bonnie St. Johnstone stands on Tay.*

He's done him into her father's hall,
  Edinbro', Edinbro'
And played the harp before them all,
  Stirling for aye
And syne the harp spake loud and clear
"Farewell my father and mither dear."
  Bonnie St. Johnstone stands on Tay.

And syne the harp began to sing
  Edinbro', Edinbro'
And it's "Farewell, sweetheart," sang the string
  Stirling for aye
And then, as plain as plain could be,
"There sits my sister who drownéd me."
  Bonnie St. Johnstone stands on Tay.

The harp is the prophetic voice of the yellow-haired goddess—the Muse-goddess was always yellow-haired—and she sings of love, and grief, and doom. Marvan, moreover, was careful to distinguish the fitful inspirational music of the Æolian harp from the purposeful rhythmic clatter of the smith's anvil.

I am aware that I should here be discussing the English, not the Irish, literary scene. But Irish poetry is to English poetry, as—may I say?—the Pharisaic synagogue is to the Christian Church: an antecedent which historians are tempted to forget or belittle. The English have long despised the Irish; and though generously ready to acknowledge their debt to Anglo-Saxon, French, Italian, Latin and Greek literatures, are loth to admit that the strongest element in English poetic technique (though certainly acquired at second or third hand) is the Irish tradition of craftsmanship.

When two hammers answer each other five times on the anvil—*ti-tum, ti-tum, ti-tum, ti-tum, ti-tum*—five in honour of the five stations of the Celtic year, there you have Chaucer's familiar hendecasyllabic line:

A knight ther was, and that a worthy man
That fro the tymë that he first began
To ryden out, he lovéd chivalrye. . . .

But Anglo-Saxon poetry had been based on the slow pull and push of the oar:

> Then I of myself/will máke this known
> That awhíle I was held/the Héodenings' scop,
> To my duke most dear/and Déor was my name.

The function of the Nordic *scop* seems to have been twofold. Not only was he originally a "shaper" of charms, to protect the person of the king and so maintain prosperity in the realm; but he had a subsidiary task, of persuading a ship's crew to pull rhythmically and uncomplainingly on their oars against the rough waves of the North Sea, by singing them ballads in time to the beat. When they returned from a successful foray, and dumped their spoil of gold collars, shields, casques, and monastic chalices on the rush-strewn floor of the beer-hall, then the *scop* resumed his song. The drunken earls and churls straddled the benches, and rocked to the tune: "Over the whale's way, fared we unfearful. . . ."

Anglo-Saxon poetry is unrhymed, because of the noise of row-locks does not suggest rhyme. Rhyme reached England from France. It had been brought there by Irish missionaries who recivilized Western Europe after the Frankish invasions. These missionaries wrote and talked Latin, and *The Rhythm of St. Bernard of Cluny*, the first rhymed poem of high literary pretensions written by an Englishman (during the reign of Henry I or II) follows the pure Irish tradition. Its complicated series of internal and end-rhymes, and its faultless finish, leave no doubt about this. Here are four of the three thousand rhymed lines:

> Urbs Syon aurea, Patria lactea, cive decora,
> Omne cor obruis, omnibus obstruis et cor et ora.
> Nescio, nescio, quae jubilatio, lux tibi qualis,
> Quam socialia gaudia, gloria quam specialis.

Prosodists have a Latin name for the metre: *Leonini cristati trilices dactylici*. St. Bernard's *Rhythm* has been translated into English, pretty well (though with a loss of all the rhyme pairs except the end ones, which have become monosyllables), by the Victorian hymn-writer, J. M. Neale:

> Jerusalem the Golden,
> With Milk and Honey Blest,
> Beneath Thy Contemplation
> Sink heart and voice oppressed:
> I know not, O I know not,
> What social joys are there;
> What radiancy of Glory,
> What Light beyond Compare!

Nordic verse-craft, as I was saying, is linked to the pull of the oar. Greek verse-craft is linked to the ecstatic beat of feet around a rough stone altar, sacred to Dionysus (or Hermes, or Eros, or Zeus Cronides), probably to the sound of the dactylic drum played by a priestess or a priest:

$$-\cup\cup \,/\, -\cup\cup \,/\, - \,/\, /\cup\cup \,/\, -\cup\cup \,/\, -\cup\cup \,/\, --$$

The Greeks also admitted the iambic, traditionally named in honour of lasciviously hobbling Iambe, who (you may remember) tried to coax a smile from the bereaved Demeter at Eleusis. Iambic metre may have begun with Helladic totem dances which imitated the hobbling of partridge or quail:

$$\cup- \,/\, \cup- \,/\, \cup/ \,/\, /- \,/\, \cup- \,/\, \cup- \,/\, \cup-$$

There was also the spondaic measure derived from the gloomy double-stamp of buskined mourners, arousing some dead hero to drink the libations (*spondae*) that they poured for him:

$$-- \,/\, -- \,/\, - \,/\, /- \,/\, -- \,/\, -- \,/\, --$$

A metrical line in Greek poetry represents the turn taken by a dancer around an altar or tomb, with a cæsura marking the half-way point: the metre never varies until the dancers have dropped with fatigue. Similarly in *Beowulf* and other Anglo-Saxon poems, the oar's pull and push continues mercilessly until harbour is reached, or until the drunken diners fall off their bench to the floor, unable to rise again.

The Irish concept of metre is wholly different. All poets owed allegiance to the Muse-goddess Brigid—who may be decently equated with the Helladic Moon-goddess Brizo of Delos. Brigid had three aspects: the Brigid of Poets, the Brigid of Smiths, and the Brigid of Physicians. A Brigid of Smiths may seem anomalous, because English smiths have long ranked lower in the social scale than poets and physicians. In England smithcraft ceased, with the triumph of Christianity, to be an inspired profession; it was wrested by monks from the hands of the lame Smith Wayland (who served the Goddess Freya) and registered merely as a useful trade. Even as a trade, it is dying now: wedding ring, or scythe, or steel helmet is supplied by factories where not even a superstitious vestige of the Wayland cult has gone into the making. But the pagan smith, whether goldsmith, whitesmith, or blacksmith, approached his work with enormous care and magical precaution. And it is significant that smiths were the last of the ancient craftsmen to be awarded a patron saint, Saint Elir, by the Roman Church.

The religious connexion between poetry, smithcraft, and medicine is a close one. Medicine presupposes a knowledge of times, seasons, and the sovereign properties of plants, trees, beasts, birds, fish, earths, minerals. Poetry presupposes an inspired knowledge of man's sensuous and spiritual nature. Smithcraft—for the smith was also carpenter, mason, shipwright and toolmaker—presupposes an inspired knowledge of how to transform lifeless material into active forms. No ancient smith would have dared to proceed without the aids of medicine and poetry. The charcoal used on his forge had been made, with spells, at a certain time of the year from timber of certain sacred trees; and the leather of the forge bellows, from the skin of a sacred animal ritually sacrificed. Before starting a task, he and his assistant were obliged to purify themselves with medicines and lustrations, and to placate the Spites which habitually crowd around forge and anvil. If he happened to be forging a sword, the water in which it was to be tempered must have magical properties—May dew, or spring water in which a virgin princess had washed her hair. The whole work was done to the accompaniment of poetic spells.

Such spells matched the rhythm of the smiths' hammers; and these were of unequal weight. A sledge hammer was swung by the assistant;

the smith himself managed the lighter hammer. To beat out hot metal successfully, one must work fast and follow a prearranged scheme. The smith with his tongs lays the glowing lump of iron on the anvil, then touches with his hammer the place where the sledge blow is to fall; next he raps on the anvil the number of blows required. Down comes the sledge; the smith raps again for another blow, or series of blows. Experience teaches him how many can be got in while the iron is still hot. So each stage of every process had its peculiar metre, to which descriptive words became attached; and presently the words found their own tunes. This process explains Marvan's mysterious reference to Lamiach, who appears in the English translations of *Genesis* as "Lamech." Lamech was the father of Tubal the first smith, and Jubal the first musician. Nor did the smith (as many archaeologists assume) let caprice rule the number and shape of ornaments that he introduced into his work. Whether he was forging a weapon, or a piece of armour, or a tool, or a cauldron, or a jewelled collar, every element in the design had a magical significance.

An Irish poet versified to the ring of hammers; and the fact that rhyme and regular metre had become characteristic of English poetry by Chaucer's time implies that the smithy tradition of careful thought and accurate workmanship, which these call for, had also been to some extent adopted. The metaphor of beating out one's verses on the anvil is now, indeed, a poetical commonplace. But let me put it this way: though every English poet is a smith for the greater part of the year, he takes to the sea during the brief sailing season. Chaucer may seem to be a hammer-and-anvil poet when he writes:

> A knight ther was, and that a worthy man
> That fro the tymë that he first began
> To ryden out, he lovéd chivalrye. . . .

Ti-tum, ti-tum, ti-tum, ti-tum. Then he lays down the hammer and reaches for the oar. Instead of:

> Honoùr and freédom, trùth and cóurtesy,

he writes:

Trùth and honoùr/freédom and coúrtesy,

and this has been the English verse-tradition ever since.

Skelton also reconciled the anvil with the oar in a metre which he used in his early *Lament for Edward IV*, and again at the close of his life in *Speke Parrot*. Note the Anglo-Saxon alliteration:

Miseremini mei/ye that be my frendis!
This world hath forméd me/downë to fall.
How many I endure/when that everi thing endis?
What creäture is bornë/to be eternáll?

and:

The myrrour that I tote in/*quasi diaphanum*,
Vel quasi speculum/*in aenigmate*,
Elencticum, or ells/*enthymematicum*,
For logicians to loke on/somewhat *sophistice:*
Retoricyons and oratours/in freshe humanyte,
Support Parrot, I pray you/with your suffrage ornate,
Of *confuse tantum*/auoydynge the chekmate.

The history of Shakespeare's blank verse is a progression from the careful anvil work of, say, *The Comedy of Errors*, to *The Tempest*, where the oar is pulling in a very rough sea. *The Comedy of Errors* begins:

EGEON: Proceed, Solinus, to procure my fall,
              And by the doom of death end woes and all.
DUKE OF   Merchant of Syracusa, plead no more.
EPHESUS: I am not partial to infringe our laws;
              The enmity and discord which of late
              Spring from the rancorous outrage of your Duke
              To merchants, our well-dealing countrymen,
              Who wanting guilders to redeem their lives,

Have sealed his rigorous statutes with their bloods,
Excludes all pity from our threatening looks. . . .

But in *The Tempest* the opening exchanges between shipmaster and boatswain are recognized as blank verse only because every now and then a regular line occurs to reassert the norm. (Heming and Condell in their edition of the *First Folio* print them as prose, and all cautious editors follow suit.)

(*The* BOATSWAIN *appears when the* MASTER *summons him*)

THE MASTER: Good. Speak to the mariners; fall to't yarely.
             Or we run ourselves aground. Bestir, bestir!
BOATSWAIN: Heigh my hearts, cheerily, cheerily, my hearts,
             yare, yare!
             Take in the topsail! Tend to the master's whistle!
(*to the* MASTER)
             Blow till thou burst thy wind, if room enough!

The rules of prosody apply only to anvil verse, or to sacred-dance verse, in which every syllable is evaluated and counted. Pope, for instance, says that he lisped in numbers for the numbers came; "numbers" translates the Latin *numeri*, which imply a careful count of syllables. Pope never escaped from the "numbers" theory: which posits an orderly sequence of metrical feet each with the same determined time value, every long syllable being given the value of a crotchet, and every short syllable the value of a quaver; though the Elizabethan critics, headed by George Puttenham, had emphatically rejected this theory. The only fundamental difference between Pope's notion of verse and Virgil's, or Horace's, was that the Latin convention of what made a syllable long or short had lapsed. Now, in Bernard of Cluny's *Rhythm*, for instance, the Latin rules of quantity are maintained: every syllable is regarded as long or short by nature, though a short syllable may become long by position; and a terminal vowel, or vowel plus *m*, will be elided and disappear. This, it must be realized, was a highly artificial convention: ordinary Latin speech, as heard in the home and Forum, seems from the scraps of camp songs penned by Suetonius to have been accentual, and the accent did not necessarily fall on the long vowel.

It amused educated English poets—such as Chaucer, Skelton, Ben Jonson, Milton, Marvell, Dr. Johnson, and Coleridge—to compose Latin verses in Classical style; but the freedom to observe natural speech stresses (as opposed to the laws of quantity) not only in vernacular verse but in Latin too, if they pleased, had already been won for them by the hymnologists and carolmakers and Goliardic song-writers of the Middle Ages. The first two lines of the famous medieval students' drinking song:

> Mihi est propositum in taberna mori;
> Vinum sit appositum potatoris ori. . . .

contain thirteen false quantities, and the first two lines of the equally famous hymn:

> Dies irae, dies illa
> Solvens saecla in favilla. . . .

contain eight. This is not due to ignorance. Who would dare accuse St. Thomas Aquinas of ignorance because he rhymes *natus* with *datus?* Aquinas knew well enough that rhyme was a barbarism in Classical Latin poetry—and that Cicero had made a fool of himself with the internal rhyme of:

> O fortunatam natam, me Consule, Romam!

But he also knew that these quantities had been justified by Irish metrical example; the Irish did not acknowledge quantity, they relied on accent.

Skelton, in his *Devout Trentale for Old John Clerk, Sometime the Holy Patriarche of Diss,* actually alternated correct hexameters with Goliardic verse:

> Sequitur trigintale,
> Tale quale rationale,

Licet parum curiale,
Tamen satis est formale,
Joannis Clerc, hominis
Cujusdam multinominis,
Joannes Jayberd qui vocatur,
Clerc cleribus nuncupatur.
Obiit sanctus iste pater
Anno Domini MD, sexto.
In parochia de Dis.
Non erat sibi similis;
In malitia vir insignis,
Duplex corde et bilinguis;
Senio confectus,
Omnibus suspectus,
Nemini dilectus,
Sepultus est *amonge the wedes:*
God forgeue hym his mysdedes!

Dulce melos*
Penetrans coelos.

Carmina cum cannis cantemus festa Joannis:
Clerk obiit vere, Jayberd nomenque dedere;
Dis populo natus, Clerk cleribusque vocatus.

The Elizabethan critics, humanists to a man, were a little uneasy about this divergence from Classical metric theory, but there was clearly no help for it. Samuel Daniel, in his *Defence of Rhyme* (1603), found it necessary to lay down: "As Greeke and Latine verse consists of the number and quantity of sillables, so doth the English verse of measure and accent." They admitted, in fact, that the natural accent of current English speech decides whether a syllable should be long or short—even though the same word may change its value in the same line. Thus, for instance, the pentameter:

ōffĕr hĕr/ĭcĕs, ŏr/ā/ /lōvelў cŏm/fōrtăblē/chāir

* Mĕlŏs rhyming with cōelōs.

is quantitatively correct according to Ovidian rule, but does not scan. Moreover, the Virgilian hexameter, as Thomas Nashe forcefully explained in his answer to Gabriel Harvey's recommendation of it, is not natural to English:

> The Hexamiter verse I graunt to be a Gentleman of an auncient house (so is many an english beggar); yet this Clyme of ours hee cannot thriue in. Our speech is too craggy for him to set his plough in; hee goes twitching and hopping in our language like a man running vpon quagmiers, vp the hill in one Syllable, and downe the dale in another, retaining no part of that stately smooth gate which he vaunts himselfe with amongst the Greeks and Latins.

And so a strong sense has grown up among practical English poets that the natural rhythm of speech decides where accents fall; and that, therefore, the less artificial the words, the truer the poem.

Tell a schoolchild that Keats's *Fairy Song* is an iambic poem with three four-foot lines followed by one of five feet, another of four feet, one of two feet, and finally a five-footer, rhyming AB, AB, C, C, B—and he will read it like this:

> Ah woe/is me/poor silv/er wing
> That I/must chant/thy lad/y's dirge
> And death/to this/fair haunt/of spring
> And mel/ody/and streams/of flower/y verge.
> Poor Silv/erwing/ah woe/is me
> That I/must see
> These Bloss/oms snow/upon/thy lad/y's pall.

But if the words are spoken in the manner most natural to their sense and feeling, this is how Keats will have meant it to be said; and you realize that the laws of prosody are, to verse, very much as copperplate models are to handwriting. Keats had a poet's ear for verse; as Shakespeare had; as Donne had; as Coleridge had; as Skelton had. But Keats was easily seduced. When he put on his singing robes and played at being a Classical poet, he became gorbliminess incarnate. In his *Ode to Apollo,* for example:

Then, through thy Temple wide, melodious swells
  The sweet majestic tone of Maro's lyre:
  The soul delighted on each accent dwells,—
    Enraptur'd dwells,—not daring to respire,
The while he tells of grief around a funeral pyre.

  'Tis awful silence then again;
    Expectant stand the spheres;
    Breathless the laurell'd peers,
  Nor move, till ends the lofty strain,
  Nor move till Milton's tuneful thunders cease
And leave once more the ravish'd heaven in peace.

  Thou biddest Shakespeare wave his hand,
    And quickly forward spring
    The Passions—a terrific band—
    And each vibrates the string
  That with its tyrant temper best accords,
While from their Master's lips pour forth the inspiring words.

Keats should have known that to impose an artificial word-order, or an artificial vocabulary, on poems is a lapse in poetic dignity.

There is so much to say about professional standards in verse-technique, that I shall confine myself to generalities. For instance, that though the muscular *str* and *scr* words: *strain, strength, string, strangle, stretch, struggle, strident, extravagant, screw, scrape, scrawny*, and such easy skipping words as *melody, merrily, prettily, harmony, fantasy* match sense with sound, other words are not so onomatopoeic. *A strangely striped strip of satin* is far too emphatic in sound for the sense, and *a terribly powerful Florida hurricane* is not nearly emphatic enough. Yet to alter the spirit of an original poetic thought for the sake of metre or euphony is unprofessional conduct. So the art of accommodating sense to sound without impairing the original thought has to be learned by example and experiment. Under-emphasis or over-emphasis in a word can be controlled by playing other words off against it, and carefully choosing its position in a line, and making the necessary adjustments to neighbouring lines until the ear at last feels satisfied. It is an axiom among poets that if one trusts whole-heartedly to poetic magic, one will be sure to solve any merely verbal problem or else discover that the verbal problem is hiding an imprecision in poetic thought.

I say magic, since the act of composition occurs in a sort of trance, distinguishable from dream only because the critical faculties are not dormant, but on the contrary, more acute than normally. Often a rugger player is congratulated on having played the smartest game of his life, but regrets that he cannot remember a single incident after the first five minutes, when he got kicked on the head. It is much the same with a poet when he completes a true poem. But often he wakes from the trance too soon and is tempted to solve the remaining problems intellectually. Few self-styled poets have experienced the trance; but all who have, know that to work out a line by an exercise of reason, rather than by a deep-seated belief in miracle, is highly unprofessional conduct. If a trance has been interrupted, it is just too bad. The poem should be left unfinished, in the hope that suddenly, out of the blue, days or months later, it may start stirring again at the back of the mind, when the remaining problems will solve themselves without difficulty.

Donne's chief failing as a love-poet was his readiness to continue the inspired beginning with a witty development. For instance:

> Goe, and catche a falling starre,
> Get with child a mandrake roote . . .

Here Donne paused, apparently remembered Villon's *neiges d'antan*, and went on:

> Tell me, where all past years are . . .

And then consciously searched for a rhyme to *roote*. But he had not the least idea where the poem was taking him, except into a discussion of impossibility. So he continued in quite a different key:

> Or who cleft the Divels foot,
> Teach me to heare Mermaides singing,
> Or to keep off envies stinging . . .

He paused again and apparently remembered Shakespeare's:

> Blow, blow thou winter wind,
> Thou art not so unkind
> As man's ingratitude . . .

and Dante's remarks about the bitterness of having to seek advancement from haughty patrons. So he ended the verse with the quite irrelevant:

> And finde
> What winde
> Serves to advance an honest minde.

Again he opened magnificently:

> I wonder by my troth, what thou, and I
> Did, till we lov'd? were we not wean'd till then?
> But suck'd on countrey pleasures, childishly?

Here inspiration faded and he resorted to artifice:

> Or snorted we in the seaven sleepers' den?
> 'Twas so; But this, all pleasures fancies bee.
> If ever any beauty I did see,
> Which I desir'd, and got, 'twas but a dreame of thee.

Donne is adept at keeping the ball in the air, but he deceives us here by changing the ball. Coleridge often does the same thing, for example when he fakes a sequel to the inspired opening passage of *Christabel*—but he handles the ball so clumsily that we are seldom deceived.

It is unprofessional conduct to say: "When next I write a poem I shall use the sonnet form"—because the theme is by definition unforeseeable, and theme chooses metre. A poet should not be conscious of the metrical pattern of a poem he is writing until the first three or four lines have appeared; he may even find himself in the eleventh line of fourteen before realizing that a sonnet is on the way. Besides, metre is only a frame; the atmospheres of two sonnets can be so different that they will not be recognized as having the same form except by a careful count of lines and feet. Theme chooses metre; what is more, theme decides what rhythmic variations should be made on metre. The theory that all poems must be equally rich in sound is an un-English one, borrowed from Virgil. Rainbow-like passages are delightful every now and then, but they match a rare mood of opulence and exaltation which soon fatigues. The riches of *Paradise Lost* fatigue, and even oppress, all but musicians. Rainbows should make their appearances only when the moment has come to disclose the riches of the heart, or soul, or imagination; they testify to passing storms and are short-lived.

Another professional principle is that *mimesis* should be regarded as vulgar. By mimesis I mean such *tours de force* as Virgil's:

Quadrupedante putrem sonitu quatit ungula campum,

and Tennyson's:

The moan of doves in immemorial elms,
The murmur of innumerable bees.

To these I should add the Homeric:

Autis epeita pedonde cylindeto laäs anaides,

the shameless stone of Sisyphus bounding downhill, if I did not think that this was high-spirited verbal comedy, proclaiming disbelief in the whole theory of divine punishment.

Pope's translation of the Sisyphus passage, by the way, runs:

With many a weary sigh, and many a groan,
Up the high hill he heaves a huge round stone . . .

though the corresponding lines in the *Odyssey* do not mimic Sisyphus's breathlessness. And Pope's concluding couplet is wretchedly incompetent:

The huge round stone, resulting with a bound
Thunders impetuous down and smokes along the ground.

The false internal rhymes of *round* and *bound* and the half-rhymes of *down* and *ground* effectively act as brakes on the stone's merry progress. As Blake said in one of his Public Addresses: "I do not condemn Pope or Dryden because they did not understand imagination, but because they did not understand verse."

One of the most difficult problems is how to use natural speech rhythms as variations on a metrical norm. And here we meet with the heresy of free verse. Until the time of Blake and his oratorical cadences, it was generally agreed that the reader should never be allowed to lose his sense of metrical norm. But Blake, finding the contemporary technique of poetry too cramping, burst it wide open and wrote something that was neither poetry nor prose. Whitman did much the same, though for different reasons: he epitomizes the restless American habit, first noted in the eighteenth century, of moving adventurously west across the trackless prairie, scratch-farming as one goes, instead of clinging to some pleasant Pennsylvanian farm, improving crops and stock by careful husbandry, and building a homestead for one's children and grand-children. All who, like Whitman, choose to dispense with a rhythmical norm are welcome to explore the new country which he opened up, but it now wears rather a dismal look. Robert Frost's poems, which combine traditional metres with intensely personal rhythms, show the advantage of staying put and patiently working at the problem.*

* Mr. Eliot has written about free verse:

> It is not defined by non-existence of metre, since even the worst verse can be scanned.

This is to beg the question. In so far as verse can be scanned, it is not freed of metre. He has also written:

> But the most interesting verse which has yet been written in our language has been done [sic] either by taking a very simple form, like the iambic pentameter, and constantly withdrawing from it, or taking no form at all, and continually approximating to a very simple one. It is this contrast between fixity and flux, this unperceived evasion of monotony, which is the very life of verse.

Interesting to some, embarrassing to others, like a jaunt in a car after

A dogma has recently been planted in English schools that the King James version of the Bible is poetry. It is not. The polishing of the English translation was, of course, admirably done by a team of capable University scholars, trained in the oratorical art. Sometimes they even included a perfectly metrical line:

How art thou fallen from Heaven, O Lucifer, son of the morning!

And:

> Come down and sit in the dust; O virgin daughter of Babylon,
> Sit on the ground. . . .

But one might as well call *The Times* leaders poetry, because they are written by skilled journalists and because they contain a high proportion of blank-verse lines, sometimes as much as 30 per cent.

Ben Jonson told Drummond of Hawthornden that "for not keeping of accent"—that is to say, allowing his readers to lose the sense of metrical norm—"Donne deserved hanging." Jonson had also said that Donne was "the first poet in the world in some things," and that he had a few of his early poems by heart. It is difficult to reconcile these statements. But Jonson seems to be referring to the *Satyres*, where Donne at times deliberately changes the metre—as when a competitor in a walking race shamelessly bends his knees and breaks into a short run:

> . . . So in immaculate clothes, and Symetrie
> Perfect as circles, with such nicetie
> As a young Preacher at his first time goes
> To preach, he enters, and a Lady, which owes
> Him not so much as good will, he arrests,

mixing a little water with the petrol to make it go by fits and starts. I was never interested in that sort of experiment; I expect verse to be verse, and prose to be prose; agreeing with Robert Frost who once said about Free Verse: "One can, of course, play tennis without a net but that's not much of a game, is it?"

And unto her protests, protests, protests;
So much as at Rome would serve to have throwne
Ten Cardinalls into the Inquisition;
And whispers by Jesu, so often, that A
Pursevant would have ravish'd him away
For saying of our Ladies psalter. But 'tis fit
That they each other plague, they merit it . . .

In the same satire, Donne also makes the units of sense play havoc
with the units of metre:

. . . No, no, Thou which since yesterday hast beene
Almost about the whole world, hast thou seene,
O Sunne, in all thy journey, Vanitie,
Such as swells the bladder of our court? I
Thinke he which made your waxen garden, and
Transported it from Italy to stand
With us, at London, flouts our Presence, for
Just such gay painted things, which no sappe, nor
Tast have in them, ours are; And naturall
Some of the stocks are, their fruits, bastard all.

But let me speak up for Donne. There are, of course, certain
familiar proprieties in English poetry. Accent must be kept, which
means, as I have shown, that however the metrical norm may be
varied, it should stay recognizable—one must not write lines that
go off into another metre altogether. Rhyme must be kept within
certain decent limits, and the consonantal part of rhyme must be
regarded as more important than the vowel. It is, for instance,
indecent to rhyme *charm* with *calm*, or (*pace* W. H. Auden) *bore*
with *mother-in-law*; though *love* and *prove*, *all* and *usual*, *fly* and
extremity are traditionally countenanced. Three-syllable rhymes are
indecent, so are mixed metaphors, and what Corinna called "sow-
ing with the sack"—namely over-ornamentation of every kind. Again:
an even level of language should be kept: one must decide to what
period each poem belongs and not relapse to an earlier, or anticipate
a more modern, diction. Thus it is indecent to address *you* and *thee*
in the same verse to the same person—even if Pope and Marvell are

quoted in justification. And, most important, there should be no discrepancy between the sound and the sense of a poem. It would be difficult, for instance, to quarrel on technical grounds with a simple iambic stanza such as this:

> Mother is dead; my heart to pieces torn,
> I hear my kinsmen weep—
> Uncle, niece, nephew, cousin, who convey her
> Unto her last long sleep.

But turn this into dactyls, and the effect is ludicrous:

> Mother is dead and my heart is in pieces,
> Hark how the friends of the family weep!
> Cousins and uncles and nephews and nieces
> Accompany her to her last long sleep.

These are elementary rules, a few chosen at random from what I may call the Common Law of English Verse. But, in English satire, all rules can be deliberately broken. Byron's satiric comment on Keats's death, for example:

> Strange that the soul, that very fiery particle,
> Should let itself be snuffed out by an article. . . .

is emphasized by the deliberate use of the three-syllabled rhyme.

And comically inexact rhyme is the strength of Siegfried Sassoon's squib, written in the palmy days of George V, which he has generously allowed me to resurrect:

> Because the Duke is Duke of York,
> The Duke of York has shot a huge rhinoceros;
> Let's hope the Prince of Wales will take a walk
> Through Africa, and make the Empire talk
> By shooting an enormous hippopotamus,
> And let us also hope that Lord Lascelles
> Will shoot *all* beasts from gryphons to gazelles
> And show the world what sterling stuff we've got in us.

The word *satire* is not derived, as most people suppose, from the witty, prick-eared satyrs of the early Greek comedy, but from the Latin phrase *satura lanx,* or "full platter." Latin satire was a burlesque performance at a harvest festival, in which full-fed countrymen would improvise obscene topical jokes to a recurrent dance tune—as many islanders of Majorca still do to the *copeo,* at their annual pig-killing. The harvest atmosphere was free and easy; anything went. Urban satire, as Horace or Juvenal or Persius wrote it, was quite a different affair: Greek in origin, and bound by the same rules as epic or pastoral verse. Samuel Butler's *Hudibras* is fascennine; so are Donne's satires. Donne, in fact, did not 'deserve hanging' if he failed to keep his accent in the satires; he could plead privilege.

Pope, who modelled himself as a satirist on Horace, thought fit to regularize Donne's lines:

> Thou, who since yesterday hast roll'd o'er all
> The busy, idle blockheads of the ball,
> Hast thou, oh Sun! beheld an emptier sort,
> Than such as swell this bladder of a court? . . .

> Thus finish'd and corrected to a hair,
> They march, to prate their hour before the fair.
> So first to preach a white-glov'd chaplain goes,
> With band of lily, and with cheek of rose,
> Sweeter than Sharon, in immac'late trim,
> Neatness itself impertinent with him. . . .

The difference between these two versions is that Donne's is readable, and Pope's is not; the regularity of the metre defeats its object after the first fifty couplets. Its readers remain unmoved; they sigh, and fall gently asleep. And this suggests another subject.

The Irish and early Welsh bards had made a discovery, which the Greeks and Romans had never made, and which reached England very late; namely, that regular verse, though a wonderful aid to memory, is soporific unless frequent changes occur in the metre; and that though, say, Virgil's *Æneid* or Homer's *Iliad* may contain numerous poems, the verse which links these poems together, because written in the same metre, robs them of their force. What jeweller would display a pearl, unless perhaps a black one, in mother-of-pearl setting? The Irish bards, while vellum was prohibitively dear, recorded their chronologies, their treatises on geography, husbandry, and so on, in mnemonic rhyme. Yet their tales (of which they had to know nine hundred or more) were prose; and these the poet told in his own way, to keep them fresh and individual and up to date; until he reached a dramatic climax, and this was a traditional poem which he had to know by heart.

Mother-of-pearl, though a noble material for cutting and engraving, is not pearl. The greater part of every long poem, even Spenser's *Faerie Queene,* is necessarily mother-of-pearl. Ben Jonson, hinted at this in his *Discoveries.* He wrote:

> Even one alone verse sometimes makes a perfect poem as when Aeneas hangs up and consecrates the Armes of *Abas* with this inscription:

> *Aeneas haec de Danais victoribus arma . . .*

and calls it a *Poeme* or *Carmen.*

This drawing of attention to the poems included in a long work written in set stanzas—as Dante enthusiasts point to *The Death of Ugolino* and similar pearls—suggests that the rest is not up to sample. And how can it be, if the same metre is insisted on throughout?

In blank verse drama one can easily mark off the poems from the roughage. Not only is blank verse capable of almost infinite variations, but prose is allowed to supply comic relief or passages which further the plot. Shakespeare, for instance, makes Trinculo and Stephano in *The Tempest* speak familiar quayside prose, which Caliban answers in poems. But it is manifestly impossible that a long narrative poem which contains genealogy, description of scenery, battles, love-passages, laments, and so on, can be reduced to a single metre without dilution of the poetic content. Long poems are like old French or Spanish tapestries: the design and colour and needlework may be charming but there is no sharpness of detail, no personal characterization, no difference in quality or colour between foreground and background.

Are there any anthropologists present? If so, they may recall the giant yam of Abulam. At Abulam in New Guinea, yams for ordinary eating are planted and tended by the women, but every planting season a tense competition arises among the men: who can grow the yam of the year. This is a purely ritualistic yam, like the Harvest Festival marrow in an English village. The winning exhibit is said to be of approximately the size and shape of a bull-hippopotamus (discounting its head and legs) and perfectly inedible. It provides, in fact, an emblem of the literary epic, which was still being cultivated in Victorian days. With the passing of this Epic, followed by the formal Elegy, and the Ode addressed to heedless nightingales, rocking-chairs, abstractions, and noblemen, of what does poetry now consist? It is reduced, at last, to practical poems, namely the lyrical or dramatic highlights of the poet's experiences with the Goddess in her various disguises. The prose setting is withheld; and, because of this, professional standards demand that it should either explain itself fully, or present a note, as schoolchildren do who arrive late or without some necessary part of their school equipment.

Before closing, I must tell you about a girl who is reading English here under Professor X.* I asked her: "What poems do you enjoy most?" and she answered with dignity: "Poems are not meant to be enjoyed; they are meant to be analysed." I hope you do not think that I subscribe to this heresy.

* Professor Leavis.

Dame Ocupacyon

In my last lecture I raised the problem of the poet's public, meaning: How large or small can this be in his lifetime? As large, I should say, as the widest possible extension of his circle of potential friends, or as small as the narrowest number of these potential friends to become aware of his work. Friends: not neighbours, not relatives, not business acquaintances: friends. People with roughly the same background of birth, environment, education, emotional propensities and intellectual prejudices. Friends, because, though they need not know the poet personally, they should feel at their ease with the poem. A poet may use any means that offer to make his work available to them. But if he tries to win a larger public by writing down to it, he is guilty of professional misconduct. I will go further: he should not consider his public at all, until the poem is written.

The medical profession supplies an analogy to this paradox. A true physician, obsessed with his work, will not regard himself as morally bound to any particular practice or hospital; he will readily move to another practice, or another hospital, which offers him more favourable working conditions, even if the pay is smaller. His chief interest lies in the diagnosis and cure (or palliation) of disease; and his chief loyalty is to the Goddess Hygieia, not to a particular group of sick people who need medical attention. The poet's chief interest lies, similarly, in the conception and working out of poems, and his chief loyalty is to the Goddess Calliope, not to his publisher, or to the booksellers on his publisher's mailing list. What the subsequent fate may be of the poems he writes should never influence their conception; as the act of love should be uncomplicated by thoughts of rich godparents for the child to be, perhaps, conceived. Also, the poet's approach to the Goddess is a personal one: he comes as himself, not in fancy-dress or borrowed clothing; and does not rant at her as though she were a public meeting, but speaks gently, clearly, intimately—they are closeted alone together. . . . By the way, I heard an answer today to the platitude: "There's no money in poetry." It was: "There's no poetry in money, either."

Epitaphs and elegies are a good test of poetic seriousness; because they may tempt the poet to hollow rhetoric. I have already quoted Skelton's *Epitaph on Edward IV*, and Clare's *The Dying Child* and, by contrast, Dryden's fancy-dress *Epitaph on Lord Hastings*. Here are two more poems of the same solemn category from opposite ends of the social scale. What makes Surrey's *Epitaph on Clere of Cleremont* a good poem is that he remains uncompromisingly himself, with all the faults and virtues of his nobility, and that he feels a sincere grief:

> Norfolk sprang thee, Lambeth holds thee dead;
> Clere, of the County of Cleremont, thou hight.
> Within the womb of Ormond's race thou bred,
> And saw'st thy cousin crownéd in thy sight. . . .
> Shelton for love, Surrey for Lord, thou chase;
> (Aye me! while life did last that league was tender)
> Tracing whose steps thou sawest Kelsall blaze,
> Laundersey burnt, and battered Bullen render,
> At Mottrel gates, hopeless of all recure,
> Thine Earl, half dead, gave in thy hand his will;
> Which cause did thee this pining death procure,
> Ere summers four times seven thou couldst fulfill.
>   Ah! Clere! if love had booted, care, or cost,
>   Heaven had not won, nor earth so timely lost.

What makes *The Night Before Larry Was Stretched*, a late eighteenth-century Dublin street-ballad, a good poem is that the writer, whoever he may have been (and one Harefoot Bill is generally credited with it) also remains uncompromisingly himself, with all the faults and virtues of his villainy, and he too feels a sincere grief:

The night before Larry was stretched,
　　The boys they all paid him a visit;
A bit in their sacks too they fetched,
　　They sweated their duds till they riz it;
For Larry was always the lad,
　　When a friend was condemned to the squeezer,
Would fence all the togs that he had
　　Just to help the poor boy to a sneezer,
　　　　And moisten his gob 'fore he died. . . .

The boys they came crowding in fast;
　　They drew their stools close round about him,
Six glims round his trap-case they placed;
　　He couldn't be well waked without 'em.
When we asked, was he fit for to die
　　Without having truly repented?
Says Larry, "That's all in my eye,
　　And first by the clergy invented
　　　　To get a fat bit for themselves."

. . . Then the deck being called for, they played
　　Till Larry found one of them cheated.
A dart at his napper he made,
　　The lad being easily heated.
"So ye chates me because I'm in grief;
　　O, is that, by the Holy, the rason?
Soon I'll give you to know, you black thief,
　　That you're cracking your jokes out of sason,
　　　　I'll scuttle your nob with my fist."

> . . . When he came to the nubbling chit,
> He was tucked up so neat and so pretty;
> The rumbler jogged off from his feet,
> And he died with his face to the city.
> He kicked, too, but that was all pride,
> For soon you might see 'twas all over;
> And after the noose was untied,
> Then at darky we waked him in clover,
> And sent him to take a ground sweat.

What (by your leave) makes *Lycidas* a bad poem, when judged by the same standards, is that Milton has put on Theocritan fancy-dress; and, as Dr. Johnson first pointed out, it must "not be considered the effusion of real passion."

Dr. Johnson observes:

Among the flocks, and copses, and flowers, appear the Heathen deities; Jove and Phœbus, Neptune and Aeolus, with a long train of mythological imagery, such as a college easily supplies. Nothing can less display knowledge, or less exercise invention, than to tell how a shepherd has lost his companion, and must now feed his flocks alone, without any judge of his skill in piping; and how one god asks another god what is become of Lycidas, and how neither god can tell. He who thus grieves will excite no sympathy; he who thus praises will confer no honour.

He might have added that Milton's chief interest while writing *Lycidas* was an experiment in adapting Welsh verse-theory to English.

About obscurity. Obscurity is often charged against a poem by readers for whom it was not intended, because they are outside the poet's natural circle of friends. They feel aggrieved at having wasted their money or time. This is foolish. Since I am neither scientist nor philosopher, I should not venture to call any scientific or philosophical treatise obscure. If for some reason or other I find myself bogged down in a technical passage which someone has pressed into my hands, I assume that the terms are beyond me, and make no complaints; unless the fault lies clearly in the careless or illogical use of English prose, which has certain agreed semantic principles.

Unhistorically-minded readers, not at home in a mid-sixteenth-century English castle, or a late-eighteenth-century Dublin thieves' kitchen, may find *The Epitaph on Clere* or *The Night Before Larry Was Stretched* obscure; Calliope, to whom they are directly addressed, does not. She is no snob about class, or dialect, or a poet's occupational obsessions. True poems have been written by oyster-dredgers and gangsters and cricketers. But when casually off-target lines are addressed to her (as the present fashion is), with an invitation to get a general atmospheric sense of what her poet means instead of reading them attentively, she feels insulted. This Impressionistic technique, like most other modernisms in poetry, has been borrowed from French painting theory. Another kind of Impressionism presents her with a series of stark images—as it might be natural objects that strike the week-ender's attention on a country walk—but leaves her to inter-relate them. And then there is the Expressionist technique, which relies on the perverse associations that some words have for a particular poet; he does not trouble to consider whether Calliope will find them acceptable. And by the way, this is the first time in history that poets have been dependent on painters for their inspiration; it used to be the other way about.

Expressionism raises a professional problem: what references are legitimate in a poem? A poet may, of course, thrust a poem in the hands of his personal muse, with: "Dear love, this is for your eyes only," and then intimate and far-fetched jokes shared between them are in order. And I must admit that old acquaintance is not always necessary for the understanding of obscure references. One may achieve a surprising rapport with a stranger, whose imaginative processes are similar to one's own—for example while playing "The Game"—I mean the Hollywood charade game, to which I am partial. The player has to convey a song title, or a book title, or a newspaper headline, or whatever it may be, to members of his team by a rapid use of dumbshow, and is timed for speed. Try it, and you may find that one of your team, of the opposite sex, will divine instantly, against all the accepted rules of semantics, what you are acting for them. For instance, you catch her eye, and paying no attention to the other members of your side, you adopt the stance of a *banderillero,* then pinch your nose, claw the air with purposeful stripes and wave your hand enthusiastically above your head. You have been asked to convey the song-title: "Three cheers for the Red, White, and Blue"—and *she* knows that in the fish-market at Barcelona, which has the best bull-ring in Spain, fish are classified according to their colour as red, white and blue. . . . Or *you* know, when she pretends to be a cricketer and goes through the motion of asking for middle-and-leg, and (after a few other gestures) sits on the floor, her head tilted at a certain angle, that she represents Michelangelo's Sybil—the last two syllables of the word *"possible,"* and you guess that the newspaper headline which she has been asked to convey is *Probables v. Possibles.* A strong, irrelevant love-element may be present on these occasions—an intellectual equivalent of the telepathic signals exchanged by certain insects when they mysteriously summon each other from a dozen miles away for an ecstatic nose-rubbing. It is a very pleasant feeling, because of its intimacy, and because no other player has understood. According to Irish legend, Cuchulain and Emir had this same experience when he wooed her in the presence of her women. He had never addressed her before, yet she guessed the kennings of all his poetic riddles and answered him in kind. The women sat gaping and non-plussed. But this is private poetry; trespassers are prosecuted.

Now, the Goddess of Fame, according to Skelton's *Garland of Laurell,* employs a registrar called Dame Ocupacyon; when one brings her a poem, it is she who decides whether to enrol it in the public records. Dame Ocupacyon has a good general education, reasonableness, and a sympathetic heart. She takes a shrewd look at your lines, and if they make sense and demand no telepathic knowledge of your more capricious thought-processes, give them her *imprimatur.* She will pass, for example, a reference to Isabella-coloured satin, because whoever the original Isabella may have been (some say she was the Archduchess who swore not to change her shift until Ostende fell), Isabella is generally recognized as a sort of greyish yellow. But "dressed in Susan-coloured satin" will not pass her scrutiny. Dame Ocupacyon knows many Susans, of widely-varying complexions, eyes and hair, and therefore with different tastes in dress; whereas this poet seems to know only one Susan who always wears, perhaps, the same lavender-grey—or is it brown-red?

To the Impressionist, Expressionist, Futurist, and Surrealist techniques, a Byzantine technique has recently been added: let me call it the Lycophronic. In current English this would be called the *quiz* technique, because it makes the reader humbly ashamed of the gaps in his education. But Dame Ocupacyon will have none of it. She rejects all over-erudite references in the poems offered her. For instance, she would be very sticky with these lines:

> As Hymenoptera jinked by Isaria
> (Which are Torrubia's conidia)
> So we are kimed and huffed.

Ocupacyon finds, on examination, that these lines make public sense —they compare the annoying attacks directed by one genus of low life on another, with similar attacks on the writer and his friends by petty enemies. But she holds that a less far-fetched metaphor with a closer and more exact relevance to the personal situation could surely have been hit upon. And that the reader who knows the meaning of "jinked," "kimed," and "huffed" will be unlikely to know what *Isaria* or *conidia* are; and *vice versa*. It is easy for a quiz-poet to acquire a reputation as a polymath by borrowing recondite words and phrases from various specialized books and mixing them up Lycophronically. I am far from being a polymath myself; and, in fact, to knock together the *Hymenoptera* verse just quoted, I was lazy enough to use only the H–K volume of *The Oxford English Dictionary*.

An absorbing subject is the poetry-reader's notion of boredom. Some readers, with theatrical rather than poetic interests, are entranced by tricks of rhetoric, and expect from the poem a wide range of fantasies, irrelevant to its central statement. Personally, I expect poems to say what they mean in the simplest and most economical way; even if the thought they contain is complex. I do not mind exalted language in poetry any more than I mind low language, but rhetoric disgusts me. I confess that I am equally allergic to oratorical prose: I read for information only, and cannot manage even Gibbon's *Decline and Fall* with patience, though it is a book of great interest, its ideas well marshalled, and the language chaste. I don't at all mind what are called dull books, so long as they are factual, accurate, and unpretentious: Brazilian politics, the digestive apparatus of sea-urchins, the art of wig-making—all is reading matter to me.

I don't even mind the so-called dull poems—such as Clare's Nature poems—if they ring true; but at the least touch of rhetoric or insincerity I close the book without marking the page. What duller poem, for example, could you imagine than an early nineteenth-century description in heroic couplets of a retired village grocer and his wife, written by the authoress of *Twinkle, Twinkle, Little Star?* Yet Jane Taylor's *The Mayor and Mayoress* happens to ring true as a poem because the appalling dullness of the theme struck her between the eyes, and she recorded it with devilish female exactness:

> In yonder red-brick mansion, tight and square,
> Just at the town's commencement, lives the mayor.
> Some yards of shining gravel, fenc'd with box,
> Lead to the painted portal—where one knocks:
>
> There, in the left-hand parlour, all in state,
> Sit he and she, on either side the grate.
> But though their goods and chattels, sound and new,
> Bespeak the owners *very well to do,*
> His worship's wig and morning suit betray
> Slight indications of an humbler day. . . .
>
> That long, low shop, where still the name appears,
> Some doors below, they kept for forty years:
> And there, with various fortunes, smooth and rough,
> They sold tobacco, coffee, tea and snuff. . . .
>
> Her thoughts, unused to take a longer flight
> Than from the left-hand counter to the right,
> With little change are vacillating still
> Between his worship's glory and the till.

Rhetoric may be the boast of the theatre—as Christopher Fry's admirers claim—but it is the curse of poetry. This must be emphasized, especially here at Cambridge where rhetoric was at one time the principal subject of study; after all, the Universities owe their existence to the medieval need for trained priests and lawyers. Rhetoric is the art of persuasion by a public speaker. When the primitive Christian Church went Greek, its leaders decided to abandon, as impractical, Jesus's strict injunctions: that his disciples should not premeditate when confronted with the enemies of their faith, but should rely on the inspiration of the Holy Spirit. Gentile Christian priests were then trained in the pagan schools of rhetoric, where the curriculum was based on close observations of the psychology of juries and public meetings—observations which helped the trained orator to make a poor, or even a bad, cause appear good. With the adoption of Christianity as a state religion, the schools of rhetoric passed under Church control; but the pagan models were preserved. It is no business of mine to evaluate the damage done to simple faith by the tropes, tricks, and traductions of rhetoric; but I am convinced that poets who rely on rhetoric rather than inspiration are behaving unprofessionally. However, I must be careful not to overstate my case. A University education in rhetoric does, of course, make students properly conscious of accidence, syntax and emphasis, and the rhythm and weight of their phrases, and the history and concealed meanings of individual words —all of which are useful in poetic composition. It is the *direction* of these studies which is anti-poetic; the student remains perpetually conscious of an imaginary audience whose resistance to argument he must beat down.

A poem (must I say it again?) is addressed to the Goddess. She smilingly forgives clumsiness in the young or uneducated—early poems have a nap, or bloom, not found in later ones. And she appreciates the loving care put into a poem by the more experienced; she dislikes slovens. But she insists on truth, and ridicules the idea of using argument or rhetorical charm to overbear her intuition of truth. Milton fell from grace because he allowed his rhetorical skill, learned at Christ's, to dull his poetic sense. While reading his "minor poems" one becomes aware of poetry still struggling against the serpent coils. It is the unhappy flutterings of her wings in *Comus* and the Nativity Ode—I am thinking particularly of *Sabrina Fair* and "the yellow-skirted fays"—that give these poems their poignant and, on the whole, distasteful character. Earlier, when writing the sixth poem of his Latin *Silvae*, at the age of twenty-three, Milton could energetically argue the cause of the "Golden Muse" against his father, on whom he depended for his allowance. Milton's father, a scrivener and a well-known musician, held that poetry was a pleasant relaxation for grave scholars and noblemen in the afternoon of their life, but that his son should choose some other sort of profession. Milton flatters him by saying: "Apollo made you a musician, and me a poet." Here is Skeat's translation:

> . . . Hence it is that as sire and son we win
> Dividual lot in his divinity.
> To hate my gentle Muse though thou dost feign,
> Thou canst not hate her, Father, I maintain:
> Since thou hast ne'er bid me to go where lies
> The broad highway and easier field of gain,
> Where hopes gleam sure of coin in mounded heap;
> Not hal'st me to the Bar and laws we keep—
> Too often wrench'd; nor with distasteful cries
> Mine ears dost peal: but seeking only power
> My mind well-stor'd with richer wealth to dower
> In deep retirement from the city's roar,
> Lettest me thus in jocund leisure stride
> As if at Phœbus's side,
> With benediction from our Muses' shore.

The poem ends with Milton's promise to celebrate his father's kindness in immortal verse.

So we come to the Theme of Fame. Skeleton raised it; but only in joke. *The Garland of Laurell*, an account of his induction into the Temple of Fame, is a comic fantasy written for the Countess of Surrey, the Ladies Isabel and Miniall Howard, Lady Ann Dakers of the South, and his other women-friends at Court. Fame was no joke for Milton, but an obsession, as appears throughout the *Silvae,* especially in his letter to Manso, and in *Lycidas.* Thirst for fame explains much that is dishonest and ruthless in his life, besides his passionate cultivation of polemical oratory. Milton appears never to have loved anyone, after the death of his friend Charles Diodati, except himself; and certainly had no women-friends with whom he could be on joking terms. Men became the objects of his adulation or execration only as they advanced or impeded his career. While an undergraduate, he wrote two elegies on bishops, and a Fifth of November poem in which he sentenced to "pains condign" (though the dupes of Satan) the treasonable wretches who tried to encompass the death of our devout King James; he had his eye, it seems, on a Royal Fellowship. But when the coveted fellowship went elsewhere, and a Bishop, a former tutor with whom he had quarrelled, proved to have been responsible, Milton lost all respect for bishops. In *Eikonoclastes* he justifies the judges who sentenced King James's devouter son Charles to similar "pains condign" at the block. His adulation of Queen Christina of Sweden in *The Second Defence of the English People* contrasts so revoltingly with his obscene libels on Charles in *The First Defence,* that nothing which he wrote later when influenced by the Muse "of Horeb and Sinai" can persuade me of his poetic sincerity; grapes are not gathered from thistles.

Poets have aimed at two kinds of poetic fame: the first, contemporary fame, is suspect because it is commonly acquired by writing for the public, or for the representatives of the public, rather than for the Muse—that is to say for poetic necessity. The second, posthumous fame, is irrelevant; though, if the poet falls in love and becomes obsessed with terrors of death, he may be forgiven (as we forgive Shakespeare) for contemplating the immortality bestowed on his beloved by means of a poem. Milton was obsessed by thoughts of his own fame. His strongest reaction to the news of Lycidas's drowning was: "Heavens, it might have been myself! Cut down before my prime, cheated of immortal glory!"

I grant that a poet cannot easily imagine a future in which he is no longer active; and poets do tend to live in a timeless world, where their predecessors are as real to them as their contemporaries. But I find that the predecessors whom I love, and for whom I might thoughtlessly lay a place at the supper table, are not those who, when they wrote, had designs on me as their posterity, but those who lived in the present and trafficked with the past. As I wrote once:

> To evoke posterity
> Is to weep on your own grave. . . .
>
> And the punishment is fixed:
> To be found fully ancestral,
> To be cast in bronze for a city square,
> To dribble green in times of rain
> And stain the pedestal.
>
> Spiders in the spread beard;
> A life proverbial
> On clergy lips a-cackle;
> Eponymous institutes,
> Their luckless architecture.
>
> Two more dates of life and birth
> For the hour of special study
> From which all boys and girls of mettle
> Twice a week play truant
> And worn excuses try. . . .

Poetic integrity. Of what does it consist? I should not like to think that integrity once lost is, like a maidenhead, irrecoverable. The young may, I believe, become actively engaged in non-poetic activities, and then repent, to re-establish themselves firmly on poetic ground. By non-poetic activities I mean those that prejudice the poet's independence of judgement; such as a religious life which imposes ecclesiastical control on his private thoughts; or politics, which bind him to a party line; or science, if it is ill-advised enough to deny the importance of magic; or philosophy, if he is expected to generalize about what he knows to be personally unique; or school-mastering, if he must teach what he considers neither true nor necessary. Ideally, poets should avoid enrolling themselves in any club, society, or guild: for fear they may find themselves committed to group action of which they cannot individually approve.

Many solutions have been found to the problem of how to separate oneself from the non-poetic world without turning anti-social. The fact is, that in this carefully organized country no poet can altogether avoid the responsibilities of citizenship, even if he should be unfit for military service; though to be a poet is a whole-time occupation to which all else must be subordinated. William Davies had solved his problem by becoming a common tramp, until he lost a foot (stealing a ride on an American railway truck)—then wrote his *Autobiography* and lived quietly by his pen in London; nevertheless, he was summoned one day for jury service. He described his experiences in a poem, *The Inquest*, which I have always admired both for its passionate detachment from the matter in hand (namely the assessment of factual evidence about a child's death); and for the troubled ambiguity of the: "So help me God! I took that oath!"

> I took my oath I would inquire,
>   Without affection, hate, or wrath,
> Into the death of Ada Wright—
>   So help me God! I took that oath.
>
> When I went out to see the corpse,
>   The four months' babe that died so young,
> I judged it was seven pounds in weight,
>   And little more than one foot long.
>
> One eye, that had a yellow lid,
>   Was shut—so was the mouth, that smiled;
> The left eye open, shining bright—
>   It seemed a knowing little child.
>
> For as I looked at that one eye,
>   It seemed to laugh and say with glee:
> "What caused my death you'll never know—
>   Perhaps my mother murdered me."

> When I went into court again,
>   To hear the mother's evidence—
> It was a love-child, she explained,
>   And smiled, for our intelligence.
>
> "Now, Gentlemen of the Jury," said
>   The coroner—"this woman's child
> By misadventure met its death."
>   "Aye, aye," we said. The mother smiled.
>
> And I could see that child's one eye
>   Which seemed to laugh, and say with glee:
> "What caused my death you'll never know—
>   Perhaps my mother murdered me."

Davies's main difficulty was that, once he had written his auto-biography, little remained to sell but his poems, of which he wrote and published too many; however, this was not a mortal sin—the unnecessary ones drop out, the necessary ones remain.

Once a poet has known the excitement of conceiving a poem and taking it through various drafts, still under the same excitement, the craving will always be with him. When it becomes oppressive, he often puts himself into a receptive posture, keeps pen and paper handy, and waits for the miracle of the Muse Goddess's appearance; then grows impatient, begins doodling with words (as you give the planchette a little push to make it start), and soon finds a promising rhyme or phrase. Thus he contrives a visitation—not of the Goddess but of one of those idle, foolish, earth-bound spirits that hover around the planchette board, or the pillows of sick men. An extraor-dinary difference in quality can be seen, for example, between Coleridge entranced and Coleridge unentranced—between *Kubla Khan* and *Frost at Midnight* on the one hand, and on the other *Lewti, The Nightingale,* and *The Old Man of the Alp*—all written in the same year (1798). Every poet knows in his heart which are the necessary and which the unnecessary poems. But too often he tries to fool himself that all are necessary. Necessary poems are rare; and poems in which the original necessity has not been blunted by unskilful elaboration are rarer still. Ideally, only these should be published, but flawed gems are none the less gems, and no poem is entirely flawless; so it should be enough in a *Collected Poems* to eliminate at least the glass and synthetic stones. Yet few poets are sufficiently ruthless to make a thorough job even of this.

A poet has certain natural loyalties—say, to a village where he spent his childhood, to a University where he was well treated, to a regiment with which he saw active service, to his family if they have respected his intransigeance. Such ties of affection need not prejudice his critical judgement, and he must take care never to join an organization where he will be expected to condone actions or attitudes of which he disapproves; or be told where he must live, how he must dress, and what sort of friends to avoid. A young poet down from the University is often tempted to go in for broadcasting, or publishing, or literary journalism. Yet he would be well advised to ask the B.B.C. for a job only as messenger or sound-technician, or the publishing house for a job as a packer or vanman, and the literary weekly for a job in the circulation department. Any position that makes him condone the printing or broadcasting of poems which he himself would not choose to print or broadcast is a dangerous one.

It is often said that poetry is unconcerned with morals; but this needs amendment. Of course, François Villon, Harefoot Bill, and Billy Gashade (author of the *Jesse James* ballad) seem to have little in common, morally speaking, with Richard Rolle, Thomas Traherne, and Henry Vaughan. But the first three were at least true to the principles of honour which prevail among thieves, and the remaining three to the principles of sainthood; their poems were honest declarations of personal integrity. Had Harefoot Bill turned stool-pigeon or Methodist preacher, it would have been as shocking as if Traherne had been caught robbing coaches on Hounslow Heath; or if either had tried to imitate the fashionable writers of his day.

And though it may be argued that no acceptable code of sexual morals can be laid down for the poet, I am convinced that deception, cruelty, meanness, or any violation of a woman's dignity are abhorrent to the Goddess; and that she loathes the deliberate sexual perversion which has male self-sufficiency for its object, and which has never been more boldly pursued by would-be poets than today.

It may also be argued that no acceptable religious code can be laid down for the poet. All I propose to say here is that one of the several strands in the Christian Faith, namely the mystery of the ever-Virgin Mother and her Son—the crucified king whose seasonal birth, initiation, death, and resurrection are celebrated by countryfolk—is wholly poetic. But other strands—the theological, the ecclesiastical, the liturgical—I find equally unpoetic. Anonymous carol-makers of pre-Reformation days did not find it hard to reconcile poetry with faith, because popular Catholicism was still closely connected with the pagan cult of "Our Lady"—the Goddess as Queen of Elphame, who initiated Thomas the Rimer into her mysteries. Take, for instance, the sixteenth-century carol *The Fawcon Hath Born my Mak Away:*

Lully, lulley; lully, lulley;
The fawcon hath born my mak away.

He bare hym vp, he bare hym down;
He bare hym into an orchard brown.

In that orchard ther was an hall,
That was hangid with purpill and pall.

And in that hall ther was a bede;
Hit was hangid with gold so rede.

And yn that bed ther lythe a knyght,
His wowndes bledying day and nyght.

By that beddes side ther kneleth a may,
And she wepeth both nyght and day.

And by that beddes side ther stondith a ston,
"Corpus Christi" wretyn theron.

Though in a North Staffordshire version the lady is described as the Virgin Mary, an earlier Scottish version calls her, more cautiously, a *leal maiden:*

> With silver needle and silken thread
> Stemming the wounds where they did bleed.

And the knight is not Christ, he is the Queen of Elphame's sacrificed lover: call him Arthur, or Robin Hood, or the Young Cordwainer, or what you will.

I do not know the present attitude of the Roman Church to poetry, but in 1916, when I was recovering from wounds near Quarr Abbey in the Isle of Wight, the good Benedictine monks tried to persuade me to join their Order after the War. One tempting argument was that they had a wonderful library of 20,000 volumes —on every possible subject—agriculture, music, history, mechanics, printing, mathematics. . . . But I asked Father Blanchon-Lasserve, the Guest-master: "What about poetry?" "No, my son," he answered, "we have no poetry. It is not necessary." As for the Protestant Church: a number of English clergymen once wrote most unecclesiastical poems—William Stevenson ("Back and side go bare, go bare"), Herrick and Swift among them—but this merely meant that in their days a priest could be a poet and forget about his priesthood. Since the early nineteenth century such an act of oblivion has been exceedingly difficult to perform. The last poet to do so was the gifted and strange Canon Frederick Langbridge of Limerick, who spent a great deal of his time writing lyrics for Edwardian musical comedies, and whose poems, *The Power of Red Michael,* published more than forty-five years ago, were as impressive as they were heretical.

A poet's integrity, then, consists of his not forming ties that can impair his critical independence, or prevent him from telling the whole truth about anything, or force him to do anything out of character. It consists also in his refusal to pay more respect to persons than decency demands, or their attainments permit. This does not, of course, give him the right to argue with a parson in the pulpit; or fail to rise in a public place when *God Save the*

Queen is played; or show contempt of Court by incivility to a magistrate. But he will not permit a parson to lecture him from anywhere else but the pulpit; or the Crown to curtail his traditional liberties; or a magistrate to insult him out of court. He will also stubbornly resist all editorial attempts to alter any line of his poetry, unless the editor clearly has a better sense of the poem's needs than himself; which is possible, though unlikely.

And he will never include in his budget the money he gets from the sale of poems. If poems happen, let them be bought and published by whatever journal asks for them. If they gradually pile up, let them be published in volume form. If reputable anthologies then want to reprint a few, why not? But any money paid for a poem should, I believe, be regarded as if it were an unexpected legacy from a distant relative, whose favour one has not courted and whose death one has not anticipated. It should be spent on things of which the Goddess would approve: such as plain texts of the better poets, or the planting of a mulberry tree. . . . Let prose, or some other activity, pay the grocer and the gas collector.

According to one school of thought, a poet's life should be full of action, sexual adventure, and social event. Byron wrote to Thomas Moore:

> I think very highly of Hogg as a poet; but he, and half of these Scotch and Lake troubadors, are spoilt by living in little circles and petty societies. London and the world is the only place to take the conceit out of a man—in the milling phrase . . . Lord, Lord, if these home-keeping minstrels had crossed your Atlantic, or my Mediterranean, and tasted a little open boating in a white squall—or a gale in "the Gut"—or the Bay of Biscay, with no gale at all—how it would enliven and introduce them to a few of the sensations!—to say nothing of an illicit amour or two upon shore, in the way of an essay upon the Passions, beginning with a simple adultery, and compounding it as they went along.

It is true that small provincial circles are most restrictive unless the members happen to be well chosen. And London until, say, 1914, was a wonderful place for polishing one's wits. Friends were not too busy making a living; or too fatigued by the noise of traffic, or too short-handed in the house to spend long hours together.

But Byron is over-stating the case for physical sensation: I doubt whether Shakespeare, when his early deer-stealing days had ended, ever so much as hired a wherry for a visit to the Isle of Dogs. And as for compound adultery: it never did Byron himself much good, and poets have written well enough without it.

Perhaps the nearest approach to an acceptable, all-purpose moral code for a poet is Swift's:

> Stoop not to int'rest, flattery or deceit,
> Nor with hired thoughts be thy devotion paid;
> Learn to disdain their mercenary aid.
> Be this thy sure defence, thy brazen wall,
> Know no base action, at no guilt turn pale.

Let me say a word or two about parody. A parody is not a poem, of course, yet the Muse at times commissions a parodist, such as Calverley or Lewis Carroll, to express her disapproval of poets who have behaved ridiculously. Parody is a form of destructive magic, like that employed by Russian forest-witches: the witch walks silently behind her victim, mimicking his gait, his carriage, and his gestures. After establishing a complete rapport with him, she pretends to stumble over a tree root. The victim inevitably does the same; but while the witch falls soft, he falls hard. No true poem can be parodied; because no true poem can be imitated. Calverley parodied Morris's *Two Red Roses Under the Moon* with his *Butter and Eggs and a Pound of Cheese*; and Carroll parodied Southey's *Old Father William*; in each case so successfully that the originals could never be recited again without a blush. But Jane Taylor's *Twinkle, Twinkle, Little Star* survives, undaunted by *Twinkle, Twinkle, Little Bat*.

Wordsworth often parodied himself so unmercifully that J. K. Stephen's lines are supererogatory, if just:

> Two voices are there: one is of the deep;
> It learns the storm cloud's thunderous melody,
> Now roars, now murmurs with the changing sea,

Now bird-like pipes, now closes soft in sleep:
And one is of an old half-witted sheep
Which bleats articulate monotony,
And indicates that two and one are three,
That grass is green, lakes damp, and mountains steep:
And, Wordsworth, both are thine. . . .

And Tennyson, late and early, also parodied himself.

She stood upon the castle wall,
　　Oriana:
She watch'd my crest among them all,
　　Oriana:
She saw me fight, she heard me call,
When forth there stept a foeman tall,
　　Oriana:
Atween me and the castle wall,
　　Oriana.

Calliope once passed word to substitute the brutal phrase *"Bottom Upwards!"* for the romantic invocation *"Oriana!"* Try it for yourselves, especially from the point where Tennyson writes:

The battle deepened in its place,
But I was down upon my face,
　　Oriana.

They should have stabb'd me where I lay,
　　Oriana!
How could I rise and come away,
　　Oriana?
How could I look upon the day?
They should have stabb'd me where I lay,
　　Oriana—
They should have trod me into clay,
　　Oriana.

These Be Your Gods, O Israel!

I was never one to stroll down the street with a catapult and break windows just for the fun of hearing the tinkle of glass and seeing furious faces peering out as I scuttled away. But to break windows *from the inside* amounts, at times, to a civic duty. One smells gas, bursts open the kitchen door, turns off the oven tap, wraps a towel around one's fist and breaks every pane in the kitchen window; for which a commendatory word or two may be expected from the magistrate—or from the coroner, according as the suicide was successful or not.

An anonymous leader-writer in *The Times Literary Supplement*, discussing the poetry of today, has described ours as an "Age of Consolidation." I find "Consolidation" too active a word, and should prefer "Age of Acquiescence" or "Age of Acceptance"; which, of course, in the Welfare States, covers a wider range of subjects than poetry and literature in general. Most of my younger contemporaries have been acquiescing in an organized attempt, by critics, publicists, and educationalists, to curtail their liberty of judgement, and make them bow the knee before a row of idols, whose rites are quite in-compatible with devotion to the Muse herself.

Idolatry is nothing new. The Goddess, or the God, being held too mysterious and exacting a figure for public worship, idols are set up as intermediaries—like the hero-images in Classical Greece—to focus the vague yearnings and aspirations of the unenlightened mass. As Isaiah remarks:

> He maketh a god even his own graven image and falleth down unto
> it and prayeth unto it and saith: "Deliver me, for thou art my God!"

Yet the ancients did at least wait until Homer and Virgil were de-cently dead before they paid them heroic honours. The living poet-hero is a modernism; I think I am right in saying that Petrarch was the first poet to receive quasi-divine honours during his lifetime. And once an idol is set up it cannot easily be removed; but slowly moulders down the years, as Byron's and Wordsworth's have done. Tennyson's idol began to moulder soon after his death; it had be-come identified with much that was unpopular in Victorianism. Thus Thomas Hardy wrote in his *An Ancient to Ancients* twenty-five years later:

> The bower we shrined to Tennyson,
>   Gentlemen,
> Is roof-wrecked; damps there drip upon
> Sagged seats, the creeper-nails are rust,
> The spider is sole denizen;
> Even she who voiced those rhymes is dust,
>   Gentlemen!

In 1910, when I first made poetry the most important interest in my life, no idols were forced on me. English literature did not form part of the curriculum at Charterhouse, and I could go foraging for myself in blessed freedom. Moreover, war broke out just when I should have gone to Oxford; I volunteered and took a commission in an unliterary line-regiment, where I spent the next four and a half years. I had never met a poet of my own generation until, by a stroke of luck, Siegfried Sassoon was posted to my battalion; and through him and Edward Marsh (who had befriended me while I was still at school) I came to know several of the real poets then extant—including Hardy, William Davies, and Wilfred Owen.

A wave of popular excitement had been raised, two or three years before the War, by Masefield's bold use of the word "bloody" in his *Everlasting Mercy;* but so dim were the other poetic lights of the period that he was the only modern poet whom Max Beerbohm found topical enough for inclusion in his *Poet's Corner—* except the insufferable Kipling (swapping 'ats with 'is gal Britannia on 'Ampstead 'Eath). Max wrote:

> A swear word in a rustic slum
> A simple swear word is to some,
> To Masefield, something more.

A second wave of popular excitement was raised by the death of Rupert Brooke during the Dardanelles campaign. Brooke's patriotic sonnet "If I should die . . ." was included in Edward Marsh's *Georgian Poetry,* and the subsequent three volumes set poetical taste for the duration of the War, and for some years after.

But there were no living idols even in the early 'twenties. Thomas Hardy was known mainly for his novels; Charles Doughty for his *Arabia Deserta;* William Davies for his *Autobiography of a Super Tramp;* A. E. Housman for his Latin scholarship. I was still young then, yet could regard them as my friends and colleagues; simply because the current text-books of English literature stopped at Tennyson and Swinburne—we were all equally post-Canonical. Thus, though I had been attracted at the age of sixteen by the soft music of Yeats's *Countess Cathleen* and *Wanderings of Oisin,* he was not yet a "required" poet; and I had felt no compunction about going behind him to literal translations of the Irish texts from which he quarried.

How things have changed since those days! Contemporary English literature has insinuated itself into the Public School and Secondary School curriculum. It is now recognized by the University Faculties too. Even I have my niche in any popular text-book: I am briefly mentioned with the Georgian War Poets of 1914–18 (*see* p. 1), successors to the Imagists (*see* p. 11) and themselves superseded (*see* p. 21) by the Modernist Movement of the 'twenties; which merged (*see* p. 111) into the Left Wing Movement of the 'thirties; which was suffocated (*see* p. 141) by the 1939–45 War; which gave a pause for reflection, the new poets being few and inhibited. And for the setting up of five living idols—namely Yeats, Pound, Eliot, Auden, and Dylan Thomas (*see separate chapters devoted to each*).

Men and women of culture in England today are expected not only to regard these five as the most "significant" modern writers but to have read all the "significant" literature that has grown up about them; because "Age of Consolidation" implies "Age of Criticism." The educational emphasis is now on appreciation of contemporary as well as ancient literature, and since to appreciate no longer means "to evaluate," as it did in earlier days, but has become a synonym for "to admire," there must be recognized objects of official appreciation—namely idols.

Ladies and gentlemen, relax! None of this lore is necessary for your salvation, once you have satisfied the examiners. There are only poems, very few of these in any generation, and there are periodic verse-fashions. And as for the old-clothesman of literature, the critic who starts by writing his D.Phil. on such subjects as *W. H. Auden and the Freudian Theory of Transference,* or *T. S. Eliot as Anticipated by Duns Scotus;* and who then applies for a Foundation Research Fellowship, because he is compiling a scholarly edition (with cancelled first drafts) of all Dylan Thomas's advertisement copy for Messrs. J. Walter Thompson's *Night Custard* account; or perhaps a polyglot concordance to Pound's *Pisan Cantos* —as for the old clothesman, leave him to his industry! Waste no money on books *about* poetry; not even on mine. Build up a library of plain texts: the poet who pleads his case before Dame Ocupacyon is expected to present a plain, unannotated text of his poems, with no supporting documents or testimonials whatsoever. I am here to remind you that poets are not idols, nor are idols poets; and that the Muse alone deserves your love. The idols are well swaddled against anything less destructive than a cobalt bomb; and all my iconoclastic zeal, so far from turning the whole temple blue, will not so much as dent a protective sandbag. Nevertheless, here it comes.

First, William Butler Yeats. The younger Yeats had wit, industry, a flexible mind, a good ear, and the gift of falling romantically in love—admirable qualities for a beginner. His less admirable qualities were greed, impatience, and a lack of proportion, or humour, for which no amount of wit can compensate. Yeats's father once confided to my father: "Willie has found a very profitable little by-path in poetry"; and this was fair enough. The early poems fall short of the pathetic only by their genuine feeling for Ireland and their irreproachable anvilcraft. They are the work of a negligently-dressed, misty-eyed, murmuring Dubliner, living in the Fenian past; "a darling man" to his friends Douglas Hyde, Dr. P. W. Joyce, A.E., J. M. Synge, Lionel Johnson, Lady Gregory, and the rest, who supplied him with certain up-to-date convictions. What he would most have liked to do was what his American contemporary, Vachel Lindsay, had done—to hawk his own ballads about the countryside; but he lacked Lindsay's simple courage. And how good a poet Lindsay could be, when he really said what he meant—as in *Bryan, Bryan, Bryan*—and was not being corny or coy! A literary event which startled critics in the 'twenties was the emergence of a new, well-groomed, cynical Yeats, with a manly voice, florid gestures, and an attractive wife, who had cast his singing robes away and his wild harp flung behind him. Yeats explained that he had been plagued by a swarm of imitators; this new technique was the only way to be rid of them. It is now claimed that the transmogrification was largely the work of Ezra Pound, who persuaded Yeats that the Celtic Twilight belonged to yesterday, and that to-day's sun beamed on the buccaneer and smart-stepping salesman. But Yeats needed little persuasion; he had written to Sturge Moore that he preferred the violent expression of error (as in Bernard Shaw or Schopenhauer) to the reasonable expression of truth which corrupts by its lack of pugnacity.

When I returned to Oxford, after the War, Yeats was lodging

above the Shamrock Tearooms in Broad Street; but curiosity never drew me there. Now, Yeats was Irishman enough to realize that, however great a man's industry, however careful his craftsmanship, all is sounding brass and tinkling cymbal, unless divine "grace" is added. "Grace" is the presence of the Muse Goddess; but she does not appear unless her poet has something urgent to say and to win her consent a poet *must* have something urgent to say. Yeats had a new technique, but nothing to say, unless one counts the literary ballads written for the Irish War of Liberation—in which he took no active part. Instead of the Muse, he employed a ventriloquist's dummy called Crazy Jane. But still he had nothing to say. What will a poor countryman do if he has no sheep of his own to shear and badly needs a warm waistcoat? He will go out with a bag into his neighbour's fields and collect strands of wool from hedges and brambles. This Yeats did.

Raymond Mortimer recently called Yeats "a bower bird collecting bright coloured rags and pebbles from the Hebrew *Kabbalah*, the *Vedanta*, the *Mabinogion*, the alchemists, Swedenborg, Blake, Nietzsche, and the Theosophists."

That is correct. He was now using his wife as a medium, and took the spirit babblings of a certain sixteenth-century Moor, a previous incarnation of his own, as inspiratory material for his poems. This explained a dialogue reported to me by an undergraduate visitant to No. 4. Broad Street, which had seemed a *non sequitur*:

UNDERGRADUATE: Have you written any poems recently, Sir?
YEATS: No, my wife has been feeling poorly and disinclined.

A few years later Yeats came to Majorca with an Indian disciple, and worked there on an English version of the *Upanishads*. That was the period of his Voronoff operation and its tragi-comic sequels, which were café gossip there for months. He confessed:

> You think it horrible that lust and rage
> Should dance attendance upon my old age;
> They were not such a plague when I was young;
> What else have I to spur me into song?

While in Majorca, he wrote asking Laura Riding and myself, as co-authors of *A Survey of Modernist Poetry*, for advice: which younger English poets should he include in his new anthology? We suggested James Reeves, whose first book we had just published. Yeats rejected Reeves with this really devilish comment:

> Too reasonable, too truthful. We poets should be good liars, remembering always that the Muses are women and prefer the embrace of gay, warty lads.

So we declined to contribute ourselves.

Raymond Mortimer goes on to say that Yeats could turn any rubbish borrowed from the planchette, or Rosicrucianism, or Mme. Blavatsky, into hard and burnished gold, and that few poets have written verse so strong in the three virtues of terseness, tensity, and eloquence.

Yes; Yeats thought of himself as an alchemist, but (as I have written somewhere) the alchemists never succeeded in making gold out of anything but gold; though they did manufacture muriatic acid, a solvent for gold. They disguised their secret formulae in a mythological cypher, which delighted Yeats and has since excited Jung, though neither of them was chemist enough to crack it. The early-medieval German monk Rugerus wrote:

> The Gentiles (Arabs) have an underground house walled with stones above and below, with two very small apertures, hardly wide enough to admit light. Here they place two old cocks of twelve to fifteen years old and feed them well. When they are fattened, the heat of their good condition makes them come together and lay eggs. The cocks are then removed and toads introduced to hatch them; these are given bread for food. Chickens then emerge like hens' chickens, but after seven days grow serpent's tails, and but for the stone pavement would disappear into the earth. To guard against this, the owners take large, round, narrow-mouthed brass vessels, perforated all over, and put the chickens inside, closing the mouths with copper and burying them underground, where the creatures are fed for six months by the fine earth which enters by the holes. They then take the vessels out and heat them under a generous fire until

the creatures are completely burned. The corpses are then left to cool, removed, carefully ground, mixed with the third part of the blood of a red man which has been dried and pulverized. . . .

And so on. The cocks here are sulphates of copper and iron; the eggs are lumps of gold ore. The chickens are fumes of sulphuric acid. The toad is nitrate of potash. The blood of a red man is muriate of ammonia. Fine earth is muriate of soda. . . . If Yeats had got hold of this passage, what fun he would have had with it! What tersity, what tensity, what eloquence—what hard, burnished rubbish!

Rugerus and his fellow-alchemists (I repeat) never made gold out of anything but gold: as poets can never make poems out of anything but poetry. However, the alchemists and their less mystical successors invented numerous glittering alloys, one of which is pinchbeck. The elder Pinchbeck (died 1732), who was an honest craftsman, produced some very pretty necklaces and brooches; but went to prison because his salesmen tried to pass them off as gold. The younger Pinchbeck, who was no craftsman but more careful of the law, mass-produced what is now called "costume-jewellery." "Pinchbeck's curious metal" contains five parts copper to one of zinc. I mention this because copper is a metal traditionally sacred to the Love-goddess, as gold is to her royal victims. But zinc, the intrusive metal which lends copper that hard, bright, delusive brilliance, has no poetic sanctity.

Here is Yeats in his early copper period:

> Who dreamed that beauty passes like a dream?
> For these red lips, with all their mournful pride,
> Mournful that no new wonder may betide,
> Troy passed away in one high funeral gleam,
> And Usna's children died. . . .

Who ever would have thought that the author would live to introduce the low word *bum* into a Classical fantasy? Or to combine blasphemy with obscenity in *The Stick of Incense*, a *double-entendre*

about St. Joseph? Well: here is the new-model Yeats, em-Pounded
as far as he was capable, writing a poem called *Chosen*:

> I struggled with the horror of daybreak,
> I chose it for my lot! If questioned on
> My utmost pleasure with a man
> By some new-married bride, I take
> That stillness for a theme
> Where his heart my heart did seem
> And both adrift on the miraculous stream
> Where—wrote a learned astrologer—
> The Zodiac is changed into a sphere. . . .

He has taken bold poetic licences: *astronomer* rhymes with *sphere*
—though, by the rule on which he was brought up, even if one
rhymes (say) *verily* with *sigh*, *sigh* must come in the first rhyming
line and *verily* in the second. He also here rhymes *on* with *man*,
which can be done decently in Scotland alone; the convention
being (I think) that half-rhymes are justified by poetic necessity
only where a prevailing mood of gloom, doubt, mental stress or
confusion would be denied by too perfect an answering chime. And
in his younger days, Yeats would not have dared publish three lines
as imprecise as these:

> . . . If questioned on
> My utmost pleasure with a man
> By some new-married bride. . . .

where the awkward syntax suggests, at first, that he was questioned
about his utmost pleasure with some man while someone else's bride
lay close by. Even after the reader has mentally corrected this confused image, he is still left with a question by the new-married
bride which seems to pre-suppose sexual commerce between Yeats
and a man, not her husband. The imprecision is developed by the
astrologer's remark that "The Zodiac is changed into a sphere," to
which Yeats supplies the following note:

The "learned astrologer" was Macrobius, and the particular passage was found for me by Dr. Sturm, that too little known poet and mystic. It is from Macrobius's comment upon "Scipio's Dream" (Lib. I, Cap. XII, Sec. 5): ". . . when the sun is in Aquarius, we sacrifice to the Shades, for it is in the sign inimical to human life; and from thence, the meeting-place of Zodiac and Milky Way, the descending soul by its defluction is drawn out of the spherical, the sole divine form, into the cone."

But suppose we also happen to have read Macrobius, who is not everyone's meat, what then? Macrobius does not say that the *Zodiac* becomes turned into a sphere, or anything of the sort. He says that the *soul* when it reaches a certain point in the Zodiac, conceived as a girdle, is drawn from the spherical form into the conical. But what *that* means, even Dr. Sturm has not elucidated.

Yeats's reference to *Usna's children,* in the early poem I quoted, can be defended: the tale of *The Three Sons of Usna* was familiar to his Gaelic Revivalist readers. But, as I was saying last week, to publish a poem strewn with references to which not one reader in ten million has the key, is regarded as impudence by Dame Ocupacyon. The case becomes worse when the poet misquotes; as so often happens with Ezra Pound.

Pound, an Idaho man, left America with a patchy education and settled in London while Edward VII still sat firmly on the throne. London was then the acknowledged literary centre of the English-speaking world. Pound's early poems were influenced by William Morris, Browning, and Yeats, particularly Yeats. Pound wrote in Yeatsian style:

> For I was a gaunt, grave councillor
> Being in all things wise, and very old,
> But I have put aside this folly and the cold
> That old age weareth for a cloak. . . .

But Pound had no inkling of English tradition, and when he tried to write a Villonaud in eighteenth-century English style, could get no closer to it than the shockingly illiterate:

> Drink we a skoal to the gallows tree,
> François and Margot and thee and me,
> Drink we to Marienne Ydole
> That hell brenn not her o'er cruelly . . .
> Those that we love shall God love less
> And smite always at their faibleness?

He ordered his songs to cock a snook at Mr. Strachey, Editor of *The Spectator;* and published among them a Latin poem in which the future indicative of *gaudeo* was given as *gaudero;* and wrote *Maelids* for *Meliads* in a poem allegedly based on Ibycus. The Thames was not set on fire.

Before his arrival on these shores he had been teaching English Literature in a small mid-Western college, where he was not appreciated, and left soon after his arrival. It is my impression that Pound never forgave his country this rebuff, and that he thereafter ranked himself as a great teacher whose talents were too stupendous for the classroom and at whose knees all illuminated rebels would gather. He made his peace with Walt Whitman, whom he had hitherto despised, and wrote in Whitmanesque vein:

> Go, my songs, seek you praise from the young and the
>   intolerant,
> Move among the lovers of perfection alone.
> Seek ever to stand in the hard Sophoclean light.

With T. E. Hulme and others he issued the *Imagiste* manifesto, which offered a hard, precise image as the *summum bonum* of poetry; but Imagism never caught on here. It seemed both precious and metrically undisciplined, and (worse) could not be harnessed to the war effort of a nation in arms. Slowly the frustrated Pound went mad-dog, and bit the other dogs of his day; he even, as I have said, fastened his teeth in Yeats's hand, the hand that had fed him.

I did not meet Pound until 1922, in T. E. Lawrence's rooms at All Souls'. He happened along for a discussion of Provençal poems, on which Lawrence was an authority. Lawrence introduced us: "Pound, Graves; Graves, Pound; you'll dislike each other." From his poems, I had expected a brawny, loud-voiced, swashbuckling American; but he was plump, hunched, soft-spoken and ill-at-ease. with the limpest of handshakes. Afterwards I asked Lawrence: "What's wrong with that man?" Lawrence answered cryptically: "Pound has spent his life trying to live down a family scandal: he's Longfellow's grand-nephew."

Gilbert Highet parodied Pound in 1942:

> . . . And there sat the well-oiled fire-engine
> all ready to strain its gutmost
>   eek ow ouf honk honk
> unable to think, but ready to quote and paraphrase
>   in six languages
> including Provençal . . .
> ei didl didl
>   li chat e li fidl
>   it took a man like Ezra to kill Provençal poetry
>   for us . . .

"The well-oiled fire-engine" is T. S. Eliot's tribute to Pound's verse technique. And again:

> the Emperor is at Ko
> but No
> silken strings shiver no longer, clashing of smilax, dark
> nuts on the dry bough, nuts on wet earth, nuts
> it's lonesome too being the only one who understands Caius
>   Properzius,
>   'Alkaios,
>   Li Pu,
> all great guys,
> an' I *know* 'em, see? . . .

However, Pound's bravado paid in the long run. He knew little Latin, yet he translated Propertius; and less Greek, but he translated Alcaeus; and little Anglo-Saxon, yet he translated *The Seafarer*. I once asked Arthur Waley how much Chinese Pound knew; Waley shook his head despondently. And I don't claim to be an authority on Provençal; but Majorcan, which my children talk most of the time and which I understand, is closely related to it. When my thirteen-year-old boy was asked to compare a Provençal text with Pound's translation, he laughed and laughed and laughed.

Pound's admirers explain that his translations should not be read as such; that his free treatment of the original has supplied him with many interesting new ideas. Well, I don't know. . . . It is true that Michelangelo advised young painters to seek inspiration (when at a loss) from the damp patches and cracks on their bedroom ceilings. But the corresponding source of poetic inspiration would, I suppose, be the litter left behind by foreign students in a Bloomsbury hostel; it seems unfair on Alcaeus and Li Po and Propertius to treat them so cavalierly. Pound's passionate feelings became centred later in politics and popular economic theory: he even succeeded for awhile in persuading Yeats of the brutal virtues of Fascism. He also convinced himself that the Jews had invented usury, and that the jew (with a small j) was the evil genius who degraded our superior Christian culture, from which only a revolution of intellectual aristocrats could dislodge him. It is an extraordinary paradox that Pound's sprawling, ignorant, indecent, unmelodious, seldom metrical *Cantos*, embellished with esoteric Chinese ideographs—for all I know, they may have been traced from the nearest tea-chest—and with illiterate Greek, Latin, Spanish, and Provençal snippets (the Italian and French read all right to me, but I may be mistaken) are now compulsory reading in many ancient centres of learning. If ever one comes across a relatively simple Blake-like passage in the *Cantos*, sandwiched between direct quotations from history text-books, and snarling polyglot parentheses, this is how it sounds. Forgive me; but we are all adults here:

S_____t on the throne of England, s_____t on the Austrian
    sofa,
In their soul was usura and in their minds darkness
    and blankness, greased fat were four Georges

Pus was in Spain, Wellington was a jew's pimp [*small j*]
and lacked mind to know what he effected.
"Leave the Duke, go for gold!"
In their souls was usura and in their hearts cowardice,
In their minds was stink and corruption.
Two sores ran together, Talleyrand stank with shanker,
and hell pissed up Metternich.
Filth stank as in our day . . .

Even Whitman's barbaric yawp was hardly as barbaric as that.
But remove the layers and layers of cloacinal ranting, snook-cocking,
pseudo-professional jargon and double-talk from Pound's verse, and
what remains? Only Longfellow's plump, soft, ill-at-ease grand-
nephew remains!

T. E. Lawrence wrote in 1912 to his brother Will, who had come
under Pound's influence:

Pound has a very common American affectation of immense learning in strange things. If you can read history and *Bertrand* together
you would not dream of following him. . . . I think *The Goodly
Fere* is by far his best thing. . . .

Bertrand de Born was a Provençal hero whom Pound used as one
of his own *personae*, or masks; but who deserved a better fate.
Lawrence means that *The Goodly Fere*, a rousing old-world Salva-
tionist ballad about Jesus Christ, the muscular fisherman, is honest
Longfellow: by *Blind Bartimaeus* out of *The Work of the Hesperus*.
T. S. Eliot omitted it from his critical edition of Pound's poems with
the lame, if aristocratic, excuse that it was "too well known."

T. S. Eliot, another American, had been a graceful writer of
songs and conventional poems at Harvard (until he read philosophy
and ceased for awhile). He came to Europe a year or two before the
First World War and found it a more congenial continent than his
own. Yet even so he was bored to screaming by tea-parties, and art-
students' chatter, and lodging-house society, and cocktail-bars, and
London fog, and hymns in London churches; already he began to feel
bald and old and useless. This reaction accounts for *Prufrock* (pub-

lished in 1917). I first met Eliot in 1916: a startlingly good-looking, Italianate young man, with a shy, hunted look, and a reluctance (which I found charming) to accept the most obvious phenomenon of the day—a world war now entering its bloodiest stage, and showing every sign of going on until it had killed off every man in London but the aged and neutrals. I was due to return to the Somme any day, and delighted to forget the war too in Eliot's gently neutral company.

When the Armistice delivered us all, he had no war-neurosis to slough off, and stepped forward as a prophet of the uninhibited, anti-Romantic early 'twenties. In *The Hippopotamus* he guyed the Church irreverently:

> Flesh and blood is weak and frail,
> Susceptible to nervous shock,
> While the True Church can never fail,
> For it is based upon a rock. . . .
> The hippo's feeble steps may err
> In compassing material ends,
> While the True Church need never stir
> To gather in its dividends.

He was as polyglot as Pound: Greek, Latin, French, German, Italian, Sanscrit tags alternate in his poems, but he took decent care to check their accuracy, and had a far better ear for verse.

Pound accepted Eliot as a disciple, or Poundling, and was rewarded for his blue-pencilling of *The Waste Land* by the dedication: *Il miglior fabbro.* This celebrated poem was, I believe, the first to apply the current art-fashion of *collage* to English verse—*collage* being the technique of pasting, say, autumn leaves, bus-tickets, metal shavings, cigar bands, fur, playing cards, and artificial flowers on a sheet of paper, in order to create a "significant" composition. What the composition is "significant" of, is never explained. Here Eliot pasted fragments of the Elizabethan ornate against skilfully chosen examples of the modern nasty (though never using words which would have barred him from the drawing-room); and in his notes asked the reader to find, despite the continual change of subject and metre, a connecting thread of sense. Dame Ocupacyon will not be pleased when she reads:

> Not only the title, but the plan and a good deal of the incidental symbolism of the poem were suggested by Miss Jessie L. Weston's book on the Grail legend: *From Ritual to Romance* (Cambridge). Indeed, so deeply am I indebted, Miss Weston's book will elucidate the difficulties of the poem much better than my notes can do; and I recommend it (apart from the great interest of the book itself) to any who think such elucidation of the poem worth the trouble. To another work of anthropology I am indebted in general, one which has influenced our generation profoundly; I mean *The Golden Bough*; I have used especially the two volumes *Atthis Adonis Osiris*. Anyone who is acquainted with these works will immediately recognize in the poem certain references to vegetation ceremonies.

Eliot had meanwhile been encouraged by Pound to voice the anti-Jewish obsession:

> My house is a decayed house
> And the jew [*small j*] squats on the window sill, the
>   owner,
> Spawned in some estaminet of Antwerp
> Blistered in Brussels, patched and peeled in London. . . .

(Eliot himself, though afterwards patched and peeled in London, was not spawned, but decently begotten by a God-fearing Christian father.) And again, in the Venice poem, we find:

> The rats are underneath the piles
> The jew [*small j*] is underneath the lot.
> Money in furs. The boatman smiles. . . .

(Eliot's family kept clear of the fur trade: machinery was more respectable.)

Well, the libertarian movement of the 'Twenties got bogged, as the text-books explain, in the political 'Thirties; and before these

were over, Eliot who, unlike Pound, had no grudge against the
world, but only a shyness of it, made his peace with the Hippopotamus and was well on his way to Rydal Mount. Instead of *The
Ecclesiastical Sonnets* he wrote *Murder in the Cathedral,* and *The
Rock*—the Rock against which he had stubbed a toe—in aid of
ecclesiastical charities:

> With Seneca, with Cicero,
>   With cockney fun he makes amends;
> The cheerful clerics grin, not slow,
>   To gather in fresh dividends.

He became a churchwarden, edited Kipling, and recanted his former
aspersions on Milton. Kathleen Nott has wickedly said: "He reminds
me of a dignified landlady who, without a word, retrieves the tribal
ornaments from the cupboard where the guest has hidden them, and
puts them back on the mantelpiece."

Eliot, being an ex-banker and less naïve in his economics, resisted
Pound's anti-usury fixation—for once he was penny-wise, not Pound-
foolish—and matured into a rugged, if retiring, businessman. Yet he
had once been, however briefly, a poet—I refer to the haunting blank
verse passages in *The Waste Land*—and if he found the demands of
the Goddess too severe, who can blame him? I shall always be grateful to Eliot for having been the only publisher in London with the
courage to print my long *White Goddess.* And his rejection of *The
Nazarene Gospel Restored* was charming: he explained that he
"would have published it if it had been more drily written." And I
admire Eliot's courageous loyalty to old friends in trouble: he was the
prime mover in a protest against the unceremonious treatment accorded to U.S. Traitor Pound when the G.I.'s caught up with him
in Italy at the end of the War. Eliot asked me to sign, but I make
it a rule not to interfere with the domestic affairs of another nation.

The Four Quartets, which had appeared in the middle of the
War, correspond with Wordsworth's *River Duddon* volume, in so far
as they were written to reassure Eliot's public that he still had a
pen in his hand:

O dark dark dark. // They all go into the dark . . .
The captains, merchant bankers, // eminent men of letters . . .
Distinguished civil servants, // chairmen of many com-
   mittees . . .
And dark the Sun and Moon, // and the Almanach de Gotha
And the Stock Exchange Gazette, // the Directory of
   Directors,

So here I am, in the middle // way, having had twenty
   years—
Twenty years largely wasted, // the years of *l'entre deux
   guerres*—
Trying to learn to use words, // and every attempt . . .
Is a new beginning, // a raid on the inarticulate
With shabby equipment // always deteriorating . . .

I suppose he mentions the two Wars because the unusual passions they aroused provoked him to write on wholly personal subjects. But why is he complaining? Who forced him, during the Battle of the Somme, to attend London tea-parties presided over by boring hostesses? Or, in after years, to become a chairman of many committees, and figure in *The Directory of Directors*, instead of serving the Muse? Does he require our commiseration because his shabby equipment is always deteriorating and because he wasted twenty years in publishing the books of others instead of writing his own? In the passages I quote he is true to a boyhood's admiration for Longfellow's *Evangeline*; but has decided that Longfellow's smooth hexameter coach-wheels run just a bit too tediously, he shortens and sufflaminates them to suit the present bumpy age. For my part, I wish that he had stopped at *The Hollow Men*, his honest and (indeed) heartbreaking declaration of poetic bankruptcy, to the approved Receiver of poetic bankruptcy, the Hippopotamus Church.

We are the hollow men
We are the stuffed men
Leaning together
Headpiece filled with straw. Alas!
Our dried voices, when

We whisper together
Are quiet and meaningless
As wind in dry grass
Or rats' feet over broken glass
In our dry cellar

Shape without form, shade without colour,
Paralysed force, gesture without motion;
                    For Thine is the Kingdom . . .
                    Life is very long . . .
                    For Thine is the Kingdom . . .

Eliot's introduction to Pound's *Poems* reveals that both based their a-metrical practices on the example of Laforgue. But he does not explain the need. That Laforgue tried to wriggle out of the strait-jacket of the French Classical alexandrine seems irrelevant to the case; English has worn no strait-jacket since the Age of Obsequiousness, and if strait-jackets exist only to be wriggled out of, why did both Pound and Eliot set such immense store on Pope, admiration for whom Eliot (in this introduction) makes the test of a truly poetic mind? Am I being obtuse? At any rate, what I like most about Eliot is that though one of his two hearts, the poetic one, has died and been given a separate funeral, in Jewish style (capital J) he continues to visit the grave wistfully, and lay flowers on it.

I have never met W. H. Auden—and, so as far as I recall, have never written to him more than once. During 1928–9 I was printing books by hand, and he subscribed to them. I had to suggest that the half-guinea he paid for Laura Riding's *Love as Love, Death as Death,* gave him no right to borrow half lines and whole lines from them for insertion in his own verse.

LAURA RIDING: The standing stillness,
                        The from foot-to-foot . . .
                        Is no real fever . . .

W. H. AUDEN: This gracious greeting,
                        "Good day. Good luck,"
                        Is no real meeting . . .

LAURA RIDING: "Yes!" to you is in the same breath
                 "No! no!" to Death.
                 But such love turns . . . *etc.*

                 After we have fictitiousness
                 Of our excess,
                 All will be as before
                 We shall say, love is no more
                 Than waking, smiling,
                 Forcing out "Good morning,"
                 And, were it more, it were
                 Fictitiousness or nothing.

W. H. AUDEN: From yes to no,
                 For no is not love; no is no,
                 And saying yes
                 Turns love into success . . .
                 And were this all, love were
                 But cheek to cheek
                 And dear to dear.

He is as synthetic as Milton, who borrowed his inspiration in *Paradise Lost* from Browne, the two Fletchers, Davies, Silvester and a host of others. Like Tennyson (whom he has admiringly edited), Auden went to Spain in warlike ardour by a comrade's side; like Tennyson he saw no fighting. But, unlike Tennyson, he played plenty of ping-pong in a hotel at Sitges. Just before World War II he emigrated to the United States, subsequently becoming a U.S. citizen, and there developed his real talent, which is for light verse. His Phi Beta Kappa poem (Harvard, 1946) is a *tour de force:*

                 Ares at last has quit the field,
                 The bloodstains on the bushes yield
                     To seeping showers,
                 And in their convalescent state
                 The fractured towns associate
                     With summer flowers.

Encamped upon the college plain
Raw veterans already train
    As freshman forces;
Instructors with sarcastic tongue
Shepherd the battle-weary young
    Through basic courses.

Among bewildering appliances
For mastering the arts and sciences
    They stroll and run,
And nerves that never flinched at slaughter
Are shot to pieces by the shorter
    Poems of Donne. . . .

The cockney rhyme of *slaughter* and *shorter* expresses his contempt of the young fools who allowed themselves to get caught in
the War. There are, by the way, no fighting men among the idols—
no successors to Ben Jonson who once "killed his man in the sight
of both armies"; which is paradoxical in an age that has sentenced
every second man to ordeal by battle. Auden's is now the prescribed
period style of the 'fifties, compounded of all the personal styles
available; but he no longer borrows whole lines, as for his first
volumes, or even half-lines. It is a word here, a rhythm there, a
rhetorical trope, a simile, an ingenious rhyme, a classical reference, a
metrical arrangement. Auden's zinc-bright influence is even stronger
than Yeats's, Pound's, or Eliot's. He has been saluted as the Picasso
of contemporary English poetry; and, indeed, if Auden's verse makes
me feel uncomfortable so, I confess, does a Picasso design, however
firmly drawn, when I recognize the source, or sources, of his inspiration—a fourteenth-century Spanish plate, a wooden mask from the
Congo, a Hittite seal, a Baffinland Eskimo ivory, an Etruscan tomb
painting, a Carthaginian clay figure, an Aztec calendar illustration.
"Ah, yes," says his admirers, "these ignorant savages anticipated
him."

So we come to the last of the modern idols: Dylan Thomas. At
what interval after the death of a young poet is it decent to tell the
truth about him? Despite the splendid orations spoken at his grave,

more eulogistic than any poet has earned since Byron's death at Missolonghi, was Thomas either a master-poet or a "great Christian gentleman"? He himself never pretended to be anything more than a young dog—witty, naughty, charming, irresponsible, and impenitent. But he did give his radio-audience what they wanted.

Thomas had all the rich musical eloquence of a South Welshman. Did anyone ever hear a Welsh choir, either in a concert hall, or a chapel, or when fortuitously assembled in a motor-bus or railway carriage, sing out of tune? It is a Welsh national characteristic to sing in tune and be eloquent: just as the Egyptian *fellah* lays a tennis-court dead flat without the aid of a spirit-level, or the old Majorcan shepherd never misses his mark with a sling-stone. But the Welshman seldom really cares what the tune is, whether *Marchog Jesu,* or *Saspan Fach,* or *Roll out the Barrel,* so long as he can sing it as a part-song.

Dylan Thomas was drunk with melody, and what the words were, he cared not. He was eloquent, and what cause he was pleading, he cared not. He had a rich voice, could put on the *hwyl* like any Rev. John Jones, B.A., Bangor, albeit in English as spoken in Langham Place; and, when I listened to his broadcasting, I had to keep a tight hold of myself to avoid being seduced. As when once, in 1916, I listened to a war speech given by Lloyd George to the Honourable Society of Cymrodorion.

I never met Thomas; but when he was sixteen, he sent me from Swansea a batch of his early poems. I wrote back that they were irreproachable, but that he would eventually learn to dislike them. I forget what more I said; but I remember thinking that whereas musical prodigies like Mozart, or mathematical prodigies like William Rowan Hamilton, are not uncommon (and, when they grow up, continue happily as they began), poetic prodigies are monstrous and ill-omened. Young poets stumble and make a thousand clumsy errors, and though one may hope or guess that they will be something in the end, there is only promise, not performance. A sense of poetic protocol develops very slowly indeed. (The sole exceptions are such inspired young women poets as Juana de Asbaje, or Christina Rossetti; but a girl is often a woman while her elder brother is still a child.) Even experts would have been deceived by the virtuosity of Dylan Thomas's conventional, and wholly artificial, early poems.

In order to conceal this defect in sincerity, he learned to introduce a distractive element. He kept musical control of the reader without troubling about the sense. I do not mean that he aimed deliberately off-target, as the later Yeats did. Thomas seems to have decided that there was no need to aim at all, so long as the explosion sounded loud enough. The fumes of cordite would drift across the target and a confederate in the butts would signal bull after bull. Nevertheless, as in double-talk, a central thread of something like sense makes the incrustations of nonsense more acceptable. Listeners, as opposed to readers, are easily convinced, in such cases, that they are obtuse and slow to follow the workings of the interlocutor's mind, especially when the musical content is so rich. But professionally-minded English poets ban double-talk, except in satire, and insist that every poem must make prose sense as well as poetic sense on one or more levels. The common report that most of Thomas's poems came out of the beer barrel cannot be accepted. It is true that he drank a great deal of beer, and that beer is a splendid drink before one takes one's place in a male voice choir; but the poems show every sign of an alert and sober intelligence. The following typical stanza is nonsense, but Dylan's golden voice could persuade his listeners that he was divulging ineffable secrets:

> If my head hurt a hair's foot
> Pack back the downed bone. If the unpricked ball of my
>   breath
> Bump on a spout let the bubbles jump out.
>
> Sooner drop with the worm of the ropes round my throat
> Than bully ill love in the clouted scene.*

---

* When I delivered this lecture, I offered a £1 note to anyone who could make sense of these lines. The ingenious Mr. M. J. C. Hodgart of Pembroke, a member of the Cambridge English Faculty, has since come forward to claim the award. He suggests that the child about to be born is here addressing his mother. The child cries out that if he is to cause her any pain by his

Stephen Spender, who often prognosticates next year's poetic skirt-length or waist-line long before the autumn collections, wrote of Thomas in 1946:

> He is a poet who commands the admiration of all [sic] contemporary poets. He has influenced a number of writers who see in him an alternative to the intellectual [sic] writing of Auden. Of the poets under forty-five, he is perhaps the only one capable of exercising a literary influence as great as that of Auden.

Yeats, Pound, Eliot, Auden, and Thomas are credited with having delivered English poetry from the shackles of the past. And the

---

birth, let him not be born at all. "If I were to hurt so much as a hair of your head in process of birth push my downy, but bony, head back into the womb." . . . Birth (Mr. Hodgart adds) is represented here as a violent movement like a bouncing ball; and the child's breath before birth is compared to an unpricked bubble. Therefore: "If even this soft bubble of breath should hurt you by bouncing on your spouting blood, prick it and let my life run out in bubbles." And: "I would sooner be born hanged with my navel-string coiled around my throat than bully you when I appear on a scene made wretched by baby-clouts, or clouts on the head."

There are flaws in this argument. The hair's foot, misleadingly identical in sound to *hare's* foot, is not a hair's *root*. Also, the physical situation is blurred by the apparent contact of the baby's downy head with the mother's hairy one, and by the description of the navel-string as "the worm of the ropes"—why "ropes" in the plural? And by the metaphor of an unpunctured ball bouncing on the top of a spout—as in pleasure fountains; how the bubble of breath could bounce on the flow of lochial blood is not easy to see (blood is not mentioned in the poem). And why should the unpricked bubble become "bubbles"? And is the infant experienced or ignorant? If ignorant, how can it anticipate baby-clouts, and balls bouncing on fountains? If experienced, how can it make so absurd a suggestion as that the mother should push its head back again to relieve her labour pains? And if it is so considerate and saintly as Mr. Hodgart suggests, why should it ever turn bully?

I have a conscience about paying my debts, but though Mr. Hodgart may have identified the thin thread of sense on which the enormous and disgusting hyperboles of the child's address are strung, this is not enough: the five lines taken as a whole remain nonsensical.

people said: "These be thy gods, O Israel, which brought thee up out of the land of Egypt!"

Need I also dwell on the lesser idols now slowly mouldering: on sick, muddle-headed, sex-mad D. H. Lawrence who wrote sketches for poems, but nothing more; on poor, tortured Gerard Manley Hopkins?

Despite the great spate of commercial jazz, there has always been a small, clear stream of living jazz music; despite the great out-pouring of abstract or semi-abstract art (the more abstract, the more imitative and academic) there has likewise been a thin trickle of admirable painting and sculpture. The same is true of poetry. To take only the United States: Robert Frost, E. E. Cummings, John Crowe Ransom, Laura Riding, have all written living poems in their time. I refrain from invidiously singling out their English counter-parts still alive, who are no fewer in number. But I do find it remark-able that the extraordinary five years of Siegfried Sassoon's poetic efflorescence (1917–21) should be utterly forgotten now. For the rest it will be enough to say that William Davies, though at times his simplicity degenerated into artfulness, put his near-contemporary Yeats to shame; and that Norman Cameron, who died last year within a month or two of Thomas, and worked in the same office for a while, was indisputably the truer poet; and that so was Alun Lewis, killed during the Second World War.

This is Alun Lewis writing from the Welch Regiment in Burma to his Muse in Wales:

. . . My longing is more and more for one thing only, integrity, and I discount the other qualities in people ruthlessly if they lack that fundamental sincerity and wholeness.

. . . And although I'm more engrossed with the *single* poetic theme of Life and Death, for there doesn't seem to be any question more directly relevant than this one, of what survives of all the beloved, I find myself quite unable to express at once the passion of Love, the coldness of Death (Death is cold), or the fire that beats against resignation, "acceptance." Acceptance seems so spiritless, pro-test so vain. In between the two I live.

With this quotation, I make my bow, and thank you for your continued patience. If, in the course of these lectures, I have said anything out of order, pray forgive me doubly; I am no longer a stranger here.

Dr. Syntax and Mr. Pound*

DR. SYNTAX: Now for our Propertius translation, boys. This morning we begin with the lines:

> Multi, Roma, tuas laudes annalibus addent
> Qui finem imperii Bactra futura canent.
> Sed, quod pace legas, opus hoc de monte Sororum
> Detulit intactâ pagina nostra viâ.

(*Dr. Syntax consults his teachers' crib, which reads:* "Multi, Roma, many men, O Rome, addent, shall add, tuas laudes annalibus, praises of thee to the annals, qui canent, prophesying, Bactra futura, that Bactria shall form, imperii finem, thine imperial frontier [i.e. that the Parthian empire shall be absorbed], sed, but, pagina nostra, my page, detulit, has brought down, hoc opus, this work, de monte Sororum, from the mountain of the Sisters [i.e. the Muses of Parnassus], viâ intactâ, by an untrodden path, quod legas pace, for thee to read in time of peace [i.e. I

* Prompted by *The Poet as Translator; The Times Literary Supplement*, Sept. 18, 1953. Quotations from the *T.L.S.* eulogy of Pound are here printed in SMALL CAPITAL LETTERS.

alone have not joined the cavalcade of popular war poets]." *He sighs and looks about him.*)

THE BOYS: Only to the bottom of the page, Dr. Syntax, Sir.

DR. SYNTAX: Ha! Very well. Let me see! Whom shall I put on to construe first? Surely our celebrated transatlantic scholar Ezra Pound who only yesterday, perhaps inspired by George Borrow's felicitous pseudo-translations from the Armenian and Polish, distinguished himself by rendèring

Unde pater sitiens Ennius ante bibit

as if *sitiens* meant "sitting," not "a-thirst." Quiet, boys, no merriment! Come on, Pound; my Fabian *libra* of twelve *asses* in one, ha, ha! I can see you are yearning to outdo yourself.

POUND (*virtuously*): Please, Dr. Syntax, Sir! I have translated the whole passage into free verse. I call it *Homage to Sextus Propertius,* Sir.

DR. SYNTAX: Eh, what? How very industrious and thoughtful of you! Proceed! We are all attention.

POUND: (*declaims*):

Annalists will continue to record Roman reputations.
Celebrities from the Trans-Caucasus will belaud Roman celebrities
And expound the distentions of Empire,
But for something to read in normal circumstances?
For a few pages brought down from the forked hill unsullied?

DR. SYNTAX: BREATHTAKING MAGNIFICENCE, Pound, BRILLIANT PARAPHRASES. I am delighted that you scorn to use Kelly's *Keys to the Classics.* You are, I see, DELIBERATELY DISTORTING THE STRICT SENSE IN ORDER TO BRING OUT VIVIDLY PROPERTIUS'S LATENT IRONY. I would go farther: I would say that you have expanded a facile and rather petty pair of elegiac couplets into what MUST SURELY PROVE TO BE A DURABLE ADDITION TO, AND INFLUENCE UPON, ORIGINAL POETRY IN THE ENGLISH LANGUAGE IN THIS CENTURY. But, pray, would you be kind enough, for the benefit of the slower-witted members of the Fourth Form, to give a literal, unpadded, word-for-word translation of the Latin, however bald? I suspect that "CELEBRITIES FROM THE TRANS-CAU-

CASUS" ARE A BRIGHT NOTION OF POUND'S OWN, SUGGESTED PER-
HAPS BY THE SINGLE WORD BACTRA?

POUND: O, no, Dr. Syntax, Sir. Please, Sir, it goes like this. *Multi tuas laudes,* many of your praises, *Roma,* O Rome, *addent annali-bus,* will be added by annalists, *qui,* who, *Bactra futura,* being Bactrians of the future (this is a bit like Macaulay's New Zealander, isn't it, Sir?), *canent,* will sing, *fines imperii,* about your fine empire. *Sed,* but, *quod,* what about, *legas,* reading matter, *pace hoc opus,* when all this work is at peace? And then in apposition, Sir: *via,* a few, *intacta paginâ,* unsullied pages, *detulit,* brought down, *de monte Sororum,* from the hill of Soritis (I looked it out, Sir, and it means "a forked complex of logical sophisms").

DR. SYNTAX: Great! This MAY SET THE ACADEMIC CRITICS ALL AGOG, but it will certainly earn you a four-column eulogy in *The Times Literary Supplement.* The anonymous reviewer will compare you with Marlow, and say even kinder things about your genius than I have dared.

(*Dreamily.*) Talking of Dog-Latin, my boys, you all doubtless recall Virgil's immortal lines beginning:

> Vere novo gelidus canis sub montibus umor
> Liquitur . . .*

Unlike good Citizen Pound, I claim no talent for free verse, but I think I can knock up a pretty fair Shakespearean line: *Vere novo,* Strange yet how true, *gelidus canis,* the dog with chills and fevers, *sub montibus liquitur,* Makes water at the lofty mountain's foot, *umor,* For a mere jest. Silence, boys, or I shall give you a hundred lines apiece! And while I am on the subject of discipline, my Poundling, let me remind you to visit my study tonight after school prayers; and mind you, *fili dilectissime,* no padding—ha, ha!

POUND (*mutters vindictively*): Pedant, Jew, pluto-democratic usurer!

---

* When spring is young, cold mist runs to water below the hoary mountains.

Mother Goose's Lost Goslings

Mother Goose is famous for her nursery rhymes, but not many of them were composed as such. Sometimes what appears to be nonsense is no more than long out-of-date topical satire; sometimes the nonsense element has been added later, either because the original words were garbled or forgotten, or because their meaning had to be suppressed for political or moral reasons. Two or three hundred years of oral tradition in the nursery had played havoc with the texts before Haliwell collected and printed them in 1846.

Deliberately nonsensical rhymes for children first appeared in the eighteenth century, as a reaction against the over-decorous verse of the over-sane Augustan Age, and even these were a fairly restrained sort of nonsense, based on puns and manifest self-contradiction. It was not until the time of Edward Lear and Lewis Carroll that nonsense of brilliant inconsequence studded with newly invented words came to be composed. Typical of the eighteenth century is:

> There was a man of London Town
> And he was wondrous wise:

> He jumped into a quickset hedge
>   And scratched out both his eyes.
> But when he saw his eyes were out,
>   With all his might and main
> He jumped into another bush
>   And scratched them in again.

The metre supplies the date. Goldsmith used it in his satire on Madam Mary Blaize. In her youth,

> Her love was sought, I do aver,
>   By twenty beaux or more;
> The King himself has followed her—
>   When she has walked before.

Also typically eighteenth-century in their restraint are:

> The man of the wilderness asked of me:
> "How many strawberries grow in the sea?"
> I answered him as I thought good:
> "As many red herrings as grow in the wood."

and:

> On Paul's Cathedral grows a tree
>   As full of apples as can be.
> The little boys of London Town,
>   They come with hooks to pull them down;
> Then they run from hedge to hedge
>   Until they come to London Bridge.

But these must be distinguished from such mildly satiric rhymes as *The Grand Old Duke of York* and *Little Jack Horner*.

> The Grand Old Duke of York,
>   He had ten thousand men.
> He marched them up to the top of the hill
>   And he marched them down again.

> And when they were up, they were up,
> And when they were down, they were down,
> And when they were only half-way up
> They were neither up nor down.

H.R.H. Frederick Augustus, Duke of York—and incidentally Bishop of Osnaburg since infancy—commanded the British Army in Flanders successfully enough from 1793 to 1795; and though he failed in the Helder expedition of 1799, that was not altogether his fault. In 1809 he was obliged by the Whig Opposition to resign his appointment as Commander-in-Chief of the Forces because his mistress, the notorious Mary Anne Clarke, had taken bribes to secure promotion for Army officers. The rhyme is an undeserved Whig libel on his military capacity. It may have been composed to offset the thanks voted him by both Houses of Parliament at the conclusion of the Napoleonic Wars.

A companion piece has survived only in two very nonsensical versions. It runs:

> King William was King James's son
> And many a gallant race did run,
> And on his breast he carried a star
> And that's the way to the pickle-jar!

or—I owe this one to Miss Alice R. Benson, who recorded it in Virginia:

> King William was King James's son
> By the royal race he run:
> Upon his breast he wore a star
> That points the way to the Governor's door.
>
> Go choose your east, go choose your west,
> Go choose the one that you love best;
> And if she will not take your part,
> Go choose another with all your heart.
>
> Down on this carpet you must kneel,
> As sure as the grass grows in the field.

The star and the name William suggest the Sailor King William IV, sometimes called "King Tarry-Breeks," who was King George III's son and famed for his amours and drinking. The last line of the first version has originally, I think, been borrowed from Hogg's: "That's the way for Billy and me." The lines which explain "many a gallant race" seem to have been variously censored by parents or nurses; but the Virginian version develops the love interest in the second stanza. The original may have run:

> Prince William was King George's son
> And many a gallant race did run.
> Upon his breast he carried a star—
> That was the way of Billy the Tar.
>
> For all the ladies upon the shore
> It shone the way to the Governor's door,
> And down on the carpet they must kneel
> As sure as the grass grows in the field.
>
> Go sail to east, go sail to west,
> Go choose the lass that you love best,
> And if she will not play the part,
> Go choose another with all your heart.

Little Jack Horner has been quoted as another Whig satire, with "Jack" substituted for "Frank":

> Little Jack Horner
> Sat in a corner
>   Eating his Christmas pie.
> He put in his thumb
> And pulled out a plum
>   And said: "What a good boy am I!"

Francis Horner, Scottish economist and member of Parliament during the Napoleonic Wars, was one of the few thoroughly honest statesmen of his day; he even refused a Treasury secretaryship in 1811 because he could not afford to live on the salary. In 1810 as

secretary to the Parliamentary Committee which investigated inflation he had persuaded the House to check the issue of paper-cur-
rency unsupported by bullion. Horner exercised a moral as well as
an intellectual influence on his fellow-members, which galled the
Whig Opposition. A "plum" in the slang of the time was £100,-
000; it appeared even in such sober reports as: "The revenue is about
£90 plum, to be increased by funding." But here critical caution is
needed. Though the Whigs may have mischievously applied the
rhyme to Horner, as an accusation that he had secretly enriched
himself by bribes from the City, while protesting his incorruptibility,
it was already at least a century old. Henry Carey quotes it in his
Namby Pamby satire on Ambrose Phillips in 1725. The Wiltshire
Horners were a rich family who had profited from Henry VIII's
dissolution of the monasteries, and seem to have been notorious for
their self-righteousness.*

The nearest to deliberate nonsense written in the seventeenth
century had been the Bedlamite verse put in the mouth of "Poor
Tom" or his sweetheart "Merry Mad Maudlen"; but this was no
more than wild fancy, not in the least Jabberwocky, nor even self-
contradictory in the eighteenth-century style.

Mad Maudlen's song:

> My staff hath murdered Gyants,
>   My Bag a long Knife carries
> To cut Mince-pyes from Children's thighs
>   With which I feast the Fairies,

is of the same order of extravagance as the contemporary dancing
song:

> If all the world were paper
> If all the seas were ink,
> If all the trees were bread and cheese,
>   What would we do for drink?

> If all the vessels ran-a
> And none but had a crack,

* I have to thank Peter and Iona Opie, authors of the *Oxford Dictionary of
Nursery Rhymes,* for putting me right on this point.

> If Spanish apes ate all the grapes
> What would we do for sack?

"If all the world were paper, if all the seas were ink" (originally a Rabbinic formula) points to the Inns of Court as the place of composition; the law-students were weary of quill work and wanted to drink and dance.

Another fanciful rhyme, of about the same date, is:

> Four and twenty tailors
> Went to catch a snail,
> Even the bravest of them
> Durst not touch her tail—
>
> She stuck out her horns
> Like a little Kyloe cow.
> Run, tailors, run
> Or she'll get you all ere now.

This is a simple popular satire on the supposed cowardice of tailors; Kyloe lies in Northumberland. As for:

> There were three cooks of Colnbrook.
> And they fell out with our cook:
> It was but for a pudding he took
> From those three cooks of Colnbrook—

I should date this to the Civil Wars. Colnbrook in Buckinghamshire was far too small a place to have supported so many cooks except for a week or two in November 1642; then the Royalist Army encamped there while Charles I negotiated with Parliament. The tune is a bugle-call, which suggests that the cooks were regimental ones stealing from one another in the old Army tradition. It is perhaps the earliest of a long series, mostly mid-Victorian, which now includes the officers' mess-call:

> Officers' wives have puddings and pies,
> But soldiers' wives have skilly;

the no-parade call:

> Hooray, hooray, hooray,
> There's no parade today!
> The Colonel's got a belly ache
> And the Adjutant's gone away.

and the post-call, which ends:

> A postcard from your mother-in-law
> And a letter from Lousy Lou.

The jingle about Little Miss Muffet and the spider can safely be dated to the second half of the seventeenth century. One Dr. Muffet wrote the treatise *A Theatre of Insects* which, in 1658, was bound up with the Rev. E. Topsell's *History of Four-footed Beasts and Serpents*. In it Muffet eulogized the Spider as follows:

> The skin of it is so soft, smooth, polished and neat that she precedes the softest skin'd Mayds and the daintiest and most beautiful Strumpets. She hath fingers that the most gallant Virgins desire to have theirs like them, long, slender, round, of exact feel, that there is no man, nor any creature, that can compare with her.

Dr. Muffet (as W. S. Bristowe, the arachnologist, has pointed out) had a daughter named Patience who probably did not share her father's entomological enthusiasms; but the occasion of the rhyme may have been the sadly comical incident, recorded in Dr. Muffet's diary, when a swarm of wasps spoilt his family picnic in Epping Forest.

Another satiric rhyme:

> I do not like thee, Dr. Fell.
> The reason why I cannot tell,
> But this I know, I know full well,
> I do not like thee, Dr. Fell.

is known to have been written in 1678 by Thomas Brown of Christ Church, Oxford. Brown merely translated Martial's epigram:

Non amo te, Sabidi, nec possum dicere quare . . .

changing Sabidius's name to that of Dr. Fell, then Bishop of
Oxford and the energetic Dean of Brown's own college. Dr. Fell is
best remembered now as the designer of the Fell type, one of the best
English founts, and for his having, albeit reluctantly, expelled the
philosopher Locke from Oxford.

The rhyme *Goosey-goosey-gander*, made nonsensical only by its
corruptions, was coined, I suspect, at the same mint. That its first
mention in print is 1816 signifies nothing; "chamber" had been
obsolete in the sense of "room" for a hundred years. Though recalling
five lines of *The Image of Hypocrisy*, an anti-clerical poem in
Skeltonic verse written about 1535:

> Doctor Bullatus
> Will brabble and prate thus:
> How Doctor Pomander
> As wise as a gander
> Wots not where to wander,

Goosey-goosey-gander should be read as a mocking chorus sung in
1689 by anti-Papal undergraduates to bait the Rev. Henry Gandy,
an Oxford University Proctor who had remained loyal to the de-
posed King James II. "Goosey," apparently suggested by "Gandy,"
had meant "stupid" since the time of Chaucer. After holding out for
a year, Gandy was deprived of his Oriel fellowship for refusing to
take the oath of allegiance to William III. (In 1716 he became one
of the Rev. Jeremy Collier's private creation of non-juror Jacobite
bishops.) The "old man who would not say his prayers" must be
Gandy himself, and the prayers, those that he refused to offer for
King William and Queen Mary; but since he was no more than forty
at the time of his deprivation "old man" is perhaps a nursery
simplification of   "proctor," which makes a pleasant alliteration
with "prayers." For "my Lady" we should read "thy Lady." It is not
clear, however, whether he is here accused of intrigue—if he had a
powerful patroness; or of immorality—Oxford fellows were not
allowed to marry and usually kept mistresses in disreputable St.

Ebbe's; or of secret Romanizing—if "thy Lady" refers to the Virgin Mary. Probably the charge is immorality, since in those days a gander meant a lecherous fellow and the "gander-month" was the month of a woman's lying-in when the husband considered himself justified in illicit love-making. It is the sort of charge that undergraduates would delight in bringing against their proctor whose main business it was to keep them out of taverns and brothels. On the other hand, "thy Lady's chamber" may be St. Mary's Hall, then an undergraduate lodging house adjoining Oriel, now the "Stimmery Quadrangle" of the College and adorned with the Cecil Rhodes statue. The original perhaps ran:

> Gandy, Goosey-Gander,
>   Whither dost thou wander?
> Upstairs, or downstairs,
>   Or in thy Lady's chamber?
>
> If e'er we catch a proctor
>   That will not say his prayers,
> We'll take him by his long legs
>   And fling him downstairs.

The Lion and the Unicorn can be dated by its metre to half a century earlier, and goes to the popular ballad-tune of *Cuckolds all a-row*.

> The Lion and the Unicorn
>   Were fighting for the Crown;
> The Lion and the Unicorn
>   All round the town—
> Some gave them white bread,
>   Some gave them brown,
> Some gave them good plum cake
>   And drummed them out of town.

Commentators have hitherto been content to point out that the Lion and the Unicorn, the supporters of the Royal Arms of England and Scotland, are turned rampant towards each other as if contending for the Crown. But the Lion heraldically represents England; and the Unicorn, Scotland; and these beasts did fight fiercely for the Crown after the execution of Charles I in 1649. What happened was that the Scots proclaimed Charles II as the King not only of Scotland but of England, though England was now a Commonwealth. When Cromwell's hands were free of other business he marched against Charles and beat him at Dunbar on September 3, 1650. But the victory did not prove decisive: in the New Year Charles was crowned at Scone, and in April moved south at the head of another Scottish army. On September 3, 1651, Cromwell met him again at Worcester and it was at this town that the Lion beat the Unicorn so unmercifully. Charles fled in disguise to the Continent, and his Restoration nine years later doubtless accounts for the nonsensical way in which the ballad now ends. I amend it as follows, remembering the pride of the New Model Army in their buff-coloured uniforms and their scorn of the gay Highland plaids.

> The Lion and the Unicorn
>   Were fighting for the Crown;
> The Lion met the Unicorn
>   Nigh Worcester Town—
> One Clad in Hyland Plaid,
>   One Clad in Brown—
> Roll Prince Charlie in the Mire
>   And Drub him out of Town!

The metre of:

> Hark, hark, the dogs do bark
>   The beggars are coming to Town;
> Some in rags and some in jags
>   And some in a velvet gown,

also points to seventeenth-century England. Here again there is no nonsense, only satire. At the Restoration, survivors of ruined Cavalier families swarmed to Court to petition rewards for their loyalty and compensation for their losses; some of them almost in

rags. With them, however, came many petitioners who had kept on
good terms with Cromwell and were as well off as before the Civil
Wars, which accounts for the "velvet gown." It is from this rhyme
that the last four lines of the familiar version of *The Lion and the
Unicorn* seem to have been borrowed, to replace the merciless Roundhead ones; but further softened by the substitution of "good plum
cake" for "a good horse-whip."

There is no mystery about how these political and topical rhymes
came to be accepted among Mother Goose's goslings. Nursemaids
and parents will sing the first thing that comes into their heads, to
keep children amused or send them to sleep. I remember my old
nurse, about the year 1898, crooning to the tune of *Quibbs was
a Quaker:*

> Our dear little Bobby,
> Our wide-awake Bobby,
> Our dear little Bobby,
>   Has turned out the Whigs.

She must have been in her 'teens when Sir Robert Peel, who had
founded the Conservative Party in 1831, was returned to power
ten years later amid great popular enthusiasm. The particular Whigs,
celebrated in the song, whom he turned out were the Whig Ladies
of the Bedchamber; he considered them to have an injurious effect
on young Queen Victoria's politics. But I knew nothing of this at
the time. And when my married daughter in New Zealand croons
to her children as she baths them:

> Whiter than the snow,
> Whiter than the snow!
> Wash me in the water
> Where you washed your dirty daughter
> And I shall be whiter than the snow.

they are certainly unaware that this is a parody of a Salvation Army
hymn which I picked up in the trenches in World War I and used
to sing to their mother on similar occasions. The fifth line is really:

Where the Lamb was led to slaughter.

Yankee Doodle entered the English nursery at the conclusion of the American War of Independence. It had long been used to sing Revolutionary children to sleep, being almost the only song that the American Army knew. But the English had a scurrilous parody, composed by the unfortunate Major André, whom Washington hanged as a spy, and it was this that they brought back to Europe with them.

Several "Mother Goose" rhymes of Northern origin have been altered for the benefit of Southern children who would not have understood them otherwise. For example, the painstakingly non-sensical:

> There was a man and he had naught,
> Yet robbers came to rob him.
> He climbed up to a chimney pot
> And then they thought they had him . . .

can easily be returned to the late eighteenth-century Yorkshire original:

> There was a man and he had nowt,
> Yet robbers came to rob him.
> He climbed up by a gutter-spout
> And there they thowt to nob him. . . .

Then there is the famous rhyme:

> How many miles to Babylon?
> Threescore miles and ten!
> Can I get there by candlelight?
> Yes, and back again.
> If your feet be nimble and light
> You can get there by candlelight.

This is revealed as eighteenth-century Scottish—and incidentally robbed of all its magic—when one recognizes *Babylon* as *Baby Land,*

and restores the whimsical comment on the threescore and ten years
which separate childhood from second childhood.

> Hoo mony miles tae Babby Lond?
>   Three scair miles an' ten.
> Sall I win yon by condle-licht?
>   Ay, and hame agen.
> Gin your feet be nimble and licht
> Ye sall be hame before the nicht.

Once the original date and provenience have been fixed for a
lost poem that has fallen into the rag-bag of nonsense, and the
text has been amended accordingly, the strangest things may shine
out. For example:

> Two grey kits and the grey kits' mother
> All went over the bridge together.
> The bridge broke down and they all fell in—
> "The rats go with you!" says Tom Boleyn.

The rhymes "mother" and "together" point to a Scottish or
Northern English origin, though the poem has survived only in the
United States. Tom Boleyn, or Tomalyn, is easily recognized as
Thom o' Lin or Tomalyn, a mysterious popular hero who has given
his name to a country dance, first recorded in 1549; and is shown
in the ballad of *Young Tam Lin*, first recorded in 1558, to have been
connected with the British witch cult. The grey kits and their
mother were witches—two witches and their queen, or a witch and
her familiars. Grey or "brinded" was the favourite colour of witch
cats, as Shakespeare mentions in *Macbeth* and *King Lear*. "The
rats" seems to be a worn-down form of "Auld Scratch," or "Auld
Scrat," the Devil. Witches were made powerless by being immersed
in running water. So the rhyme is a sixteenth or early seventeenth-
century charm against witches:

> Twa grey kits and the grey kits' midder
> A' went ower the brigg togidder.
> The brigg brak doon and they tummelled in.
> "Auld Scrat gae wi' ye!" says Tam o' Lin.

Then again:

> Grey goose and gander,
> Waft your wings together
> And carry the good king's daughter
> Over the one-strand river.

In a recent London newspaper correspondence about its sense, the only solution offered was that *strand* did not mean *thread*, but *shore*, and that the "one-strand river" was the ocean. This was correct up to a point, but did not explain either the geese or the king's daughter, which were dismissed as charming fancies.

The metre cannot be later than the middle sixteenth century and, to judge by the rhymes "together" and "river," the poem comes from Scotland or the Scottish Border. The recovery of the original text is perhaps best shown in three stages of emendation.

> FIRST STAGE: Grey goose and gander,
> Waft your wings togidder,
> And carry the gude King's dochter
> Owre the ane-strand river.

No: in the ballad-poetry of Scotland and the Border *gander* would never have rhymed with *dochter;* also *gander* was usually spelt *ganer. Daughter* has evidently been suggested by the "King of Spain's daughter" in another of Mother Goose's rhymes, or by the "King's daughter of Norraway" in the *Ballad of Sir Patrick Spens.* The rhyme needed is *banner,* or *baner* as it was then spelt.

> SECOND STAGE: Grey goose and ganer,
> Waft your wings togidder
> And carry the gude King's baner
> Owre the ane-strand river.

No: *waft* means "blow gently" and is likely to be a Southern English modification of the vigorous Northern *wap*, which is what wild geese in flight do with their wings. And the heavy alliteration of the other lines is missing in the third, which suggests that *carry* has been substituted for *bear ye*. But why should wild geese in their summer flight across the cold Northern ocean to their breeding grounds in the Arctic Circle, or near it, be asked to carry a King's banner?

Surely, because a banner goes ahead of the king's army, and because the wild geese in British folklore are the *Cwm Annwm*, or Hounds of Hell, a ghostly pack used by the Wild Hunter—Arawn, Bran (hence the names "*Brant*-goose" and, by metathesis, "*Barn*acle-goose"), Herne, Gwyn, Gabriel, or what you will—when he conducts the souls of kings and heroes (and, in later popular tradition, the souls of unbaptized children or suicides or excommunicated heretics) to the pre-Christian Otherworld at the back of the North Wind. In Scotland he was known as Arthur, or "Arthur of the Bower," and to die was to "rest in Arthur's bosom." The cry of the barnacle-goose is almost indistinguishable from the music of a pack of hounds on a hot scent. To quote the *Whitby Glossary* (1876):

> *Gabriel Hounds:* the flocks of wild-geese high in the air migrating southward in the twilight evenings of autumn, their cry being more audible than the assemblage is visible. As the foreboders of evil, people close their ears and cover their eyes until the phalanx has passed over.

The Hounds of Hell are also variously known as "Yeth Hounds," "Wish Hounds," "Yell Hounds," "Gabriel Ratchets," "Gobble-ratches" and so on. Hounds and Wild Hunter are carved in stone outside the church door of Stoke Gabriel in Devon. The "ane-strand river" is, in fact, the ocean of Death, across which no traveller can hope to return.

Then at what time in the sixteenth century did a Royal Scottish banner need to be conveyed by wild geese across the one-strand river? The history books supply only one answer. On September 9, 1513, near Flodden Edge, in battle with the Earl of Surrey, James IV was killed fighting at the head of almost the entire chivalry of Scotland. So dreadful was the carnage dealt by the English "brown bills" that the royal corpse was not found for some days after; and when finally it was recognized by a glove and plaid, it could not be given Christian burial because the Pope had excommunicated James for his unprovoked attack on his "brother," King Henry VIII of England. There remained only a single refuge for the unhouseled soul: the ancient pagan paradise of his royal ancestors.* Indeed, he had no choice; for as a Scottish rhyme says:

> The King o' Scots wi' a' his power
> Canna stop Arthur o' the Bower.

But why "grey goose"? Because the grey goose is also known as the "lag" from its habit of lagging behind when the barnacle-goose has migrated to its breeding grounds in Spitsbergen and other varieties have flown to Iceland, Greenland, and Lapland. In early September the "lag" would be the only wild goose likely to be encountered by a poet in the neighbourhood of Flodden.

> FINAL STAGE: Grey goose and ganer,
>   Wap your wings togidder
>   And bear ye the gude King's baner
>   Owre the ane-strand river.

* On November 29, 1513, the Pope, at King Henry's request, gave permission for James's body to be buried with regal honours in St. Paul's Cathedral. But, as we read in Stow's *Survey of London*:

    . . . after the battle the body of the said king being found, was enclosed in lead, and conveyed from thence to London, and so to the monastery of Shene in Surrey, where it remained for a time, in what order I am not certain; but since the dissolution of that house, in the reign of Edward VI . . . I have been shown the same body so lapped in lead, close to the head and body, thrown into a waste room amongst the old timber, lead, and other rubble. Since the which time workmen there, for their foolish pleasure, hewed off his head; and Launcelot Young, master glazier to her majesty, feeling a sweet savour to come from thence, and seeing the same dried from all moisture, and yet the form remaining, with the hair of the head and beard red, brought it to London to his house in Wood street, where for a time he kept it for the sweetness, but in the end caused the sexton of that church [St. Michael's, Wood Street] to bury it amongst other bones taken out of their charnel. . . .

Gif ye wad ask me guhy this sang was made and quhilk was his maker, I answer: Ye man understond that whenas our brave King Jamie iiii was slaine fechting dughtely at the heid of his grand battaile of Skottishe lairds and knichtis, on the morowe ane auld menstorall fortuned to come be fflodden hylls and Brankstone Muir quhair lay the lykis of the foresaid King and his deid lairds and knichtis, all manglit in peses and abandonat starke nakid amang the wods and scrogs. Quhairat he made meikle dule that the sowl of King Jamie, and the sowlis of them that holp him, being excomminicat by the Pope of Rome, micht na be receivit intil the Paradise of our swete Saviour Jesu Crist. Bot espying ane parcel of grey geese quhilk swom upon a water nere to hand (as fouls slow to flee after ther kin to the heich court and bower and septemtrionall tiltyard of him quhilk men call Arthur) this same auld menstorall waefully strook the stringis of his harp and, being inspirit of the Muse Calliope, made him the sang quhairof I tell yow.

Juana de Asbaje*

Every few centuries a woman of poetic genius appears, who may be distinguished by three clear secondary signs: learning, beauty, and loneliness. Though the burden of poetry is difficult enough for a man to bear, he can always humble himself before an incarnate Muse and seek instruction from her. At the worst this Muse, whom he loves in a more than human sense, may reject and deceive him; and even then he can vent his disillusion in a memorable poem—as Catullus did when he parted from Clodia—and survive to fix his devotion on another. The case of a woman poet is a thousand times worse: since she is herself the Muse, a Goddess without an external power to guide or comfort her, and if she strays even a finger's breadth from the path of divine instinct, must take violent self-vengeance. For awhile a sense of humour, good health, and discretion may keep her on an even keel, but the task of living to, for, and with herself alone, will sooner or later prove an impossible one. Sappho of Lesbos, Liadan of Corkaguiney, and Juana de Asbaje belonged to this desperate sisterhood: incarnations of the Muse-

* Afterwards JUANA INES DE LA CRUZ (with two of her poems).

goddess, cut off from any simple gossiping relation with their fellow-women, who either adored them blindly or hated them blindly, and from any spiritual communion with men on equal terms. Though a woman so fated cannot help feeling physical desire for a man, she is forbidden by her identity with the Goddess from worshipping or giving herself wholly to him, even if he desires to worship and give himself wholly to her. It is possible that Clodia was another of these unfortunates, so that the harder Catullus tried to please her, the more despairingly she fought him off: playing the society harlot rather than consent to burn with him in a mutual flame.

About Clodia little is known, and about Catullus no more than his poems reveal. Even the story of Sappho survives only in fragmentary form. We learn that she was early married on Lesbos to one Cercolas, a man of no distinction, and bore him a daughter; that her learning and inventive faculties were memorable; that she tutored girls of literary promise; that she rejected the advances of Alcaeus, the leading poet of his day; that she fled to Sicily from some unnamed trouble and, after an unhappy affair with one Phaon, a common sailor, "took the Leucadian leap": which implies some spectacular act of self-destruction. The inter-relation of these bare facts remains obscure; yet it seems that a possessed woman poet will rather subject herself to a dull husband or ignorant lover, who mistrusts her genius and may even ill-treat her physically, than encourage the love of a Catullus or Alcaeus, which demands more than it is hers to give.

The story of Liadan is also fragmentary. She was a brilliant young Irish *ollamh* (or master-poet) of the seventh century A.D., privileged to make semi-royal progresses from one great mansion to another, preceded by a peal of golden bells, and followed by a train of lesser bards and pupils. On one progress she went to Connaught, where the *ollamh* Curithir welcomed her to an ale feast. After the long exchange of riddling poetic lore in Old Goidelic, customary on such occasions, he burst out suddenly: "Why should we not marry, Liadan? A son born to us would be famous." She was startled into answering: "Wait until my progress is done; then visit me at Corkaguiney and I will come with you." He did so, only to find that Liadan, regretting her lapse, had meanwhile taken a religious vow of chastity. In despair and anger, Curithir took a similar vow, and when they went away together, as agreed, it was to the monastery of Clonfert, where Liadan insisted on placing herself under the spiritual direction of St. Cummin, a hard and severe abbot. Curithir followed suit. Cummin found them two separate cells, offering Curithir the choice of either seeing Liadan without addressing her, or addressing her without seeing her. He chose the second alternative; and Liadan consented to this arrangement. They were then each in turn allowed to wander around the other's wattled cell; until Liadan persuaded Cummin to grant Curithir greater freedom, of which she must have known that he would try to take advantage. As a result, he was banished from Clonfert, and sailed away to the Holy Land; but Liadan let herself die of remorse, because she had foolishly involved him in her ruin.

Unlike Sappho and Laidan, Juana de Asbaje was born into a society where she must have seemed as portentous as a talking dove, or a dog which does long division. Neither in Lesbos nor ancient Ireland had limits been set to a woman's learning. Sappho was no freak, but merely the truest of several famous women poets. Liadan, to win her peal of golden bells, had passed the *ollamh's* twelve-year course in literature, law, history, languages, music, magic, mathematics, and astronomy—one of incredible stiffness—and that a woman should so distinguish herself was not considered abnormal. In seventeenth-century Mexico, however, the Church had gained such a stranglehold on learning and literature that women, doctrinally debarred from the priesthood, and despised as the intellectual and moral inferiors of their fathers and brothers, could nurse no aspirations beyond a good husband, many children, and a Christian death. Only at the Viceregal Court might a lady read poems or romances, and thus equip herself for the games of chivalry in which etiquette required her to assist the courtiers; but even so, a confessor always stood by to check all signs of vanity or immodesty.

Juana, born on November 12, 1651, was the daughter of Don Pedro Manuel de Asbaje, an immigrant Basque, and Dona Isabel Ramirez, whose father, the head of a family long established in Mexico, owned a substantial estate near Chimalhuacán and seems to have been a man of some cultivation. Juana's mother, however, could neither read nor write and, when she died some thirty years later, it transpired that Juana and her two sisters had all been born out of wedlock: presumably because the father had left behind a wife in Spain. Though he seems to have legitimized the three of them before they grew up, it has been suggested that the shame of having been born a bastard encouraged Juana to excel as a poet, while it soured her against marriage; but this is mere speculation.

One morning, when she was three years old, her sister said: "Mother cannot have you about the house today. Come with me to school and sit quietly in a corner." Juana went . . .

. . . and seeing that they gave my sister lessons, I so burned with a desire to know how to read that, deceiving the teacher, as I thought, I told her that my mother had ordered her to give me lessons. She did not believe this, as it was incredible, but to humour me, she acquiesced. I continued to attend and she to teach me, not in mockery now, because experience had undeceived her; and I learned to read in such short time that when my mother (from whom the teacher had hidden the matter in order to give her the pleasure and receive the reward all at once) found out, I was already proficient. I, too, had concealed it, thinking that they would whip me for acting without orders. She who taught me still lives, God preserve her, and can testify to the truth. . . . I recall that in those days I had the appetite for sweets and delicacies that is common at such an age, but that I abstained from eating cheese because I had heard it said that taking this made one dull-witted; for my desire to learn was stronger than the wish to eat, which ordinarily is so powerful in children.

At the age of six or seven, she pleaded to be enrolled at Mexico City University and, since the statutes barred women from taking the course, to have her hair cut and be dressed as a boy. When her mother laughingly refused, Juana took possession of her grandfather's library, which no punishment could deter her from reading; and when she found that the most desirable books were in Latin, mastered the elements in fewer than twenty lessons and, before she was eight, could read and enjoy Plato, Aristophanes, and Erasmus. Juana now made life so difficult for her mother that she was sent to her uncle's house in Mexico City, where she taught herself literature, science, mathematics, philosophy, theology, and languages. At the age of thirteen she was presented at Court by the uncle; there her exceptional talents, vivacity, and beauty—wide-set chestnut-coloured eyes, broad brow, quick smile, straight nose, determined chin, delicate fingers—qualified her to be the darling and first lady-in-waiting of the Vicereine. For three years Juana took part in all the gallant diversions of the Viceregal Court, the cultural centre of the New World, and became its principal ornament, next to the regal pair themselves: studying every book that came to hand, and writing a profusion of court verse in Castilian, Latin, and Aztec—besides theatrical sketches, satires, verses of commendation and occasional trifles, some of them "highly seasoned"; and finding time for poetry of a truer and more personal kind. A great many well-born young men asked her hand in marriage, but she behaved with admirable discretion and refused their offers, though the Viceroy and Vicereine would doubtless have provided a dowry.

When she reached the age of sixteen, the Viceroy heard her decried as having only a smattering of knowledge, and therefore summoned forty learned men—University professors, theologians, poets, mathematicians, and historians—to examine her in their various subjects. He afterwards recorded with satisfaction:

> Like a royal galleon beating off the attacks of a few enemy sloops, so did Juana fight clear of the questions, arguments and objections that so many specialists, each in his own department, propounded. . . .

Father Calleja, of the Society of Jesus, her first biographer, asked Juana what impression this triumph, capable of puffing up even the humblest soul to self-importance, had made upon her. She replied: "It left me with no greater satisfaction than if I had performed a small task of hemstitching more neatly than my embroidery-teacher." About this time she first expressed a total aversion to marriage. Her motives have ever since been hotly debated. Father Calleja suggests that she recognized the glitter of Court life as empty delusion; never fell in love with a man; and soon realized that only service to God could give her lasting happiness. This is still the view of the Church, despite her plainly autobiographical love-poems, written at the age of sixteen: *Este amoroso tormento que en mi corazón se ve,* and: *Si otros ojos hé visto, matenme, Fabio, tus airados ojos;* and the poems of disillusion which followed, especially the famous:

> Hombres necios que acusáis
> a la mujer sin razón;

and the two scorching farewell sonnets to Silvio, whom she hates herself for having loved so well.

Juana presently decided to become a nun, although, as she wrote later: "I knew that the estate implied obligations (I am referring to the incidentals, not the fundamentals) most repugnant to my temperament." In this course she was encouraged by her confessor, Father Antonio Nuñez de Miranda, to whom "she broached all her doubts, fears, and misgivings." Her first attempt failed: after three months as a novice among the Barefoot Carmelites, her health broke down, and she withdrew on doctor's orders. Fourteen months later, however, she was well enough to enter a Jeronymite convent and in February 1669, having completed a short novitiate, took the veil as Sor Juana Inés de la Cruz, the name by which she is now generally known.

Father Antonio did not insist that she should abandon her studies and, since the Jeronymites were the most liberal of the Orders in seventeenth-century Mexico, her cell soon became an academy, lined with books and filled with the instruments of music and mathematics. Juana learned to play several instruments, wrote a treatise on musical harmony, made a name as a miniaturist, became proficient in moral and dogmatic theology, medicine, canon law, astronomy, and advanced mathematics. Her library swelled to four thousand books, the largest in the New World, and it is recorded:

> . . . the *locutorio* of the Jeronimas was frequented by many of the highest in Mexico, thanks to the renown of Sor Juana. She had loved solitude but [her presence] brought her many distinguished

visitors. Not a Viceroy of that epoch but desired to know her and, from the highest to the lowest, they all consulted Juana on weighty affairs. A natural affability and graciousness made her lend herself with good will to these fatiguing visits.

Juana continued to write verses, though none for publication: mostly birthday and name-day greetings addressed to her friends at Court, dedications, epitaphs, commemorations, rhymed letters of thanks for books or musical instruments—all smooth, eloquent, and highly rhetorical. To these she added sacred sonnets, dirges, roundelays, carols, panegyrics of saints, lively allegories, and religious plays. She was also a famous cook and for ever sending her friends gifts of confectionery: almond rings, nuns' sighs (to use the politer phrase), cakes, and puff pastry of every kind. Accompanying these went humorous verses, such as this:

To Her Excellency again, with a shoe embroidered in
Mexican style, and a parcel of chocolate:

A cast glove is challenge:
Contrariwise,
A cast shoe, my Lady,
Surrender signifies.

Frequent balls, concerts, and ballad-recitals were given in the Convent and patronized by the Viceregal pair who never failed to attend vespers there as an excuse for amusing and instructive conversation with the "Mexican Phoenix." It was an easy life, since no limit was put on the number of Indian serfs owned by the sisters; one convent of a hundred nuns had five hundred such serving-women working for them. Juana was unlucky, at first, to be under a jealous and narrow-minded prioress, at whom she once shouted in exasperation: "Hold your tongue, you ignorant fool!" The prioress complained to the then Archbishop of Mexico who, as an admirer of Juana, endorsed the prioress's complaint with: "If the Mother Superior can prove that this charge is false, justice will be done."

Juana performed all the religious tasks laid on her, though not greedy of ecclesiastical advancement and, when on one occasion unanimously elected prioress, declined the honour. The gay times at the Convent seem to have ended with the Viceroy's term of office; but her "passion to know" remained as strong as ever, and this, she wrote, subjected her to more criticism and resentment than the massive learning she had already acquired. On one occasion a "very holy and candid prelate" ordered her to cease from her studies. She obeyed in so far as she read no more books . . .

> . . . but since it was not within my power to cease absolutely, I observed all things that God created, the universal machine serving me in place of books.

During the three months of the prelate's continuance in office, she studied the mechanics of the spinning top, and the chemical reactions of convent cookery, making important scientific discoveries. Later, when she fell seriously ill, the doctors also forbade her to read, but . . .

> . . . seeing that, when deprived of books, her cogitations were so vehement that they consumed more spirit in a quarter of an hour than did four days' reading,

they were forced to withdraw their prohibition.

Juana's confessor, still the same Father Antonio, now tried to dissuade her from seeing and writing to so many friends and learned laymen, on the ground that this was irreconcilable with her profession; and when she would not listen to him, resigned his charge. Next, she was ordered by an unnamed superior to refute an admittedly unorthodox sermon preached by a famous theologian, the Portuguese Jesuit Father Antonio Vieira; which Juana did in a letter of such masterly argument, that when it was published (without her knowledge or permission) the most learned doctors of Spain and Portugal were highly diverted to find that this Mexican nun had completely demolished Vieira's thesis; and sent her profuse congratulations. But one old friend, the Bishop of Puebla, qualified his praises with the suggestion that the letter proved how sadly she had wasted her talents in writing shallow verses and studying irrelevant and profane subjects; instead, she should have devoted herself to the unmasking of doctrinal error, now so rife in Christendom. Juana, deeply offended, replied that she made no claim to academic distinction, had written the letter only because ordered to do so and, when she saw it in print, had burst into tears, "which never come easily to me." Then, rather than become a theologian, to the exclusion of all her other studies, she grimly sold her entire library for the benefit of the poor, together with all her musical and mathematical instruments; and submitted to the severest conventual discipline, which Father Antonio, returning in joy, unsuccessfully begged her to moderate. This spectacular event created such a stir that the new Archbishop of Mexico similarly sold all his books, jewels, valuables, and even his bed.

In 1695, some of the sisters fell ill of the plague, and Juana, though weakened by nearly two years of rigorous penance, set herself to nurse them; but presently caught the infection and succumbed. The Jeronymite records contain this sentence, scratched with Juana's fingernail dipped in her own blood—because she had renounced the use of pen and ink:

> Immediately above will be noted the day, month and year of my death. For the love of God and of His Purest Mother, I pray that my beloved sisters, both those now living and those who have gone before, will recommend me to Him—though I have been the worst woman in the world.
>
> Signed: I, Juana Inés de la Cruz.

Juana de Asbaje wrote true poetry before she was seventeen; but what of her heiress and successor, Sor Juana Inés de la Cruz? We can applaud the dazzling fantasy of Sor Juana's religious verse, its perfect sense of rhythm and sure balance of phrases, its essential clarity, which shames the interlaced extravagances of contemporary Gongorists, and the universality of knowledge displayed by the incidental references. Yet the appeal is almost wholly to the intellect. Juana never became mystically involved with Christ. She accepted Him as a theological axiom, rather than as the divine bridegroom whom St. Teresa knew, and of whom the medieval Irish nun wrote:

> Jesukin, my Jesukin
> My small cell doth dwell within!
> With prelates have I nought to do:
> All's untrue but Jesukin.

She was no longer the Muse of every Mexican gallant, though flatterers continued to call her "The Tenth Muse"; and as an intelligence she now functioned in a field which the ecclesiastics, to whom she had promised obedience, were always seeking to reduce; being forced to play a religious part in which she could not wholly believe, because it was repugnant to her temperament, yet at last playing it so successfully as at once to shame them and defeat her own ends. When she had sold her books and cut herself off from the world, the only solace left was the fellowship of her ignorant sisters, and even this seems hardly to have been an unmixed blessing:

> It happened that among other favours, I owe to God an easy and affable nature and the nuns loved me for it (without taking notice, like the good people they were, of my faults) and greatly enjoyed my company; knowing this and moved by the great love I had for them—since they loved me, I loved them more—there were times when they intruded somewhat, coming to me to console themselves and to give me the recreation of their company.

It was in no spirit of mock-humility that she described herself as the worst of women; writing the confession in her own blood. She meant that when she first took the Leucadian leap by becoming a nun, it had not been into the sea of pure religion. Still keeping her intellectual pride, her thirst for scientific knowledge and her pleasure in profane authors, lay visitors and the minor pleasures of the flesh, she could remember what it had been to love and to write poetry; and her ancient powers still occasionally reasserted themselves, for instance in some of the songs, based on the *Canticles*, which enliven her religious play *The Divine Narcissus*. Juana called herself the worst of women, it seems, because she had lacked sufficient resolution either to stick it out as a Muse, or make a complete renegation in the style of Liadan.

Now, though both Liadan and Juana were young and famous women poets who took vows of celibacy and submitted to ecclesiastical discipline, it was Juana's Irishness, rather, that first led me to compare them. Juana not only combined Christian ethics with pagan emotion, and profound learning with easy lyricism, like the *ollamhs*, but had inherited their technique by way of the early medieval Latin hymns and the anti-monastic ballads of the Goliards. She too loved the short rhymed quatrain; and the internal rhymes of her *Carol to St. Peter*:

> Y con plumas y voces veloces
> Y con voces y plumas las sumas
> Contad . . .

were in the purest Bardic tradition, like St. Bernard of Cluny's *Rhythm*, which begins:

> Hora novissima, tempora pessima
> Sunt; vigilemus
> Ecce minaciter imminet arbiter
> Ille supremus . . .

Moreover, she excelled in satire of the scorching Irish sort that would raise blotches on the victim's face: her *Lines to Sour-Faced Gila* might have been written by the arch-*ollamh* Seanchan Torpest himself, notorious for having rhymed rats to death. Perhaps Juana's Basque blood was at work; an ancient tie of kinship and religion bound the Western Irish with the Northern Spanish—both peoples had worshipped the same pre-Christian Muse-goddess and the doomed hero Lugos, or Lugh, her gifted son.

POEMS BY JUANA DE ASBAJE, WITH TRANSLATIONS

Arguye de Inconsecuentes el Gusto y la Censura de los Hombres que en las Mujeres Acusan lo que Causan

Hombres necios que acusáis
a la mujer sin razón,
sin ver que sois la ocasión
de lo mismo que culpáis,

si con ansia sin igual
solicitáis su desdén
¿por qué queréis que obren bien
si las incitáis al mal?

Combatis su resistencia
y luego, con gravedad,
decís que fué liviandad
lo que hizo la diligencia.

Parecer quiere el denuedo
de vuestro parecer loco,
al niño que pone el coco,
y luego le tiene miedo.

Queréis, con presunción necia,
hallar a la que buscáis,
para pretendida, Thais,
y en la posesión, Lucrecia.

¿Qué humor puede ser más raro
que el que, falto de consejo,
él mismo empaña el espejo
y siente que no esté claro?

Con el favor y el desdén
tenéis condición igual:
quejándoos si os tratan mal,
burlándoos si os quieren bien.

Opinión ninguna gana,
pues la que más se recata,
si no os admite, es ingrata,
y os admite, es liviana.

Siempre tan necios andáis
que con desigual nivel
a una culpáis por cruel
y otra por fácil culpáis.

¿Pues cómo ha de estar templada
la que vuestra amor pretende,
si la que es ingrata ofende
y la que es fácil enfada?

Mas entre el enfado y pena
que vuestro gusto refiere
bien haya la que no os quiere
y dejaos en hora buena.

Dan vuestras amantes penas
a sus libertades alas,
y después de hacerlas malas
las queréis hallar muy buenas.

¿Cuál mayor culpa ha tenido,
en una pasión errada,
la que cae de rogada,
o el que ruega de caído?

¿O cuál es más de culpar,
aunque cualquiera mal haga,
la que peca por la paga
o el que paga por pecar?

Pues ¿para qué os espantáis
de la culpa que tenéis?
Queredlas cuál las hacéis
o hacedlas cual las buscáis,

Dejad de solicitar
y después, con más razón,
acusaréis la afición
de la que as fuere a rogar.

Bien con muchas armas fundo
que lidia vuestra arrogancia,
pues, en promesa e instancia
juntáis diablo, carne y mundo.

AGAINST THE INCONSEQUENCE OF MEN'S DESIRES AND THEIR CENSURE OF WOMEN FOR FAULTS WHICH THEY THEMSELVES HAVE CAUSED

Ah stupid men, unreasonable
In blaming woman's nature,
Oblivious that your acts incite
The very faults you censure.

If, of unparalleled desire,
At her disdain you batter
With provocations of the flesh,
What should her virtue matter?

Yet once you wear resistance down
You reprimand her, showing
That what you diligently devised
Was all her wanton doing.

With love you feign to be distraught
(How gallant is your lying!
Like children, masked with calabash,
Their own selves terrifying),

And idiotically would seek
    In the same woman's carriage
A Thais for the sport of love,
    And a Lucrece for marriage.

What sight more comic than the man,
    All decent counsel loathing,
Who breathes upon a mirror's face
    Then mourns: "I can see nothing."

Whether rejected or indulged,
    You all have the same patter:
Complaining in the former case,
    But mocking in the latter.

No woman your esteem can earn,
    Though cautious and mistrustful;
You call her cruel, if denied,
    And if accepted, lustful.

Inconsequent and variable
    Your reason must be reckoned:
You charge the first girl with disdain;
    With lickerishness, the second.

How can the lady of your choice
    Temper her disposition,
When to be stubborn vexes you,
    But you detest submission?

So, what with all the rage and pain
    Caused by your greedy nature,
She would be wise who never loved
    And hastened her departure.

Let loved ones cage their liberties
    Like any captive bird; you
Will violate them none the less,
    Apostrophizing virtue.

Which has the greater sin when burned
  By the same lawless fever:
She who is amorously deceived,
  Or he, the sly deceiver?

Or which deserves the sterner blame,
  Though each will be a sinner:
She who becomes a whore for pay,
  Or he who pays to win her?

Are you astounded at your faults,
  Which could not well be direr?
Then love what you have made her be,
  Or make as you desire her.

I warn you: trouble her no more,
  But earn the right to visit
Your righteous wrath on any jade
  Who might your lust solicit.

This arrogance of men in truth
  Comes armoured with all evil—
Sworn promise, plea of urgency—
  O world, O flesh, O devil!

VILLANCICOS EUE SE CANTARON EN LA CATEDRAL DE MÉXICO,
EN LOS MATINES DEL PRÍNCIPE DE LA IGLESIA,
SEÑOR SAN PEDRO,
EL AÑO DE 1677

Estribillo

Serafines alados, celestes jilgueros,
templad vuestras plumas, cortad vuestros ecos,
y con plumas y voces aladas,
y con voces y plumas templadas,
cantad, escribid de Pedro los hechos;

y con plumas, y voces
   veloces,
y con voces y plumas
   las sumas
cantad, escribid de los hechos de Pedro.

Coplas

Reducir infalible
quietud, del viento inquieto las mudanzas,
es menos imposible,
que de Pedro cantar las alabanzas,
que apenas reducir podrán a sumas,
de las alas querúbicas las plumas.

Más que al Cielo de estrellas
número hay de excelencias, que le asista;
¿pues qué diré de aquellas,
que imperceptibles son a nuestra vista?
¿si a decir las sabidas no acertamos,
cómo podré cantar las que ignoramos?

Poner Pedro la planta
adonde Cristo la cabeza puso,
misterio es, que adelanta
el respeto que el Cielo nos impuso:
pues de besar el pie Cristo se precia
a Pedro por cabeza de la Iglesia.

Que él es Pedro, responde
Cristo cuando el Dios vivo le ha llamado;
porque tal gloria esconde
este nombre de Pedro venerado,
que no hallando a su fe, que satisfaga,
sólo en llamarle Pedro Dios le paga.

No le dijo, que él era
cabeza de la iglesia militante,

ni que era la primera
puerta para pasar a la triunfante,
ni que a la redondez; que alumbra el día;
su pescador anillo ceñiría.

Ni que entre justos tantos
tendrá el primer lugar entre los hombres;
gocen allá otros Santos
de gloriosos altísimos renombres,
cual la palma inmortal, cual verde cedro,
que a mi Pedro le basta con ser Pedro.

Pues si tal enseñanza
nos muestra vuestro título y nobleza,
y que vuestra alabanza
encierra en vuestro nombre más grandeza,
no quiero yo alabaros de otro modo:
Pedro sois, y en ser Pedro la sois todo.

Carol Sung in the Cathedral of Mexico City at the Matins of Our Lord Saint Peter, Prince of the Church, A.D. 1677

Winged seraphin, celestial linnets,
Trim your feathers, still your echoes,
And with feathers and winged voices
Sing, write the deeds of Peter:
O, with feathers and voices
    Swift-flying,
O, with voices and feathers,
    Singing and writing,
Sum the deeds of Peter!

What? Reduce to infallible quiet
The shifts of the unquiet wind?
Even that were less impossible

Than to sing Peter's praises
Which the very feathers of the cherubs' wings
Could scarce reduce to a sum.

More than the stars of Heaven in number
Are the merits that attend him.
How then to celebrate such finenesses
As must elude our vision?
If we cannot certify things known to us,
How chant of things we know not?

That Peter his sole rested
Where Christ rested His head,
Is a mystery enhancing
Awe which Heaven has upon us laid:
Since by Christ's kissing of that foot
Peter was hallowed as the Church's head.

"Thou art Peter," Christ replied
When greeted by him as the Living God—
For the reverend name of Peter
Enshrines such glory
That, finding other fee too poor,
God recompensed his faith with this alone;

And did not manifest him as the head
Of the Church Militant,
And the first gate wherethrough
The Church should pass triumphant,
Nor told him that the Fisherman's ring would loop
The round horizon beamed upon by day;

Nor that of all men ever born
He would hold first place among the just.
O then, let other Saints in Heaven enjoy
Honours most glorious and most high,
Be it deathless palm, or cedar evergreen;
My Peter it suffices to be Peter.

Envoie

Wherefore, since Christ's Own declaration
Blazoned your title and nobility,
And since your praise must rest upon
The supreme grandeur which your name encloses,
I would not praise you otherwise than thus:
"Peter thou art and, being so, art all!"

The Old Black Cow

Pawb yn llosgwrn ei henfon, "every man to the tail of his cow," as the Welsh say, and the cow whose tail Professor Gwyn Williams* follows is the old black bardic Llywaidwr which gives whey instead of milk: not shining white Olwen, "she of the white track," known in Ireland as the Glas Gabnach. This Olwen was a moon-cow and once yielded creamy milk in such rivers that it formed the Milky Way.

I was introduced to Welsh poetry nearly fifty years ago, when my father became an enthusiastic pan-Celt; and, this noun being new to Merioneth where we lived, he had a famous argument with Mr. Postoffice-Griffiths as to whether it would count as one word in a telegram, or cost a half-penny more as two words. Mr. Postoffice-Griffiths finally conceded the point: "Very well, sir, one half-penny it shall be: on the analogy of a pancake I shouldn't wonder." To our house came numerous Welsh bards, including

---

* *An Introduction to Welsh Poetry from the Beginnings of the Sixteenth Century,* By Gwyn Williams. Faber, 25s.

Ceiriog ("the Welsh Wordsworth") whose non-Bardic name I forget, and who was a stationmaster on the Cambrian Railway; also gentle Canon Owen Edwards, whose Bardic name I forget; and the formidable, booming Arch-Druid Dyfed himself. It amused Canon Edwards to teach me the ninety-odd rules for writing the Bardic *englyn,* which is to the Welsh what the *tanka* is to the Japanese; and in 1906 my father took me to the Carnarvon Eisteddfod where I watched his friends (dressed up in antique druidic robes, with Sunday-go-to-meeting boots and trouser-legs showing underneath, and bowler hats on their heads against the soft summer rain) assemble for the mock-antique opening ceremony.

But by then I was reading the *Mabinogion,* in Lady Charlotte Guest's translation; and an inspired fishmonger from Criccieth had brought its wonders to life for me. He took me up into the hills and pointed out, on the enormous panorama of Merioneth and Carnarvon stretched before us, by what road a King of Dyfed once pursued the wizard Gwydion in an attempt to recover his pigs; and where the refugees fled from the drowned *cantrevs* of Gwynedd in the days of Prince Seithenyn; and, turning about, showed me the distant knoll of Mur-y-Castell, the scene of Llew Llaw's murder by the treacherous Flower-goddess Blodeuwedd. So Welsh poetry for me now meant the *Mabinogion,* not the Eisteddfod contest for the Chair; though, as I knew from Canon Edwards, *eisteddfod* contests were of very ancient origin, and *englynion* in a primitive form dated back to the Battle of Catraeth—fought as long ago as 565 B.C., and celebrated by Aneirin in his *Gododdin,* a Cymric poem not unlike the *Chanson de Roland.*

It is not generally known that the Cymry were once as much foreigners in Wales as the hated Saxons who followed them. Soon after the Romans decamped, an army of adventurers from Kirkcudbright and Wigtown invaded North Wales under King Cunedda and, linking up with their Brythonic kinsmen in mid-Wales, imposed a barbarous aristocracy on the Goidelic and pre-Celtic peoples who then occupied the country. The Goidels were Aryans, like the Cymry, but being in numerical inferiority to the pre-Celtic tribes, had been converted to their matrilineal culture and accepted institutions which the battle-scarred Cymry rejected with scorn. Presently the Cymric kings, still behaving as foreigners, became Christianized, and the master-poets of the old religion—tellers of the earliest *Mabinogion* tales—were driven from their seats of learning, replaced by ecclesiastical bards of inferior education and powers, and forced to become wandering minstrels, or *kerddorion.*

Professor Williams is referring to the effects of this literary revolution when he writes:

> In Wales, to say that a man is a poet immediately induces an attitude of respect for him . . .

and goes on to explain:

> Most of the poetry of the present century has been written by Nonconformist ministers and University professors.

This respectability he traces to Hywel the Good, a tenth-century King of North Wales who claimed descent from Cunedda, and whose laws regulated Welsh society before the coming of the Normans:

> Poets ranked high in the civil service of the Welsh kings. According to the laws of Hywel Dda, a poet became a *penkerdd,* or chief poet, when he won a chair, that is a seat in the immediate entourage of the king or prince. In the hall he then sat next but one to the *edling,* or heir to the throne, the priest sitting between them.

But on reaching down a dusty copy of *Cyvreithiau Hywel Dda*—"how *do* you manage for books in Majorca, Mr. Graves?"—from my legal shelf, I find that Professor Williams has not been quite accurate. Hywel Dda himself seems to have had little respect for poetry, since in the earliest version of the *Cyvreithiau* (Peniardd MS. 28) the *penkerdd* is not mentioned as having any place at court, and a version called the Demetian Code denies his right to one. Moreover, in the late Venedotian Code, the seat allotted him carries less honour than those of such minor functionaries as chaplain, steward, chief falconer, chief groom and page of the chamber;

his worth is six score and six kine—not above that of the porter and the queen's candle-bearer.

In Ireland, where Christianity was not forcibly imposed on the Courts, and the master-poet, who was required to attend a twelve-year university course in the arts and sciences, exercised corresponding power, the Welsh bard would have been derided as an unqualified practitioner—and, indeed, that is the meaning of "bard" in Irish. He had served only a short apprenticeship and, as the Anomalous Laws suggest (Book iv, 2, p. 397) had been appointed directly by the king—for his morals rather than his poetic qualities. He held his chair on the understanding that he praised God Almighty and his lord at set times, in set metres, in set diction, and that he avoided all "untruth"—meaning any exercise of the imagination that would puzzle the Chief of the Household's mead-sodden brain or bring a frown to the mutton-gorged chaplain's brow. Poetry was defined for him as: "Grammatically accurate expressions, clothed in exalted diction, beautified with becoming and approved epithets, signifying praise of good, dispraise of evil." He might also, as a dispensation, write poems more proper to the *teulwr*, or poet of the second category (namely gnomic stanzas, upright and stereo-typed amatory verse, and rhymed lives of the saints), but nothing else. He never ceased to be under the strict moral control of the Chaplain and Chief of the Household, and could be fined or imprisoned for satire, parody or mimicry; for speaking disrespectfully of religion; for dicing in taverns; for quarrelsomeness; or for suggesting that any woman in Wales would ever, under any circumstances, behave with impropriety. His use of mythology was restricted to the "Triads of Wales," a dry *memoria technica*, already meaningless, of the ancient pre-Cymric tales which had been banned by the Church as "untruths." Thus a *penkerdd* might praise his prince as having "the might of Aergwl, the disposition of Alexander, the strength of Alun, the energy of Beli, the sword-stroke of Peredur, and the courtesy of Medrod"—without in the least knowing who these personages were. The Irish master-poet, on the other hand, was required to know three hundred and fifty ancient historical tales, each of them a night's entertainment, and could recite any one of them correctly at a moment's notice.

Professor Williams, while dwelling proudly on the official bards of Wales, has no word of praise for the *kerddorion,* the descendants of the dispossessed pre-Cymric master-poets, from whom royal favour continued to be withheld—and who managed to preserve a few of the old tales, despite all efforts to suppress them; yet one *kerddor,* Geoffrey of Monmouth's "Bledhericus," or Bleiddriw, introduced the tales to the Norman-French *trovères,* thus setting a fashion of Arthurian romance throughout Western Europe. And it was these same outcasts—rather than, as Professor Williams would like to think, the *teuluwr*—whose obstinate adherence to their ancient poetic principles brought about the fourteenth-century renascence in Welsh poetry. When Professor Williams briefly mentions the *Preiddeu Annwfn,* "The Spoils of Tartarus," because of a reference to King Arthur's harrowing of Hell, he allows his readers to suppose that it is official verse, rather than a poem of "untruth"—a biting satire by a *kerddor,* who called himself Gwion Bach of Llanfihangel, on the ignorance, cowardice and boastfulness of the official bards.

This would pass as old-fashioned conservative obscurantism, were it not for the praise which Professor Williams inconsistently showers on the fourteenth-century Dafudd ap Gwilym who, being a real poet, behaved exactly as a *penkerdd* should not. Like his gifted friends Gruffudd ap Ada and Madog Benfras, Dafudd used non-Classical metres, versified tales of untruth, diced, whored, blasphemed:

> For God's sake, no more bread and water,
> Throw aside Lenten watercress,
> For Mary's sake, cease your thin prayers,
> The Romish monks' religion:
> Be not a nun in Springtime,
> The grove is better than a nunnery . . .
> Come to the spreading birch
> The cuckoo's woodland church,
> Where none will mock at us
> For seeking Heaven in a green grove;
> Keep Ovid's book in mind
> And pray, not too much faith!

and when he should have roused the Welsh to perish magnificently in a rebellion against the English oppressors, was exchanging *en-glynion* with charming but disreputable Gwerfil Mechain—who had written:

> I am the hostess of the irreproachable Ferry Tavern,
> A white-gowned moon welcoming
> Any man who comes to me with silver—

about his and her sexual anatomy. Dafudd often refers to himself as a wandering minstrel; but since he came of a noble family, and towards the end of his life humorously reverted to the twenty-four Classical metres—the Job's potsherd with which Welsh bards still scrape themselves—used by his more respectable contemporaries, his moral shortcomings are here ascribed to the breakdown of Welsh social life after the conquest of Wales by the English. "When a nation is defeated," Professor Williams observes charitably, "there are sensitive spirits for whom politics and religion cease to be serious concerns."

Besides, Dafudd is long dead, poetry in dangerously free metres has come and gone, respectability is respectable again:

> The competition for the Chair at this year's Eisteddfod requires a poem of not more than three hundred lines in full *cynghanedd* [a form of balanced cross-alliteration] employing any number of Davydd ap Edmwnd's measures [Davydd ap Edmwnd was the bard who, in 1451, tightened up *cynghanedd* to a pitch of craziness], including at least one *awdl* measure; and the winner may well be a shepherd, a postman, a preacher, or a journalist.

As Gwion Bach, who had taken the trouble to give himself a proper poetic education in Ireland, remarked on a similar occasion about eight hundred years ago:

> Ni obrynaf lawyr llen llywiadur—

meaning: "I have a poor opinion of official Welsh literature."

Legitimate Criticism of Poetry

Some people call this a critical, as opposed to a creative age. I doubt whether it is either. Certainly, so many thousands of professed poets write and publish, that a great need has arisen for critics to assess their worth; but the criticism racket, to judge from the advanced literary journals that people send me, is about as bankrupt as the poetry racket. Poetry ceases to be happily creative, because most poets are seldom thinking of the poem itself, but worrying how to provide interesting material for critical discussion. And it also seems to me that because critics are seldom thinking of the poems they are supposed to assess, but only of the art with which they will write their criticism—they, rather than the poets, have become the happy creators.

Mount Holyoke is an institution where girls learn to think for themselves; after having spent some years at schools, run by ed-ucationalists, where thought was not always obligatory. Education-alists are honest characters charged with feeding useful information to half-empty minds. They rightly believe that no student is fit to attend college before getting exposed to English poetry from, let us say, Chaucer to Yeats. The student may dislike poetry—may regard it as time-wasting, useless nonsense—but at least she should be given a chance to sample it. So the educationalists choose an anthology edited by some reputable judge of poetry, and use it as a text-book. The students are then asked to "appreciate" its contents.

Be very careful with the word "appreciate," which originally meant "to calculate the quality, or worth, or amount of a thing." Thus Burke wrote in 1769: "Let us calmly appreciate these dreadful and deformed gorgons and hydras." In the earlier sense of "appreciation," the student should not consider herself obliged to write: "This is a swell poem: it makes me feel fine. Milton surely knew how to write." Some such critical judgement as: "This poem is punk, for the following reasons," would also come under the heading "appreciation." But it is only in the debased sense of the word: "I certainly would appreciate" (i.e. be mighty glad to get) "a loan of five hundred bucks"; or "I welcome any attempt to appreciate" (i.e. to enhance) "the value of tobacco shares"—a solecism first current in the United States around 1799—it is only in this sense, I fear, that most honest educationalists require their students to "appreciate" poems.

Poetry (need I say?) is more than words musically arranged. It is sense; good sense; penetrating, often heart-rending sense. Children who delight in verse-jingles are not reliable critics of poetry, and though a few nursery-rhymes happen to be poems, most have nothing but their engaging rhythms to recommend them. Yet how few students ever get beyond the jingle-loving or, at best, the music-loving stage, of poetic appreciation! How few give any thought to the sense of a poem, though it often has layer after layer of meaning concealed in it!

I dislike generalizing, unless I can support my argument by practical examples. Has anyone here read Milton's *L'Allegro?*

Most of you? Good. But I, for one, hadn't read *L'Allegro* carefully until the other day, when my thirteen-year-old daughter Lucia, finding herself obliged to learn it by heart (as I had done at the same age) asked me: "Isn't this rather a muddle, Father?"

How could I deceive an innocent and intelligent girl? I admitted, after a closer scrutiny of the text, that *L'Allegro* was indeed a dreadful muddle, and that most of it could be "appreciated" only in the Burkian sense, as one appreciates deformed gorgons and hydras.

Lucia's anthology version began straight away with:

> Haste thee, Nymph, and bring with thee . . .

leaving out the ponderous introduction, written in a somewhat different style. This seems to have been tacked on later, when *L'Allegro* became a companion-piece to *Il Penseroso:*

> Hence loathèd Melancholy, etc., . . .

*

> But come thou Goddess fair and free . . .

So I started my appreciation of the anthology text before me with:

> Haste thee, Nymph, and bring with thee
> Jest, and youthful Jollity. . . .

(There was something awkward about *"youthful* Jollity," I felt at once—it must have been put there for some dishonest reason.) Then the same Nymph was asked to bring along two other allegorical figures:

> . . . Sport that wrinkled Care derides,
> And Laughter holding both his sides.

Jest, Jollity, Sport, Laughter—four characters not easily distinguished, as one (say) distinguishes the plaster saints in a Catholic repository by the emblems they bear: Peter's keys, Isidore's spade, Lawrence's grid-iron, and so on. I found this conjunction rather fuzzy.

One way of appreciating a poem is first to write it out in longhand; then to imagine oneself composing the lines, and so creep inside the poet's skin. The process of getting a rough verse draft into presentable form will be familiar to most of you. And with practice one can often deduce, from some slight awkwardness surviving in the final version, what the grosser faults of the original were. Well, when I tried the longhand test, my little finger told me (and I never argue with my little finger) that Milton had written:

> Hasten, Mirth, and bring with thee
> Jest and Youth and Jollity,
> Sport that wrinkled Care derides
> And Laughter holding both his sides . . .

Afterwards he had wondered whether the difference between Mirth and Jollity could be justified or, alternatively, the difference between Mirth and Laughter. He shook his head, changed "Mirth" to "Nymph," and kept her anonymous. Then, disliking the two *n*'s of "Hast*en*, Nymph," he changed this to "Haste thee, Nymph"— not noticing another "thee" at the end of the line—and went on:

> And in the right hand lead with thee
> The Mountain Nymph, sweet Liberty . . .

But it was clear that some lines were needed to separate this couplet from the first one, in which he had not only used the same rhyme —*with thee* and *Jollity*—but also the word *Nymph*. So between the figures of Mirth, Jest, Youth, Jollity, and their companions, Sport, Care and Laughter, he introduced a crowd of impersonalized nouns:

> Quips and Cranks and Wanton Wiles,
> Nods and Becks and gleeful Smiles . . .

And, to prove that he was a Cambridge graduate, Milton added a mythological reference to Hebe, Goddess of Youth. Having decided on Hebe, he prudently removed the figure of Youth from the second line by changing *Youth and Jollity* to *youthful Jollity*. I suspect that the first draft ran:

> Wreathed about sweet Hebe's cheek
> Which is dimpled, fair and sleek . . .

but Milton realized that *"Wreathed about sweet Hebe's cheek"* was far too heavy for a tripping measure, and that *wreathed* made an ugly assonance with *sweet* and *cheek*. So he substituted *wreathed smiles* for *gleeful smiles* and let the next line read:

> Such as hang on Hebe's cheek . . .

Clearly smiles don't hang on cheeks, and wreaths don't either, and Milton knew it; but the revised line was much more musical, with its alliteration of *hang* and *Hebe;* and in these minor poems Milton always put music before sense, if he got stuck. Besides, all nouns were capitalized in his day (whether common or proper); so Quips, Cranks, Wiles, Nods, Becks and Smiles could be read as allegorical imps or animalcules. Smiles, for example, might be tinsy, whimsical little atomies, wearing wreaths around their heads, and hanging merrily from Hebe's cheeks. He hoped to get by with that.

Re-reading:

> Which is dimpled, fair and sleek . . .

Milton disliked the three adjectives in a row, immediately after all those nouns in a row—Quips, Cranks, Wiles, Smiles, etc. He considered:

> And love to live on skin so sleek . . .

But the double alliteration—*love, live; skin, sleek*—was excessive; so he decided to retain the dimples and let the tinsy whimsical little Smiles keep house in them. He wrote:

> And love to live in dimple sleek . . .

Cheek, not *cheeks,* for the sake of the rhyme; and *dimple,* not *dimples*—because of dimples sleek. Though it was only natural to suppose that Hebe had two cheeks (with a smile-infested dimple in each), a hoary old Latin verse-convention allows the use of singular for plural, and Milton took advantage of it. And he knew, of course, that dimples aren't sleek; however, another hoary Latin verse-convention, called "transference of epithet," allowed him to call the *dimple* "sleek," instead of the cheek. But this is not honest English.

That it was a "tripping measure" suggested the next line:

> Come and trip it as you go . . .

The rhyme would be *toe,* meaning *toes.* I think Milton first wrote:

> Fantastically on the toe . . .

but disliked the extra syllable at the beginning. He tried:

> Fancifully on the toe . . .

but that wasn't quite strong enough; so he used another transferred epithet, making *fantastic* govern *toe,* as in Latin one might get out of an awkward difficulty of scansion by writing:

> Ibimus ad ludos, heu, lacrumante pede . . .
> ["We shall go to the games, alas, with a weeping foot."]

meaning: "we shall walk weeping to the games." But this is not honest English either. In English, feet don't "weep"; nor are toes "fantastic," unless one is a Charles Addams monster, or has been forced to wear tight shoes as a child.

So Milton was now back at:

> And in the right hand lead with thee
> The Mountain Nymph, sweet Liberty . . .

and rattled on:

> I'll live with her, and live with thee
> In unrestrainèd pleasures free . . .

He then thought of his Puritanical father, who was allowing
him to stay at home and write poems in their cottage at Horton,
rather than enter the family scrivener's office down in Bread Street.
What would Father say about *"unrestrainèd"*? He changed it to
"unreprovèd," which made the line sound less orgiastic. Yet condona-
tion of wanton wiles, including a derision of serious, careworn men,
still seemed a bit dangerous, so he dissociated himself from the
poem by making it describe *L'Allegro*—the ideal, mirthful man—
and not himself, John Milton.

The next trouble was that he had carelessly repeated the *"with
thee-ee"* rhyme. He corrected this by inserting two more lines of
padding:

> And if I give thee honour due,
> Nymph, admit me of thy crew . . .

"Nymph," again! Very well, he'd call her by her real name and risk
it:

> Mirth, admit me of thy crew,
> To live with her, and live with thee, etc., etc.

Then the poem got under way at last:

> To hear the lark begin his flight
> And, singing, startle the dull night . . .

Now, I believe that the earliest draft of the poem had begun,
without any allegorical invocation, as follows:

> Hark: the lark begins his flight
> And singing startles the dull night,
> Hark: the cock with lively din

> Scatters to rear the darkness thin,
> Come, dear heart, in spite of sorrow,
> And at my window bid good-morrow . . .

But he did not want anyone to think that he had borrowed *"Hark the lark"* from Shakespeare, so he cut out *"Hark."* And, fearing that his father might suspect him of dalliance at dawn with sorrowful milkmaids, he also cut out his *"dear heart"* altogether, and instead conjured up the harmless allegorical figure of Mirth— though few of us feel particularly mirthful at 3 A.M., even in June, unless we have been making mirth all night and the spicy nut-brown ale is still going round. He tied up this *"Haste thee, Nymph"* address with the discarded *aubade* to his dear heart.

Milton now asks Mirth's permission (unnecessarily, I think) to hear the lark begin his flight and sing, etc., until the dappled dawn doth rise; and then to come and bid her good-morrow at his window, peering out through the sweet brier, vine, or twisted eglantine, while the cock in the barnyard crows and stoutly struts before his dames. So far, not so bad. But as he is distractedly bidding good-morrow, at the window, to Mirth, with one ear cocked for the hounds and horn, he sometimes, we are told, goes *"walking, not unseen, by hedgerow elms, on hillocks green."* Either Milton had forgotten that he is still supposedly standing naked at the open window—the Jacobeans always slept raw—or else the subject of "walking" is the cock who escapes from the barnyard, deserts his dames, ceases to strut and, anxiously aware of the distant hunt, trudges far afield among ploughmen and shepherds in the dale. But why should Milton give twenty lines to the adventures of the neighbour's wandering cock? And why *"walking, not unseen"*? Not unseen by whom?

This really is a puzzle. Let me read the lines aloud, to refresh your memory:

> And if I give thee honour due,
> Mirth, admit me of thy crew,
> To live with her, and live with thee,
> In unreprovèd pleasures free;

To hear the lark begin his flight,
And, singing, startle the dull night,
From his watch-tower in the skies,
Till the dappled dawn doth rise;
Then to come, in spite of sorrow,
And at my window bid good-morrow,
Through the sweet-brier or the vine,
Or the twisted eglantine;
While the cock, with lively din,
Scatters the rear of darkness thin;
And to the stack, or the barn-door,
Stoutly struts his dames before:
Oft list'ning how the hounds and horn
Cheerly rouse the slumb'ring morn,
From the side of some hoar hill,
Through the high wood echoing shrill:
Sometime walking, not unseen,
By hedgerow elms, on hillocks green,
Right against the eastern gate
Where the great Sun begins his state,
Robed in flames and amber light,
The clouds in thousand liveries dight;
While the ploughman, near at hand,
Whistles o'er the furrow'd land,
And the milkmaid singeth blithe,
And the mower whets his scythe,
And every shepherd tells his tale
Under the hawthorn in the dale.

Please, do not think that I am joking when I suggest that the last sixteen of these lines formed the sixth page of Milton's manuscript and got accidentally misplaced as the third page. (Always number your pages, girls!) Milton laid the poem aside for a few days, perhaps, while he visited London to see whether Jonson's learned sock, or socks, were on and, when he returned, did not notice the mistake.

Originally (my trustworthy little finger tells me) the second draft of the poem went directly on from the point where Milton stands at his window bidding Mirth good-morrow and hearing the lark and the cock, to the more natural, if rather artificial:

> Straight mine eye hath caught new pleasures
> Whilst the landskip round it measures . . .

The intruding sixteen lines make sense only as Page 6—way on in the poem—a continuation of the Lubber Fiend story. You will remember how an anonymous farm-hand—

> Tells how the drudging goblin sweat
> To earn his cream-bowl duly set,
> When in one night, ere glimpse of morn,
> His shadowy flail hath thresh'd the corn
> That ten day-labourers could not end;
> Then lies him down, the Lubber Fiend,
> And, stretch'd out all the chimney's length,
> Basks at the fire his hairy strength;
> And crop-full out of door he flings,
> Ere the first cock his matin rings:

And (here one turns the page):

> Oft list'ning how the hounds and horn
> Cheerly rouse the slumb'ring morn,
> From the side of some hoar hill,
> Through the high wood echoing shrill:
> Sometime walking, not unseen,
> By hedgerow elms, on hillocks green,
> Right against the eastern gate,
> Where the great Sun begins his state,
> Robed in flames and amber light,
> The clouds in thousand liveries dight;
> While the ploughman, near at hand,
> Whistles o'er the furrow'd land,
> And the milkmaid singeth blithe,
> And the mower whets his scythe,
> And every shepherd tells his tale
> Under the hawthorn in the dale.

The *"not unseen"* now explains itself: the farm-hand claims to have himself caught sight of the legendary Lubber Fiend slinking off eastward across the meadows in search of a basking place under the hot sun: though ploughman, milkmaid, mower and shepherd are busy and fail to see him.

Why Milton did not notice the misplacement may have been the verbal similarity between *Thus don the Tales, to bed they creep* and *Every Shepherd tells his tale;* and between *While the Cock with lively din* and *Ere the first Cock his Matin rings.* Milton came to despise his early non-religious work and did not consider *L'Allegro,* published in 1632, to be worthy of reprint even for the sake of amending the textual error. A correspondent who forgot to sign his name, recently reassured me that I was perhaps not unique in my amendment of the text. He wrote:

> . . . I possess an edition of Milton's *Minor Poems* with illustrations by the mid-Victorian painter-etcher Samuel Palmer. One of these is entitled "The Eastern Gate." It shows the Ploughman at his toil, with eyes turned towards the rising sun while, full in his line of vision, walks the "Lubber Fiend," looking like a bear on his hind legs, or an Abominable Snowman. This need not be taken to contravene your thesis: that it takes a poet to understand a poem. Palmer was a great student of Milton; but he had also, in his childhood, been well acquainted with William Blake, whose influence on him was a lasting one. Perhaps Blake anticipated you?

I should be proud to think so.

I expect you have wondered why Milton wrote:

> Mirth, admit me *of* thy crew . . .

instead of:

> Mirth, admit me *to* thy crew . . .

and:

> Scatter the rear of darkness thin . . .

instead of:

> Scatter to rear the darkness thin . . .

In each case you will find that he was striking out the word "to" because another "to" occurred in the next line.

Well, when Milton had finished *Il Penseroso*, he took *L'Allegro* up again and found it far too countrified. In *Il Penseroso* he had sown Classical allusions with the sack; but apart from Hebe's cheek and a reference at the end to Orpheus and Eurydice, *L'Allegro* might well have been written by any poetic bumpkin (Shakespeare, poor fellow, for example—"father lost his money in the meat trade and couldn't send young Will to college"). So, as I have said, Milton tacked on that ponderous *"Hence, loathèd Melancholy"* piece to *"Haste thee, Nymph,"* and there introduced the Nymph in due Classical form as Euphrosyne; giving her, for good measure, two variant mythical parentages. He also, I believe, inserted that most un-English passage about Corydon's meeting with his boy-friend Thyrsis at the cottage between the oaks. Phillis prepares their luncheon and scurries discreetly off in pretended haste, saying that she has to bind the August sheaves, or perhaps cart the June hay, she isn't sure which. Milton, incidentally, not having access to an *Apollodorus* in the Horton cottage, misreported Euphrosyne's birth. Her mother was neither Venus nor Aurora, but the Moon-goddess Eurynome; her father neither Zephyr nor ivy-crowned Bacchus, but jolly old Father Zeus himself, with a thunderbolt in his fist and a grog-blossom on his nose.

If you think that I'm exaggerating Milton's pride in his Cambridge education, you will have to account for these lines:

> . . . thou goddess fair and free
> In Heav'n ycleped Euphrosyne,
> And by men heart-easing Mirth . . .

which made Milton an immortal and mortalized all the uneducated Horton clods who could talk only English—who called Thyrsis

"Maister Jack Melton" and Corydon "that young furriner, Maister Charley Deodati, or somesuch."

*

The legitimacy of this sort of chiselling "appreciation" is tested when one applies it to other similar songs of mirthful invocation such as Shakespeare's:

> Come unto these yellow sands,
> And then take hands . . .

or the nursery-rhyme:

> Girls and boys, come out to play:
> The moon doth shine as bright as day . . .

There the probing cold-chisel of criticism rings against the true rock of poetry. With L'Allegro, the plaster flakes away and the rubble tumbles out.

I grant that L'Allegro is very cunning verbal music—"linkèd sweetness long drawn out" as he called it—and that Milton is a cunning musician who can cheat you of your inheritance of commonsense as easily as he once cheated his Royalist mother-in-law, Mrs. Powel, of her "widow's thirds." Shakespeare, on the other hand, was an English poet, and always played fair, except sometimes when he knocked off verses too hurriedly for patching up some old play. He burlesqued the "University wits" who wrote English as if it were Latin, and never did so himself, though his grammar school education seems to have been a sound one.

I don't know whether anyone has yet pointed out that Milton's linkèd sweetness seems to be a quotation from Thomas Campion's definition of a poem as "a system of linked sounds." But Campion's poems always made good simple sense and were endowed with complexity by the linkèd music he wrote for them. Milton's purely verbal music, as I suggest, tends at times to confuse the sense.

The genius of the English language, whether transplanted to

Wales, Scotland, Ireland or America remains literal, logical, and anti-hypocritical. No sensitive poet or critic can accept without a blush Milton's pastoral affectations:

> And daffodillies fill their cups with tears,
> To strew the laureate hearse where Lycid lies . . .

in what is supposed to be an elegy for his dead college friend. Especially after Shakespeare had written in *The Winter's Tale* the wholly unpastoral lines:

> . . . daffodills
> That come before the swallow dares, and take
> The winds of March with beauty . . .

which no true poet who has lived through an English winter can read without a catch at the heart.

A poem is legitimately judged by the standards of craftsmanship implied in the form used. One expects little from a fo'c'sle ballad beginning:

> Come all you jolly mariners
> Who sail upon the sea . . .

where even false rhymes do not matter so long as the tune is brisk. But Milton was not writing a fo'c'sle ballad. Why pretend that English poetry is held in a Latin strait-jacket from which one has to wriggle out with the artful aid of grammatical and syntactical licence?

*

Wordsworth's *Solitary Reaper* is simpler to "appreciate." Milton scamped his remodelling work on *L'Allegro*; but at least he made some attempt to disguise weaknesses. Wordsworth, on the contrary, seems to have left his first draft untouched; with the plea, perhaps, that a sketch has a certain ingenuous bloom which the finished picture may lose:

Behold her, single in the field,
Yon solitary Highland Lass!
Reaping and singing by herself;
Stop here, or gently pass!
Alone she cuts and binds the grain,
And sings a melancholy strain;
O listen! for the Vale profound
Is overflowing with the sound.

No Nightingale did ever chaunt
More welcome notes to weary bands
Of travellers in some shady haunt,
Among Arabian sands:
A voice so thrilling ne'er was heard
In spring-time from the Cuckoo-bird,
Breaking the silence of the seas
Among the farthest Hebrides.

Will no one tell me what she sings?—
Perhaps the plaintive numbers flow
For old, unhappy, far-off things,
And battles long ago:
Or is it some more humble lay,
Familiar matter of today?
Some natural sorrow, loss, or pain,
That has been, and may be again?

Whate'er the theme, the Maiden sang
As if her song could have no ending;
I saw her singing at her work,
And o'er the sickle bending;—
I listened, motionless and still;
And, as I mounted up the hill,
The music in my heart I bore,
Long after it was heard no more.

For a poem of such seeming simplicity *The Solitary Reaper*
proves on examination to be peculiarly artificial:

> Behold her, single in the field,
> Yon solitary Highland Lass!

There are only two figures in sight: Wordsworth and the High-land Lass—yet he cries "Behold her!" Do any of you find that reasonable? Perhaps you think that he is telling readers merely to picture her as they sit with the book open before them? Very well! But what of the next line:

> Stop here, or gently pass!

and again:

> O listen! for the Vale profound
> Is overflowing with the sound . . .

How can readers stop, pass, or listen if they aren't there?

Very well! Let us assume that Wordsworth is soliloquizing on both occasions. Then why does he tell himself: *"Behold her!"* when he has already done so? And why: *"O listen!"*? He can hardly help listening, because the vale profound is overflowing with the sound. And why: *"Stop here, or gently pass!"*? It is not even an exclusive alternative: as we learn later. Wordsworth first stopped for awhile and then passed gently on. I'm afraid we must agree that he wrote *"or gently pass!"* for the sake of the rhyme; and that *"Behold her!"* and *"O listen!"* are Latin verse tricks. Wordsworth also was a Cambridge graduate.

Have you ever seen a squirrel "appreciating" hickory nuts? It weighs them in its little paws and flings away the light ones. Well, a good habit which I recommend to all you young squirrels as a test of your own poems, is to weigh them. You can turn it into a game called "Cables." Imagine yourselves badly off for cash and having to cable the *sense* of this first verse, at your own expense, to a friend in New Zealand. By the rules, you must use Wordsworth's own vocabulary, and leave out no word of importance. What about this?

SOLITARY HIGHLAND LASS REAPING BINDING GRAIN STOP
MELANCHOLY SONG OVERFLOWS PROFOUND VALE

Twelve words instead of forty-three! Wordsworth has (did you notice?) used four synonyms for her loneliness: *"single," "solitary," "alone," "by herself"*; and two for her sickle-work: *"reaping"* and *"cutting"*; and has mentioned her voice four times: *"singing," "sings," "strain," "sound."* All true poetry is economical of words. Try putting:

> Come unto these yellow sands,
> And then take hands . . .

or:

> Full fathom five thy father lies,
> O, his bones are coral made . . .

into cablese! You wouldn't save much money.

Wordsworth feels the need for some poetic contrast to this rugged Highland scene. Something warm and luscious:

> No Nightingale did ever chaunt
> More welcome notes to weary bands
> Of travellers in some shady haunt,
> Among Arabian sands . . .

Personally, I regard *"chaunt"* (or even *"chant"*) as an affectation when used of birds. Monks and sorcerers chant; birds sing. But let that pass. Now for the sense. It is true that occasional nightingales, or bulbuls, penetrate to the more verdurous parts of Arabia Felix, but only as winter migrants, when heavy rains provide them with grubs and caterpillars, and never nest there; consequently they do not *"chaunt."*

Then Wordsworth thinks up a poetic contrast to perpetually sun-smitten Arabia—something bitterly cold and frozen:

> A voice so thrilling ne'er was heard
> In spring-time from the Cuckoo-bird,
> Breaking the silence of the seas
> Among the farthest Hebrides . . .

"*Cuckoo-bird*" is pretended innocent baby-talk for "cuckoo," on the analogy of "dickey-bird." Occasional cuckoos do get so far north as the Hebrides; but in springtime the Hebridean seas, which Wordsworth seems to imagine as icebound, are at their noisiest—the islands enjoy a remarkably temperate climate, because of the Gulf Stream; and the cuckoo's arrival coincides with the equinoctial gales. Moreover, Wordsworth does not seem to have considered that all the Outer (or Farther) Hebrides are inhabited by other loud-voiced Highland Lasses singing in competition with the cuckoo.

He goes on:

> Will no one tell me what she sings?

Who could? Nobody is present except Wordsworth and the single, solitary girl, all alone and by herself, whom he is too shy to accost.

> Perhaps the plaintive numbers flow . . .

"*Plaintive numbers*" is utterly wrong in this Ossianic context. The Highland Lass, who seems to have sung her lay in Gaelic (since Wordsworth didn't understand a syllable of it, however loud she sang), could certainly not be described as singing in "*numbers.*" "Numbers" are a translation of the Latin *numeri,* which implies a strictly observed metrical scheme; whereas Gaelic lays are wild and fitful as the breeze.

> For old, unhappy, far-off things,
> And battles long ago . . .

"*Old,*" "*far-off,*" "*long ago*": three near-synonyms. Yet the two lines have an innocent compelling ring, the only justification of the poem —until prosily interrupted by:

> Or is it some more humble lay,
> Familiar matter of today?
> Some natural sorrow, loss, or pain,
> That has been, and may be again?

Wordsworth gives up the problem:

> Whate'er the theme, the Maiden sang
> As if her song could have no ending;
> I saw her singing at her work,
> And o'er the sickle bending;—
> I listened, motionless and still;
> And, as I mounted up the hill,
> The music in my heat I bore,
> Long after it was heard no more.

I leave you to play "Cables" with this last verse, too; though, after the first six lines, which can be reduced to nine words, your cable will run you into money:

> CANCEL PREVIOUS COMMUNICATION STOP SONG
> DID NOT OVERFLOW PROFOUND VALE STOP
> CEASED TO HEAR IT LONG BEFORE MOUNTING
> HILL BUT BORE MUSIC IN HEART

*

I should define a good poem as one that makes complete sense; and says all it has to say memorably and economically; and has been written for no other than poetic reasons. By "other than poetic reasons" I mean political, philosophical, or theological propaganda, and every sort of careerist writing. Careerism is the plague of modern poetry, as it was of the early nineteenth century. Wordsworth, when he had written the *Lucy* poems and others in the same vein, which are good if a trifle clumsy, turned careerist. Though I thought of "appreciating" his sonnet "Great men have been among us . . . ," I shall refrain. You can make that one of our vacation tasks. But Wordsworth has plenty to answer for. Largely because of him the old-fashioned terms "great poet," "major poem," "higher stature," still persist; and in the United States especially, where there is enough loose money about to make poetical careerism profitable, poetry has become a dog-eat-dog game. Here poets no longer compete in writing good poems, they are all trying to be listed as "great new experimental masters in the line of Eliot and Pound."

Neither Eliot nor Pound are, however, great experimentalists, except in the sense that they once tried adapting modern French poetic theory to English verse; and Pound-Eliot experimentation of the early 'Twenties is already as dated as a streamlined pogo-stick with gay decorative motifs from Tutankhamen's tomb—a reference, which, I fear, most of you are too young to get. Many Americans of that day thought it cleverer to go French in verse (and German in scholarship) than to develop their predominantly English tradition in an American sense; yet the true American masters of experiment were such poets as John Crowe Ransom and Robert Frost. Their experiments do not date, because each adapted his individual speech-rhythm and diction to agreed verse-forms—as Shakespeare did—and produced something startlingly new and lasting.

I remember my delight in 1922, when I first opened Frost's *North of Boston*, and came across:

THE MOUNTAIN

The mountain held the town as in a shadow.
I saw so much before I slept there once:
I noticed that I missed stars in the west,
Where its black body cut into the sky.
Near me it seemed: I felt it like a wall
Behind which I was sheltered from a wind.
And yet between the town and it I found,
When I walked forth at dawn to see new things,
Were fields, a river, and beyond, more fields.
The river at the time was fallen away,
And made a widespread brawl on cobble-stones;

> But the signs showed what it had done in spring:
> Good grass-land gullied out, and in the grass
> Ridges of sand, and driftwood stripped of bark . . .

And I remember my delight when John Crowe Ransom sent me from Nashville, Tennessee, his hitherto unpublished *Ilex Priscus:*

> He is a tower unleaning. But he may break,
> If Heaven in a rage try him too windily;
> And what uproar tall towers concumbent make;
>
> More than a hundred years, more than a hundred feet
> Of timeless trunk that is too vast to shake;
> Only the temporal twigs are abashed on their seat,
>
> And the frail leaves of a season, which are susceptive
> Of the mad humours of wind, and turn and beat
> Ecstatic round the stem to which they are captive.
>
> But he casts the feeble generations of leaf,
> And naked to the spleen of the cold skies eruptive
> That howl on his defiant head in chief,
>
> Bears out their frenzy to its period,
> And hears in the spring, a little more rheumy and deaf,
> After the tragedy, the lyric palinode . . .

I always find it far easier to say why a poem is bad, than why it is good. Criticizing a good poem, as both of these are, is like trying to scale a tower of such perfectly fitted masonry that one can find neither finger-hold nor toe-hold.

Not long ago I denounced a widespread critical plot to make "great" a better epithet than "good." An English critic had written that one becomes "great" by presenting "a diploma piece" of "major form"—such as Eliot's *Four Quartets*, or Pound's *Hugh Selwyn Mauberley*. I protested that, according to the logicians, nothing is better than the truly good, not even the truly great; therefore, what is not truly good, however great, must be either to some degree evil (an active denial of good) or to some degree bad (a falling short of good). It followed that all truly "great" diploma pieces, unless truly bad, were likely to be truly evil—inspired by ambition, the vice which caused Lucifer's downfall. But it was my opinion, I said, that *The Four Quartets* could hardly be called either bad or evil. Their chief appeal was a macabre one, as when one observes zombies still working posthumously on the old sugar plantation. And as for Pound's *Mauberley*, I found the poetic technique poor, the thought muddled, and the emotions vulgar.

To this the English critic (whose name, by the way, was Mr. Wharton) replied that it was unseemly for me to discuss "major form"; because, though I had written excellent lyrics within my self-imposed limitations, my work contained no diploma pieces. Then he offered me a "major lyric" of Ezra Pound's to illustrate what he meant:

> O Lynx, guard this orchard
> Keep from Demeter's furrow
> This fruit has a fire within it,
>   Pomona, Pomona,
> No glass is clearer than are the globes of this flame
> What sea is clearer than the pomegranate body holding
>   the flame?
>   Pomona, Pomona.
> Lynx, keep watch on this orchard
> That is named Melagrana
> or the Pomegranate field
>   The sea is not clearer in azure
>   Nor the Heliads bringing light
> Here are lynxes   Here are lynxes,
> Is there a sound in the forest
>   of pard or of bassarid
>   or crotale   or of leaves moving?

I was grateful to be given a text for discussion; but, though I am as smart as the next man in looking through a brick wall, I could not get beyond where a lynx is improbably asked to keep from Demeter's furrow a clear flaming pomegranate-like fruit in an

orchard sacred to Pomona. There the trail went cold, despite
Heliads, pards and bassarids "such as any college library will supply"
(Dr. Johnson on *Lycidas*). *Crotale* is probably an approximation to
crotalon, the Greek word for "rattle"; as *Melagrana* probably is to
Malagranata, the mediaeval Latin for "pomegranate." The Greek
for "pomegranate-field" would probably be *rhoiōn*, on the analogy
of *ampelōn*, "a vineyard"; and why use mediaeval Latin in this
Classical Greek context—even if the speaker is supposed to be so
drunk that he telescopes his sentences? And what is Pomona, the
Latin Goddess of Fruit-trees, doing here? There were no pards,
lynxes, or bassarids in her Italian territory; and the pomegranate
was a solemn fruit sacred to Infernal Persephone (or Proserpina),
not associated with the revels of the bassarids, or with Dionysus's
pards.

If this was a major lyric, I said, might I never write one!

Modern poetical experiment has been influenced by non-representational painting and sculpture; especially in the abandonment
of metre. Everyone can make what experiments he pleases, but
poetry is necessarily linked with metrical forms designed to create
in the listener, or reader, a hypersensitive awareness of the meaning.
Personal rhythmic variations can be, and should be, made on the
metrical norm—I have quoted Frost and Ransom—just as one expresses one's personality by an individual variation of copperplate
handwriting. Verse forms are elastic and may be subjected to great
stress under poetic emotions, but they have their breaking point.
When broken, and called "free verse," there is no metrical norm
left to make variations on.

Eliot has written about free verse:

> It is not defined by non-existence of metre, since even the worst
> verse can be scanned . . . But the most interesting verse which has
> yet been written in our language has been done either by taking a
> very simple form, like the iambic pentameter, and constantly with-
> drawing from it, or taking no form at all, and constantly approxi-
> mating to a very simple one. It is this contrast between fixity and
> flux, this unperceived evasion of monotony, which is the very life
> of verse.

I can make nothing of Eliot's cautiously negative remark—free verse "is not defined by non-existence of metre, since even the worst verse can be scanned." If verse *can* be scanned, it is not freed of metre; and whether it may be good or bad seems irrelevant to the argument. As for Eliot's suggestion that "the most interesting verse which has yet been written in our language has been done [*sic*] either by taking a very simple form . . . and constantly withdrawing from it, or taking no form at all, and constantly approximating to a very simple one"—well, "doing" that sort of verse is interesting to some, but embarrassing to others, like a jaunt in the family car after mixing a little water with the gasoline to make it go by fits and starts. I was never partial to such experiments. I expect verse to be verse, and prose to be prose. Keeping the demands of verse should be an easy burden to a poet, unless he puts himself in a strait-jacket of metres so strict that they allow him no imaginative play at all—as the court bards of Wales, for instance, did.

The experimental change-over from metre to free verse began around 1911, when English poetry was in the doldrums and very few poets were about. With it went a reaction against the habits persisting from the time when Pope and his Francophile followers tried to "freeze" poetry in gentlemanly forms. This convention had been widened by the Romantic Revivalists, who sanctioned new metres and an enlarged vocabulary; but it remained false. The poet still put on his singing-robes and laurel crown and made as if to twang the property lyre; the use of *thou* and *thee*, which elsewhere survived only among hymn-writers and Quakers was encouraged; and so were inversions of noun and adjective, *mountains cold* or *vale profound*, and such obsolete words as *whene'er, whate'er, flowerets, roundelays, darkling,* and the like. The *vers libre* reformation was soon followed by a counter-reformation among the traditionalists—the so-called "Georgians"—who tried to get behind Milton to a simple, unaffected English manner. The *vers-librists* howled them down, and I must admit that the Georgians who won the literary prizes were a pretty dull lot.

After the First World War, as I was saying, many young American poets went over to Paris and *vers libre;* with the result that, when the Depression sent them home again, those who thought it would now be smart to try metre had never learned the art of accepting metrical discipline while keeping their individuality. Their ill-success with verse led them through new *isms* and new stylistic excesses, to the point where legitimate criticism breaks down altogether; the author, modelling himself on the non-representational artist, attempts no coherent statement, but merely a significant abstract arrangement of sounds and emotional phrases. Now, "significant" is a word that once carried a burden on its back. Rheumatic pains were found significant of approaching rain. Double vision was significant of having drunk too much. Posting a letter in one's own mailbox was significant of schizophrenia. But nowadays the word has dropped its burden. "This is a significant picture," pronounces the art-dealer. "This is a significant poem," writes the magazine editor. If critics are not told what the picture or poem is "significant" of, they are baffled. And the baffling of criticism has become a world-wide sport. So, as I say, the critics turn creative in self-defence.

I repeat that careerists are the plague of poetry: especially the modern careerist, who doubts whether he can make his name by traditional writing, yet shrinks from becoming a whole-hearted abstractionist. He will commit himself neither to a metre on which he can make his individual variations, nor to precise images and an accepted syntax; but takes Eliot's irresponsible advice and teases the critic by constantly approximating to sense and rhythmic pertinence, and then constantly withdrawing into deliberate nonsense.

I beg you younger people to preserve your critical integrity. Always "appreciate" in the earlier sense of the word. Never accept shoddy work offered you as "great," however dearly you may love the donor or the author. Keep tight hold of that critical cold-chisel, and strike it home without mercy: on my work too, if you please.

Good poets are exceedingly rare; "great poets" are all too common. The poet who accepts his limitations but works to the point of exhaustion on getting every word of a poem into place, may yet fail, for one reason or another, to be as good as he intends:

> Yet shall he mount and keep his distant way
> Beyond the limits of a vulgar fate:
> Beneath the Good how far—but far above the Great . . .

The White Goddess

I shall tell you frankly how the White Goddess affair started for me, how it continued, and what I really think about it all.

Though a poet by profession, I make my living by writing prose —biographies, historical novels, translations from various languages, critical studies, ordinary novels, and so forth. My home has been in Majorca since 1929. When temporarily exiled because of the Spanish Civil War, I wandered around Europe and the United States; and the World War found me in England, where I stayed until it ended; then I returned to Majorca.

In 1944, at a Devonshire village called Galmpton, I was working against time on a historical novel about the Argonauts and the Golden Fleece, when a sudden overwhelming obsession interrupted me. It took the form of an unsolicited enlightenment on a subject I knew almost nothing of. I stopped marking across my big Admiralty chart of the Black Sea the course which (according to the mythographers) the *Argo* had taken from the Bosphorus to Baku and back. Instead, I began speculating on a mysterious "Battle of the Trees," allegedly fought in pre-historic Britain, and my mind worked at such a furious rate all night, as well as all the next day, that my pen found it difficult to keep pace with the flow of thought.

The obsession resembled one that overtook Friedrich August Kekule von Stradonitz, the chemist, one day in 1859, when he had a vision of serpents waltzing around, tail to mouth, in a ring. Somehow he *knew* what they meant; so he sat down, and furiously wrote out his "closed ring" theory of the constituents of benzene. This, fortunately for my argument, is everywhere admitted to be the most brilliant piece of prediction—for though Kekule *knew,* he had no proof—in the whole range of organic chemistry. "Fortunately," because I can now mention Kekule (who thought he was going crazy) in self-justification. If a chemist may be granted a practical vision, why not a poet? Well, within three weeks, I had written a 70,000-word book about the ancient Mediterranean Moon-goddess whom Homer invoked in the *Iliad,* and whom one of his sons, or (as some prefer to think) one of his daughters, invoked in the *Odyssey:* and to whom most traditional poets ever since have paid at any rate lip-service.

The other day I came across the manuscript of my book, which has since swelled to four times the original size; and the uncanny excitement that held me throughout those critical weeks flooded back. I had called it *The Roebuck in the Thicket,* after one of the leading emblems in the Goddess's cult—a white stag (or roebuck) in Wales, Greece and Ireland, an antelope in Libya; I likened my historical hunt to the chase of that enigmatic beast.

The enlightenment began one morning while I was re-reading Lady Charlotte Guest's translation of *The Mabinogion,* a book of ancient Welsh legends, and came across a hitherto despised minstrel poem called *The Song of Taliesin.* I suddenly knew (don't ask me how) that the lines of the poem, which had always been dismissed as deliberate nonsense, formed a series of early mediaeval riddles, and that I knew the answer to them all—although I was neither a Welsh scholar, nor a mediaevalist, and although many of the lines had been deliberately transposed by the author (or his successors) for security reasons.

I knew also (don't ask me how) that the answer must in some way be linked with an ancient Welsh poetic tradition of a "Battle of Trees"—mentioned in Lady Charlotte Guest's notes to *The Mabinogion*—which was occasioned by a lapwing, a dog, and a white roebuck from the other world, and won by a certain god who guessed the name of his divine opponent to be Vron, or "Alder." Nobody had ever tried to explain this nonsense. Further, that both these texts would make sense only in the light of ancient Irish religious and poetic tradition. I am not an Irish scholar, either.

Since there has never been any lunatic streak in my family, I could not believe that I was going crazy. More likely, I was just being inspired. So I decided to check up on the subject with the help of a shelf-ful of learned books on Celtic literature which I found in my father's library (mainly inherited from my grandfather, an Irish antiquarian) but which I had never read.

To cut a long story short, my answer to the riddle, namely the letter-names of an ancient Druidic alphabet, fitted the not-so-nonsensical *Song of Taliesin* with almost frightening exactitude; and *The Battle of the Trees* proved to be a not-so-nonsensical way of describing a struggle between two rival priesthoods in Celtic Britain for control of the national learning. You see, I had found out that the word *"trees"* means "learning" in all the Celtic languages; and since the alphabet is the basis of all learning, and since (as I remembered from Julius Caesar's *Gallic Wars*) the Druidic alphabet was a jealously guarded secret in Gaul and Britain—indeed, its eighteen letter-names were not divulged for nearly a thousand years—well, the possession of this secret must have been something worth struggling about. I had also found out that the alphabet in Caesar's day was called the *Boibel-Loth*, because it began with the letters B.L.; and that as a result of the Battle of the Trees, the *Boibel-Loth* had displaced an earlier, very similar, and equally secret Celtic alphabet, the *Beth-Luis-Nion*, whose eighteen letters were explained as referring to a sequence of forest trees—including the Alder. This sequence, I found, served a dual purpose: as an alphabet and as a sacred calendar—the tree-consonants standing for the months of which their trees were characteristic; the tree-vowels standing for quarterly stations of the Sun, its equinoxes and solstices. It is a calendar which can be proved, by a study of the festal use of trees throughout Europe, to have been observed in the Bronze Age (and earlier) from Palestine to Ireland, and to have been associated everywhere with the worship of the pre-Aryan Triple Moon-goddess —sometimes called Leucothea, the White Goddess.

Then I found that the eighteen-letter Celtic tree-alphabet could, for various reasons, be regarded as a Celtic counterpart of the eighteen-letter Greek Orphic alphabet, associated with moving trees; the Orphic alphabet is known to have preceded the Classical Greek alphabet, the characters of which betray its Phoenician origin. Also, I found that the Triple Moon-goddess Brigit, or Bride, of ancient Ireland and Scotland (patroness of poetry, smithcraft and medicine) whose counterpart in Wales was the powerful Ninefold Muse-goddess Caridwen, could be identified with the Triple (or Ninefold) Muse-goddess of Greece; and again with the Italian Goddess Carmenta (who is said to have invented the Latin alphabet); and with the Nine Scandinavian Norns, who dispensed their runes under the World Tree Yggdrasil. All these cults seemed to have been basically the same.

My conclusions have not been condemned at universities; but then neither have they been approved. Scholars blush and turn their heads away when they are mooted. Of course, this should have been a subject for wide and deep research by university teams of specialists; and to show that I was merely a single, ignorant poet, I did not write in scholarly language, nor even provide an *apparatus criticus*. But I had at least marked out a new field of investigation, in case any university folk might one day feel inclined to exploit it. All that has happened so far is that dozens of intelligent strangers—students in Celtic literature, in botany, arboriculture, archaeology, anthropology, and so forth, but none of them holding university chairs—have helped me to amend and enlarge the book; and that I have incorporated their findings in the latest edition.

Don't mistake this for a grievance. Poets neither compete with professional scholars, nor do they solicit sympathy from them. Granted, I seem to have stumbled on the central secret of neolithic and Bronze Age religious faith, which makes sense of many otherwise inexplicable myths and religious customs; but this discovery is not essential to my central theme—namely the persistent survival of this faith among what was loosely called "romantic poets." Their imagery, I have shown, is drawn either consciously or unconsciously from the cult of the White Goddess, and the magic their poems exert largely depends on its closeness to her mysteries.

The most important single fact in the early history of Western religion and sociology was undoubtedly the gradual suppression of the Lunar Mother-goddess's inspiratory cult, and its supersession not by the perfunctory cult of a Sky-god, the god of illiterate cattle-raising Aryan immigrants, but by the busy, rational cult of the Solar God Apollo, who rejected the Orphic tree-alphabet in favour of the commercial Phoenician alphabet—the familiar ABC —and initiated European literature and science. It is no secret that, towards the end of the second millennium B.C., Apollo's people captured the Moon-goddess's most revered shrines and oracles, including Tempe, Delphi and Delos; and so limited her worship that the great raging Ninefold Mountain-mother of Parnassus was at last converted into a choir, or ballet, or troupe, of nine tame little Nymphs, "the Muses," with Apollo as their art-director and manager. Apollo also triumphed over the Italian Goddesses Minerva and Carmenta, when the Romans went all Greek under the late Republic.

Much the same thing happened elsewhere among other European nations. Early in the sixth century A.D., certain muscular Christians from Strathclyde marched south into Wales, and dispossessed the Muse-goddess Caridwen, who had hitherto been served there by highly educated poet-magicians: supplanting these with untrained scalds and hymn-writers. In Ireland, Christianity also triumphed, but only as the result of slow, peaceful penetration, not of war; and the ancient poetic traditions, closely allied with those of the ancient Welsh, survived until mediaeval times outside the English settlements. Brigit, the Goddess of Poetry, who may be the same as the Greek Goddess Brizo of Delos (there were strong cultural connexions between Bronze Age Greece and Ireland) became Christianized as St. Bridget, and her ancient fire still burned at Kildare until the reign of King Henry VIII.

This general view led me to differentiate between Muse poetry and Apollonian poetry: written respectively by those who rely on inspiration, checked by commonsense, and those who rely on intellectual verse decorated by the artificial flowers of fancy. Before pursuing this subject, I must make four rather odd disclosures.

Now, I am no mystic: I studiously avoid witchcraft, spiritualism, yoga, fortune-telling, automatic writing, and so on. I live a simple, normal, rustic life with my wife, my children, and a wide circle of sane and intelligent friends. I belong to no religious cult, no secret society, no philosophical sect; but I do value my historical intuition, which I trust up to the point where it can be factually checked. There's nothing so strange about that, surely? Every good business-man in the service of the mercantile god Hermes knows what a "hunch" is, and will always explore its possibilities with statistical care. Moreover, every great mathematic or scientific discovery has begun as pure hunch: substantiated later by careful calculation.

I have told you about the sudden obsession that overcame me at Galmpton. The fact is, while working on my Argonaut book, I found the figure of the White Goddess of Pelion growing daily more powerful, until she dominated the story. Listen to this: I had in my work-room several small brass objects from the Gold Coast—bought from a dealer in London—gold-dust weights, mostly in the shape of animals, among them a hump-backed man playing a flute. I also had a small brass box, with a lid, originally used (so the dealer told me) to contain the gold-dust itself. I kept the humpback seated on the box. In fact, he is still seated on the same box; but I knew nothing about him, or about the design on the box-lid, until ten years later. Then I learned that the humpback represented a herald in the service of the Queen-mother of an Akan State, prob-ably Asante; and that every Akan Queen-mother (there are some still reigning today) claims to be a direct incarnation of the Triple Moon-goddess Ngame. The design on the box-lid is a spiral con-nected by a single line to the rectangular frame enclosing it—the frame having nine teeth on either side—and means: "There is none greater—in the world—than the Triple Goddess Ngame." These gold weights and the boxes for containing the gold dust were made before the British conquest of the Gold Coast, by craftsmen sub-servient to the Goddess, and regarded as highly magical.

Very well: put it down to coincidence. Deny that there was any connexion at all between the hump-backed herald on the box (proclaiming the magnitude of the Triple Moon-goddess of West Africa and surrounded by brass animals representing Akan clan totems) and myself, who suddenly became obsessed by the White Goddess of Europe, wrote of her clan totems in the Argonaut context, and now had thrust upon me ancient secrets belonging to her cult in Wales, Ireland and elsewhere. Believe me: I was wholly unaware that the box celebrated the Goddess Ngame. Or that the Helladic Greeks, including the early Athenians, were racially linked with Ngame's people—Libyan Berbers, known as the Garamantians, who moved south from the Sahara to the Niger in the eleventh century A.D., and there intermarried with negroes. Or that Ngame herself was a Moon-goddess and shared all her attributes with the White Goddess of Greece and Western Europe. I knew only that, according to Herodotus, the Greek Athene was the same goddess as Libyan Neith.

I completed *The White Goddess* in 1946, when I returned to Majorca soon after the War, and there wrote more particularly about the Sacred King as the Moon-goddess's divine victim; holding that every Muse-poet must, in a sense, die for the Goddess whom he adores, just as the King died. Old Georg Schwarz, my next-door neighbour—a German-Jewish antiquary—had meanwhile passed away and bequeathed me five or six more gold weights of the same provenience. These included a small, mummy-like figurine with one large eye. It has now been identified by experts on West African art as an Akan King's *okrafo* priest. I had suggested in my book that the King in primitive Mediterranean society was, to begin with, merely the ruling Queen's handsome young consort, and doomed to be sacrificed at the end of his term. But, by early historical times (to judge from Greek and Latin myths) he had won executive power as the Queen's representative, or King, and the privilege of sacrificing a substitute. The same governmental change, I have since learned, took place among the matriarchal Akan, after their southern migration. In Bono, Asante, and other states similarly constituted, the King's victim was called the *"okrafo* priest." This particular gold weight happened to be early and unique; the famous Danish expert on African native art, Kjersmeier, who has handled ten thousand gold weights, tells me that he never saw another like it. Dismiss it as a coincidence, if you like, that the *okrafo* figurine lay beside the herald on the gold box, while I was writing about the Goddess's victims.

After *The White Goddess* had been written, a friend in Barcelona, who knew nothing about the book, asked me to choose myself a gem for a seal-ring, from a collection of Roman gems he had bought. Among them I found a stranger—a banded carnelian seal of pre-Trojan War Mitannian provenience—and the design was a royal stag with a moon on its flank, galloping towards a thicket! Dismiss that as a coincidence, too, if you like.

This reminds me of a cross-examination by Sir Edward Marshall Hall, the celebrated K.C., of a witness in a London murder trial:

MARSHALL HALL: What would you call it if you were walking along a street one Monday morning, and as you passed a certain house a brick fell on your head?

WITNESS: I should call it an accident.

MARSHALL HALL: Very well. And if you walked along the same street on the Tuesday, at the same time of day, and as you passed the same house another brick fell on your head? What would you call that?

WITNESS: I should call it a coincidence.

MARSHALL HALL: Very well. But if it happened a third time? You walked along the same street on the Wednesday, at the same time of day, and as you passed the same house a third brick fell on your head. What would you call *that*?

WITNESS: I should call it a habit.

*

Chains of more than coincidence happen so often in my life that if I am forbidden to call them supernatural hauntings, I must call them a habit. Not that I like the word "supernatural"; I find these happenings natural enough, however superlatively unscientific. The avowed purpose of science is to banish all lunar superstitions and bask in the pure light of solar reason. Superstitions are magical beliefs which (as the word conveys) *survive* from some banned faith—being so deeply rooted that to challenge them gives one a most un-

comfortable feeling. Usually, the new faith incorporates old superstitions in its religious dogma. I think it is foolish to defy any superstition unless one feels very strongly about either its inconvenience
or its irrationality—like a Scottish atheist I knew, who had suffered
so much from a rigidly Puritan upbringing that he would strop his
razor every morning on the leather-bound family Bible. Myself, I
wouldn't do that for a thousand dollars. Also I hate sitting down
thirteen to table. The Church refers this superstition to the Last
Supper, as a result of which Judas, the thirteenth guest, hanged himself; but it is far older than that. In fact, it refers to the ancient
British calendar-alphabet where the tree of the thirteenth month,
the tree of death, with its ragged leaves and corpse-like smell was
the Elder—the elder on which, according to British mediaeval legend,
Judas hanged himself (though, of course, elders do not grow in
Palestine). Nor do I ever fail to bow to the new moon, disregarding
the scientific presumption that the moon is merely a dead satellite
of Earth; for the moon moves the tides, influences growth, rules
the festal calendar of Judaism, Islam and Christianity, and possesses
other unaccountable magic properties, known to every lover and
poet.

Let me get this straight. Mr. Randall Jarrell, the American poet
accredited this year to the Library of Congress, has generously
declared that I write good poems; but holds that what I say about
the White Goddess is grotesque nonsense, a personal fantasy of
my own. If he had said that my poems were bad, I should not
contradict him, because everyone is entitled to his likes and dislikes
and, anyway, no poem is absolutely good. Yet I venture to suggest
that, despite my superstitions (inherited from an Irish father)
and despite my habit of noting more-than-coincidences, Mr. Jarrell
cannot accuse me of *inventing* the White Goddess, or any facts
about her worship in ancient days. He views me as a triumphant
vindication of Freud's and Jung's psychological theories; and bases
his analysis on *Good-bye To All That*, an autobiography which I
wrote twenty-eight years ago. "Few poets have made better pathological sense," he reports—adding that my world picture is a projection
of my unconscious on the universe.

Well, I shall not repudiate the autobiographical facts of *Good-*

bye To All That; but I should be a triumphant vindication of Freud's and Jung's theories only if I did not know exactly what my poems were about—if I had to get them psycho-analysed in order to find out what ailed me. The truth is that I read Freud as long ago as 1917—critically, too, and found him most unscientific. Freud, indeed, never realized to his dying day that he was projecting a private fantasy on the world, and then making it stick by insisting that his disciples must undergo prolonged psycho-analytic treatment until they surrendered and saw the light. Much the same goes for Jung. My world picture is not a psychological one, nor do I indulge in idle myth-making and award diplomas to my converts. It is enough for me to quote authentic myths and give them historical sense: tracing a certain faith through its vicissitudes—from when it was paramount, to when it has been driven underground and preserved by witches, travelling minstrels, remote country-folk, and a few secret heretics to the newly established religion. Particularly by the endowed Irish poets and their humble colleagues, the Welsh travelling minstrels—descendants of the poets expelled by the Christian Cymry, and preservers of the pre-Christian *Mabinogion* myths.

In scientific terms, no god at all can be proved to exist, but only beliefs in gods, and the effects of such beliefs on worshippers. The majority of scientists, however, are God-worshippers, if no more than metaphorically and for social convenience. The concept of a goddess was banned by Christian theologians nearly two thousand years ago, and by Jewish theologians long before that. The universities have naturally followed suit; though I can't make out why a belief in a Father-god's authorship of the universe, and its laws, should be considered any more scientific than a belief in the inspiration of this artificial system by a Mother-goddess. In fact, granted the first metaphor, the second follows logically. If these *are* no more than metaphors. At all events, the scientists attached to universities continue to respect their theological colleagues. Protestant Doctors of Divinity in particular, who posit the literal existence of an all-powerful God and regard supernatural happenings (many of them scientifically ill-attested) as a proof of His existence. But they would raise their eyebrows at anyone who posited the literal existence of a goddess. Here they are, I admit, on safe political and sociological ground. Except in a few scattered, semi-civilized tribes, such as those of West Africa and Southern India, the Goddess is everywhere refused official recognition; nor are the times propitious for reviving her worship in a civilized world governed (or mis-governed) almost exclusively by the ambitious male intelligence. So when people write to me, as they often do—not only from what is called the "Screwy State", but also from the hinterland of this highly intellectual Empire State—asking me to help them start an all-American Goddess cult, I reply discouragingly. I beg them not to mistake me for a Joseph Smith junior, a Mary Baker Eddy, or that sort of person.

My task in writing *The White Goddess* was to provide a grammar of poetic myth for poets, not to plan witches' Sabbaths, compose litanies and design vestments for a new orgiastic sect, nor yet to preach matriarchy over a radio network. Certainly, I hold that critical notice should be taken of the Goddess, if only because poetry which deeply affects readers—pierces them to the heart, sends shivers down their spine, and makes their scalp crawl—cannot be written by Apollo's rhetoricians or scientists. Two outstanding scientists of the early nineteenth century—Sir William Rowan Hamilton, the mathematician, and Sir Humphrey Davy, the chemist, tried their hands at poetry. Hamilton's work was ludicrously sentimental; while Davy's was pompously academic. But I am grateful to Davy for epitomizing the conflict of solar reason and lunar inspiration, in these defiant and egotistical stanzas:

> Like yon proud rock, amidst the sea of time,
> Superior, scorning all the billows' rage,
> The living Sons of Genius stand sublime,
> The immortal children of another age.
>
> For those exist, whose pure ethereal minds
> Habiting portions of celestial day
> Scorn all terrestrial cares, all mean designs,
> As bright-eyed eagles scorn the lunar ray . . .

[*minds* and *designs*, though, are a rather unacademic rhyme.]

True poetic practice implies a mind so miraculously attuned and illuminated that it can form words, by a chain of more-than-coincidences, into a living entity—a poem that goes about on its own (for centuries after the author's death, perhaps) affecting readers with its internal magic. Since the source of creative power in poetry is not scientific intelligence, but inspiration—however this may be scientifically accounted for—why not attribute inspiration to the Lunar Muse, the oldest and most convenient European term for the source in question?

Let me be plainer still. It is a commonplace of history that what happens on earth gets reflected in theological dogma. When the Chief Priestess of a matriarchal state has been dethroned by patriarchal invaders, the event becomes recorded in religious myth—as the Theban Sphinx-goddess is said to have committed suicide on Oedipus's arrival from Corinth, where a Hittite Sun-cult had taken root; or as Jehovah (according to Isaiah) cut in two with his sword the Sea-serpent Rahab—the ancient Mediterranean Sea-and-Moon-goddess of Palestine whom the Jews banished from Jerusalem. And when a dozen small states, some with patrilineal, some with matrilineal royal succession, form a federation for mutual convenience, this gets recorded in myth as a heavenly family of gods and goddesses—as happened in Greece during the second millennium B.C. We can be pretty sure that the divine feastings which were said to have taken place on Mount Olympus reflected the feastings at Olympia in the Peloponnese—the sacred centre of the Confederation where the various state representatives met under the Zeus-like High King of Mycenae. And if a revolution breaks out within a matrilineal state, such as Athens, and descent is thereafter reckoned through the father, not the mother, the State-goddess is said to have been re-born from the Father-god's head—as happened to Athene at Athens.

The progress of patriarchy in ancient Greece can be gauged by the fortunes of the divine Olympian family. The Achaean Zeus humbled Hera, the Goddess of Argolis, whom he denied all her former powers but that of prophecy; Athene declared that she was "All for the Father"; Apollo pushed his twin Artemis into the shade; Heracles was admitted to Heaven despite Hera's protests; Hestia the Hearth-

goddess vacated her seat on the Council in favour of Dionysus; and
Aphrodite had become the butt of obscene jokes by the time that the
Odyssey was written. Only the Fertility-goddess Demeter kept her
dignified position, and even she had to employ a male priesthood at
the Eleusinian Mysteries, and allow the demi-god Dionysus his part
in them—according to legend, the Athenians who tried to keep him
out were ignominiously smitten with piles. These events recorded a
steady deterioration in the general position of women—they were
pushed out of trade, industry, justice, and local government; and the
rise of Platonic philosophy, coupled with the homosexual cult, set
them back still further.

The divine honours presently given to world conquerors—a field
in which no woman could compete—made women (always the outraged victims of this royal sport) seem of less account than ever. At
last, military need forced the Roman Emperor Constantine to humour his predominantly Christian legionaries and junior officers and
let them march behind the Cross. Thereupon the long-discredited
Olympians were banished for ever (apart from a brief come-back
under the Emperor Julian) and superseded by the all-male Christian
Trinity. Women then went down in status still further, since Christianity brought with it the Hebrew myth of Adam's rib and Eve's
apple; and they could not even point to Sappho's poems and say:
"Well, at least a woman wrote these!"—because the Church had been
at great pains to hunt out and burn all the copies, on the untenable
excuse that Sappho was a Lesbian in more senses than one. But
the bottom of the trough had been reached, and women's social
position improved markedly about the eleventh century A.D. This
change has been attributed to the abolition of slavery and to the
continuous wars that followed the break-down of central government in the West; and particularly to the Crusades, which obliged
the warrior-princes and nobles to leave their small and independent
estates in the hands of their ladies while they were away. The ladies
had to keep accounts, buy and sell, see that the fields were sown
and the crops fetched in, watch the work of the castle artisans,
manage the brewing, weaving, and other necessary crafts, educate
the children, learn to be physicians and surgeons. In earlier days,

these matters would have been attended to by a trusty slave or freedman.

It was in this period that Romantic poetry began, under Saracen influence, but nourished on the ancient Arthurian myths of Wales and Brittany. King Arthur's legend is partly historical, partly derived from the pre-Christian myth of the sacrificed King who is taken to the Apple-tree Fairyland by the White Goddess Morgan le Fay. Normans carried the Arthur legend to countries as distant as Scotland, Majorca and Sicily—since when the locals have claimed that King Arthur lies concealed under this hill or that in their own territory, waiting for his eventual resurrection. And the Virgin Mary, hitherto a dim figure—but for the heretical sects of the Middle East who had identified her with the dethroned Goddess—suddenly rose in theological esteem as incarnate Wisdom. She would have risen still further but for the check she received in certain vigorous male-minded Protestant regions, such as Southern and Eastern England (where the hatred of Mariolatry was a leading cause of the Roundhead Revolution), Eastern Germany, parts of the Low Countries, and New England. Nevertheless, the Catholic Church has given the Virgin many of the attributes that belonged to the ancient Triple Moon-goddess; and she can now legitimately be saluted as "the Queen of Heaven"—the very title borne by Rahab (the Goddess Astarte), against whom the prophet Jeremiah declaimed in the name of his monotheistic Father-god Jehovah.

While the present technological civilization, which is largely of Protestant impulse, maintains itself, with men holding the key positions in industry, law, trade, medicine, science, and government, the Virgin cannot rise beyond the rank conceded her. But if this system collapses—or if, instead, it reaches the stage of perfect nuclear automation, in which men do not need to work so hard as now to provide and distribute the necessities of life—then social changes may well follow: changes that will obviously be reflected in religious dogma. The new Heaven may house two gods and a goddess; or even, as in pre-Christian Rome, pre-Exilic Jerusalem, and pre-Roman Carthage, two goddesses, one of intuition, one of fertility, aided by a technological male god of the Vulcan type.

I offer this merely as speculation. Yet the growing popularity of

Muse-poets (as opposed to Apollonian poets who glorify male intelligence, male courage, male energy) and the growing mistrust of
orthodox Christian dogma among the educated classes throughout
the Western World, suggest that such a religious revolution may
already be brewing. Meanwhile, in all Christian Churches, the Virgin
is allowed no female characteristics which might threaten male
supremacy; she is merciful, gentle, pure, patient, obedient—making no
parade of wisdom and promoted to motherhood without having
loved in ordinary female fashion. If wise, she modestly hides her
wisdom, and though her bodily Assumption to Heaven is now dogma
at Rome, she has no priestesses to perform her mysteries, but only
priests of the triune male God. The Welsh ministrels dared, at one
period, to identify the Virgin with their pagan Muse-goddess Caridwen; but this heresy could come to nothing, because Caridwen had
been very far from being a nun. In fact, the White Goddess has
never been monogamic and has never shown pity for the bad, the
ineffective, the sterile, the perverted, the violent, or the diseased:
though loving and just, she is ruthless. Her symbol is the double-
axe—consisting of two moon-like blades, one crescent, one decrescent, set back to back and fitted with a haft. The crescent blade
represents blessing, increase, joy; the decrescent blade represents
cursing, plague and sorrow that punish human folly and disorder.
The Muse-poets have always recognized those two blades: poetry
proper is the constructive side of their profession, satire the destructive side.

Mr. Jarrell accuses me of a sort of schizophrenia in thinking so
highly of women and cheerfully accepting the more disagreeable side
of their nature, although, as he points out, I have been, in my day,
a boxer, a full-back at football, and a fighting soldier. But is that so
strange? Was it not the code of mediaeval chivalry, which the trou-
badour poets extolled in the Virgin's name, to be a parfit gentle
knight: a lion in battle, a lamb in the bower, however cruel one's
mistress? Have British soldiers fought less gloriously when they
served under a queen rather than a king—Elizabeth, Anne, Victoria?
It is a complete fallacy that the toughest fighter is the cave-man who
knocks his women about. The most miraculous victory against odds
in Classical times was won by the Epizephyrian Locrians of

Calabria against their neighbours of Croton; and these Locrians were then the only people in Europe who still had a matrilineal constitution, with the women politically in the ascendant and a supreme Moon-goddess their sole deity.

I am aware that the Protestant dogma reflects well enough the sociological set-up of, say the United States Bible Belt, Nonconformist Britain, and the Dutch Reformed Church in Holland and South Africa. Most of the devout Christian women in those Churches are perfectly content with their social position, and therefore with the Virgin Mary as a representative of womankind. They look up to their husbands, give in to them, take motherhood seriously, do not consider themselves the equal (let alone the superiors) of man, restrain their wayward passions, support good causes, neglect their own looks, and do not grudge men their monopoly of the priesthood. They sometimes even take a masochistic delight in being ill-treated, abused and betrayed by extravagantly swaggering he-men, while they pinch and scrape. They are not to be either praised or pitied—that's how they come. But they cannot appreciate Muse-poetry. For them the Apollonian poet, even the fraudulent rhetorician, or the prosy hymn-writer, suffices. Yet it is a question how far Chaucer's "Patient Griselda," or Bunyan's Christiana, or David Copperfield's wife Agnes, are the results of domestic conditioning; whether they differ in circumstance, rather than in nature, from the numerous predatory women of our own day, born in unhappy homes and soured by the patriarchal system, who enjoy breaking up insecure marriages and making a living from male weakness and credulity.

Some of you are looking queerly at me. Do I think that poets are literally inspired by the White Goddess? That is an improper question. What would you think, should I ask you if, in your opinion, the Hebrew prophets were literally inspired by God? Whether God is a metaphor or fact cannot be reasonably argued; let us likewise be discreet on the subject of the Goddess. All we can know for sure is that the Ten Commandments, said to have been promulgated by Moses in the name of a Solar God, still carry religious force for those hereditarily prone to accept them; and that scores of poems written in the Muse-tradition still carry the authentic moon-magic for those hereditarily prone to accept that. Apostles of

Solar Reason "scorning the lunar ray" may reject such poems as idle or nonsensical; but respectable anthropologists (and anthropologists are scientists) now give *de facto* if not *de jure* recognition to all sorts of crazy deities, male and female—such as the Voodoo deities of Haiti (some of African origin; others renegade Catholic saints)—whose invocation causes ecstatic behaviour in their worshippers and produces if not miraculous, at least inexplicable, phenomena.

By ancient religious theory the White Goddess becomes incarnate in her human representative—a priestess, a prophetess, a queen-mother. No Muse-poet can grow conscious of the Muse except by experience of some woman in whom the Muse-power is to some degree or other resident; just as no Apollonian poet can perform his function properly unless under a monarchy or a quasi-monarchy. (Under a republic he tends to turn seedy and philosophical.) A Muse-poet falls in love, absolutely, and his true love is for him the embodiment of the Muse. In many cases the power of absolutely falling in love soon vanishes; if only because the woman takes no trouble to preserve whatever glory she gets from the knowledge of her beauty and the power she exercises over her poet-lover. She grows embarrassed by this glory, repudiates it, and ends up either as a housewife or a tramp; he, in disillusion, turns to Apollo who, at any rate, can provide him with a livelihood and intelligent entertainment—and goes out of circulation before his middle twenties. But the real, perpetually obsessed Muse-poet makes a distinction between the Goddess as revealed in the supreme power, glory, wisdom and love of woman, and the individual woman in whom the Goddess may take up residence for a month, a year, seven years, or even longer. The Goddess abides; and it may be that he will again have knowledge of her through his experience of another woman.

Mr. Jarrell, having read my autobiography, concludes that when the woman in whom the Goddess was once resident for me abdicated, I identified myself for all intents and purposes with the Goddess. He writes, very naughtily: "There is only one Goddess, and Graves is her prophet, and isn't the profit of the White Goddess the nearest thing to the White Goddess?"

I flatly deny that, even though Mr. Jarrell claims to have found general confirmation of his theory "in Volume Seven of Jung's *Col-*

lected *Works*—the second part of the essay entitled 'The Relations
Between the Ego and the Unconscious.' " No, my autobiography was
written nearly thirty years ago, and much has happened to me
since, as he might well have deduced from my later poems. Being in
love does not, and should not, blind the poet to the cruel side of
woman's nature—the decrescent axe-head—and many Muse-poems
are written in helpless recognition of this by men whose love is no
longer returned.

"As ye came from the holy land
    Of Walsinghame,
Met you not with my true love
    By the way as ye came?"

"How should I know your true love,
    That have met many a one
As I came from the holy land,
    That have come, that have gone?"

"She is neither white nor brown,
    But as the heavens fair;
There is none hath her divine form
    In the earth, in the air."

"Such a one did I meet, good sir,
    Such an angelic face,
Who like a nymph, like a queen, did appear
    In her gait, in her grace."

"She hath left me here alone,
    All alone, as unknown,
Who sometime did me lead with herself,
    And me loved as her own."

"What's the cause that she leaves you alone
    And a new way doth take,
That sometime did you love as her own,
    And her joy did you make?"

> "I have loved her all my youth,
> But now am old, as you see:
> Love likes not the falling fruit,
> Nor the withered tree."

It will be noticed that the Elizabethan poet who makes this pilgrimage to Mary the Egyptian at Walsinghame, the mediaeval patron saint of lovers, has loved one woman all his life, and is now old. Why is she not old, too? Because he is describing the Goddess, not the individual woman. The same is true of Wyatt's:

> They flee from me who sometime did me seek
> With naked foot stalking within my chamber . . .

It is not *"She flees from me,"* but *"They flee from me"*: namely the women who were in turn illumined for Wyatt by the lunar ray that commanded his love—beginning with Anne Boleyn, later Henry VIII's unfortunate queen.

I hesitate to delve into Mr. Jarrell's emotional biography as a means of discovering how far he regards romantic falling-in-love as a grotesque pathological event. But I cannot think the act unmanly, or discreditable, far less grotesque. Nor am I a prophet of the Goddess. A prophet is, by definition, one who speaks in the name of a deity, like Moses or John the Baptist, or Mohammed, with: "Thus saith the Lord!" No man can decently speak in a woman's name. The Pythian Priestess at Delphi did not give clever, ambiguous, political answers to her visitants (instead of genuine oracles) until Apollo captured the Goddess Gaia's oracular stool and installed his own docile nominees. To acknowledge the Goddess's power is a very different matter from saying in a ringing baritone: "Thus saith the Goddess!" A simple loving declaration: "There is none greater in the universe than the Triple Goddess!" has been made by every Muse-poet in the English language (and by countless others, down the centuries, in various European, African and Asian idioms); though the Goddess is sometimes, of course, given such cautiously abstract titles as "Nature," "Truth," "Beauty," or "Poetry." Myself, I think it most unlikely that this grotesque habit will end for a few centuries yet.

You think perhaps that I am holding out on you by not trying to account for the hauntings? But surely it is enough to record what there is no logical means of evaluating? When a simple citizen, who is neither very good, very wicked, nor very anything else, is struck dead by lightning while running for shelter to the Subway, and is the only victim of the storm, what do people call that? They call it an act of God: meaning that it was a blind accident. Well, in that case, what should you call a more-than-coincidence of the sort I have described?

This brings me to another disclosure. I offered *The White Goddess* in turn to the only publishers I knew who claimed to be personally concerned with poetry and mythology.

The first regretted that he could not recommend this unusual book to his partners, because of the expense. He died of heart failure within the month.

The second wrote very discourteously, to the effect that he could not make either head or tail of the book, and could not believe it would interest anyone. He died too, soon afterwards.

But the third, who was T. S. Eliot, wrote that it must be published at all costs. So he did publish it, and not only got his money back, but pretty soon was rewarded with the Order of Merit, the Nobel Prize for Literature, and a smash hit on Broadway.

Very well, call these coincidences. But I beg you not to laugh yet! Wait! I beg you not to laugh, unless you can explain just why the second publisher should have dressed himself up in a woman's panties and bra one afternoon, and hanged himself from a tree in his garden. (Unfortunately, the brief report in *Time* did not specify the sort of tree.)

Was that a blind *act of God*, or was it a calculated *act of Goddess*? I leave the answer to you; all I know is that it seemed to me natural enough in its horrid way.

I must end this talk which, I hope, answers more questions than it raises, by driving home my main point. A poem which is moon-magical enough to walk off the page—if you know what I mean—

and to keep on walking, and to get under people's skins and into their eyes and throats and hearts and marrows: that is more-than-coincidence at its most miraculous. And Solar Apollo, for all his new thinking-machines and rhyming dictionaries and analytic courses in poetry-writing, can't begin to imitate it.

Sweeney Among the Blackbirds

There comes a time when a man realizes that it is too late to start
doing a lot of things he half-wishes he had done years and years ago.
Learning Hebrew, for instance, or becoming a champion figure-skater,
or working his passage round the world in a tramp steamer, or fighting bulls, or mastering the guitar, or (if he happens to have been a
model husband and is now a decrepit widower) entering on a long
string of pleasantly casual love-affairs. Too late!

There are exceptions, of course. Narses, the Byzantine Emperor
Justinian's eunuch palace-chamberlain, embarked on his military
career when he was over seventy and pursued it gloriously for another twenty years. Jean-Henri Fabre, a provincial schoolmaster, lost
his job at much the same age and subsequently earned world-wide
fame by turning natural historian. But most elderly men are content to say: "Too late, too late. I must leave it for my next incarnation, if I have one."

Being now sixty-two myself, I confess to few regrets for accomplishments untried or abandoned, though if I could drive a car at least as well as I can ride a horse, which is not very well, that would be useful; or if I understood the first thing about electricity— but once, long ago, I was dealt a dangerous electric shock and am still too scared even to mend a fuse.

The most unlikely of all professions to take up late in life must be poetry: one might as well try ballet or football. Hold on to that pronouncement for a moment, please, until I circle round to it again; I still have a few words to say about the after-life.

The heathen Anglo-Saxons believed in a Hell of ice and bare rocks, where crowds of blue-nosed, shivering ghosts wandered aimlessly around for ever in thick mist without ever seeing so much as a fir-tree, a crow, an Arctic fox, or a snow-rabbit. Consequently, when St. What's-his-name came to preach to King Offa's Mercians and dwelt on the eternal and quenchless bonfire blazing in the Christian Hell, he found an unexpectedly appreciative audience. "We shall be warm, we shall be warm!" the thegns shouted in delight.

Myself, I consider it greedy to ask for more than one life in this space-time continuum, where obviously everything has its proper place in order to avoid duplications and collisions; and if I have wasted what life has been allotted me, whose fault is that? Nor will I philosophize about time and space; both of which I am content to accept as useful human conventions. They can, of course, be by-passed in an emergency. On occasion I have extemporized objects that did not exist, such as a foothold on a bare rockface to avoid killing myself; or an unscheduled train when I needed to reach a certain town in a life-and-death hurry. Startling events, which gave me the feeling that we infantrymen often experienced after those fearful creeping barrages in the First World War: two lone un-wounded survivors would stare amazed at each other and say: "Blimey, chum, we must be in God's pocket!"

As I say, I dare not ask for a second helping of life, much as I should enjoy it, when the ration seems to be only one. Being human and mortal, however, and brought up by pious parents in the hope of a Christian Paradise, I find it comforting to picture an ideal after-death location, a suitable sequel to the life I have hitherto lived.

Yet I could not presume to invent one; my conscience would insist that it was a mere subjective fiction, and leave me feeling lonelier than before. T. E. Lawrence once told me that when we have discounted every cosy social convention of marriage or friendship, we must find ourselves, each by each, separate and alone. But this discounting of cosy conventions gave Lawrence a sense of being lost in his own private world—around which he had raised such a prickly fence that nobody could enter, and thus forfeited the capacity of being in love.

Myself, I have never *not* been in love since boyhood; and what irks me about the many after-worlds invented by mystics and philosophers is the absence in them of any *grande passion*. The Moslem Heaven of sherbet, tiled baths and anonymous, plump, well-depilated, complaisant houris . . . The Norse Valhalla with its endless battles and mead-orgies—as one of the Sagas has it:

> All the mighty champions
> Housed in Odin's barracks
> Crack one another's pates, day after day,
> Then gather up the dead, as always,
> Ride back from battle
> And sit together healed and sound
> At the great mead-board . . .

The Judaeo-Christian Heaven of golden temples, angelic choirs, and no sea except a crystal one: a region where there is no marrying nor giving in marriage, and only a chaste sodality reigns. . . . The perilous Egyptian Hell, peopled with hawk-headed Sphinxes, dog-headed apes, ibises, crocodiles and monstrous spotted serpents, as described in that yellow-leaved morticians' manual: *The Book of the Dead*. . . . The listless, twilit Greek Hell, from which even the great champion would rather return to earth as a landless, hungry serf, than rule as a prince over the twittering shades. . . . The featureless, perfect Indian Nirvana, of which Ramprasad Sen, the eighteenth-century Sakta poet, wrote:

> Sugar is good, yet I have no desire
> To become sugar . . .

I know of no Paradise myths conceived by poets, nearer than the Polynesian Islands. My favourite has always been the ancient Celtic one: "Apple Island" or "Avalon," where a fine moated castle was reached by a glass bridge, and ruled over by a lovely, fair-haired, white-throated, gold-crowned Queen. At this castle, built among oaks, birches, apple-trees and grassy meadows, gathered a distinguished, brave, witty, youthful company in variegated clothes: with horses to ride, streams to fish, exquisite food for belly-cheer, music for beguilement, brimming mead-vats for inspiration, and fine red beds to lie on when the stars came out. "Mine" and "thine," we read, were words unknown there—so generous the castle-folk; and love remained free of guilt or reproach. When I come to die, may it be with that picture of Avalon before my eyes, brightly coloured like the miniatures of a mediaeval Irish missal, and in the hope of recognizing among the golden-brooched, crimson-cloaked, ever-youthful crowd the impassioned faces of those I have loved best.

No individual love, no grass, no trees, no birds or animals— that is what makes most Otherworlds so disastrously dull. And also what makes most modern poems so disastrously dull. Poetry fashions are set in the big cities. The countryside, of course, has no monopoly of love; but if ever true passion burns in cities, it burns despite civically-cleaned sidewalks, well-controlled traffic, hygienic elevators, and huge, impersonal office-buildings: must constantly refresh itself by raids on the surrounding country, or the parks, or the riverside, or the narrow, dirty, lively streets where immigrants, criminals, and the very poor live their desperate and uncivic lives. If there are poets who succeed in holding down a regular job in the city, yet somehow keep the poetic flame from being snuffed out by a city-bred miasma; who can plant their imaginations with tangled forests and stock them with wild game, and go hunting through the glades in gold-brooched, crimson-cloaked chosen company—they are few; and, necessarily perhaps, schizophrenic.

"Nature abhors a straight line," it is said. The sea's horizon is pleasantly curved; and so is the track of an arrow through the air;

and the fishing-line drying between its posts. For, as the author of a
Victorian mathematical text-book once noted in an unconscious burst
of poetry:

> No lateral force, however great,
> Can stretch a cord, however fine,
> Into a horizontal line
> That shall be absolutely straight . . .

Moreover, even the taut linen-thread spun by the Fates has its
roughnesses; and motes dance golden along the edge of every sun-
beam. Table-tops smoothed by a hand-plane are far from level;
only machines, working on metal or marble, can produce a line that
is to all intents and purposes straight, or a surface that is to all intents and purposes flat. This feat is looked upon as a triumph of
science; yet I believe that closer research into human fatigue-reac-
tions would show that perfectly straight lines and perfectly flat
surfaces, perfect circles, and exact right angles, induce between
them much of the mental illness for which functionally-built modern
cities are notorious. They impose a tyrannous discipline on the eye,
from which it has no relaxation but the television screen. Old-
fashioned, hand-constructed cities are safer to work in and to make
love in; since they suffer less from rectangularity, rectolinearity, and
the mercilessly perfect circle. One day, perhaps, architects will
realize with a startled "Oh!" that a major function of functionally-
designed houses and offices is to preserve the mental health of the
inhabitants; whereupon they will try to counteract the monotony of
the rectangle and the straight line by inventing machines capable of
building houses and offices with a slight curve or a wobble. However, the human eye will not be deceived; only man's fallible hand
can pleasurably serve it with lines and curves that convey a *living*
waywardness. One great fault of modern building-technique is that
hard timber has fallen into disuse. Steel is exploited, the cruellest of
metals; lifeless concrete; frivolous plastics. But hardly any timber; few
stones even. And no love at all.

These views of mine explain why I prefer to live in an industrially backward country and see only trees and rocks and the sea from my workroom window. Once a year I pay a brief visit to England or the States, as a self-reminder that I am a confirmed rustic and have no clue (except from the newspapers) what this modern world is about; secure in the knowledge that it's far too late for me to find out by enrolling for a last-minute scientific education. I'm no Jean-Henri Fabre, and no Narses.

"No fool like an old fool," is a sound proverb, and I have always been convinced that poetry (what I call poetry at any rate, and everyone is entitled to his definition) cannot be separated from the state of being in love. I substantiate this theory in a long, complicated book of mine called *The White Goddess;* the central figure being the ancient Goddess of Life in Death, and Death in Life, the Goddess of Love and the Sea, and Trees, and Moonlight, who once ruled Europe and great parts of Africa and Asia. Any poem having that magical quality which differentiates it from barbaric saga, or rhetorical verse, or parlour entertainment, or verbal experimentation based on aesthetic theory—any such simple poem is written, either wittingly or unwittingly, under the Goddess's influence. True poets are not in God's pocket: they are in the Goddess's crane-skin bag.

However (and here I come to an awkward point), this love magic makes sense, it seems, only in the context of young and vigorous life: the woman still young, wild, and beautiful, not yet a sedate matron nor one whom marriage has passed by; the man still hale and vigorous—able to bear arms, box and wrestle, and acceptable as a lover to the same young, wild, beautiful woman. Surely it is almost indecent for anyone after the age of, say, fifty to attempt such poetry, even if he has been writing it for thirty years? All but very few poets die young—as poets: the men in their middle or late twenties, the women even earlier. You may remember the Gravedigger's Song in *Hamlet:*

> For Age with his stealing steps
> Hath clawed me in his clutch . . .
> And hath shipped me intil the land
> As if I had never been such . . .

This stanza was misquoted by the Gravedigger from an original poem, which ran:

> I loathe that I did love,
>   In youth that I thought sweet,
> As time requires for my behove,
>   Methinks they are not meet.
>
> My lusts they do me leave,
>   My fancies all are fled,
> And track of time begins to weave
>   Grey hairs upon my head.
>
> For Age with stealing steps
>   Hath clawed me with his crutch,
> And lusty life away she leaps
>   As there had been none such.
>
> My Muse doth not delight
>   Me as she did before;
> My hand and pen are not in plight,
>   As they have been of yore.
>
> For reason me denies
>   This youthly idle rhyme;
> And day by day to me she cries:
>   "Leave off these toys in time!"
>
> The wrinkles in my brow,
>   The furrows in my face,
> Say: "limping Age will lodge him now
>   Where Youth must give him place . . ."
>
> A pickaxe and a spade,
>   And eke a shrouding sheet,
> A house of clay for to be made
>   For such a guest most meet . . .
>
> Thus must I Youth give up,
>   Whose badge I long did wear;

> To them I yield the wanton cup,
>   That better may it bear.
>
> Lo, here the baréd skull,
>   By whose bald sign I know,
> That stooping Age away shall pull,
>   Which youthful years did sow.
>
> For Beauty with her band
>   These crookéd cares hath wrought,
> And shippéd me into the land,
>   From whence I first was brought . . .

The author of this poem was Thomas, Lord Vaux, who wrote it not long before his death in 1556, at the age of forty-six. Of course, a man's life-expectancy was very much lower in Tudor times. Shakespeare said his farewell to poetry with *The Tempest*, probably written when he was forty-six. Nearly all magic poems in English are the work of young people: the young Donne, the young Coleridge, the young Blake, the young Christina Rossetti. If Keats had survived, he would probably have turned into a Victorian monster long before reaching forty-six; there are warning symptoms in *Hyperion*, and more in his *Cap and Bells*.

The poet, as he grows old and reasonable, tends to lose his power of falling in love, or even of remaining in love. Half-appalled, half-relieved by this discovery, he tells himself: "No fool like an old fool!"

> For Reason me denies
>   This youthly idle rhyme;
> And day by day to me she cries:
>   "Leave off these toys in time!"

Nevertheless, anyone who has acquired a name as a young poet— "promising" is the best that the cautious critics of the Literary Establishment will allow him—feels that he ought to go on. The Literary Establishment has a bright label for what he then produces, if he follows the right models energetically enough. It is "Major Poetry"

—which casually consigns the magical poems of his early manhood
to the category "Minor Poems." Having by this time graduated as
a solid member of society, the new major poet transfers his allegiance
from the White Goddess of inspiration to Apollo, the god of musical
and artistic achievement—the all-too-reasonable upstart godling who
dethroned the great Ninefold Muse-goddess of Greece, reduced her
to nine little obedient Muses, like bric-à-brac plaster-saints from a
Catholic repository, and assigned different departments to each of
them.

Very well: consider what subjects of knowledge are respectable, if
a trifle dry, and ask to be brightly adorned and furbished for
the ordinary earnest citizen by a man with technical training as a
poet? Philosophy? Ethics? Theology? History? Yes; and in the seventeenth and eighteenth centuries even Geography, Botany, and
Anatomy were included in the list. For Apollo is invoked by major
poets for his harmonious architectural concepts, his scientific exactness, his musical masonry—Apollo's lyre had made Troy rise, the
Greeks claimed.

Though these subjects of knowledge are of no concern to the
White Goddess, long poems about them have always been welcomed
by educationalists, on the ground that men of manners and experience who obligingly enhance the cultural programme, deserve to be
honoured in a way that no froward young romantic, even dead
and buried, ought ever to be. Hence the term "major."

Nevertheless, some thirty years ago, educationalists began to think
that quite enough long poems had perhaps already been written.
The Classics, of course, remained: *Paradise Lost, The Dunciad,
Idylls of the King, Hiawatha* even; but would it not be wise to admit
that the main excuse for long poems—namely that the information
which they contain is easily memorized by illiterates—was no longer
valid? If ordinary earnest citizens needed a grounding in philosophy,
or theology, or ethics, or history, why then, simple, well-written prose-
works on these subjects had now become available at a low price;
and illiteracy had almost disappeared. The word went round: "Long
poems are out!" and, indeed, they were ceasing to be a commercial
proposition; which left minor poets who stood on the brink of their
majority in a difficult position. If they published dramatic epics, at

258   ON POETRY: COLLECTED TALKS AND ESSAYS

their own expense, could they count on a *succès d'estime?* Or even on
a *flop d'estime?* It looked as though they would have to quit. Most
of them did. The last major poems in English to be commercial prop-
ositions were John Masefield's *Reynard the Fox,* Robert Bridges'
Testament of Beauty, and Stephen Vincent Benet's *John Brown's
Body.* Long works also formally enrolled Robinson Jeffers and Edward Arlington Robinson among the seeded group of American
poets. But that was quite a time ago; the titles do not spring to the
lips of the younger generation who are well acquainted with Ezra
Pound's more newsworthy *Cantos.* These *Cantos* have already attained sufficient length in the aggregate to rank as major works, but
fall under the heading of vaudeville rather than education. They
were published serially, like Dickens's *Pickwick Papers,* and written
hand-to-mouth with the same careless gusto. Architecturally, ethically, or musically they invite no serious criticism; being, by your
leave, a random sequence of sighs, coos, Bronx cheers, rhetorically
garbled scraps of history, quotations from foreign tongues, falsetto
screams and indecent eructations.

Here we strike a paradox. Though major poems in the old architectural, ethical, musical, Apollonian sense are no longer viable,
yet the Cultural Establishments both of the United States and the
United Kingdom feel ashamed that the present era of rapid material and scientific progress has been glorified by no bearded bard
of Whitman's stature, or Tennyson's. They cast around for a name
to fill this gap, preferably one approved by the younger intellectuals.
Pound is not politically respectable, but what about T. S. Eliot? *The
Wasteland* has been their beacon for the last thirty years, and
Eliot's record is academically clean: he unsaid his harsh judgement
of Milton, and cannot be accused of writing any love poems since
his school days. True, *The Wasteland* is not really a long poem, or
even a long short poem, but a *collage* of lyrical and dramatic pieces
connected by a thread as tenuous as that which links the mystificatory
scenes of *The Cocktail Party.* However, Eliot's *Four Quartets,* taken
in a lump, are lengthy enough and adult enough and religious enough
and philosophical enough to pass as a masterpiece. So the *Four
Quartets* ("with *The Wasteland* taken into consideration," as the
Courtroom reporters put it) have elevated Eliot into a major poet. I

use the word "masterpiece" without irony, in its original technical sense: which is a borrowing from the German *Meisterstück*—a piece of work done by a journeyman which satisfies his guide-authorities that he is henceforth entitled to rank as a master, or full member of the Establishment. Here's a quotation dating from 1658: "Taylors suffer none to set up his trade unless he have first made the masterpiece."

Eliot's trade is well set up now. The British Establishment awarded him the Order of Merit, the highest cultural award in its gift—reserved for major operators in the arts and sciences. Minor operators, however talented, cannot hope for an Order of Merit. Nevertheless, about forty years ago the Establishment created a secondary Order, the Companionship of Honour, so as to prevent (it is said) a busy and ambitious man of letters, named Robertson Nicoll, from attaining an Order of Merit that had fallen vacant. The Prime Minister's consultants did not think him worthy of wearing it. The Companionship of Honour can be reasonably conferred on distinguished verse-writers who loyally support the Establishment, for instance the late Sir Henry Newbolt, a patriotic rhymester in the Kipling tradition. The Order of the British Empire was a creation of the First World War: a means of encouraging the civic spirit among minor executives, businessmen, and so forth, and of keeping such higher Orders as the Bath, or the St. Michael and St. George, decently exclusive. The public at first scorned the Order of the British Empire, which became known as "The Order of the Bad Egg"; but now accept it as cheerfully as they do the naval and military Distinguished Service Order, created during the Boer War—when D.S.O. was commonly read as "Damned Stupid Officer."

Minor poets who happen also to be professors of literature, or museum curators, are sometimes made Commander of the British Empire, or C.B.E. A minor poet, whom I know very well, was offered one the other day because his name had so often appeared in our literary weeklies that the Establishment hoped he might eventually mature and qualify for a Companionship of Honour, or even an Order of Merit. However, he declined the honour on the ground that politicians have no right to distribute poetry prizes, even in the name of Her Gracious Majesty Queen Elizabeth II; and because he felt loth to deprive some retiring stationmaster, or Assistant Commissioner in Lunacy, of a reward earned by a lifetime of loyal public service. Virginia Woolf had set him a precedent: when offered a Dameship of the British Empire, she replied by postcard that her mother had once warned her never to accept candy from strange men.

Yes, indeed. The writing of poetry is a private and non-competitive task commissioned by the Muse herself; no board of poets has any right to award diplomas, still less has the English faculty of any university—and as for a Prime Minister, especially when he is a publisher by trade . . . ! Here is a minor poem that came out of the incident:

BARABBAS'S SUMMER LIST

Barabbas, once a publisher
But currently Prime Minister,
Writes—not of course in his own fist—
"May we include you in our List"
(Across the *Times* in glory spread
With Baths and Garters at its head)?
"Your graceful lyric work," says he,
"Fully deserves a C.B.E."

I ask my agents, Messrs. Watt,
Whether I should accept or not.
Few agents are so tough as these
At battling with Barabbases:
The mongoose in his cobra-war
Provides a perfect metaphor.
"Barabbas ought to raise his price
By five per cent," is Watt's advice.

*

So much for that. The political-honours racket is one you Americans did well to scotch when you proclaimed your Independence. Now let me ramble on. The point from which I started, and which

I began to develop until I got sidetracked again, was that minor poetry, so called to differentiate it from major poetry, is the real stuff; but that, with rare exceptions, it has always been written by young men—men under early middle age. Me, I took a vow to the Muse when I was fifteen and as I say have now reached my Grand Climacteric, which is regarded as a man's final goodbye to youth. What excuse have I for continuing to write in a vein that I should have finished with at least thirty years ago? I don't know the answer to this. It may be that my later poems are no good: artificial, patched, phoney. Yet Thomas Hardy still wrote true poems—*Winter Words* was the title of the last collection—well into his seventies when he had grown frail and thin-blooded; and Robert Frost is far from mute either.

I once had the great good fortune to spend a night with Hardy at his Dorchester house, when I was a young poet, and he a very old one; a wise old man who had somehow retained the juvenile power of being in love. And only last May I had the equally good fortune to meet Robert Frost again, after a lapse of forty-two years, and recognized the same power in him. We discussed poetry and poets we had known—I was delighted to find so many of my own brash verdicts supported by his veteran judgement—but the conversation also rambled around the countryside, and trees, and different strains of apple. The curly maple and the hickory are the timber of Frost's poems; and his apples are the old-fashioned "sheep's noses" and "sops-in-wine." It meant a great deal to me: meeting a poet of the generation above mine for whom I could feel respect and deep affection, and with whom I could talk at ease about poetry and trees.

Now to discuss women poets. The capacity for being continuously in love, common among girls, but is unusual among adult women once they have secured their niche in society; and how few women dare remain outside and earn the suspicion of their families, neighbours and friends! I hardly need mention the obvious but extraordinary change that comes over women when they become mothers. To have children by a man she loves is considered a marvellous thing by a woman; yet Nature, to preserve the race, has arranged that a stronger and tenderer love shall burn in her for the child than for the man. I can find no evidence of *poetry* in this love, however strong and tender it may be. Poetry—minor poetry, if you like—is by definition non-domestic; it has to do with the state of being moon-struck, of seeking one's true love in the dark forest, among perils and trials, death threatening. A girl may conceive in this poetic mood, but once she has her child safely tucked up in the cradle, she becomes a new woman: the woman at home. Since no women, except those who have converted themselves into hard-faced intellectuals, can resist the tug at their hearts which children give, and since hard-faced intellectuals cannot appreciate poetry anyhow, the few women poets who come up for serious discussion (correct me, if I am wrong) have all been childless when they wrote their best work. Fatherhood is a serious enough matter, if only because, as a rule, the father provides for the child's care and education, and sometimes plays the nurse-maid as well. But no physical change takes place in him at father-hood; indeed, he may be quite unaware of his condition—a prisoner of war, for instance, or a sailor who has had a casual love-affair in a foreign port. Thus fatherhood does not prevent a poet from continuing to write poems. It may happen, though, that the mother of his child was the nymph to whom he swore eternal faith under the moon, and that, finding her heart now more than half engaged to the child, he will sheer off and let his fancy stray. Or else he still sees her as the nymph he loved, showers irrelevant kisses on her and tries to lure her out into the forest at the first convenient full moon. After a while, she may consent and it will be, between them, almost as it was before—but never quite. Then what of his eternal vows? I wrote somewhere that the White Goddess is the perpetual "other woman".

To remain childless after her twenties can seldom be a triumph for a woman poet, even if she proclaims it so. Emily Dickinson was an exception. She remained true to her first unconsummated love for a young married preacher, whose home she could easily have broken, but did not. A sense of power and virtue sustained her as a poet until the end. Other women poets either go dry, or go religious, or go Lesbian, or present themselves as major prophetesses; or, in desperation, throw their gift of poetry out of the window, and make common clay of themselves.

A grim proverb occurs in *The Triads of Ireland:* "It is death to insult a poet, death to love a poet, death to be a poet." And a simpler English proverb runs: "All poets are mad." There is truth here too, because the nature of a poet's vow to the Goddess involves him in constant experiences of death; and to court death is madness. One morning, last September, when I was vaguely thinking of what to tell you tonight, I strolled into my garden to see whether enough cherry-crab-apples had fallen for another preserving-panful of jelly; and whether there would be enough carobs to keep Isabella the donkey fed until this September; and whether the walnuts were ripe enough to knock down; and whether the figs, which should have been ripe, were still hard and small and green; and how soon the wild-olive shoots growing from the trunk of a wind-felled tree beside the grape arbour would be sturdy enough for grafting with sweet-olive. You know, I daresay, that one cannot *plant* a sweet-olive tree; there is no such thing. A sweet-olive must always be grafted on an oleaster, or wild-olive stock; the original graft was a gift to Athens by Athene, her Goddess. This provides a neat emblem for poetry: poetry not being a gift granted at birth, but a graft made by the Goddess on a likely wild tree at adolescence.

As I stood there in the garden, a portent occurred: a nightingale began singing from our olive grove across the road. I called the girls from the house to listen, in case I had misheard the note. Nightingales have no right to sing in September; they must stop short at the end of June when the nesting season closes. The girls agreed that, yes, ¡mira!, it *was* a nightingale. I thought this a happy portent indeed, because the nightingale is pre-eminently the bird of poetic love, and if he can sing on a September morning as passionately and sweetly as at night-time in May, there is still hope for me.

Now let me tell you about *Sweeney and the Blackbirds:* the real Sweeney, Suibne Geilt, spelled s–u–i–b–n–e—not APENECK s–w–e–e–n–e–y, the character celebrated by T. S. Eliot in two sordid poems which you all know only too well. At the close of *Sweeney and the Nightingales* occur six lines of Classic felicity, by way of contrast to the portrait of a brutal, ape-like, urban American, already depicted in *Sweeney Erect.*

> The nightingales are singing near
> The Convent of the Sacred Heart,
>
> And sang within the bloody wood
> When Agamemnon cried aloud
> And let their liquid siftings fall
> To stain the still dishonoured shroud . . .

Lines which have earned Eliot much applause, especially in that district of New York where the Nightingales are neighbours, and bitter rivals, of the Sacred Heart girls—on 81st Street, isn't it?—and a hidden reference is therefore suspected. But the wood at Mycenae was not "bloody." Agamemnon was murdered on the City acropolis in the Palace bath house, not in the wood; and Classical authority, quoting Deinias the historian, insists that the murder took place on the thirteenth day of Gamelion, which fell towards the end of January; a time when nightingales are silent, even for poets.

Let us forget about Eliot's *Sweeney*—broad-bottomed, pink from nape to base, who pays no attention to his hysterical wife in the adjacent bedroom, but wipes the suds around his face and tests the razor on his leg, waiting until the shriek subsides. . . . Instead, let us consider the real Suibne, Suibne Geilt, the poet-king of Dal Araidhe. This is the Suibne about whom an anonymous ninth-century Irishman composed a prose tale, *The Madness of Suibne*, incorporating a sequence of dramatic poems based on certain seventh-century originals which were attributed to Suibne himself. In the tale, as it has come down to us, Suibne was driven mad because he had twice insulted St. Ronan: first, by interrupting the Saint as he marked out the site of a new church without royal permission, and tossing his psalter into a stream; and next, by flinging a spear at him as he tried to make peace between the High King of Ireland and Suibne's overlord, just before the Battle of Magh Rath. The spear hit St. Ronan's mass-bell, but glanced off harmlessly. St. Ronan thereupon cursed Suibne with the flying madness. Evidence found in three early chronicles, however, suggests that Suibne's second insult was directed not at St. Ronan but at an ollamh, or sacrosanct poet, who was trying to make peace on the eve of the Magh Rath battle between the rival enemy army-commanders, namely King Domnal the Scot, and Domnal High King of Ireland. In the seventh century, such peacemaking was an ollamh's function, not a priest's. Perhaps Suibne's spear struck the branch of golden bells which were the ollamh's emblem of office; and the ollamh vengefully threw in his face a so-called "madman's wisp" (a magical handful of straw), which sent him fleeing madly from the battlefield. At any rate, Suibne's wife Éorann had tried to restrain him from this act of folly, and was therefore spared the curse. The flying madness is described as making his body so light that he could perch in the tops of trees, and leap desperate leaps of a hundred feet or more without injury. Mediaeval Latin philosophers described the condition as *spirituali-zatio, agilitas* and *subtilitas,* and applied it to cases of levitation by ecstatic saints. Feathers then sprouted on Suibne's body, and he lived like the wild things: feeding on sloes, holly-berries, watercress, brook-lime, acorns; sleeping in yew-trees and rocky clefts of ivy-clad cliffs, and even in hawthorn and bramble bushes. The slightest noise would startle him into flight, and he was cursed with a perpetual distrust of all men.

Suibne had a friend, Loingseachan, who constantly went in pursuit, trying to catch and cure him. Loingseachan succeeded temporarily on three occasions, but Suibne always relapsed: a fury known as "the Hag of the Mill," would soon tempt him to renew his frantic leaps. During a lucid interval after seven years of madness, Suibne visited Éorann, who was being forced to marry his successor the new king—and one most moving dramatic poem records their con-versation:

SUIBNE: "At ease you are, bright Éorann,
            Bound bedward to your lover;
            It is not so with Suibne here—
            Long has he wandered footloose.

         "Lightly once, great Éorann,
            You whispered words that pleased me.
            'I could not live,' you said, 'were I
            Parted one day from Suibne.'

"Now it is clear and daylight clear,
How small your care for Suibne;
You lie warm on a good down bed,
He starves for cold till sunrise."

EORANN: "Welcome, my guileless madman,
Dearest of humankind!
Though soft I lie, my body wastes
Since the day of your downfall."

SUIBNE: "More welcome than I, that prince
Who escorts you to the banquet.
He is your chosen gallant;
Your old love you neglect."

EORANN: "Though a prince may now escort me
To the carefree banquet-hall,
I had liefer sleep in a tree's cramped bole
With you, Suibne, my husband.

"Could I choose from all the warriors
Of Ireland and of Scotland,
I had liefer live, blameless, with you
On watercress and water."

SUIBNE: "No path for his belovéd
Is Suibne's track of care;
Cold he lies at Ard Abhla,
His lodgings cold are many.

"Far better to feel affection
For the prince whose bride you are,
Than for this madman all uncouth,
Famished and stark-naked."

EORANN: "I grieve for you, toiling madman,
So filthy and downcast.
I grieve that your skin is weather worn,
Torn by spines and brambles . . ."

"O that we were together,
And my body feathered too;
In light and darkness would I wander
With you, for evermore!"

SUIBNE: "One night I spent in cheerful Mourne,
One night in Bann's sweet estuary.
I have roved this land from end to end . . ."

The tale continues:

Hardly had Suibne spoken these words when the army came marching into the camp from all directions. He sped away in wild flight, as he had often done before; and presently, when he had perched on a high, ivy-clad branch, the Hag of the Mill settled close beside him. Suibne then made this poem, describing the trees and herbs of Ireland:

Bushy oak, leafy oak,
You tower above all trees.
O hazel, little branching one,
Coffer for sweet nuts!

You are not cruel, O alder.
Delightfully you gleam,
You neither rend nor prickle
In the gap you occupy.

Blackthorn, little thorny one,
Dark provider of sloes.
Watercress, little green-topped one,
From the stream where blackbirds drink.

O apple-tree, true to your kind,
You are much shaken by men;
O rowan, cluster-berried one,
Beautiful is your blossom!

O briar, arching over,
You never play me fair;
Ever again you tear me,
Drinking your fill of blood.

Yew-tree, yew-tree, true to your kind,
In churchyards you are found;
O ivy, growing ivy-like,
You are found in the dark wood.

O holly, tree of shelter,
Bulwark against the winds;
O ash-tree, very baleful one,
Haft for the warrior's spear.

O birch-tree, smooth and blessed,
Melodious and proud,
Delightful every tangled branch
At the top of your crown . . .

Yet misery piled upon misery, until one day, when Suibne was
about to pluck water-cress from a stream at Ros Cornain, the wife of
the monastery bailiff chased him away and plucked it all for herself,
which sent him into utter despair:

Gloomy is this life,
In lack of a soft bed,
To know the numbing frost,
And rough wind-driven snow.

Cold wind, icy wind,
Faint shadow of a feeble sun,
Shelter of a single tree
On the top of a flat hill.

Enduring the rain-storm,
Stepping along deer-paths,
Slouching through greensward
On a day of grey frost.

A belling of stags
That echoes through the wood,
A climb to the deer-pass,
The roar of spumy seas . . .

Stretched on a watery bed
By the banks of Loch Erne,
I consider early rising
When the day shall dawn.

Then Suibne thought again of Éorann. The story goes:

Thereafter Suibne went to the place where Éorann was, and
stood at the outer door of the house wherein were the queen and
her womenfolk, and said again: "At ease you are, Éorann, though
ease is not for me."

"True," said Éorann, "yet come in," said she.

"Indeed I will not," said Suibne, "lest the army pen me into the
house."

"Methinks," said she, "your reason does not improve with time,
and since you will not stay with us," said she, "go away and do not
visit us at all, for we are ashamed that you should be seen in this
guise by those who have seen you in your true guise."

"Wretched indeed is that," said Suibne. "Woe to him who trusts
a woman. . . ."

Suibne resumed his fruitless wanderings, until befriended by a
cowman's wife, who would secretly pour a little milk for him into
a hole she had stamped with her heel in the stable cowdung. He
lapped the milk gratefully, but one day the cowman mistook him
for her lover, flung a spear, and mortally wounded him. Then
Suibne regained his reason and died in peace. He lies buried beneath
a fine headstone which the generous-hearted St. Moling raised to
him . . .

This improbable tale conceals a true one: that of the poet obsessed by the Hag of the Mill, another name for the White Goddess.
He calls her "the woman white with flour" just as the Greeks
called her Alphito, "Goddess of the Barley Flour." This poet quarrels

with both the Church and the bards of the Academic Establishment, and is outlawed by them. He loses touch with his more practical wife, once his Muse; and though, pitying his misery, she admits that she loves him still, he can no longer reach her. He trusts nobody, not even his best friend, and enjoys no companionship but that of the blackbirds, the stags, the larks, the badgers, the little foxes, and the wild trees. (Not the nightingales—the nightingale never visits Ireland, for some unjust reason.) Towards the end of this tale Suibne has lost even the Hag of the Mill, who snaps her neck-bone in leaping along with him; which means, I suppose, that he breaks down as a poet under the strain of loneliness. In his extremity Suibne returns to Éorann; but her heart has gone dead by now, and she sends him coldly away.

The tale seems to be devised as an illustration of the *Triad* I quoted. Suibne found it death to insult a poet; and death to be a poet; Éorann found it death to love a poet. Only after he had died in misery did Suibne's reputation flourish again.

This must be the most ruthless and bitter description in all European literature of the obsessed poet's predicament. The woman-poet's predicament is described in an almost equally poignant tale: *The Loves of Liadan and Curithir*: in which, as I have said elsewhere, Liadan, the she-ollamh of Corkaguiney, falls in love with the ollamh Curithir. When Curithir asks her to marry him, remarking truly, but somewhat tactlessly: "Should you consent, my children will be famous," she realizes that by marrying him she would lose her gift of poetry, and then his love. She therefore takes a vow of chastity. Liadan's end, I regret to say, is as sorrowful as Suibne's.

But let us not wallow in these griefs and flying-madnesses. A poet writes, as a rule, while he is young, and has the spell of the White Goddess on him.

> My love is of a birth as rare
>   As 'tis by nature strange and high:
> It was begotten by despair
>   Upon impossibility.

In the result, he either loses the girl altogether, as he rightly feared; or else he marries her and loses her in part. Well, why not? If she makes him a good wife, why should he cherish the poetic obsession to his own ruin? Again, if a woman-poet can get a healthy child in exchange for the gift of poetry, why not? The sovereign White Goddess dismisses both deserters with a faintly scornful smile, and inflicts no punishment, so far as I know; but then neither did she praise and cosset and confer Orders on them while they served her. There is no disgrace in being an ex-poet; if only one makes a clean break with poetry, like Rimbaud, or (more recently) Laura Riding.

Yet, is the alternative between service to the White Goddess, on the one hand, and a respectable citizenship, on the other, quite so sharp as the Irish poets presented it? Suibne in his tale has an overriding obsession about poetry; so has Liadan in hers. But was either of them gifted with a sense of humour? Doubtless not, or they would never have punished themselves so cruelly. Humour is the one gift that helps men and women to survive the stress of city life. If he keeps his sense of humour, too, a poet can go mad gracefully, swallow his disappointments in love gracefully, reject the Establishment gracefully, die gracefully, and cause no upheaval in society. Nor need he indulge in self-pity or cause distress to those who love him; and that goes for a woman-poet also.

Humour is surely reconcilable with devotion to the White Goddess; as it is, for example, with perfect sanctity in a Catholic priest, whose goings and comings are far more strictly circumscribed than a poet's, and whose Bible contains not one smile from *Genesis* to the *Apocalypse*. It has been said of the Goddess (by one of her Scottish devotees on trial for witchcraft): "She can be young or old, as it pleases her," and, indeed, she reserves a delightful seven-year-old giggle for those who are not daunted by her customary adult marble glare. She may even allow her poet an eventual happy marriage, if he has taken his early tumbles in good part. For though she is, by definition, non-human, neither is she altogether inhuman. Suibne complains about a snowstorm which caught him without clothes in the fork of a tree:

> I am in great distress tonight,
> Pure wind my body pierces;
> My feet are wounded, my cheek pale,
> Great God, I have cause for distress!

Yet his sufferings were by no means the whole story. He enjoyed life to the full in better weather: his meals of wild strawberries or blueberries, the swift flight by which he would overtake the wood-pigeon, his rides on the antlers of a stag or on the back of a slender-shinned fawn. He could even say: "I take no pleasure in the amorous talk of man with woman; far more lovely, to my ear, is the song of the blackbird." Nobody can blame Éorann for asking Suibne politely to begone, when he had reached that stage. What preserved her, what he lacked, namely that blessed sense of humour. Éorann's earlier wish for a feathered body in which she could fly around with him, suggests that she too began as a poet, but sensibly resigned when the time for poetry had gone by.

Pulling a Poem Apart

If I thought that any poem of mine could have been written by anyone else, either a contemporary or a forerunner, I should suppress it with a blush; and do the same if I ever found I had been imitating myself. Every poem ought to be new, unexpected, inimitable, logical, incapable of being parodied or pulled apart. The poet's first rule must be never to bore his readers; and his best way of keeping this rule is never to bore himself—which, of course, means to write only when he has something urgent to say. He must constantly scrutinize poems written years ago and ask: "Is this poem really necessary?" If it can't justify itself, out it goes! But self-deception cannot always be avoided, and then someone else must pull the poem apart. The pulling apart of poems, other than my own, has often got me into trouble with the educational authorities: I have never hesitated to say exactly why a poem was bad if it seemed so to me, whoever the author.

Poems must always be judged in their historical context. Thus I would not, for example, venture to criticize the permissibly inexact rhymes of cowboy ballads or capstan chanties. Nor would I quarrel with Coleridge's use of "honey-dew" in *Kubla Khan*—"for he on honey-dew hath fed, And drunk the milk of Paradise." When Coleridge wrote this poem, nobody knew the nature or origin of honey-dew—a sticky, sweet substance that messes up the bonnet and hood of a car left parked for a few hours under an English lime-tree. Gilbert White, in his *Natural History of Selborne*, thought it a peculiar form of dew, like the Biblical manna that fell upon the Wilderness; Pliny, in his *Natural History*, had explained it as a sweet distillation of the stars. Entomologists, however, now have discovered honey-dew to be the watery excrement of plant-lice; as manna is the solid excrement of the scale-insect (*trabutina mannipara*), which infests tamarisk-trees in Sinai. Myself, I should never use "honey-dew" in a poem to denote delicious food of supernatural origin. Honey-dew is not really tasty, even if one forgets its unappetizing origin, though Alpine bees in bad seasons mix it with pine-blossom honey—and so impair their own digestions.*

Poems reflect a poet's contemporary world of reference, and even the blackest Protestants can admire Old English carols written by pious Catholics in the days before religious doubt set in. Nor do Chaucer's or Shakespeare's or Donne's unscientific beliefs about medicine, geography or physics destroy the value of their work. Yet the mere antiquity of a poem seems a very poor excuse for faulty construction or feebleness of thought. No poet, however much of a classic, is above criticism. I have always deplored the practice of making students admire indifferent work that happens to have been written by long-dead poets as politically respectable, say, as Wordsworth or Milton.

Recently someone upheld Wordsworth's sonnet "Great men have been among us," as the kind of poem that nobody is great-hearted enough to write in these degenerate days. I refrained from immediate comment, but sat down and copied out the lines in long-

* It has now been discovered that both honey-dew and manna are subject to ergot, a minute hallucinogenic fungus which is the basis of lysergic acid or "LSD." This accounts for Coleridge's ecstatic poem and for the absurd account of "manna from heaven" found in the *Book of Exodus*; which must be eaten fresh "before it breeds worms and stinks."

hand as though I were composing them myself—a useful technique for testing the integrity of a poem. If my pen runs on without check or hesitation, well and good; if not, I ask myself: "what is wrong?"

This sonnet proved peculiarly difficult to copy out, though I found it had been praised, by educationalists, as "one of that splendid series of generally impressive and universally intelligible poems dedicated to national Liberty and Independence."

> Great men have been among us; hands that penned
> And tongues that uttered wisdom—better none:
> The later Sidney, Marvell, Harrington,
> Young Vane, and others who called Milton friend.
> These moralists could act and comprehend:
> They knew how genuine glory was put on;
> Taught us how rightfully a nation shone
> In splendour: what strength was, that would not bend
> But in magnanimous meekness . . .

"Great men have been among us . . . !" "Have *been*," in Wordsworth's time, as now, suggested a short stay: "I have been in Newhaven; I have been to Venice; I have been on Capri"—as opposed to "I have *dwelt*," or "I have *lived*," which imply residence for a year or more. So I expected Wordsworth to furnish a list of distinguished foreign visitors to Britain: perhaps Julius Caesar, St. Augustine, Dante, Peter the Great, Voltaire. But apparently he meant: "have dwelt". In that case, why did he not list King Alfred, Sir Thomas More, John Hampden, and men of their calibre? Surely he could have made a less bizarre choice than Sir Philip Sidney, Sir James Harrington, Andrew Marvell and Sir Henry Vane, adding certain anonymous characters "who called Milton friend"? My pen came to a stop. Presently I realized that the "later Sidney" was not, after all, Sir Philip Sidney in his maturity (as one discusses the "later Beethoven" or the "later W. B. Yeats"); but either Algernon Sidney (1622–1688), a Commonwealth statesman or, less probably, his elder brother Philip, the third Earl of Leicester (1619–1698), another staunch Republican; and that these four men were chosen as representative friends of Milton's. So Wordsworth meant: *"Others who called Milton friend,"* not: "Others who called *Milton* friend." The sonnet, I saw, formed part of a sequence in which Wordsworth likened himself, by implication, to the great poet-prophet-republican John Milton, whose freedom-loving voice had thundered across the Continent two centuries before—when France was threatening England, as once more in 1802, despite the Peace of Amiens.

Now, about these four staunch Republicans. Algernon Sidney, whose *Discourses Concerning Government* had encouraged Thomas Jefferson and James Otis in their rebellion against Wordsworth's patron, George III, was a member of the Cromwellian Council of State, notorious for his bad temper and ambition. After Charles II's restoration to the Throne, he visited King Louis XIV at Paris and offered, for one hundred thousand crowns, to raise a revolt in England, already much troubled by the Dutch Wars. Louis found the price too high, so Sidney returned to London, where the French Ambassador paid him well to foster King Louis's interests in Parliament.

Sir Henry Vane, another member of the Council of State, and sometime Royal Governor of Massachusetts, was an unbalanced religious enthusiast distrusted by all political parties. Cromwell said of him: "O Sir Henry Vane, O Sir Henry Vane, the Lord deliver me from Sir Henry Vane!"

Andrew Marvell should have been omitted from Wordsworth's list: he was a poet, not a moralist.

Sir James Harrington, whom Cromwell made Groom of the Bedchamber when the Roundheads captured King Charles, was suspected of disloyally trying to aid his escape. Harrington's book of political theory *The Commonwealth of Oceana*, is condemned in the *Encyclopaedia Britannica* as "irretrievably dull."

Since Milton, as Cromwell's Press Censor, worked closely with the Book Censor, these four great men had to call Milton friend, if they wanted anything penned by themselves to appear. At any rate Wordsworth, my pen told me, ought to have qualified his sonorous statement about great men, by defining the period during

which there were no better than these available. He could easily
have done so by cutting out one miserably prosaic line:

These moralists could act and comprehend . . .

and turning the remaining lines around. Thus:

ON THE FRIENDS OF JOHN MILTON

Algernon Sidney, Marvell, Harrington,
  The younger Vane, each calling Milton friend;
  Such great men lived among us, hands that penned
And tongues that uttered wisdom—better none,
From Cromwell's usurpation to his end.

This change would have dispelled the ambiguity of "better
none" which, as it stands, could well mean that it is always preferable
to have no tongues at all speaking wisdom—on the ground, perhaps, that Algernon Sidney and Sir James Harrington were both
eventually executed for High Treason and Sir Henry Vane imprisoned. The vagueness of "They knew how genuine glory was
put on," also troubled me. Did "put on" mean "worn like a
crown," or could it mean "cleverly faked"?

The end of the sonnet came as a surprise. I had been expecting a
reasoned justification of Wordsworth's rash thesis that these four
men "taught us what strength was, that would not bend but in
magnanimous meekness." Or else, perhaps, a complaint that Wordsworth himself lacked friends as noble as those who surrounded
Milton during his Latin Secretaryship; Coleridge, Southey and Crabb
Robinson may have seemed to him poor fish by comparison. Instead,
however, I found a wholly irrelevant sestet, salvaged perhaps from
a discarded poetical tirade of the *Gott strafe Frankreich!* sort popular
at the turn of the century when the war was not going well for
England:

> . . . France, 'tis strange,
> Hath brought forth no such souls as we had then.
> Perpetual emptiness! unceasing change!
> No single volume paramount, no code,
> No master spirit, no determined road;
> But equally a want of books and men!

Here Wordsworth presents the surprising view that France in all its long history has never produced a single great soul comparable to the four English ones listed, or a single book comparable to any written by them. If he means modern Revolutionary France, he ought to say so. (I cannot blame him for failing to anticipate the introduction, two years later, of the *Code Napoléon;* but surely he should have revised the sonnet in his *Collected Works,* despite the difficulty of finding another rhyme in *ode?*) He is, I suppose, outdoing Milton, who wrote in *Areopagitica:*

> What does God then but reveal Himself to His servants
> and, as His manner is, first to His Englishmen?

At the same time, Wordsworth is studiously recanting his former attachment to the French Revolution, while holding fast to old-fashioned English republicanism. He damns France with all the greater violence because he feels an overpowering sense of guilt: guilt for having deserted not only the Girondist cause but also Annette Vallon, the daughter of his French host at Blois, whom he has got with child. The poetic result is confused, confusing, and false-hearted.

"Ah, but," you plead, "it's a war-time poem; and at least it *reads* well."

"Yes, perhaps! As we often used to say at breakfast in 1940–1945: 'it's war-time jam, and at least it *spreads* well.'"

The Dedicated Poet

I thank those of you members of Congregation who, last February, disregarded the warning of London's best-known literary weekly: to the effect that, though a poet, Mr. Graves could have nothing either novel or important to say from this Chair—which, it was added, might be better occupied by a Russian or French savant or, better still, by a bright young lecturer from a red-brick university. The same editorial insisted that the Professor you chose to address what would be predominantly an undergraduate audience, should adopt a serious moral attitude consonant with the dignity of his, or her, position. I do not dispute this last point; but poetic morals can surely be best discussed by poets, who, in the course of their labours, suffer pricks of professional conscience at which a Muscovite savant, or a bright young red-brick lecturer, cannot do more than guess.

This Chair, the only elective one at Oxford, has been linked by statute with the School of English Language and literature—albeit of far older foundation. The occupant is therefore expected to make no pronouncement irreconcilable with the view of poetry that tutors and examiners require from undergraduates. It may thus be called a

Siege Perilous: because Ben Jonson, of glorious memory, to whom
the young wits of Oxford used to flock when in his old age he held
forth at Great Tew, allowed poets alone the faculty of judging
poems; and few English School tutors have been practising poets.
. . . As Domingo Ortega, the veteran bullfighter, remarked the
other day (the translation is mine):

> Bullfight critics ranked in rows
>   Crowd the enormous Plaza full;
> But only one is there who *knows*
> And he's the man who fights the bull.*

Of course, to be a practising poet is not necessarily to be a good one.
I know my own poetic limitations well enough, and shall never
forget the gentle rebuke once addressed to me by a personal Muse:

> Forgive me, giver, if I destroy the gift!
> It is so nearly what would please me
> I cannot but perfect it.

Nevertheless, only a poet of experience can hope to put himself in
the shoes of his predecessors, or contemporaries, and judge their
poems by re-creating technical and emotional dilemmas which they
faced while at work on them. The method may be called "analeptic
mimesis": one slowly copies out the poem by hand, as if it were a
first draft of one's own. When the pen checks at a word or a phrase,
one becomes intuitively aware of laziness, doubt, stupidity, or some
compromise with moral principle.

Yes: I know that Dr. Samuel Johnson sturdily rejected Ben
Jonson's view. He licensed non-poets to judge any poem, on the
ground that a man has a right to scold his carpenter for making him
a bad table. But this surely begs the question? Granted that if Dr.
Johnson bespoke a table, giving detailed instructions for its manufacture, he had every right to complain if these were disobeyed;
but not since Sir Roger Newdigate founded his Prize, in the early

---

* This was quoted by President Kennedy at his first press conference, but attributed in error to the Spanish philosopher Ortega y Gasset.

nineteenth century, has it been seriously believed that even Universities have a right to bespeak poems. I am lucky, I confess. My Oxford English School colleagues still preserve the undogmatic and indulgent spirit I found displayed here soon after the First World War, when Sir Walter Raleigh was Merton Professor, and Mr. Percy Simpson my tutor. They neither encourage nor discourage undergraduates who choose to swim in the foul tidal basin of modernism: merely requiring from them a close attention to the primitive roots of our language and the long history of our literature. Yet this cannot be said of certain other English Schools. Besides, it is always tempting for tutors to commend the set Classics as worthy of a praise which few of them deserve—even if judged as literary fashion-plates, rather than as reading matter. And I have observed elsewhere that for most examinees the word "appreciate" has lost its original sense of "evaluation," and come to mean "admire."

The earliest and clearest example of the dedicated poet is John Skelton, one of Oxford's greatest glories, whom I discovered by accident in 1916, while on short leave from the Somme trenches, and on long leave from St. John's College. What heightened my shock of delight was that nobody else, it seemed, had felt as I did about him during the past four centuries.

Skelton, it is true, began his studies at Cambridge and probably took his B.A. there; but for a final academic polish came to "Oxforth" where, as he writes:

> By whole consent of their Senáte
> I was made Poet Laureate. . . .

This degree, taken in October 1488, according to Professor William Nelson, implied a diligent study of mediaeval grammar and rhetoric, though the *Poeta Laureatus* need not have written any poems— except perhaps a hundred Virgilian hexameters, and a Latin comedy, both eulogizing Oxford, to prove that he had mastered Latin prosody and the Aristotelian unities. Yet in old age, after being created *Orator Regius,* a sort of Latin Secretary, by his former pupil King Henry VIII, Skelton made a startling public avowal of devotion to the Muse-goddess, when he appeared wearing a white and green Court dress embroidered with the golden name CALLIOPE. He chose Calliope ("lovely face") rather than any of the Goddess's eight other names because, as he writes in an *amplificatio* of Diodorus Siculus' *History*, Calliope combines "incomparable riches of eloquence with profound sadness."

Why Wear Ye "Calliope" Embroidered With Letters of Gold?
Skelton Laureate, Orator Regius, Maketh His Answer.

Calliope,
As ye may see,
Regent is she
    Of poets all,
Which gave to me
The high degree
Laureate to be
    Of fame royál.

Whose name enrolled
With silk and gold
I dare be bold
    Thus for to wear
Of her I hold,
And her household.
Though I wax old
    And some-deal sere,

Yet is she fain,
Void of disdain,
Me to retain
    Her serviture:
With her certáin
I will remain
As my sovereígn
    Most of pleasure—
Maulgré touz malheureux. . . .

He adds a *"latinum carmen,"* which I shall translate:

Calliope, who rules over prophetic poets, her white robe embroidered with glittering gold, crowning Pierian devotees with laurel: it is she whom I, a Pierian, shall ever account worthy of the greatest honour while I still have life. And though I grow old and my body slowly decays, yet I swear still to wear this loyal pledge of her love, and yield to her gentle poetic inspiration. Famous Calliope, whose image is next to my heart! Thus speaks a Pierian, one more free than any Spartan, since Calliope the most excellent, most beautiful, most shapely of the Muses, presides over my heroic verses.

Historians will dismiss this as early Tudor rhodomontade; but wrongly. "More free than any Spartan" gives the clue. It refers to the famous stand of the Spartans at Thermopylae, and Skelton is claiming as a poet the liberty of thought and action which King Lycurgus' proto-Fascist discipline denied even the most patriotic Spartans. (By the way, they sent only a token force against the Persians—300 out of the many thousands they could put into the field.) Skelton explains in his play *Magnificence:*

> To live under law it is captivity:
> Where dread leadeth the dance there is no joy nor pride.
> Or how can you prove there is felicity
> An you have not your own free liberty
> To sport at your pleasúre, to run and to ride?

He made good his claim to freedom by being the one man in England who, at the height of Cardinal Wolsey's power—when Dread led the dance—dared oppose him in cruelly satiric verses as a traitor to King, Church, and people. And though appointed Rector of Diss in Norfolk, by Royal favour, Skelton did not hesitate to take what was then called a "remedy" for his celibate condition—a regular concubine—with whom he lived until his death, and by whom he had several children. The following "Merry Tale of Skelton," a version which appeared while he was still alive, may well be authentic:

Skelton went into the pulpit to preach and said: "*Vos estis, vos estis,*" that is to say: "You be, you be!" "And what be you?" said

Skelton. "I say that you be a sort of knaves, yea and a man might say worse than knaves, and why I shall show ye. You have complained of me to the bishop that I do keep a fair wench in my house. I do tell you that if you had any fair wives, it were somewhat to help me at need. I am a man as you be. You have foul wives and I have a fair wench, of the which I have begotten a fair boy, as I do think, and as you all shall see."—"Thou wife," said Skelton, "that hast my child, be not afraid! Bring hither my child to me!" The which was done.

And he, showing his child naked to all the parish said: "How say ye, neighbours all? It hath nose, eyes, hands and feet as well as any of yours: it is not like a pig or a calf, nor like no fowl nor no monstrous beast. If I had," said Skelton, "brought forth this child without arms or legs or that it were deformed, being a monstrous thing, I would never have blamed you to have complained to the bishop of me. But to complain without a cause—I say, as I said before in my antethem, *vos estis,* you be, and have been, and will and shall be, knaves, to complain of me without a cause reasonable. . . . If that you exalt yourselves and cannot be contented that I have my wench still, some of you shall wear horns, and therefore *vos estis,* and so farewell!"

Nevertheless, Skelton's pledge to Calliope presumes his knowledge of a different sort of love than the carnal Remedy—the old solace which the parish of St. Ebbe's used to offer Oxford Fellows under the ancient celibacy rule; and this is evidenced by his *Divers Ditties Solacious.* No more direct and sincere love poems had yet been written in English. In his old age he called himself the "British Catullus." The historic parallel is close, if only because Catullus had dared satirize Julius Caesar in the height of his power, and displayed the heart of a true lover. Skelton writes with profound sadness to his unnamed Muse:

> Remorse have I of your most goodlihood,
>   Of your behaviour courteous and bening,
> Of your bountee and of your womanhood
>   Which maketh my heart oft to leap and spring
>   And to remember many a pretty thing;
> But absence, alas, with trembling fear and dread
> Abasheth me, albeit I have no need.

You I assurë, absence is my foe,
    My deadly woe, my painful heaviness.
And if ye list to know the cause why so,
    Open mine heart, behold my mind express! . . .
    I would ye could! Then should ye see, maistress,
How there nis thing that I covett so fain
As to embrace you in my armës twain.

    Nothing earthly to me more désiróus
    Than to behold your beauteous countenance.
But, hateful Absence to me so envious,
    Though thou withdraw me from her, by long distánce.
    Yet shall she never out of rémembránce—
For I have gravèd her within the secret wall
Of my true heart, to love her best of all.

His *Garland of Laurell* addresses to a bevy of young Court ladies,
are well known. To Margery Wentworth:

    With marjoram gentle
      The flower of goodlihood
    Embroidered the mantle
    Is of your maidenhood. . . .

To Margaret Hussy:

    Merry Margaret
    A midsummer flower
    Gentle as falcon
    Or hawk of the tower. . . .

(By the way, he gets his own back on Mistress Gertrude Statham,
with whom he has had a tiff:

    Though you were hard hearted
    And I with you thwarted
    With wordës that smarted. . . .

by wishing her the happy fate of Dame Pasiphaë—a cruel mythological reference which she will certainly have missed.)

Here I must distinguish, as I have done before, between devotees of Apollo and those of the Muse. Apollonian poetry is composed in the forepart of the mind: wittily, should the occasion serve, always reasonably, always on a preconceived plan, and derived from a close knowledge of rhetoric, prosody, Classical example, and contemporary fashion. It may, of course, disguise simple statement in masquerade dress, but if so, observes all masquerade conventions; whether the dress chosen be mediaeval doublet and hose, pastoral smock, Roman toga, or pseudo-Homeric armour. The Apollonian allows no personal emotions to obtrude, and no unexpected incident to break the smooth musical flow of his verse. The pleasure he offers is consciously aesthetic.

Muse poetry is composed at the back of the mind: an unaccountable product of a trance in which the emotions of love, fear, anger, or grief are profoundly engaged, though at the same time powerfully disciplined; in which intuitive thought reigns supralogically, and personal rhythm subdues metre to its purposes. The effect on readers of Muse poetry, with its opposite poles of ecstasy and melancholia, is what the French call a *frisson*, and the Scots call a "grue"—meaning the shudder provoked by fearful or supernatural experiences.

If every Englishman were content to undergo a normal education, work hard in a regular job, order his life reasonably, marry a sensible woman, pay his taxes when required, be socially co-operative and count himself happy in such well-doing, then there would be little need for Muse poets. This sort of Englishman has never, as a matter of fact, been typical of our race. But since he is widely assumed as typical, it may be argued on his behalf: "Should we not esteem accomplished Apollonian poems above these products of morbid psychology? If the formal discipline of verse can endow a concept with grace and memorability, should we not regard loyal odes to the Sovereign, celebrations of rural pleasure, epic accounts of heroic feats, elegies for the dead, and stately epithalamia, as worthy of the highest honour?"

My answer is: No reason at all, if you have never felt a grue or *frisson* in your life, never fallen desperately in love, never faced personal disaster, never questioned the religious tenets of your childhood—no reason whatsoever, except perhaps this practical one; that the flowery age which bred such exercises is now long over-blown. Apollonian masterpieces may still arouse historic interest, but they have lost contemporary relevance—ask any librarian or publisher what demand there is for them, unless as required school or college text-books, or as morocco-bound prizes. To be honest: the refinement of quick, clean prose down the centuries, encouraged by cheap printing and universal literacy, and with it the provision of countless sharper, brighter pleasures than were ever before known, has made the formal Apollonian poem a dead bore to all but specialists. There is still room in modern life for the epigram, the topical squib, the *memoria technica*, the rhymed advertisement; but for what else? That a distinguished English bard* has just published his autobiography in the form of a long blank-verse poem, does not weaken my contention: he is displaying once more his whimsical nostalgia for the irrecoverable past. But as the Apollonian poem fades away—despite bold attempts to revive its rhetoric by modernistic art-techniques borrowed from impressionism, expressionism, surrealism, or existentialism—so the Muse poem comes into its own.

Let me speak as a poet, rather than a professor—in mythical language. An ancient Greek prophecy is being fulfilled before our eyes. Apollo, the god of Science, having formed a palace conspiracy with his half-brother Hermes, god of Politics, and his uncle Plutos, god of Money, has emasculated Almighty Zeus with the same curved sickle, laid up at Sicilian Drepane, that Zeus used on his father Cronus. Zeus still remains propped on his throne, but a Regency Council of Three has taken over his powers. In this new anarchical era anything may happen. That the Divine Triumvirate are suspicious of one another, and that their rival ambitions have made them careless of mankind, is proved by the absurd cold war now being waged between East and West, with the massive resources of Science, Money, and Politics. They have cut civilization loose from its moorings: familiar coasts of orthodox religion, philosophy, and economics fade in the dusky distance. Crazy new cults are preached, old ones

* John Betjeman.

revived; ghosts supposedly laid centuries ago creep out of their graves, not only at dusk but by broad daylight. And the ancient sovereign Goddess, who has been waiting these last three thousand years to return with power, observes her opportunity. The political and economic emancipation of women, which was needed to implement Zeus's downfall, has had unforeseen consequences. Despite the successful conversion of a great many of them, especially business women and civil servants, not into matriarchs but into pseudo-patriarchs, a small but powerful minority find themselves free to be simply women, clear of male tutelage. With these newcomers woman's magical power over man, so long curbed, reappears in something of its primitive glory and ferociousness; and the uglier the anarchy caused by this demise of Father Zeus and the quarrels of his successors, the better become the Goddess' chances of persuading mankind that she can offer a wholesome change from the wholly negative cult of scientific pluto-democracy. It is possible, of course, that the Triumvirate will patch up their differences, make common cause, and try to hang the Goddess from the vault of Heaven once more, with anvils tied to her feet, which was Father Zeus's way; or banish her to a nunnery, which was the Church Fathers' way: but this can be no easy task. Meanwhile, Muse-poets who understand what is happening, and what is at stake, even more clearly perhaps than historians and anthropologists, can provide the emotional physic to which the rising generation, many of them painfully caught in the Goddess' net, will take recourse. . . . I hope I have not startled or offended you. My old friend Max Beerbohm made an even direr prophecy in his *Zuleika Dobson*: that of all young Oxford none but the ignoble Noakes shall be proof against the Goddess' cruel spell. . . . And that afterwards she will look up the trains for Cambridge.

Back to Skelton, whose era was also one of change: the Renaissance and the Breach with Rome having given the Muse a foothold at Court, which she kept until dislodged by Cromwell's Ironsides; and Skelton was her servant. It is true that, as priest, scholar, and Court official, he could not avoid writing ornate Apollonian verse in earnest of his professional capacities—as Catullus had done—but he did so with a covert half-smile at the understanding Muse. For example, his *Prayer to the Father of Heaven*:

O radiant Luminary of light intermináble,
  Celestial Father, potential God of might,
Of heaven and earth, O Lord incomparáble
  Of all perfections the essential most perfíte!
  O Maker of Mankind, that formèd day and night
Whose power imperial comprendeth every place—
  Mine heart, my mind, my thought, my whole delight
Is, after this life, to see thy glorious face.

Whose magnificence is incomprehensible,
  All arguments of reason which far doth exceed,
Whose Deity, doubtless, is indivisible,
  From whom all goodness and virtue doth proceed;
  Of Thy support all créatures have need.
Assist me, good Lord, and grant me of Thy grace
  To live to Thy pleasúre in wordë, thought and deed,
And, after this life, to see Thy glorious face.

Which leaves us dazzled, but cold; we even suspect that Skelton has been naughtily ambiguous in his "*potential* God of might," and in "Whose Deity, *doubtless*, is indivisible."

He also addressed the Second Person of the Trinity:

O bening Jesu, my sovereign Lord and King,
  The only Sonnë of God by filiation,
The Second Person, withouten béginning,
  Both God and man (our faith maketh relation)
  Mary, thy Mother, by way of incarnation—
Whose glorious passion our soulës doth revive
  Against all bodily and ghostly tribulation,
Defend me with thy piteous woundës five!

"Both God and man (our faith maketh relation)": another line of possible ambiguity. For Skelton had doubts about the Real Presence, if we can believe the story of a palfrey lent him by Bishop Stephen

Gardiner. Instead of returning the beast as desired, Skelton sent the Bishop a verse letter:

> Non meministi
> Quod mihi scripsisti
> De corpore Christi?
> Sic tibi rescribo
> De tuo palfrido:
> "Crede quod habes, et habes."

"Do you not remember what you wrote to me about Christ's body? I write back the same thing about your palfrey: 'Believe that you have it, and you have it.'"

Yet when Skelton adopts an ancient sacrificial theme inspired by the Goddess, his lines are emotionally aflame:

> Woefully arrayed
> And shamefully betrayed.
>   My blood, man,
>   For thee ran,
> It may not be nayed:
>   My body blue and wan
> Woefully arrayed. . . .
>
> Thus naked am I nailèd, O man, for thy sake.
> I love thee, then love me. Why sleepest thou? Awake!
> Remember my tender heart root for thee brake,
> With painès my veinès constrainèd to crake.
>   Thus tuggèd to and fro,
>   Thus wrappèd all in woe,
>   Whereas never man was so
> Entreated thus in most cruel wise:
> Was like a lamb offered in sacrifice,
>   Woefully arrayed.
>
> Of sharp thorn I have worn a crown on my head,
> So painèd, so stainèd, so rueful, so red:

Thus bobbèd, thus robbèd, thus for thy love dead,
Unfainèd not deignèd my blood for to shed.
  My feet and handës sore;
  The sturdy nailës bore;
  What might I suffer more
Than I have done, O man, for thee?
Come when thou list, welcome to me,
  Woefully arrayed.

But the flame dies down again, and flickers out in ecclesiastic homily:

Dear brother, no other thing I of thee desire
But give me thine heart free to reward mine hire.
I wrought thee, I bought thee from eternal fire.
I pray thee, array thee toward my high empire
  Above the orient
  Whereof I am regént
  Lord God Omnipotent,
With me to reign in endless wealth.
Remember, man, thy soulës health.

To banish from his nostrils the odour of incense and sweating Norfolk congregations, Skelton wrote *Philip Sparow*. He used Goliardic verses, blithely parodying the most sacred of Catholic Church rites: including the *Commendatio Animae,* the *Officium Defunctorum,* the *Missa pro Defunctis,* the *Absolutio super Tumulum;* and all in honour of Jane Scroop's pet sparrow eaten by the Convent cat at Carrow near Norwich. (It is, of course, an elaboration of the *Passer mortuus est meae puellae* by Catullus, whose *editio princeps* had been recently published.) Jane was not a little girl, as is often assumed, but a beauty in her early twenties; and Skelton, the middle-aged incumbent of nearby Diss, had fallen in love with her. He makes Jane dwell on tender memories of Philip's tricks and sports, and utter furious curses on the assassin:

Vengeance I ask and cry,
By way of exclamation,
On all the wholë nation

Of cats both wild and tame:
God send them sorrow and shame!
That cat especially
That slew most cruelly
My little pretty sparrow
That I brought up at Carrow. . . .
The léopards saváge,
The lions in their rage,
Might catch thee in their paws
And gnaw thee in their jaws;
The serpents of Libany
Might sting thee venomously;
The dragons with their tongues
Might poison thy liver and lungs;
The man-tigers of the mountaíns
Might feed them on thy brains . . .
Of Inde the greedy grypes
Might tear out all thy tripes;
Of Arcady the bears
Might pluck away thine ears;
The wild wolf Lycaon
Bite asunder thy back bone!
Of Etna the brenning hill
That day and night brenneth still
Set in thy tail a blaze
That all the world may gaze
And wonder upon thee,
From Ocean, the great sea,
Unto the Isles of Orcady,
From Tilbury Ferry
To the plain of Salisbury,
So traitorously my bird to kill
That never owed thee evil will. . . .

The humorous violence of this outburst is a measure of Skelton's true feelings for Jane, whom he here boldly deifies as the Muse herself! H. R. L. Edwards, a leading authority on Skelton, emphasizes that in the passage entitled *Commendations,* which is a direct praise

of Jane's beauty, he has substituted *Domina* for *Domine* in all his
Biblical quotations. "Deal bounteously with thy servant, that I may
live, and my lips shall praise thee. Teach me, Lady, the way of thy
statutes. As the hart panteth for the water brooks, so longeth my
soul for thee, Lady. Remember thy word to thy servant—and I am
thy servant." (John Donne similarly substituted *Domina* for *Domine*
in a Biblical quotation written above an early portrait, discovered
the other day, which shows him in a love-trance "with folded arms
and melancholy hat.") Skelton writes of his Muse:

> Her eyën grey and steep
> Causeth my heart to leap,
> With her browës bent
> She well may represent
> Fair Lucrece, as I ween,
> Or else fair Polyxene . . .
> Her beauty to augment
> Dame Nature hath her lent
> A wart upon her cheek
> That seemeth from afar
> Like to a radiant star—
> All with favour fret
> So properly is it set.
> She is the violet,
> The daisy déléctable
> The columbine cómmendáble
> The jélofer ámiáble.
> For this most goodly flour
> This blossom of fresh colóur
> (So Jupiter me secure)
> She flourisheth new and new,
> In beauty and virtúe,
> *Hac claritate gemina,*
> *O gloriosa femina,*
> *Bonitatem fecisti cum servo tuo, Domina,*
> *Et ex praecordiis sonant praeconia.*

> "Thou hast dealt kindly with thy servant, Lady,
> And from his heart rings out thy commendation."

Twenty years later, in his *Garland of Laurell* (1523), Skelton finds himself obliged to defend *Philip Sparow*: for although Jane originally asked him to write it, and although she fed his poetic flame, she now complains that he has insulted her—being by this time, alas, a respectable widow, relict of Thomas Brews, Esq., at whose side she lies on a funeral brass in the parish church of Little Wenham.

To know the Muse well, is to have experienced betrayal: the inevitable penalty of aspiring to her love. Skelton has not omitted to record this cruel aspect.

> "My darling dear, my daisy flour,
>   Let me," quoth he, "lie in your lap."
> "Lie still," quoth she, "my paramour,
>   Lie still, hardelý, and take a nap."
> His head was heavy, such was his hap,
> All drowsy dreaming, drowned in sleep,
> That of his love he took no keep,
>   With "lullay, lullay, like a child
>   Thou sleepst too long, thou art beguiled."
>
> With "ba, ba, ba," and "bas, bas, bas,"
>   She cherished him both cheek and chin,
> That he wist never where he was;
>   He had forgotten all deadly sin.
>   He wanted wit her love to win.
> He trusted her payment, and lost all his pay,
> She left him sleeping, and stole away
>   With "lullay lullay, like a child
>   Thou sleepst too long, thou art beguiled."
>
> The rivers rowth, the waters wan,
>   She sparèd not to wet her feet;
> She waded over, she found a man
>   Who halsèd her hartly and kissed her sweet.
>   Instead of a cold she caught an heat.
> "My love," she said, "rowteth in his bed.

Ywis he hath an heavy head"—
With "lullay lullay, like a child
Thou sleepst too long, thou art beguiled."

What more natural than that Skelton should have earned the opprobrium of two prime English Apollonians, Milton and Pope? Milton, in his *Areopagitica*, even wanted Skelton's works censored! His outrageous low-life satire, *The Tunning of Elinour Rumming*, was the excuse for their attacks; but they clearly resented his earthy humour, reckless courage, poetic independence, and dedication to a personal Muse. No Apollonian dares lampoon a public figure of Cardinal Wolsey's stature or parody Church ritual, or drink in country taverns with rogues and trollops, or publish scurrilous songs—nor does he wear CALLIOPE embroidered on his white and green Court dress. Though scorned as a mountebank, Skelton possessed higher scholarly distinctions than any of his traducers—degrees at Oxford, Cambridge (the only Laureate ever created there), and Louvain. The great Erasmus had hailed him in Latin verse as worthy of unfading laurels, as inspired by Calliope, sweeter-throated than the dying swan, the rival of Orpheus himself. Britain (Erasmus insisted) should admit that her debt to Skelton equals that of Greece to Homer, Mantua to Virgil; for it was he who first introduced the Muses to his fellow-countrymen, who first taught them to speak their own language accurately and purely.

This is of course hyperbole. Skelton never claimed to be the father of English poetry, and acknowledged his filial affection for Chaucer, Gower, and Lydgate; though, as he rightly pointed out, "they lacked the laurel": the emblem of learning in the humanities. He was, however, not only the first scholar to write popular English verse, but the first Muse-poet to appear in England. (I am well aware that Chaucer toyed with the artificial French tradition of courtly love in his prologue to *The Legend of Good Women*; but long association with City merchants while Comptroller of Customs made a cynic of him. In *Troilus and Cresyde*, he plainly aligns himself with Pandarus, who persuades his niece that fine words butter no parsnips, and that she should take a practical view of her future.) A study of the *Oxford English Dictionary* will show that Skelton enriched our vocabulary more than any other poet before or since, even Chaucer. He also wrote the teasing, inconsequential, passionate *Speake Parot!*—its rolling stanzas liberally sprinkled with polyglot pseudo-learning, which Professor Ian Gordon calls the first modernist poem in England. Yet it is cut wholly from native cloth, in native fashion, and makes perfect sense to the informed reader—none of which things can be said of twentieth-century Anglo-American modernism.

In the bibliography attached to his *Garland of Laurell*, Skelton characteristically not only lists such Apollonian works as *The Book of Honorous Estate, The Book of the Rosary, Dialogues of Imagination,* his translations of Cicero's *Ad Familiares* and Diodorus Siculus' *History*—but interlards them with his wilder extravagances:

Of Mannerly Mistress Margery Milk and Ale,
  To her he wrote many matters of mirth,
Yet (though I say it) thereby lieth a tale:
  For Margery wincèd and brake her hinder girth.
  Lord, how she made muchë of her gentle birth!
With "Gingerly, go gingerly!" Her tail was made of hay;
Go she never so gingerly, her honesty's gone away.

The Duke of York's creauncer when Skelton was,
  Now Henry the Eighth, King of Engeland,
A treatise he devised and brought it to pass,
  Called *Speculum Principis,* to bear in his hand,
  Therein to readë, and to understand
All the demeanour of princely estate
To be our King, of God preordinate.

Also *The Tunning of Elinour Rumming*
  With *Colin Clout, John Jew,* with *Joforth Jack.*
To make such trifles it asketh some cunning,
  In honest mirth, pardee, requireth no lack;
  The white appeareth the better for the black,
And after conveyance as the world goes
It is no folly to use the Welshman's hose.

"After conveyance as the world goes" means "since trickery is now in fashion"; "to use the Welshman's hose" means to take liberties with solemn texts—a Welshman's hose, like a shipman's hose, is one that will fit any leg.

> The umbles of venison, the bottle of wine,
>   To fair Mistress Anne that should have been sent,
> He wrote thereof full many a pretty line
>   Where it became, and whither it went,
>   And how that it was wantonly spent,
> The Ballad also of the Mustard Tart—
> Such problemës to paint, it 'longeth to this art.

Skelton could not repudiate the world unless perhaps by turning hermit like his saintly predecessor Richard Rolle of Hampole; and he enjoyed life too much for that. A dedicated poet is "a man as you be," who needs food, drink, lodging, and even domestic happiness—none of which benefits are bestowed on him without payment. But though he may make concessions to authority by wearing academic robes, or Court dress, or even a cassock, he must never smother poetic principle; must feel free to swap jokes with Mannerly Margery Milk and Ale, John Jew, Joforth Jack, Elinour Rumming, and "Mistress Kate, that farley sweet, Who wones at the Key in Thamës Street."

Dedicated poets cannot exist in a vacuum, discarding all tradition, all knowledge, rejecting society. They must be at least as well grounded as was Shakespeare, whose Petty School *A.B.C. with the Catechism,* his *Primer and Catechism,* his *Book of Common Prayer* and *Psalter,* assisted him later to a self-education in more readable works. But Shakespeare was a special case; and so was John Clare, who had an equally limited schooling. I believe that every poet should read our English Classics, master the main grammatic rules before daring to bend or break them; should travel abroad, be at ease among all sorts and conditions of men, and experience not only the horrors of thwarted passion but, if he is fortunate, the tranquil love of an honest woman. The supreme gift bestowed on him by the Muse is that of poetic humour: a grasp of the identity of opposites, the wearing of Welshman's hose. Sometimes, in fact, when a poem has been assiduously refined and refined under the white blaze of inspiration, its final draft becomes so perfect in its ambivalence as to make the poet humorously doubt whether the insertion of a simple "not" will perhaps improve it.

Good manners demand that visitors should respect the laws of whatever society has courteously entertained them—court, university, public house, or gipsy camp; and poets, by their nature, are perpetual visitors. Skelton, like Naaman, bowed in the House of Rimmon, his fingers humorously crossed. I piously follow his example; and look with disgust on the so-called beatnik poets whose boast is that they conduct themselves with equal bad manners in all societies.

Erasmus referred to Skelton as a *vates,* and the inscription on Skelton's tomb at St. Margaret's, Westminster, ran: *Joannes Skelton, vates Pierius, hic situs est. Vates,* though occurring as a conveniently spondaic synonym for *poeta* in the *Gradus ad Parnassum,* means a good deal more than "poet." A *vates* is a prophet, one divinely possessed; one who must speak the truth, however strange or distasteful, and is sometimes granted visions both of the future and the past. *Pierian* means a native of Pieria, the district lying below Olympus, which was the birthplace not only of the poet Orpheus, but of the Ninefold Muse herself. The true Pierian limits his loyalties to those reconcilable with his worship of the Goddess "Whose service is perfect freedom"—a phrase, oddly enough, borrowed by St. Augustine from Apuleius' address to Isis, and by Thomas Cranmer from St. Augustine. The fewer the poet's affiliations, political, social, ecclesiastical, or scholastic, the better his chances of doing good work. Every gainful trade or profession has its characteristic occupational deformity: I have already mentioned Chaucer's Comptrollership of Customs. Shakespeare even regretted his actor-managership, complaining in a sonnet that the player's hand was dyed by it. And to avoid adopting a gainful trade or profession is difficult. Nevertheless, so long as a poet distinguishes Love from Remedy, and Wisdom from Learning; so long as he expects no rewards from the Muse nor any pity, never allows his business or domestic affairs to erase her name from the "secret wall of his true heart," never enlarges his public figure at the expense of his private self, the poetic trance may recur, from time to time, throughout his life. "Poor Devil" or "Lucky Devil"; it does not matter which you call him—the coin spins evenly.

Poets who decide to live by poetry, and remain otherwise uncommitted, should not understand "live by" in a financial sense. Until yesterday, or the day before, they were tempted to graduate as major poets—all Muse poetry is minor poetry, if length be the criterion—by writing verse plays or long philosophical works destined for posterity. Apollo would make them rich and famous, would secure them an honourable place in the curriculum—even name Ages after them. As I wrote once: "To invoke posterity is to weep on your own grave."

> And the punishment is fixed:
> To be found fully ancestral,
> To be cast in bronze for a city square,
> To dribble green in times of rain
> And stain the pedestal.
>
> Spiders in the spread beard;
> A life proverbial
> On clergy lips a-cackle;
> Eponymous institutes,
> Their luckless architecture.
>
> Two more dates of life and birth
> For the hour of special study
> From which all boys and girls of mettle
> Twice a week play truant
> And worn excuses try. . . .

Skelton pictures himself in *The Garland of Laurell* as conducted triumphantly to the Hall of Fame, where a whole crowd of authors—including such second-raters as Aulus Gellius, Sallust, Quinctilian, Quintus Curtius, Macrobius, Propertius, Poggio, and John Bochas—wait to greet him. Yet this is an elaborate joke against himself. Skelton knew just how good his writing was, and though he may have expected to live posthumously "where breath most breathes, even in the mouths of men" (a thought later borrowed by Shakespeare from Ennius), he cannot have been unaware that the mouths of men are highly unselective: filled with worthless tags from the least worthy of Apollonians—and even from anti-poets.

The Anti-Poet

In my first address, a *captatio benevolentiae* suitable to the occasion, I spoke about the dedicated Muse poet, taking John Skelton as my chief example. Today, secure I hope in this captured benevolence, I shall deal with the Apollonian anti-poet, his precise opposite; and though this will break an eight-hundred-year-old academic tradition at Oxford, my example must be Publius Virgilius Maro, *alias* Virgil, who has for two thousand years exercised an influence over Western culture out of all proportion to his merits either as a human being or as a poet. Virgil's pliability; his subservience; his narrowness; his denial of that stubborn imaginative freedom that the true poets who preceded him had valued; his perfect lack of originality, courage, humour, or even animal spirits—these were the negative qualities which first commended him to government circles, and have kept him in public favour ever since.

A brief biography. Virgil was born (70 B.C.) at Andes, a marshland village near Mantua, in Transpadine Gaul. Although of military age when Julius Caesar's legions crossed the Rubicon and swept through the province, this dark-complexioned, heavily-built man

never bore arms either for or against Caesar: a weak digestion, a delicate throat, bleeding piles and frequent headaches offered sufficient
excuse. He avoided the loud, obscene tavern talk of military friends,
and his girlish shyness presently earned him the nickname "Parthe-
nias" ("the maiden"). Virgil's father, a bee-keeper and hired man to a
magistrate's clerk, had succeeded in marrying the clerk's daughter;
which helped him to improve his property by buying up woodlands
and selling the timber.

Virgil attended school at near-by Cremona, and there discovered a
facility for versification. Beginning on epigrams, he was soon penning
narrative pieces of some length. From Cremona the proud family sent
him to Milan; thence to Naples, where he studied Greek, the language of higher education; and finally to Rome, where he completed his rhetorical studies under the best available professor: Syron
the Epicurean. If Virgil's Greek was rather poor, as his occasional
misrenderings of Homer prove, this must be pardoned him: a course
at Athens would have been beyond the family's means.

Two centuries before, Greek rhetoric and poetry had been imported
to Rome and, by Virgil's day, young Roman noblemen usually
travelled abroad to study. Though more attracted to rhetoric, as a
means of political advancement, than to poetry, they could not avoid
the required course in Poetics, which meant learning by heart as
much as possible of Homer's *Iliad* and *Odyssey*. They thus became
aware of the strict Greek laws governing scansion. Their own native
Saturnian metre, as handled by Naevius, the father of Latin poetry,
enjoyed so much rhythmic freedom that it now looked barbarous to
them—like the old Roman habit of building temples by eye, not by
the rules of geometry, mensuration and the Golden Section. They
could hardly point to a single "normal" line in all Naevius, whose
scansion was accentual as opposed to quantitative. That is: instead
of depending, as Homer did, on the calculated length of each syllable
(doomed to be either short or long), and allowing so many short or
long syllables to each foot, Naevius depended on the natural stresses
of speech—as in English ballad poetry. That the same word could
be accentuated differently in different parts of the same poem, chang-

ing from short to long and back again according to stress, seemed
arbitrary and illogical to these Roman students.

They shamefacedly renounced their natural ballad inheritance and
went all Greek. Naevius found no literary successors. Depressed by
the encroachment of Greek and a gradual falling-off in the standard
of pure colloquial Latin, he had written his own epitaph, as a slow
march:

> Mortales immortales
> Flere si foret fas,
> Flerent divae Caménae
> Naevium poetam.

Itaque:

> Postquam est Orcino
> Traditus thesauro
> Obliti sunt Romae
> Loquier Latina lingua.

which means:

> Were deathless gods permitted
> Weeping for dead mortals,
> Each Muse divine would weep for
> Naevius, her poet.

And so:

> Since to Hell's own storehouse
> He has been committed,
> Rome is grown forgetful
> Of her native Latin language.

Ennius, the first Roman (so far as I know) to experiment
with a quantitative hexameter, became the stepfather of Latin
poetry; educating it by sternly suppressing its natural inclinations.

304 ON POETRY: COLLECTED TALKS AND ESSAYS

The results will, at first, have sounded as comic as those English ones which Edmund Spenser composed:

> Nŏble Alĕxāndĕr//when he cāme to the tŏmb of Achīllēs
> Sīghing spăke with a bīg//voīce ō thrīce blēssèd Achīllēs
> Thăt such a trŭmp, sō grēat//sō lŏud sō glōrious hăst fŏund
> As the renŏwnēd ănd, sūrprīsīng ārch-poet Hōmer!

Fortunately, the attempt to force English poetry into a Classical strait-jacket failed. George Chapman wrote, in his *Shadow of Night*:

> . . . Sweet poesy
> Will not be clad, in her supremacy.
> With those strange garments (Rome's hexameters)
> As she is English; but in right prefers
> Our native robes (put on with skilful hands—
> English heroics) to those antique garlands.

In establishing his new metre, Ennius had to create a special poetic vocabulary of dialect or obsolete forms to assist versification. His trouble was that a number of Latin words were excluded by their scansion from the hexameter. I have elsewhere instanced the famous Roman name Domitius Ahenobarbus. "Domitius" contains four short syllables in a row, and "Ahenobarbus" has a short syllable hopelessly imprisoned between two long ones. So if one wished to write the hexameter: "And Domitius Ahenobarbus also came," the only way out would be to address him in the vocative—*Domiti*—which is a manageable word; and to use the historical present for "came"; and to explain "Ahenobarbus" as meaning "Brazen Beard":

> Tū-que venīs, Domitī, quēm sīgnat ahēnea bārba . . .
>
> (And thou comest also, Domitius, whom a brazen
> beard distinguishes.)

And because the word *āudiŭnt* ("they hear") cannot be used in a hexameter, third persons plural must always "perceive with their ears," *aūrīs pērcipiūnt* instead of simply "hearing," or use the past tense.

Virgil employed numerous other tricks and evasions for supplying manageable words. Also, as I shall show, he further divorced poetry from common sense by the exploitation of "poetic licence." An "olde worlde" vocabulary, unnatural grammatic inversions, and poetic licence were among the many curses bequeathed to English Apollonian poetry by the Virgil cult. Nevertheless Latin accentual verse remained fixed in popular song—the Legions used it—and eventually triumphed in such sacred chants as *Dies irae, Dies illa* and in drinking songs like *Mihi est propositum in taberna mori.*

Virgil's four principal predecessors, the poets Naevius, Ennius, Lucretius and Catullus, were men of determination, and had something urgent to say. Naevius, a First Punic War veteran, satirized the haughty Metellians who then dominated Rome, and served a prison sentence for it. Ennius fought as an infantry captain in Sicily and re-engaged for the Aetolian campaign; his surviving verse fragments show a tough spirit and imaginative magnificence. A gap of more than a century separated Ennius from Virgil's elder contemporaries Lucretius and Catullus.

Lucretius, a forthright Calabrian provincial, used Ennian hexameters, now at last naturalized, for preaching scientific godlessness to the religious-minded Romans. Since he chose a most difficult theme, *The Nature of Things,* and since Latin was still singularly barren of abstract words, he faced linguistic problems that had not troubled Ennius; but his passion often broke through the philosophic argument in lines of unmistakable beauty.

Catullus, a young Veronese nobleman, had learned from the Alexandrian critics that all long poems have their boring passages, and that to bore is the worst crime a poet can commit. He therefore wrote no epics, constantly varied his metres, and did not let metrical difficulties thwart the plain sense of a poem by driving him to clever periphrasis. Catullus lived a violent, gay life at Rome, often running into debt, and expressed his loves, hates, griefs and bawdy humour with absolute freedom. While admiring Julius Caesar, he dared publish two most offensive lampoons on him.

The timorous, inoffensive Virgil, in contrast, found so little to say of personal value that the themes of both his best-known poems, *The Georgics* and *The Aeneid,* were forced on him by patrons. He never lampooned those in power, and never got into scrapes. He bartered his talent for social security; and wrote only hexameters—to which, for the sake of elegance, he applied new constrictive rules. Nor did he ever invent where he could borrow. Quintus Octavius Avitus later published an eight-volume collection of Virgil's plagiarisms—sources and all—but this ranked as no demerit in official quarters, so long as the sources were Greek classics. And when accused of filching from Homer, Virgil replied disarmingly: "Why don't my critics try to follow my example? They will find it no easier than to steal Hercules' club." He had also plagiarized Latin contemporaries, including Parthenius, his old Bithynian schoolmaster; for no Roman copyright laws restrained him.

Thus, further evil bequests of Virgil's have been the notions that borrowing from the classics proves a poet's modesty and good sense; and that style is more important than subject. And, though verse epics have ceased to be fashionable, clever poets of the Establishment are still Virgilian enough to conceal recondite Classical beauties in their works, for the well-read reader to greet with self-satisfied smirks.

To resume the brief biography. One of Virgil's early poems, *The Gnat,* has survived. This is the plot: a certain shepherd falls asleep and is warned of a poisonous snake approaching him by a gnat, which impulsively stings his forehead. He flattens the gnat with a blow of his fist, and by good luck kills the snake at the same time. Then he builds the gnat a tomb, inscribing on it this touching epitaph:

> Poor little gnat, well-deserving! The guardian shepherd
>   now offers,
> Grateful for this kind gift, due funeral rites at your
>   tombstone.

Dissatisfied with such trifling, Virgil felt called upon to versify Roman history; perhaps because in 49 B.C., when he was twenty years old, a decree had given full Roman citizenship to all towns of the province.

Five years later, a fortunate accident launched him into fame. His family were threatened with forcible eviction from the farm at Andes by discharged veterans of Caesar's—they were planting a colony between Cremona and Mantua. The story can be read in Virgil's *Eclogues*, which are drawing-room pastorals based on the *Idylls* of Theocritus. First, he appeals for help to the poet Cornelius Gallus, who has studied beside him at Rome under Syron; and Gallus, now one of the triumvirate who have distributed land among these veterans, recommends Virgil to Asinius Pollio, the bookish Provincial Governor. "Ah, so you are a poet, too, my dear fellow?" we can hear Pollio saying. "Our common acquaintance Gallus mentions your talent, in this note. Let me see if it will justify our intervention!" Virgil hands Pollio his patriotic verses. They pass muster, and Virgil's plea is granted.

We next find him admitted to Pollio's *salon* and dutifully applauding his tragedies, though so dry-as-dust an orator can hardly have been much livelier as a poet. Virgil stood on the same easy terms with Gallus. Times had changed. The noble Scipio Africanus, who supported Polybius the historian and Terence the playwright, kept these gifted commoners at a certain distance. But when Julius Caesar broke social conventions, choosing his friends for their usefulness to him, not for their birth, all barriers were down. Gallus himself was a "New Man," the grandson of an emancipated slave from Fréjus.

Pollio's command passes to Alfenus Varus (whom commentators have confused with one Atius Varus, and make a former fellow-student of Virgil's), and Virgil hears that the farm is threatened again. He appeals for Varus' help, in an ecloque; but Varus replies that he can do nothing. Gallus then investigates the case on Virgil's behalf, accuses a local magistrate at Cremona of allowing veterans to occupy lands not mentioned in the grant, and sends Virgil with his plea directly to the Supreme Court; where Augustus decides in his favour. Virgil's eclogue of acknowledgment proffers Augustus divine honours. Later, Varus brazenly asks Virgil to make good a promise that, if he regains the property, "vocal swans shall bear thy name, Varus, to the skies!" The matter has now been arranged,

Varus says, so will Virgil please celebrate his military exploits? Not wishing to offend Pollio and Gallus by flattering the unhelpful Varus at their expense, or to offend Varus by a direct refusal, Virgil borrows a polite formula of evasion from the Alexandrian poet Callimachus. He is at present writing only pastorals, he says, "having ceased to sing of wars and kings." And a shepherd, though he may feed his flock until they are fat, slow and heavy, must not let the same thing happen to his poems—by adopting the heroic style. However, he adds, Varus will find numerous poets eager to undertake this worthy task.

One eclogue condoles with Gallus on the loss of his beloved mistress, a stage singer. Commentators inform us that she was Lycoris, in whose praise Gallus had written a whole volume of elegiac poems, and that she deserted him for the protection of Mark Antony, Augustus' powerful colleague and rival. Since, according to Suetonius' *Life of Virgil*, Virgil's *Eclogues* were stage successes, it has been plausibly suggested that Lycoris sang them. And that the provincials in applauding her were applauding her protector—and their own.

In another piece, Virgil sympathizes with the middle-aged Pollio for having failed to seduce a handsome boy. It was genuine sympathy, not toad-eating, because (Suetonius reports) Virgil himself suffered from pederastic passion. His particular favourite was an educated slave, afterwards given him by Pollio, whom he has celebrated in an eclogue as "Daphnis"; and his second favourite was young Cebes—another slave, but a poet in his own right.

Virgil encourages Pollio's perversion and applauds his tragedies. Probably he reads them aloud—"the poet Montanus," Suetonius remarks, "used to declare that verses which convinced the audience when Virgil read them with his beautiful voice, wonderful facial expression, and dramatic power, sounded flat and toneless from another's lips." We also learn that when Lucius Varus, the poet, tried to cure Virgil of his inveterate homosexuality by arranging for him to get into bed with one Plotia Hieria, he shrank from the ordeal horror-stricken.

This takes us, in our worldly wisdom, a little further. It has long been a habit of actresses and high-class courtesans to choose gentle, lonely half-men as their confidantes, and we may suppose that

Gallus, when busy at his magistrate's court or army headquarters, engaged Virgil to act as Lycoris' escort. A practical argument against heterosexual passion and rough male brawling occurs in his *Fourth Georgic:*

> But nothing so strengthens the power of a male animal, whether stallion or bull, as to restrain him from desire. A bull is therefore banished to lonely pastures beyond a hill or river; for the sight of a female slowly wastes his strength and, what is more, she often drives her proud lovers to settle their differences with clash of horns.

Virgil's fear of destructive females explains Juno, Aeneas' persecutrix in the *Aeneid;* also the savage vilification of Cleopatra, Mark Antony's seductress; and Aeneas' scarcely controlled impulse to butcher Helen of Troy.

Virgil spent three years on the *Eclogues,* before climbing into an even higher social sphere. He secured the patronage of Maecenas, Minister of Literature, Propaganda, and the Fine Arts, who had been Gallus' contact at Court when Virgil took his plea there. In 39 B.C., Maecenas, though admiring the elegance of the *Eclogues,* asked Virgil to write on a less trivial theme. Unwilling to risk his neck by attempting political projects—the quarrel between Augustus and Mark Antony was still undecided—Virgil compromised by agreeing, instead, to write a long poem in aid of agriculture. "Very well, my friend," says Maecenas, "you have proved yourself the Latin Theocritus. Now become the Latin Hesiod! Write Georgics."

Virgil had left the farm at too early an age to have acquired any practical knowledge of agriculture; and Hesiod, a sour, pessimistic, litigious Greek peasant who believed, like the author of *Genesis,* that God had invented work as a curse upon mankind, was no soulmate of Virgil's. Moreover, Hesiod's *Work and Days* provided material for only the First Book of *Georgics.* He stuck at this point until, two years later, by good fortune, the famous Roman know-all Varro began to publish a *Treatise on Agriculture.* Virgil then quarried from Varro, and from Cato's *Rustic Economy.* Though having also collected such copious Greek reference works as Aristotle's *Zoology,* Nicander's *Bestiary,* Theophrastus' *Botony,* and Eratosthenes' *As-*

tronomy, he found his task heavy enough going, and took seven years to finish it—at the average rate of one line a day. Even so, I suspect that clever little Cebes drafted plenty of them.

Nobody (except Virgil himself, in a suppressed but extant foreword to the *Aeneid*) has ever called the *Georgics* a "useful work for farmers." They come little closer to real life than the *Eclogues*. Seneca observes: "His aim is not truth but beauty; not agricultural information but literary pleasure." Guided by Virgil, the Roman city dweller could dream about simple rural joys, and feel himself at one with his farming ancestors—even if he had never in his existence handled a hoe, milked a goat, or tended more than an ornamental window-box. This waiving of factual truth has since become fixed in the popular imagination as "poetic"; and few poets have escaped the taint.

An obstinate late-Victorian tradition praises the *Georgics* for upholding the "dignity of labour," for expressing "a devotion to Rome founded on local devotion to a particular region, village, family, farm," and for reminding absentee landlords of their duty to the soil. But no modern historian can accept Virgil's picture of stout Roman yeomen ploughing ancestral acres, secure in their title-deeds, proud of gnarled parents and sturdy sons, offering pious sacrifices to old-fashioned rustic gods. "Peasants are not tempted by luxury," Virgil claims. "Justice reigns among them, and the daily round perfects their morals." A more honest poet would have anticipated Goldsmith's *Deserted Village,* in distress that Augustus' victories had dealt another heavy blow to traditional Italian agriculture by further encouraging the growth of large estates run on slave labour. Smallholders could no longer compete against the low prices at which estate owners marketed their produce. They must sell out and join the dole-collecting city rabble, or starve, or find employment as estate foremen.

"Labour conquers all!" exults Virgil, using "labour" in its most idealistic sense. Yet when he himself grew weary of Rome's noise and bustle, did he return to the family farm at Andes and sacrifice unblemished lambs of his own raising to Pales, Faunus and Picus? Indeed, no! He bought a slave-run estate at fashionable Nola, Augustus' birthplace. . . . The polished *Georgics* make simple, quaint reading where Virgil has versified the works of Cato or Varro; but here is his address to the sturdy yeomen whom he has just been lecturing on cattle-raising:

Sed fugit interea, fugit inreparabile tempus . . .

But time meanwhile is flying, flying beyond recall, while we, charmed with love of our theme, linger around each detail! Enough, now, for the herds; there remains the second part of my task, namely to describe the tending of fleecy flocks and shaggy goats. In this theme lies labour, hence hope of fame, my sturdy yeomen! And though well I know how hard it is for me to win a triumph here by crowning a lowly theme with glory, yet sweet ambition hurries me up the lonely steeps of Parnassus. How joyful it is to roam over heights where no forerunner's track slopes gently down to the Castalian spring . . .

As if the struggling peasant would care a sesterce what fame this patronizing city-man earned!

Virgil continues his lecture:

First, then, I decree that [when winter hardens] your sheep shall crop the herbage in soft pens, till leafy summer soon returns, and that you strew the hard ground beneath them with straw and handfuls of fern, lest the chill ice harm the tender flock, bringing scab and unsightly foot-rot . . .

The omissions from the Georgics are significant of complete disinterest in Virgil's ostensible theme. For example, when Varro's Treatise on Agriculture gives advice on the care of asses, pigs, and hens, Virgil hurriedly turns the page: Maecenas will not consider such topics idyllic enough. Instead, he goes elsewhere to borrow a fine purple passage about race horses, which should please the Roman Hippodrome audience—although well aware that horses formed no part of peasant economy.

Augustus, returning in triumph from Actium, paused at Atella to cure an infected throat, and there Virgil read the Georgics to him on four successive days, Maecenas taking over whenever Virgil grew hoarse or faint. Since four days of this monotonous entertainment seems a long time for a busy man to endure, we must suppose his interest to have been neither poetic nor agricultural. Rather, he was pondering Maecenas' view that Latin literature could at last challenge Greek in all fields, except the Homeric corpus of epic poetry, and that this field must likewise be conquered. Virgil, already Rome's Theocritus, had now improved on Hesiod, and would be just the man to write the official Roman epic, glorifying the divinely-descended Caesars as fated rulers of the world. The *Georgics* brought Augustus over to Maecenas' view; and Virgil hitherto reluctant to "sing of wars and kings" and "to feed his sheep until fat, slow and heavy," dared not flout the sacred wish. He accepted the *Aeneid* commission, though plainly finding this a most uncongenial task.

"Make it a mirror of both the *Iliad* and the *Odyssey*," says Maecenas. "You can draw heavily on those two, and on our own poetical history—Aeneas' visit to Dido, for example, has been celebrated by Naevius and Ennius—and on the historians Dionysius, Hellanicus, Timaeus, Cato and Varro. I can lend you the scrolls. But in describing Aeneas' struggle against the natives of Italy, try to give no offence: foreshadow the present era when every Italian is proud to call himself a Roman. Meanwhile, the Emperor will maintain you worthily. How would you like a house on the Esquiline Hill, near my gardens? . . . I trust you to sound the correct note: an appeal for national unity, peace and hard work under the aegis of Augustus Caesar, incarnate God of Success!"

Thereupon, so Suetonius tells us, Virgil drafted a prose version of the *Aeneid*, which he slowly turned into verse: dodging from book to book, as the fancy took him. He chose the easiest options first. Four years afterwards (27 B.C.) Augustus wrote from Spain demanding extracts, but Virgil excused himself: no book was ready, he answered, and he felt a fool to have undertaken so ambitious a work, especially when faced with the arduous commission of modelling his epic on far more distinguished ones. He did not mention other troubles: that ancient Roman history was a hopeless jumble of irreconcilabilities, and that he found it hard to hit upon a legend decently eulogizing Augustus' ancestor Aeneas—who, the mythographers agreed, had betrayed his overlord King Priam, and sold Troy to the Greeks at the price of a safe-conduct through their lines.

In 24 B.C., the poet Propertius gave the *Aeneid* advance publicity:

> Yield, Roman writers; yield, you Greeks; for now
> A greater than the *Iliad* has been born!

And, by the seventh year, Virgil had (like a she-bear with her cub—his own expression) licked the Second, Fourth and Sixth Books into a fairly presentable shape, and read them to Augustus. Those later books about the wars in Italy must have been a dreary assignment; but he could not avoid it. Ignorant of soldiering, he flavoured passages from Roman legend with imitations from the *Iliad,* the *Odyssey,* and Apollonius' *Argonautica.* In the *Iliad,* Achilles' horses shed tears when Patroclus dies, so in the *Aeneid* Pallas' team do the same; and the god Hephaestus forges picturesque arms for Achilles, so the god Vulcan forges even better ones for Aeneas. Virgil's chief delight was to mourn beautiful boys cut off in the flower of their youth—ah, what a waste!

> Euryalus rolls over in death. Athwart his lovely limbs runs the blood—and his drooping neck sinks on his shoulder. As when a purple flower lopped by the plough-share droops in death, or as when poppies with weary neck bow the head when weighted by some chance shower . . .

I find this much-admired passage poetically inept. Poetry must be practical. Once blood has suffused Euryalus' limbs, the purple or scarlet colour of the flower should not be stressed; after all, Euryalus' head was uninjured, and would have grown pallid in comparison with his bloody limbs. Also, the simile is false: when the root of a plant has been sliced by a plough-share, its flower gradually droops; a lopped flower, however, has no chance to do so. The alternative simile of the poppy weighted down by rain comes straight from the *Iliad*, but Virgil spoils it, changing "poppy" to "poppies," which scan better. (How hard to filch from Homer!)

Virgil's handling of the Dido and Aeneas episode reveals his character. When Aeneas' fleet reaches Carthage, Queen Dido and he fall in love with each other. But this is a mere stratagem arranged by the Goddess Venus, his mother, to protect the Trojan refugees from massacre; and Aeneas is willing to desert Dido as soon as high destiny orders a resumption of his interrupted voyage. Dido utters a passionate plea for him to stay. Aeneas answers (to quote my old schoolmaster, Mr. T. E. Page) "with the cold and formal rhetoric of an attorney." Dido, after another hysterical outburst, sinks distraught into her attendants' arms. Aeneas, stammering and "ready to say a great deal more," makes a disgusted exit. T. E. Page indignantly describes the next paragraph, which begins: *"But the good Aeneas . . ."* as one of the puzzles of literature.

I cannot agree. Women, except comfortable kindly matrons (Venus always appears to Virgil in maternal, never in erotic, guise) or sexless Amazons like the Italian heroine Camilla, left him cold; hysterics frightened him. But here is a real puzzle of literature: Aeneas' son Ascanius, when bribing Nisus to undertake a raid, promises him not twelve beautiful captive princesses skilled in all the arts, as in the *Iliad*, but "twelve captive mothers!" What on earth would Nisus want with twelve? Men of Virgil's temperament notoriously welcome a broad black-satin bosom to sob upon; yet surely *one* captive mother would have sufficed?

Commenting on the scene where Aeneas subsequently meets Dido in Hell, one of our senior literary church-wardens* has written:

> Virgil excuses himself: "I was under the God's orders," he says. "I didn't want to do it. I am sorry you took it so hard." Dido avoids his gaze and turns away, with a face like flint. I have no doubt that Virgil when he wrote these lines, was assuming the rôle of Aeneas and feeling decidedly a worm.

* T. S. Eliot.

Yet anyone who reads the passage carefully, will see that Aeneas, so far from feeling a worm, was spitefully getting his own back on Dido. He found her in the close, if shadowy, embrace of her former husband Sychaeus (or Sicharbas), who remained as yet unaware that she had injured his memory by a crazy love affair. Aeneas, a cad to the last, insults them both by bringing up the shameful adventure under cover of an apology. What is more, we learn from Justin, Servius, and Silius Italicus that Virgil is grossly libelling womankind. The original Punic legend makes Dido pursued in her widowhood by the Libyan prince Hiarbas, who offers her the choice of marriage or death. She sacrifices victims to the shade of her husband, and bravely leaps on her own funeral pyre. St. Jerome comments drily: "St. Paul thought it better to marry than to burn; Dido disagreed."

> Conticuere omnes, intenti-que ora tenebant . . .
> (They kept silence and, being attentive, held their mouths.)

This hexameter, which opens Book Two, was the first line of the *Aeneid* that Augustus heard Virgil recite. Reading it again, after a lapse of fifty years, I seemed to be back at Charterhouse, teasing gentle old Tommy Page, the Sixth Form Beak: "*Who* all kept silent, sir? And why write the same thing in two different ways? . . . Yes, sir, I know—the *notes* say that 'all' means Dido's courtiers; but why doesn't Virgil?"

Tommy replies: "You suggest, my boy, that he might have written straight out:

> Intenti comites Didonis conticuerunt . . .
> (Dido's courtiers preserved an attentive silence.)

"Well, Virgil, as it happens, thought that Lucretius and Homer, who did not mind ending a hexameter line with a single, five-syllabled verb, were inelegant; so *conticuerunt* had to begin the line and take the poetic form of *conticuere*. That suggested *onmes* as a means of removing the final 'e' by elision—*conticuer' onmes*. Virgil's readers could be allowed to guess at the meaning of *onmes*, in return for the elegant trope, borrowed perhaps from the Orient, and often miscalled *hendiadys,* of saying the same thing, differently, twice over. He uses it several times, you'll have noticed, when telling us about the Wooden Horse. The Greeks 'enclose chosen bodies of men in the sides of the horse' *and fill the mighty central cavern with armed soldiers.* When they have sailed away, the Trojans 'find the Greek camp deserted' *and the shore abandoned.* Thymoetes then orders the Trojans to push into the sea 'the wiles of the Greeks' *and the gifts they suspected* (but that's true *hendiadys,* not repetition); whereupon Laocoon hurls his spear 'into the side' *and the carved flank* of the animal; as a result of which *the stomach being struck,* its 'hollow interior makes a sound' *and the caverns groan."*

"Thank you, sir! Another thing we can't make out is what wood the Trojan Horse was really built of."

"Fir, my boy. Line 16."

"Yes, sir, it's fir in line 16, but it's maple in line 112, and oak in line 186, and pine in line 258, and oak again in line 280 . . ."

"Yes, now I remember. But in Virgil's time a poet was licenced to use any particular sort of timber as a synonym for timber generally, even if it involved him, as here, in apparent contradictions."

"Thank you again, sir!"

The child has been father to the man. My adult eye is offended by numerous other examples of poetic bad manners in the same passage, such as the verse-endings *sanguine cretus* and *cum sanguine poscunt* occurring close together, although *sanguine* means "lineage" in the first case, and "bloodshed" in the second—a similarity without relevance. And *fatur* ending one line, and *fatebor* the next; again a similarity without relevance. And three ugly lines all appearing on the same page:

Illi me comit[em] et: consanguinitate propinquum . . .
Promis[i]ultor[em] et: verbis odi[a] aspera movi . . .
Hoc Ithacus velit et: magno mercentur Atridae . . .

The English equivalent would be:

> Me as his tent-fellow *and* related to him by a blood-tie . . .
> Vengeance I promised him *and* caused hate by my eloquent rough-
> ness . . .
> Pleasing the Ithacan, *and* the Atreidae would handsomely pay
> you . . .

Homer, when he wielded this stately measure, never left an *and*
suspended in the air at the end of his half-line!

Also I come across such meaningless, if elegant, rhetoric as:

> . . . jam nox umida caelo
> Praecipitat, suadent-que cadentia sidera somnos.
> (Now damp night precipitates itself from the sky, and the descend-
> ing stars encourage sleep.)

"Damp night" probably refers to dew; but does the word *praecipitat*
mean that night is falling (as we English say)? Or does it, as in
Cicero and Ovid, mean that night is drawing to a close? The
context will not help us, neither will "descending stars": because
all night long some stars dip towards the Eastern horizon, just as
all night long others rise from the West. But the *Homeristae* had,
for centuries, made a profession of commenting on Homeric problems,
and now *Virgilistae* were herewith invited to a fresh banquet of
commentary.

When Virgil died at the age of fifty-one, worth something like
a quarter of a million pounds in modern money, the *Aeneid* was
complete but not yet published. Conscious of its defects, and perhaps
even (let us be fair to him) repentant, he asked his executors to
burn the manuscript. Augustus, of course, would not permit that.
Having invested heavily in the production, he ordered it to be published without delay. Rome chorused approval, and soon Caecilius
Epirota had fixed Virgil in the Latin school curiculum, where he
has remained ever since. The one discordant note was struck by

tough old Vipsanius Agrippa, who had not only won the Battle of Actium for Augustus, but settled the Spanish War, restored peace to Gaul, overawed Pontus, and conciliated the Jews. He said bluntly: "Virgil, a poet first foisted on us by Maecenas, has invented a new bad way of imitating the classics. Neither bombastic nor dry, he employs a restrained poetic vocabulary, which makes his failings less obvious."

Anchises' prophecy in the Sixth Book beginning *Excudent alii*, a favourite declamation of imperialists who consider themselves heirs of Augustan Rome, awards the Greeks credit for greater eloquence than the Romans in pleading causes. Unfair! Latin eloquence, as exemplified by Cicero, could give Demosthenes himself points. Virgil never mentions Cicero—even when Catilina the Criminal, whose revolt Cicero crushed, is prophetically portrayed on the shield of Aeneas; but caricatures him as the abominable "Drances" in the Eleventh Book. Cicero, it must be remembered, who upheld constitutional Republican government, had fallen a victim to Augustus' rough justice. And Virgil himself, on the sole occasion that he pleaded in a Court of Law had, Suetonius says, made a mess of things by speaking "hesitatingly and like an uneducated rustic."

But why should the name of Julius Caesar, Augustus' great-uncle and adoptive father, not be mentioned in the *Aeneid*, either? Was not Julius the most gifted, heroic and magnanimous of all Aeneas' descendants—a supreme orator, too—and the only one who had yet been deified? An oblique reference occurs in Anchises' complaint that one of the Aeneadae is destined to take up arms against his own son-in-law (Pompey), and imbrue the soil with Roman blood. Here Virgil has pandered to Augustus' envy of Julius' wider fame; and makes a pretence of forgetting that Augustus fought a civil war against his brother-in-law Mark Antony. Augustus is oddly hailed as "The Prince of Peace." True, he established peace—by hunting down the last of his Republican opponents. But the divine mystique which Virgil helped to perpetuate for him and his heirs destroyed all safeguards against absolute tyranny; thus fomenting rebellions and further civil wars in subsequent reigns.

Virgil committed a single political blunder. His former patron Gallus, sent by Augustus to Egypt after the Battle of Actium, had obliged four of Antony's legions to surrender, and then defeated Antony so soundly at Paraetonium that he did away with himself. (What became of Lycoris is not known.) Virgil thought it appropriate to eulogize Gallus in the *Fourth Georgic*. Augustus, however, grew suspicious of his Procurator. Suppose he seized Egypt and starved Rome by holding back the grain-ships? Gallus' enemies, aware of the situation, brought charges of disloyalty against him, and he knew that he was lost. On hearing of his suicide, Virgil cut out the eulogy. Now, as Professor George Duckworth of Princeton has demonstrated beyond all possible doubt, in his recent pamphlet *Mathematical Symmetry in Virgil's Aeneid*, Virgil never consulted the Muse; he only borrrowed Apollo's slide-rule. The *Aeneid* is, indeed, craftily built according to a Greek architectural theory known as the Golden Section, or the Divine Proportion, or the Golden Mean Ratio. Virgil the Apollonian, whose interest in mathematics Suetonius mentions had, Professor Duckworth shows, divided his books into three parts each, relating these parts by the Golden Mean Ratio; and these parts into lesser units, also in the same Divine proportion; and these again into speeches or incidents also in the same proportion, by a deliberate counting of lines and even of half-lines. . . . Thus, to keep the scheme correct and in order, Virgil needed to replace his discarded eulogy of Gallus with a piece of equal length. He used what reads like a discarded poem of pre-*Eclogue* vintage: the intrusive legend of Aristaeus, which has always puzzled the Virgilistae.

It has been noted that, once taken up by Maecenas, Virgil never again mentions Pollio, though he lived to a venerable age. This may be due either to ingratitude or to caution; Gallus and Pollio had been close friends. The *Fourth Eclogue*, which Virgil had addressed to Pollio when he was about to enter on his Consulship, makes a curious story. Virgil here announces that he will "now use a somewhat loftier strain." Observe the "somewhat"; and, indeed, the eclogue is couched in a familiar, bantering style. Pollio has, at last, deserted beautiful boys and sired a son on his lawful wife. Virgil hunts around for a suitable source of felicitation, and finds just the thing in the *Sibylline Oracles*. Everyone who has read early Roman history will recall that the Sibyl of Cumae (seventh century B.C.), to whose thirteenth-century predecessor Aeneas had paid a visit, bullied the Roman King Tarquinius Priscus into buying her stock of manuscript prophecies; which he thereupon placed in the Roman archives, to be consulted whenever danger threatened the State. Unfortunately, these "Sibylline Leaves" got burned during the Sulla-Marius troubles and, seven years before Virgil's birth, commissioners were appointed to secure another set. The burned manuscripts were not, in fact, the Cumaean Sibyl's own work, but borrowed by her from a more ancient prophetess, the Sibyl of Erythrae in Ionia. During their travels through Ionia, Syria and Egypt, the commissioners came across a great many Greek "Sibylline" oracles, which they brought back home, sorted and edited. That Virgil had access to this official selection cannot be proved, since Stilicho deliberately destroyed it in the fourth century A.D. But he certainly had access to a mixed bag of others, still extant, drawn from many different countries and historical periods. It happened to be a Graeco-Jewish piece that Virgil chose: one adapting Isaiah's Messianic prophecies to some Egyptian philosophic theory of a new Golden Age which succeeds each new Aeon.

The year of Pollio's consulship was a happy one: Augustus temporarily reconciled with his rival Mark Antony by the mediation of Pollio himself; and Virgil, among others, mistaking this armed truce for an end to civil war. Thus the Sibylline prophecy of a laughing child being born, of the wolf and the lamb lying down together, of the child leading bear and lion on a halter and playing unharmed with the dragon and snake—all under the benignant eye of the Universal Father—delighted Virgil. He borrowed from it piecemeal, and added for good measure excerpts from other prophecies in the same collection. Perhaps, it has been suggested, he was gently burlesquing Pollio's Orientalism.

Two hundred years later, certain Church Fathers read into the *Fourth Eclogue* an original prophecy of the Advent. Augustine and Lactantius made a pre-Christian prophet of Virgil, placing him *in limbo Patrum*; and a legend arose that St. Paul wept on his grave, grieved by the thought that this noble poet had been denied a chance to accept the Cross. As loyal Roman citizens, they would not remove Virgil from his place in the national curriculum; besides, his teachings were, at a pinch, reconcilable with Christianity. Had he not used the myth of a beneficent Father creating the Universe, in preference to Lucretius' Epicurean theory that it came about by a fortuitous combination of atoms? In the *Aeneid,* too, sensual feelings were so little stirred that Aeneas (solemnly obeying the divine voice, rather than his own desires and appetites, in his ditching of Dido) could become a prototype of all heroic saints and missionaries. They also gathered Seneca into the fold—a millionaire philosopher, the Anti-Christ Nero's tutor, and privy to the poisoning of his own patron Claudius—because Seneca had occasionally lifted moral precepts from the New Testament. They even forged a correspondence between him and St. Paul which passed as authentic for a thousand years or more!

Some Churchmen still enlarge on Virgil's having made the *Fourth Eclogue* "a blue-print of the *Aeneid,* which foreshadows the Christian ideal." But if Christians need to bolster faith in the Gospels by treating the words of Virgil and Seneca as pre-Canonical Scripture, they deserve to have the *hendiadys* quoted at them from Book Two of the *Aeneid:*

Non tali auxilio, nec defensoribus istis . . .
(Not with help such as *that,* not with *those* defenders!)

A strange phenomenon is the counter-Virgil invented by a German mediaeval Romance writer: Virgil of Toledo, the great magician who, among other marvels, made himself a talking head. He came into being partly because of Publius Virgilius Maro's ill-deserved fame as a herald of Christ; and partly because the habit of turning the pages of Homer at random and putting one's finger on a line that could be construed as a prophecy, had been successfully applied to Virgil when he displaced Homer in the schools. This counter-Virgil was a *vates,* a dedicated poet, armed with all the magical power appropriate to his calling. On one occasion, imprisoned in a dungeon, he took charcoal and with it drew a galley on the wall, persuading his fellow-captives that this vessel had come to rescue them. They stepped aboard, rowed away, and Virgil, taking the tiller, steered them, fourth-dimensionally, to safety on a mountain top; which is a pretty fair metaphor of what Muse-poems can do for their readers.

Many romantically inclined Classicists, somehow convincing themselves that Virgil was born at Toledo, not at Andes, are tempted to discover *frissons* in the *Aeneid* where none was intended. . . . I am reminded of Professor Loomis' essay on how the ruins of a wholly utilitarian Roman fort at Segontium near Caernavon, built by Agricola, became etherialized in mediaeval Welsh legend as Caer Segeint, then as Caer Seint, and finally as Sinadon—a golden-roofed hall vaulted with precious stones, where noble youths sat at chess, and Queen Helen occupied her throne of pure gold. But it is even worse to be seduced by such deliberately contrived rhetorical horripilations as:

> In summas arces Tritonia—respice—Pallas
> Insedit nimbo effulgens et Gorgone saeva.*

* Look behind you where Pallas Athene, born by Lake Tritonis, has seated
  herself in the topmost citadels,
Shining from a cloud, her aegis containing the fierce Gorgon's head.

The Personal Muse

Do you complain that I have defined the dedicated poet too narrowly? Do you insist that Virgil, for example, was dedicated to his art of political verse-making, with the surreptitious aid of Pythagoras' Golden Section? And that St. Gregory Nazianzenus was equally dedicated?—the St. Gregory in honour of whose pious lucubrations the Church authorities sought out and burned great stacks of pagan poetry, including Sappho's, as no longer convenient Christian reading? Very well: you are on firm ground. All verse compositions may be loosely called "poems"—the dictionary permits this enlarged sense of the word. One should not forget even the dedicated craftsmen who write pantomime librettos or the mottoes for Christmas crackers or rhymed advertising slogans.

In my first lecture I distinguished between verse rhetoric, the product of cold reason, and true poetry, the result of an emotional trance. For some three thousand years, the inspiration that accompanies poetic trances has been ascribed to a character called the Muse; and although the meaning of "Muse" has long been blurred by dishonest or facetious usage, what other word can replace it?

The original Muse, or Mountain-goddess, whom the pre-Classical Greeks worshipped on Olympus, Helicon, Parnassus and elsewhere did not, of course, appear by candlelight in a poet's attic and guide his pen; the Muse-trance was a collective one induced at set lunar festivals. The Goddess rode her devotees very much as the voodoo gods of Haiti now ride theirs: causing them to chant and dance ecstatically; though first, no doubt, the tribal poet felt called upon to invoke the Goddess ceremoniously, and provide a ballad refrain— which is still a tribal poet's task in the South Cameroons and other remote parts of West Africa. In Greece by the eighth century B.C., invocation of the Muse had become a formality—a claim that Sons of Homer could entrance listeners with the harp in a palace courtyard as effectively as when stamp of foot and clap of hand beat out the Goddess' dance rhythms on the slopes of a mountain.

One thing is certain: though countless dull poets in the service of politics, learning, or the Church, have since used this invocation to enlarge their literary fame, true possession by the Muse (a phenomenon which can be neither provoked nor foreseen) does occur sporadically to this day among dedicated poets.

That a Goddess so long banished to wet woods and bramble-bound ruins continues to exert a divine spell is ridiculed not only by churchmen but by scientists who find no room in their macrocosm even for Jehovah. Nevertheless, most anthropologists give primitive gods *de facto* recognition as the alleged sponsors of abnormal psychical phenomena, and welcome the public honour given to modern European poets (unendowed private citizens not even necessarily equipped with university degrees or diplomas) as a tacit acknowledgment of their control by a supernatural power. The Muse cannot, of course, be ecclesiasticized. Concerted attempts to rebuild her shrines would be inept, now that she manifests herself not collectively to a group of devotees, but to the individual poet in privacy. Although his poems may be on public sale, the readers are individuals and study them apart, also in privacy.

It is difficult to discuss the Muse concept in historic terms. Let me begin by saying that a deity must remain an idle abstraction, unless he or she has (to employ West African terms) a *sunsum* as well as a *kra*—*kra* meaning supernatural power, *sunsum* meaning an agreed personality. A *sunsum* becomes so notable that the devotee "ridden" by, say, the goddess Ntoa or the god Odomankoma, uses certain traditional gestures, tones and mannerisms at once recognized as the deity's own. Consider the Hebrew prophets—"prophet" means "one who speaks on behalf of God," not necessarily "one who forecasts the future." Though we cannot be sure whether, when acting as mouthpieces of the Palestinian Bull-god El, they adopted his *sunsum*, or merely claimed his *kra*, yet the Bible declares that genuine divine possession could be distinguished from false. We know that Zedekiah the son of Chenaanah impersonated El by providing himself with horns of iron, and that he cried: "Thus shalt thou push the Assyrians!"; but we are told that the god was clearly not riding him at the time.

When a pseudo-poet claims to be inspired by his Muse, the case is much the same. True poetic trances excite memorable images, strong personal rhythms, and a peculiar syntax which, together, transcend in emotional force the most considered rhetoric; false trances imitate these elements, but deceive no reader of sensibility. I wrote on the subject of pseudo-poets some years ago in a poem titled *Any Honest Housewife:*

> Any honest housewife could sort them out,
> Having a nose for fish, an eye for apples.
> Is it any mystery who are the sound
> And who the rotten? Never, by her lights.
>
> Any honest housewife who by ill-fortune
> Ever engaged a slut to scrub for her
> Could instantly distinguish from the workers
> The lazy, the liars, and the petty thieves.
>
> Does this denote a sixth peculiar sense
> Gifted to housewives for their vestal needs?
> Or is it failure of the usual five
> In all unthrifty writers on this head?

And any honest dedicated poet, with a nose and an eye, will take up a new volume of verse, riffle the pages through, and decide after two minutes, by a pricking of his finger-tips, whether or not the Muse has been in attendance. His tasks are to recognize her *kra* and her *sunsum;* never to write (if he can help it) except under her influence; and never to praise poems otherwise written. Attempts to supplant the Muse by worshipping Apollo have always failed—Apollo being a patron of the intellect, not of intuitive truth: of metre, not rhythm; of novelty, not of timelessness.

Fifteen years ago, when I wrote *The White Goddess,* I tried to put the Muse's *sunsum* and *kra* into clearer focus by examining her ancient rites, and reminiscences of them found in European folklore and myth. I came to the conclusion that the main theme of her worship still rules the dedicated poet. Some of you have read the book, most of you have not; so those who have must please excuse my quoting three short paragraphs from it.

The Theme, briefly, recounts the birth, life, death and resurrection of the Demigod of the Waxing Year; the central chapters concern his losing fight against the Demigod of the Waning Year, his rival for love of the all-powerful and inscrutable Threefold Goddess, their mother, bride and layer-out. The poet identifies himself with the Demigod of the Waxing Year; the rival is his twin, his second self, his weird. All true poetry—true by A. E. Housman's practical razor test: "Does it make the hairs of one's chin bristle if one repeats it silently while shaving?"—celebrates some incident or other of this ancient story; and the three main characters are so much a part of our racial legacy that they also assert themselves in dreams and paranoiac visions.

The rival sometimes appears as the tall, lean, dark-faced spectre, or Prince of the Air, who tries to drag a dreamer out through the window, so that he looks back at this body lying rigid in bed; but he takes countless other malevolent or diabolic or serpent-like forms. The Goddess is a lovely, slender woman who will suddenly transform herself into sow, bitch, mare, vixen, she-ass, weasel, serpent, owl, she-wolf, tigress, mermaid or loathsome hag. Her names and titles are multifold. In ghost stories she often figures as "The White Lady," and in ancient religions as the "White Goddess." I can think of no true poet from Homer onwards who has not recorded his personal experience of her. The test of a poet's vision, one might say, is the accuracy of his portrayal of the White Goddess, and of the secret island over which she rules. The hairs stand on end, the eyes water, the throat constricts, the skin crawls, and a shiver runs down the spine when one writes or reads a true poem: because this is necessarily an invocation of the White Goddess, or Muse, the Mother of All Living, the ancient power of love and terror—the female spider or the queen-bee whose courtship means murder. Housman offered an alternative test of true poetry: whether it matches a phrase of Keats's, "everything that reminds me of her goes through me like a spear." This has equal pertinence to the Theme. Keats was writing under the shadow of death about his personal Muse, Fanny Brawne; and "the spear that roars for blood" is the traditional weapon of the dark executioner and supplanter.

Sometimes the hairs will bristle at an apparently unpeopled and eventless scene, if the elements bespeak the Goddess' hidden presence clearly enough: for example, when owls hoot, the moon rides like a ship through scudding cloud, trees sway slowly together above a rushing waterfall, and a distant barking of dogs is heard; or when a peal of bells in frosty weather suddenly announces the birth of a New Year. . . . Despite the deep, sensory satisfaction that some readers derive from Classical poetry, it never makes the hair rise or the heart leap, except perhaps where the verseman has failed to maintain decorous composure; and this marks the difference between the attitudes to the White Goddess of Apollonian poets and dedicated poets.

The Ugarit Epic, discovered at Ras Shamra in 1926, supplies one ancient text of the Theme. Two demi-gods, Aleyan and Mot, fall in love with Anatha—*alias* Neith, a pre-dynastic Libyan goddess. Aleyan is the Bright Twin; Mot is the Dark Twin. Although the Ras Shamra tablets are fragmentary at a crucial point, we gather from analogous myths that Anatha encouraged Mot to murder his Bright Twin Aleyan, and then went off with him. As a result, all grass and herbs languished and a universal lamentation arose. Anatha then thought again, and avenged Aleyan's death by the destruction of Mot, whose body she ground in a mill, leaving the remains to carrion birds. Finally she harrowed Hell, rescued Aleyan, and set him on his throne again. The Goddess' betrayal of the Bright

Twin is a constant element in Hebrew, Greek and Celtic myth. An early non-Biblical Hebrew tradition even makes Cain murder Abel for the favours of another Eve—*alias* Hepta, or Hipatu, a Hittite goddess identified with Anatha.

The Theme originally concerned a seasonal war between the Spirit of Growth and the Demon of Drought. It seems that at the barley harvest, when the blazing Palestinian sun dried up all grass and herbs, Anatha, incarnate in a priestess-queen, annually ordered the crucifixion of her sacred consort as a means of placating the Demon of Drought; then took the executioner into her bed until the autumn rains should come—after which she destroyed him, chose another sacred king: in theory, the crucified man risen from the dead. This ritual practice ceased when the patriarchal cattle people swept down from the north-east, over-running the queendoms; and a Bull-king, or Father-god, gradually assumed the Goddess' powers. But the Theme survived in Hebrew myth and ritual. It even appears, transmogrified, in the Christian doctrine of the sacred king, betrayed by his own familiar friend, who died crucified at the harvest festival for love not of the Goddess but of the Father-god.

Orthodox Christianity marks a parting of ways between poets who serve the Muse, and non-poets who inherit from the patriarchal Hebrews prophets a mistrust of woman as the temptress: prime cause of man's fall from divine grace. By asserting an irrepressible confidence in woman, as being closer to the divine than the man, the poet imaginatively casts himself for the rôle of the sacred king destined to die at his queen's command. And the early mediaeval Church, recognizing a widespread homesickness for the Goddess, shrewdly gave this emotion vent by the sanction of Mariolatry: though extolling Mary as a virgin without blemish, and denying her membership in the Divine Trinity. Catholic poets have accepted this compromise; but the poet from whom the Muse, so far from being a virgin, presides over physical passion, will continue to pledge her his eternal faith, arbitrary and merciless though she may seem— an attitude which appears evil to Christians, and morbid to philosophers. His is a wholehearted protest against the patriarchal system: in so far as it values the intellect at the expense of instinct; and force at the expense of persuasion; and written laws at the expense of custom.

A dedicated poet sees history as a dangerous deviation from the true course of human life—an attempt to deny women their age-old moral ascendancy. A poet's absolute love, his readiness to trust in woman's wisdom, whatever may ensue, represents a nostalgia for human truth. He does not, however, love indiscriminately, but only *the* woman, the royal woman, an incarnation of the Goddess, gifted with her *kra*, who (he assures himself) is waiting somewhere to restore the lost mysteries of mankind. From this obsessive love of an unknown Muse proceed poems of trance, in which the ancient mythical elements assemble thickly. The Muse, I have said, is "the perpetual other woman," never the poet's wife; meaning that the poet-Muse relationship either precedes the patriarchal system, or looks forward to an epoch which must succeed it. Patriarchal marriage would put the Muse under his moral sway, a circumstance impossible for her to accept.

The only Christian country where a tradition of equal love between the sexes survived in the Dark Ages was Ireland. The Irish Church, having been planted by Eastern missionaries, escaped Papal interference. Kings chose bishops from among their dependents, assigning them lands for individual tenure, not in the form of Church property; and the ollamhs, or master-poets, the chief Councillors of State, still worshipped the Triple-goddess Bridget (of Poetry, Medicine and Smithcraft) in thin Christian disguise. Noble Irish women were known to have minds of their own, and encouraged to use them, as can be seen from such dramatic tales as Cuchulain's wooing of Emer, Midir's wooing of Étain, Deirdre's mourning for Naoise, the loves of Liadan and Curithir, of Créide and Cáel. The intensity of Irish love passion is shown in this ninth-century poem from *Midir's Wooing of Étain:*

> Torment I have endured a twelvemonth,
> With grief well hidden behind my eyes,
> With strength enlarged beyond belief
> To the four quarters of this earth,
> To the highest crown of heaven.

> Love is a breaking of the neck-bone
> In battle with a spectre,
> Love is a drowning in flood water,
> Love is a race against the nightly stars,
> Or hero-feats below the salt sea,
> I wooed the echo in wooing her,
> To whom, body and soul, I bound myself.

Nevertheless, the Irish poet's beloved was always presented as a woman, not a goddess—unless in plainly mythical tales, like *Oisin and Niamh of the Golden Hair* and *Grainne and Diarmat*. This unorthodox Irish view of woman as something more than a mere sexual or domestic convenience, as having thoughts and sensibilities worthy of man's close regard, came to England at third hand after the Norman Conquest: when Welsh minstrel traditions of Irish origin were woven by Breton bards into the Norman-French Arthurian romances—*Tristan and Iseult*, for example, being a version of *Grainne and Diarmat*; and *Gawain and the Green Knight* of *Cuchulain and Curoi*.

An equally important source of English love-poetry was Provence, with its extensions to Northern Spain and Italy. Many untruths are current about the troubadors—taken from Catholic propaganda against the Albigensian heresy, to which many of them seem to have been attached. These poets, of whom one hundred and eleven figure in the records, and who included twenty-three ruling princes, among them Richard Coeur de Lion, flourished from the early twelfth century to the late thirteenth, and celebrated a view of human love that cut across ecclesiastical tradition. Such sacred power was claimed for the extra-marital bond which united a troubador to his beloved, that Bernart of Ventadour—a former scullion but a leading troubador—suffered only banishment when his amours with the Viscountess of Montluçon came to light. And when the jealous Count of Castel-Roussillon murdered Guillem de Capestang, and caused Seremonda, his countess, to commit suicide by serving up Guillem's heart for her supper, all Provence rose to avenge the lovers; and pilgrims flocked to the grave in Perpignan Cathedral, where their bodies had been laid together. The adulterous loves of Guinevere and Lancelot were treated as sacred in the *Morte d'Arthur* as late as the fifteenth century; and Lord Barnard, of the Border ballad, after killing his wife and Little Musgrave when he found them making love together, laments that he has done away with the finest couple of all England. Women poets appeared among the troubadors, as they appeared in early mediaeval Ireland; one of them, Eleanor of Guienne, became Henry II's Queen.

The usual etymology of *troubador* is the Provençal word *trobar*, "to find or invent"; an alternative suggestion is the Latin *turbare*, "to stir up"; but since the editors of the *Oxford English Dictionary* are unwilling, on linguistic grounds, to accept either of these, I incline to the view that *troubador* represents the Arabic *ta rabub*, "lute player." Historians often casually mention the troubadors' debt to Arabic poets; but the Arabs were not lovers in this sacred sense. The troubadors' real debt was to Sufism—a way of thought refined by the Persians and eventually adapted to Islam, though in essence heretical. Moorish invasions of Spain and Southern France had brought along a heterogenous mass of Islamic visitors from distant Oriental lands— traces of whose cults are to be found not only in *flamenco* dancing (of Yemenite, not gipsy origin), but in the mediaeval witch records of Spain, France and Britain. By the twelfth century, Morisco lutanists clad in motley and with bells on their ankles, had gone all through Provence singing love-ditties based on the Persian; from these the troubadors, it seems, learned their code of behaviour.

The Sufis seek to eliminate by a long course of mental discipline whatever desires and beliefs are foreign to divine love. A Sufi feels superior to normal restraints and, being spiritually and physically at one with the woman who has accepted his devotion, claims a certitude that allows him to face every danger and bring seeming impossibilities to pass. Sufic thought, though its spiritual disciplines appear to have been scamped in Provence, contributed to the Albigensian heresy, against which the Catholic Church directed all the armies she could muster, in the bloodiest of Holy Wars. Church historians libel the troubadors. Thus Guillem of Poitiers, Duke of Aquitaine, is said to have roved the country seducing noblewomen with his songs; and William of Malmesbury even accuses him of having intended to found a religious house for Venus worship.

The troubadors' heretical convictions were decently ecclesiasticized when Petrarch, a clerk in Holy Orders, professed a chaste love for Laura de Noyes, Hugo de Sade's wife—after which a living Muse could encourage her poet with a distant smile, as it might be the image of a Virgin Martyr miraculously made flesh, yet not allow him so much as a hand-clasp of intimate understanding. And though Petrarch might be accused of harbouring illegitimate desires for Laura's person, his successor Dante guarded himself against a similar charge by a more prudent choice of Muse. He had felt a sudden pang of divine love for Beatrice when both of them were only nine years old; but so far as anyone knows, she never reciprocated his feelings or considered herself in the least degree affected by them. Beatrice bore her husband twelve children, and Dante had some of his own—yet even her death could not remove his obsession. Thus, despite his vehement praise, in the *Inferno,* of the troubador Arnaut Daniel, the new theory of Courtly Love remained artificial and unreal: an "Inamorato's Manual: every man his own Muse."

Sir Thomas Wyatt was the first Englishman to imitate Italian, French and Spanish verse models of Courtly Love. His titles tell the story.

The Lover for Shamefastness Hideth His Desire Within His Faithful Heart . . .

The Lover Waxeth Wiser, and Will Not Die for Affection . . .

The Abused Lover Seeth His Folly and Intendeth to Trust no More . . .

The Lover Describeth His Being Stricken With Sight of His Love . . .

The Wavering Lover Willeth, and Dreadeth, to Move His Desire . . .

How the Lover Perisheth in His Delight as the Fly in the Fire . . .

The Lover Despairing to Attain Unto His Lady's Grace, Relinquisheth the Pursuit . . .

The Deserted Lover Consoleth Himself with Remembrance that All Women Are by Nature Fickle . . .

The Deserted Lover Wisheth that His Rival Might Experience the Same Fortune He Himself Had Tasted . . .

The Neglected Lover Calleth on His Stony Hearted Mistress to Hear Him Complain Ere that He Die . . .

The Lover Having Broken His Bondage, Voweth Never More to Be Enthralled . . .

The Abused Lover Admonishes the Unwary to Beware of Love . . .

Deserted by His Mistress, He Renounceth All Joy for Ever . . .

These were graceful exercises describing different clinical stages in the fever of love, and despite a pretence of Petrarchian chastity, proved ingenious sexual lures. The Muse being both anonymous and impersonal, they could all be addressed to any woman willing to take a hand in the love game. By thus serenading susceptible Court ladies, Wyatt won numerous intimate favours; and seems neither to have loved openly in the chivalrous manner of the troubadors, flaunting his beloved's kerchief on his casque, nor to have dedicated himself to the divine Muse. Few of these poems stand out as honestly his own. An exception is *The Recovered Lover Exulteth in His Freedom*, which begins:

> I am as I am, and so will I be,
> But how that I am, none knoweth trewely—
> Be it evil, be it well, be I loved, be I free,
> I am as I am, and so will I be.
>
> But how that is, I leave to you—
> Judge as ye list, false or true,
> Ye know no more than afore ye knew
> Yet I am as I am, whatever ensue.

None "knoweth trewely," in fact, what his game is—not even the many women to whom he has dedicated himself heart and soul. *The Faithful Lover Wisheth All Evil May Befall Him if He Forsake His Lady* reads typically:

> The knot which first my heart did strain,
> When that your servant I becam,
> Doth bind me still for to remain,

> Always your own as now I am;
> And if you find that now I feign,
> With just judgemént myself I damn,
> To have disdain.
>
> If other thought in me do grow
> But still to love you steadfastly;
> If that the proof do not well show
> That I am yours assuredly;
> Let every wealth turn me to woe,
> And you to be continually
> My chiefest foe . . .
>
> If in my love there be one spot
> Of false deceit or doubleness;
> Or if I mind to slip the knot
> By want of faith or steadfastness;
> Let all my service be forgot,
> And when I would have chief redress,
> Esteem me not . . .
>
> And for the end of this my song,
> Unto your hands I do submit
> My deadly grief, and pains so strong
> Which in my heart be firmly shut,
> And when ye list, redress my wrong:
> Since well ye know this painful fit
> Hath last too long.

Too glib a statement to carry conviction, and never so intended! And at the end, when Wyatt had outgrown his amorous escapades, he fell back on self-pity. The one woman is now revealed as "they": *The Lover Showeth How He Is Forsaken of Such as He Sometime Enjoyed.*

> They flee from me that sometime did me seek,
>   With naked foot stalking within my chamber:
> Once have I seen them gentle, tame, and meek,
>   That now are wild, and do not once remember

That sometime they have put themselves in danger
To take bread at my hand; and now they range
Busily seeking in continual change.

Thanked be Fortúne, it hath been otherwise,
    Twenty times better; but once inespecial,
In thin array, after a pleasant guise,
    When her loose gown did from her shoulders fall,
    And she me caught in her arms long and small,
And therewithal so sweetly did me kiss,
And softly said: "Dear heart, how like you this?"

It was no dream; for I lay broad awaking:
    But all is turned, thorough my gentleness,
Into a strangë fashion of forsaking;
    And I have leave to go of her goodnéss,
    And she also to use new-fangleness:
But since that I so kindly am servèd:
I would fain know what she had déservèd?

John Donne likewise used love-poems as a means of seduction. He persuaded himself, at times, of his love's absoluteness; yet, when the flame had died down, declared that the spiritual identity of lovers was an illusion. His poems yield no portraits of individual women; their bright eyes always reflect his own passionate image. One of his loves, we read, sent him amusing letters, but he does not quote a line from them; and if he kept their identities secret, roundly cursing any man who guessed the secret, it was himself whom he feared to compromise.

The series begins boldly with *The Good Morrow:*

I wonder by my troth, what thou and I
Did, till we loved? Were we not weaned till then,
But sucked on country pleasures childishly?
Or snorted we in the seven sleepers' den?
T'was so; but this, all pleasures fancies be.
If ever any beauty, I did see,
Which I desired, and got, t'was but a dream of thee.

And now good morrow to our waking souls,
Which watch not one another out of fear;
For love, all love of other sights controls,
And makes one little room an everywhere.
Let sea-discoverers to new worlds have gone,
Let Maps to other, worlds on worlds have showne,
Let us possess one world, each hath one, and is one.

My face is thine eye, thine in mine appears,
And true plain hearts do in the faces rest,
Where can we find two better hemispheres
Without sharp North, without declining West?
Whatever dies was not mixed equally;
If our two loves be one, or thou and I
Love so alike that none do slacken, none can die.

But soon doubt creeps in; one woman is no better than another, and
all are faithless. He writes in *The Indifferent*:

I can love both fair and brown,
Her whom abundance melts, and her whom want betrays,
Her who loves loneness best, and her who masks and
    plays,
Her whom the country formed, and whom the town,
Her who believes, and her who tries,
Her who still weeps with spongy eyes,
And her who is dry cork and never cries;
I can love her, and her, and you and you,
I can love any, so she be not true . . .

The first stanza of *Air and Angels* does not deny his doubt. The Muse,
he explains, is his own imaginative creation, not a power recognized
by him:

Twice or thrice had I loved thee,
    Before I knew thy face or name;
    So in a voice, so in a shapeless flame,
Angels affect us oft, and worshipped be;
    Still when to where thou wert I came,

Some lovely glorious nothing I did see.
  But since my soul, whose child Love is,
Takes limbs of flesh, and else could nothing do,
  More subtil than the parent is
Love must not be, but take a body too.
And therefore what thou wert, and who,
    I bid Love ask, and now
    That it assume thy body I allow
    And fix itself in thy lip, eye, and brow . . .

He allows himself an occasional glimpse of what absolute love can mean in these stanzas from *A Valediction:*

    Dull sublunary lovers' love
      (Whose soul is sense) cannot admit
    Absence, because it doth remove
      Those things which elemented it.

    But we by a love so much refined
      That our selves know not what it is,
    Inter-assuréd of the mind,
      Care less, eyes, lips, and hands to miss.

    Our two souls therefore, which are one,
      Though I must go, endure not yet
    A breach, but an expansión,
      Like gold to airy thinness beat . . .

Absence, indeed, seems more rewarding to him than presence, when presence is the erotic abandon which he celebrates in his *Nineteenth Elegy* but depreciates in his *Farewell to Love:*

        . . . the thing which lovers so
Blindly admire, and with such worship woo;
  Being had, enjoying it decays:
    And thence
What before pleased them all, takes but one sense,
  And that so lamely as it leaves behind
A kind of sorrowing dullness to the mind.

He confesses in *Love's Alchemy:*

> Some that have deeper digged love's mine than I,
> Say where this centrique happiness doth lie:
>   I have loved, and got, and told,
> But should I love, get, tell, till I were old,
> I should not find the hidden mystery;
>   Oh, 'tis imposture all . . .

> Hope not for mind in women; at their best
> Sweetness and wit, they are but *Mummy*, possessed.

And *The Token* shows that he does not expect the woman addressed to trust him:

> . . . I beg no ribband wrought with thine own hands,
>   To knit our loves in the fantastic strain
> Of new-touched youth; nor ring to shew the strands
>   Of our affection, that, as that's round and plain,
> So should our loves meet in simplicity.
>   No, nor the corals which thy wrist enfold,
> Laced up together in congruity
>   To show your thoughts should rest in the same hold;
> No, nor thy picture, though most gracious,
>   And most desired, because best like the best;
> Nor witty lines, which are most copious,
>   Within the writings which thou hast addressed.

> Send me nor this, nor that, to increase my store,
> But swear thou thinkst I love thee, and no more.

She had been warned in his *Elegy:*

> I love her well and would, if need were, die
> To do her service. But follows it that I
> Must serve her only, when I may have choice
> Of other beauties, and in change rejoice?

"I would die to do her service" is rhetorical; Donne remained un-committed. Later, he married well; proved a faithful husband; took Holy Orders; and, after his wife's death, gave his heart to the Father-god and duly repented his sins. He writes in *A Hymn to God the Father*:

> Wilt Thou forgive that sin by which I have won
> Others to sin and made my sin their door?
> Wilt Thou forgive that sin which I did shun
> A year or two: but wallowed in, a score?
> When Thou hast done, Thou hast not done,
> For I have more.
>
> I have a sin of fear, that when I have spun
> My last thread, I shall perish on the shore;
> Swear by Thyself, that at my death Thy Son
> Shall shine as he shines now and heretofore;
> And, having done that, Thou hast done,
> I fear no more.

Must I take you through all the corpus to prove that the Tudor poet had little thought for the women he celebrated save as beautiful, complaisant bedfellows—no respect for their mind, pride or sensibility; and that if they would not succumb to his blandishments, he felt aggrieved? An anonymous poem in *Tottel's Miscellany* is put into a Court lady's mouth:

> Girt is my guiltless gown, as I sit here and sew,
> I see that things are not in deed as to the
> outward show . . .

She then speaks of a love-song:

> The author whereof came, wrapped in a crafty cloak
> In will to force a flaming fire where he could raise no
> smoke.
> If power and will had met, as it appeareth plain,
> Nor truth nor right had ta'en a place—their virtues had
> been vain.

But even poets who love humanly with all their heart's affection, and those who idealize women as distant saints, alike avoid the third and most poetic way of love: namely the recognition of the Muse-goddess as incarnate in some particular woman, who must be loved and trusted whatever happens. Though a sudden sense of the Goddess' creative power may overcome a poet when he first falls in love, and be enhanced by his rediscovery of her ancient titles and emblems, only a personal Muse can open the arcana of poetry to him.

Royal women are rare—wild, ruthless, awe-inspiring, their progress like a forest fire—the greener the wood, the fiercer the flames. For "royal" let me substitute "real." The Latin words regalis formed from *rex* (king) and *realis* formed from *res* (the thing itself) became conflated in mediaeval English since what was royal was considered noble, divinely approved and therefore authentic. Was Donne incapable of the absolute love demanded by such a Muse because male pride would not let him yield to it? Or did he never meet a woman real enough to subdue his pride? In my view he knew what this love meant, but deliberately rejected it; so that the Muse who should have claimed him as her poet, and saved his soul, went frowning away. Donne's punishment appears in an abject address to *The Father*:

> Father of Heaven, and Him by whom
> It and us, for it, and all else, for us
> Thou mad'st, and govern'st ever, come
> And re-create me, now grown ruinous:
> My heart is by dejection, clay,
> And by self-murder, red.
> From this red earth, O Father, purge away
> All vicious tinctures, that new fashionèd
> I may rise up from death, before I'm dead.

Strangely enough, the woman who came nearest to an authentic personal Muse in Tudor times was Queen Elizabeth herself, as celebrated by Sir Walter Raleigh. Though he has been accused of flattery, self-seeking and other ignoble traits in his relations with Elizabeth (who was almost twenty years older than he) and though his earlier poems of prosperity in love have disappeared, leaving only complaints of her subsequent unkindness, it is difficult after reading

The Eleventh and Last Book of the Ocean to Cynthia to challenge
the reality of the power she exercised over his heart. And the most
compelling of all Muse poems in English, *The Holy Land of Wal-
singham,* is Raleigh's.

A tremendous effort of will freed early historic man from subservience to a matriarchate and gave him the power of personal choice.
Breaking the female monopoly of arts, sciences, and religious ritual,
he consolidated his gains by a development of intellect, until he
had made women his chattels. Modern men cannot be expected
to renounce this hardly won power, and sell themselves back into
collective slavery. But they can perhaps be persuaded that the
a-moral exercise of intellect has created institutions hostile to human
happiness—total wars, uncontrolled money, denatured food, soul-
destroying machines, academicism, commercialized entertainment
—which is no great advance on prehistoric savagery.
     As I see it, a poet has only one choice: to refrain from exploiting
a bovine will-power—from forcing events to adopt intellectually conceived, and therefore unnatural, and therefore disastrous, patterns;
and, instead, learn from his Muse how to cultivate an intuitive
certitude about the fortunate course of whatever he feels impelled
to do. In a recent poem of mine, a lover addresses the Goddess:

> Your sceptre rules me, Aphrodite,
> The knot-of-wisdom in your grasp . . .

This knot-of-wisdom, or the true lover's knot, is made of two cords
so intertwined that the harder one tugs, the more tightly they knit
together. West-African queen-mothers carry silver knot-of-wisdom
sceptres, meaning "My decisions are irrevocable." Yet their decisions
are not mere exercises of female will-power; they represent the natural
certitude of rightness given them by the *kra* of their ancestress, the
Threefold Moon-goddess Nyame.
     Education tends to destroy this intuitive gift in women. Real
women are those who resist patriarchal conditioning, and are thus
recognized by poets as holding the sceptre tight in their grasp. The
Muse, no longer a collective emanation, but incarnate as an inspired,

real woman, can teach her poet how to cultivate the same certitude without damaging either his male self-esteem or his male intellect. And it may happen that, before long, a few dedicated poets, by imparting this knowledge to their fellow-men, will change the present disagreeable climate of human thought. Such, at least, is my faith; the only alternative seems to be universal catastrophe.

Many of you will know what I mean by "certitude," though your experience of it is perhaps limited to a small, private, intuitive art in which you shine—you neither know, nor ask, where the magic comes from—but which, if practised with any other object than its own perfection, slowly vanishes. And most of you must occasionally have felt, at some time or other, a peculiar sense of being "on the beam": nothing can go wrong, all your impulses are right. If you throw a stone at a tin can fifty yards away, you cannot fail to score a direct hit—because you have not mathematically computed the distance, the weight of the stone, and other problems of ballistics, but used your sense of divine assurance. I tend to choose my closest friends among those who preserve this faculty in a high degree.

The personal Muse, then, should inspire a poet with her own certitude; in return, he should acknowledge her divine *kra*, though loving her as a woman with a *sunsum* of her own. There is no cabalistic or occult element in such poet-Muse relationships, however difficult they may be to achieve and maintain. At this point I am no longer addressing a general University audience, but talking in an aside to any poets who may be listening. So few are to be found in the elder or middle generations that, doubtless, some younger ones must be growing up whose names are unknown to me. Though Donne's reasons for keeping the name of his beloved concealed do not seem to have been the right ones, the principle was right in so far as the public identification of a woman with a poet's Muse may cause her to reject him as a threat to her private royalty—because people will not readily abandon the notion that whoever actually writes the poems is the more important partner in this difficult relationship, and may persist in regarding her as a mere idol rather than the director.

Too many irresponsible young women, eager for Muse-ship, go in search of poetic recognition. Unless they have the integrity, ruthlessness, and certitude characteristic of a real Muse, they will get entangled with pseudo-poets; and the outcome is always sad, often sordid. Cunning pseudo-poets ruthlessly exploit a pseudo-Muse's innocent ambitions. Real Muses are rare indeed; and not enviable, for the ancient Irish Triad is as true today as ever it was:

> It is death to mock a poet;
> Death to love a poet;
> Death to be a poet.

Here is a message to would-be Muses—*Beware, Madam!*

> Beware, madam, of the witty devil,
> The arch intriguer who walks disguised
> In a poet's cloak, his gay tongue oozing evil.
>
> Would you be a Muse? He will so declare you,
> Pledging his blind allegiance,
> Yet remain secret and uncommitted.
>
> Poets are men: are single-hearted lovers
> Who adore and trust beyond all reason,
> Who die honourably at the gates of hell.
>
> The Muse alone is licensed to do murder
> And to betray: weeping with honest tears
> She thrones each victim in her paradise.
>
> But from this Muse the Devil borrows an art
> That ill becomes a man. Beware, madam:
> He plots to strip you bare of woman-pride.
>
> He is capable of seducing your twin-sister
> On the same pillow, and neither she nor you
> Will suspect the act, so close a glamour he sheds.
>
> Alas, being honourably single-hearted,
> You adore and trust beyond all reason,
> Being no more a Muse than he is a poet.

A poet may likewise be mistaken in his Muse: she may prove unworthy of continued trust. I have written about this, too—*In Her Praise:*

> This they know well: the Goddess yet abides.
> Though each new lovely woman whom she rides,
> Straddling her neck a year, or two, or three,
> Should sink beneath such weight of majesty
> And, groping back to humankind, betray
> The headlong power that whitened all her way
> With a broad track of trefoil—leaving you
> Her chosen lover, ever again thrust through
> With daggers, your purse rifled, your rings gone;
> Nevertheless they call you to live on,
> To parley with the pure, oracular dead,
> To hear the wild pack whimpering overhead,
> To watch the moon tugging at her cold tides,
> Woman is mortal woman. She abides.

I read the story of Anatha, Aleyan and Mot not only as an ancient seasonal myth, but as a prophecy of this new, peculiar, not yet fully explored, poet-Muse relationship. Anatha may well discipline Aleyan for showing signs of marital possessiveness: may betray him with his cruel, destructive twin as a means of asserting her personal freedom. But if Aleyan survives the ordeal, after dying cheerfully for her sake, she will surely—he tells himself—raise him up again and destroy his rival. We are no longer, of course, annually subjected to semi-famine by the droughts of summer or the frosts of winter. In a city we scarcely notice the passing of the seasons, and can fly from polar cold to equatorial heat in a matter of hours, so that the seasonal myth on which the Theme rests has lost its cursed absoluteness. But the poet as Sacred King cannot avoid a love-ordeal which puts his sense of certitude to the supreme test. And I believe, despite all adverse evidence, that there was never an epoch in which so many young men were willing to be ruled by the knot-of-wisdom sceptre—the royal pledge of absolute if unpredictable love to those worthy of it.

Poetry does not deny the intellect, or the discipline of reason: but transcends both. Young poets are often tempted to despise the formal University curriculum: I think them mistaken. A curriculum is what one makes of it. As we say of food in Majorca: "What does not poison, fattens," and the curriculum is non-poisonous, if in parts somewhat indigestible. Moreover, Oxford happens to own a peculiar *báraka*, or blessedness—a kindly, non-doctrinaire, generous spirit, unmatched anywhere else in the world. Enjoy it, maintain it!

Poetic Gold

My grandfather Charles Graves, afterwards Bishop of Limerick, won the Chancellor's Gold Medal at Trinity College, Dublin, in the eighteen-thirties; so did his two brothers, Robert Graves the physician who became famous for identifying Graves's Disease, and John Graves the Classical historian and lexicographer. These three medals, big as silver dollars and engraved by a Dublin jeweller, hung behind our drawing-room grand piano when I was a child, set in a gilt glass case against a shamrock of faded green velvet. My mother fondly hoped that since her three sons bore the same Christian names, they would one day win three medals of equal importance; yet, each in turn, we disappointed her. We all came up here to St. John's and none of us brought home any University prize whatsoever. "One ought not to consider the intrinsic value of the gold," she moralized, "because it would be wrong to sell or pawn such a medal even if on the point of starvation. Only the achievement counts. Still, gold is the noblest of metals and signifies the honour in which outstanding talents are held."

This piece of family history explains why, in January 1960, I felt my mother's ghost present with me at the Waldorf-Astoria, New York, where the National Poetry Society of America were celebrating their Golden Jubilee. Though an Englishman, I had been judged worthy of the Prince Alexander Droutzkoy Memorial Award: a gold medal for Services to Poetry. An alarming experience, since I have always considered poetry as a private and, indeed, almost anti-social obsession, and been at pains to discount its more public manifestations. There I was, in evening dress, among six hundred fellow-obsessionists as well-groomed as myself, sitting down to dinner in the great Sbert Banqueting Hall. The Committee had placed me with a row of award-winners on a lofty daïs.

The Society's medals and diplomas all carried money prizes—an aggregate of some six thousand dollars—but, on studying the list, I noticed that their cash value seldom corresponded with their billing. In fact, the greater the honour, as a rule, the less the cash. One certain deduction was that gold ranked higher than silver, and silver than bronze, as at trade and agricultural shows.

Robert Frost, the Society's Honorary President, sat near me, making mischievous *sotto voce* comments. I have known and loved him since 1914, when we first met accidentally in a London bookshop; and his carefree mood gave me courage. Marianne Moore, whom I had not known before, but always respected for her unchanging dry wit, was there too; and when the noble Jubilee Birthday Cake came sailing in, flash-bulbs illumined the three of us bending together over it. Even a much bigger cake would hardly have gone far among six hundred guests; still, I was surprised when Miss Moore, who had cut a ritual slice and blown out most of the fifty candles (Robert Frost pinched out the rest with practised fingers), did not receive so much as a single crumb or currant. The Birthday Cake sailed back to the kitchens: to be patched up, perhaps, for a subsequent Jubilee Celebration of Dentists, Wood-Whittlers, or Turkey-Raisers. . . . The surprised look on Miss Moore's face reminded me of Lewis Carroll's Alice when introduced to the Lobster at the White Queen's banquet: "Alice—Lobster; Lobster—Alice! Waiter, remove the Lobster!"

Dr. Clarence B. Decker, the genial President, glanced at a sheaf of congratulatory cables from all over the world, and read out

President Eisenhower's: to the effect that poets are vital to American progress, culture and spiritual endeavour. This being, however, a strictly national occasion, Dr. Decker did not read us a cable from the Secretary of the Russian Union of Writers, which declared that poets are vital to international culture, peace and goodwill.

After Dr. Decker had reported on the Society's fifty years of achievement, Robert Frost spoke in more personal tones about poetry. The awards were then distributed—Miss Moore won a great bronze medal engraved with a Pegasus—and some winners read their prize poems aloud. My turn came last. Dr. Decker pinned the Prince Alexander Droutzkoy Memorial Award for Services to Poetry on my lapel, everyone applauded, and I rose to speak—"for twenty-five minutes or so, if you don't mind; and please remember the microphone! Our Celebration is being broadcast to five million listeners."

Well, I had won a gold medal at last and, although in Europe no speaker is ever asked to rise at a banquet without a minimum three glasses of wine and one of brandy to sustain him, I would not chicken-out just because the ordeal must be faced in American style on strawberry ice-cream and a demi-tasse of pale coffee.

I had only a vague idea of what I ought to say, but the circumstances seemed to call for something based on my mother's moral discourse; and in my pocket lay a goldsmith's touchstone—a small diamond-shaped cube of black jasper, which I was taking over as a christening-present for an infant of that name. This made a useful starting-point. "Mr. President, ladies and gentlemen," I said, "many of you use the word 'touchstone' as a metaphor for testing the value of any poem or work of art. Perhaps few of you have ever seen a real touchstone; and because poets should avoid dead metaphors, let me show you one . . ."

I held it up, and began discoursing on gold, the royal metal, the only one found in a pure state, a metaphor for truth and integrity and, because royal and real are the same word, for reality. To be paid in gold is to be paid *really*: not in promissory notes or base metal. "The testing or assaying of doubtful gold," I went on, "has given numerous words to the English language—'touchstone,' 'acid test,' and even the word *test* itself. The original noun 'test' meant the cupel in which refiners parted gold from other metals; hence the phrase 'put it to the test.'" Hence also the phrase used by the Earl of Montrose in speaking of love:

> He either fears his fate too much,
>   Or his deserts are small,
> Who dares not *put it to the touch*
>   To gain or lose it all.

Louis Untermeyer, anthologist and jeweller, nodded sagely as I made as if to scratch the edge of my medal with the touchstone. Should the golden trace now left on the jasper, I said, be subjected to the acid test—a light application of hydrofluoric acid—it would not, like baser metals, be dissolved. . . . In the Bible, pure gold means holiness: "thou shalt overlay the ark with pure gold." And, according to the *Book of Job*, nothing exceeds pure gold in value save God's holy wisdom. . . . Pure gold is of twenty-four karat fineness. Fine gold, in English usage, goes from eighteen karats upward to twenty-four. Semi-fine gold contains no less than twelve karats; but "semi-fine" is a Gallic euphemism for the term "low gold"—everything under fine-gold standard being low gold.

I warmed to my theme, talking about karats. Karats were originally carob-seeds, employed by Jewish goldsmiths as weights: twenty-four of them equalling the sixth of an ounce which was the weight of the Emperor Constantine's *solidus,* or gold piece. But of this number only twenty represented the gold contained in the coins; the other four represented the silver or copper which hardened it—pure gold can be bent like lead—for service as practical currency. . . . In Hebrew mysticism, carobs, *alias* locust-beans or St. John's bread, are an emblem of repentance; as the parable of the Prodigal Son who was reduced to this diet shows; and the proverb "when Israel eats carobs she will turn again to the Lord"—hence John the Baptist's choice of them as a staple. Thus carob-seeds when used as measures of fineness stand for man's conscious assessment of his failure to achieve the pure gold standard of holiness. . . .

I pointed to the medal. "This," I said, "though doubtless fine gold, cannot be twenty-four karat, because gold is unworkable at more than twenty-two karat fineness. And even if it could be, the award of a pure gold medal for poetry would flatter the recipient unduly: no poem ever attains such karat purity. Few of us even succeed in reaching the fine-gold standard; a notable exception being your Honorary President, Robert Frost. . . . But I am glad to know, by this gift, that the Society considers my work to have attained a certain karat fineness. Most poetry nowadays is silver-gilt, or gold-filled bronze, or pinchbeck. . . ."

That went over pretty well, and I was rewarded after dinner with a couple of stiff drinks in the lounge, where a procession of poets congratulated me on the Award.

But an unwillingness to accept official valuations on trust has always been my curse. And I have a sensitive touch. That night, remembering the gold sovereigns I used to jingle in my pocket as a young man before the First World War, I poised the medal on my finger tips and decided that, for its size, it hardly weighed quite what it should. . . . Closer inspection revealed a small "14 k" stamped on the edge, next to the maker's name. "Not fine gold, but at least gold," I reassured myself.

Back home in Majorca, I found that an account of the celebrations had been copied from the *New York Herald Tribune* in our local papers. Several Palma citizens gave me their congratulations, including Don Carlos Pomar, whose jeweller's shop I visited one morning to have a signet ring enlarged. (That is another story. In Israel, last year, I had stubbed my little finger at Sodom against a block of salt which formed Lot's Wife's skirts—an accident of enormous interest to our village priest, since it authenticated Holy Scripture—and my ring no longer went over the middle joint.)

Don Carlos asked to see the famous medal. "Do not think me curious or impertinent, but in all my life I have never handled a medal that was *oro de ley*—fine gold of eighteen karats. Spain is a poor country since President Negrin sent her entire gold reserve to Moscow; but even before that, our medals had long been gilt bronze. Sad, how many indigent Army widows have tried to sell me their husbands' gold medals and crosses won on the field of battle. . . . America, however, possesses so much gold that she can afford to bury ingots by the thousand tons in underground vaults."

"My medal has a fourteen-karat stamp," I said.

"That is not, of course, *oro de ley;* but at least you have a gold medal. Please do me the favour of letting me examine it."

"With great pleasure, friend."

In due course I brought Don Carlos the medal. He sighed. "Once again a disappointment. . . ."

"How?"

"It is not gold of any sort. It is not even engraved; and the inscription has been written with an electric needle."

"But what of this fourteen-karat stamp?"

"I do not know what regulations are in force among the North Americans; but this medal is certainly not fourteen karat. . . . You disbelieve me? Then may I scratch, very lightly, the knob which secures the ribbon?"

"Certainly."

Don Carlos scratched, and handed me a magnifying glass: "You see: here is a delicate plating of gold; underneath lies perhaps bronze, perhaps silver. . . . Let us call it silver."

"Surely you are wrong?"

"Don Roberto, you have known me, and my father before me, for thirty years! We Pomars have been jewellers for at least three centuries. Is it likely that I would be wrong?"

"Most unlikely!"

"Why should I mislead you?"

"Do not suggest such a possibility!"

So I wrote to Dr. Decker, thanking him for the honour that this Society had done me, and for his great personal kindness. I much admired the gilt medal he had pinned on my lapel and, when I went to Switzerland, would spend the hundred-dollar cheque that came with it on a real-gold replica, taking care to use the original red ribbon and pin.

Next morning I thought: "This is the sort of letter one writes but does not mail." Nevertheless, recalling my eloquent speech about poetic gold, I felt that Dr. Decker should, in justice, have taken me by an arm and revealed the truth before the banquet ended.

So I sent my letter to Robert Frost, and asked him to forward it, or not, whichever he chose. Although the demon of plain speaking has always plagued Robert, as it plagues me, he might be reluctant to compromise his standing with the Society. . . . True, Dr. Decker was a gentleman, but a letter like mine would be putting both his courtesy and his sense of humour to a severe test—indeed, an acid test.

I realize now who had dictated the letter: my mother, grieved to see her son's outstanding talents symbolically slighted. Dear Mother! If it is true that the dead know everything, she must have been aware that the fine-gold Tara brooch, always flaunted proudly on her black silk bosom, came to me after her death; and that, when I asked Don Carlos to mend the pin, he discovered that the brooch was pinchbeck. . . .

Robert Frost ("gleefully" I hear) forwarded the letter; and in due course I got from Dr. Decker a stiff but gentlemanly reply. This medal, he assured me, was "real gold for me and my heirs." If, however, by some strange mischance, I had been given a trial piece struck in base metal, he would be glad to send me a real gold replacement. . . .

Stricken with shame and remorse, I hurried to Palma again. "Look here, Don Carlos," I said. "I trusted you as I trusted your father; but it appears that an embarrassing error has been made. The medal is gold, or so the donors swear. Why should they tell lies? Please test it once more, and then I will know whether I owe them an apology."

Don Carlos smiled: "It is unnecessary. I have seen as much as I need, Don Roberto. Why not take a second opinion? You are acquainted with Señor Cortés, I think? Consult him!"

Señor Cortés is perhaps the most experienced and most affluent member of the Palma Marranos—the former Jewish goldsmiths' guild forcibly converted to Christianity at King Philip II's orders.

I approached young Cortés, whose shop stands at the other end of the same street. He is heavily built, swarthy, grave, formal. "Senor Cortés, will you do me a great favour?"

"Always at your service, Señor Gravés."

"Tell me: is this object gold?"

He did not answer, nor even glance at the medal, but clapped his hands. "Jaimito: the touchstone and the acid!"

Jaimito, his small assistant, appeared like a genie, carrying the family touchstone (just like mine, though two inches longer) and the acid bottle.

"Will you mind if I scratch the metal, Señor Gravés?"

"Do your worst, Señor Cortés!"

He filed a minute piece from the edge, took a trace from the exposed interior with the touchstone, applied the acid, shook his head. "I regret to inform you, Señor Gravés," he said in even tones, "that this is not gold."

I wrung his hand. "I am delighted by your assay, Señor Cortés; and under a profound obligation to you!"

He looked at me in surprise; then, after a brief, suave nod of goodbye turned to show a woman tourist some matched strings of the "Manacor Pearls" for which this island is famous. There are, of course, no pearl-beds in the Mediterranean. . . .

I wrote again to Dr. Decker, informing him that the medal had now been twice assayed, and at each test proved not to be what he and I believed it was; but that, joking aside, I should always recall with pride the occasion of its bestowal. Nor should I expect him to send me a gold substitute. Though the "14 k" referred, in fact, to the karat-fineness of the plating—a trade device which, I understood, was neither unusual nor, so far as I knew, against the Law—a medal's intrinsic value could be of no consequence to the recipient.

Dr. Decker took this very well, assuring me that he would ask the metallurgists of his University to assay the stock of metals already struck for further Prince Alexander Droutzkoy Memorial Awards, and see whether or not mine had been exceptional. That was over a year ago, and I am still waiting for his report. But I notice that the Alexander Droutzkoy Gold Medal was not awarded in 1961.

You all know, I suppose, that in England no non-royal medals have been struck of gold since the First World War. It's against the Law. But I got a research-team to do a brief investigation of American gold medals for me. They report that though no legal impediment to the striking of fine-gold medals exists in the United States, such awards are now rare. The Director of the Mint licences medal-makers and jewellers to buy fine gold; yet while they must

submit detailed returns on the troy ounces of gold used in manu-
facturing their products, they need not declare how much gold
went into any particular piece. American medals, therefore, range
through all degrees of fine and low gold; nor is it illegal or un-
ethical to describe gilded bronze or silver as "gold."

If medal-makers stamp their products to indicate karat-fineness,
they are subject to the Federal Stamping Act of 1906, which tolerates
a deficiency of no more than one half-karat. This Act also regulates
the mark to be used by makers of gold-filled or rolled-gold plated
medals—two similar processes, in which sheets of gold are brazed,
welded, or soldered to base metal. Legally, a medal stamped "gold
filled" must contain gold equal to one-twentieth or more of its total
weight; a medal marked "rolled gold plate" must contain gold equalling one-twentieth or less of its total weight; and, in each case, the
stamp must indicate not only the fractional proportion of gold to
the base metal, but also its karat-fineness. However, the Act can
be interpreted in more ways than one. Until three years ago, it
was considered lawful and ethical to describe as "gold plated" any
medal cast in bronze or silver which had a gold skin at least seven
one-millionth of an inch thick—the result of having been dipped
into an electrolytic gold-solution. Makers of such medals were glad
to stamp their products "gold plated"; but rolled-gold-platers raised
an outcry, charging the electroplaters with fraud. In 1957, the Federal Trade Commission, which issues trade-practice rules for jewellers, decided that articles electroplated with a gold skin of at least
seven one-millionth of an inch, might be marked (if marked at all)
as "gold-electroplated"; and that where the thickness was even less,
they might be marked "gold-flashed" or "gold-washed." This F.T.C.
decision being unenforceable by law, the dispute has never been
resolved, and gold electroplaters now seldom stamp their products;
or, if they do, cannot, it seems, be restrained from marking them
"14 k." As Chaucer wrote: *Hyt is not al gold that glareth.*

Variations in the gold-content of medals have, naturally, been
caused by the changing price of gold. When President Roosevelt
devalued the dollar, a troy ounce of fine gold went up in price
from twenty dollars to its present level of thirty-five. The medal-
makers passed on this 75 per cent increase to the medal-donors;

and demand for high-karat awards soon weakened. Since World War Two, however, the endowment funds of most national institutions have risen more than 75 per cent in sympathy with the stock market; and fine-gold medals are no longer ruled out by economics. Nevertheless, why give fine gold when one may safely and ethically give dross? Thus, though more "gold medals" are awarded than ever before, the gilt enormously outnumber the golden; and of these, few exceed fourteen-karat fineness.

A random golden roll. The U. S. Golf Association gave Jack Nicklaus, the amateur with the lowest score in the 1960 National Open Golf Tournament, a fourteen-karat medal. Mayor Wagner collected one of the same fineness: the Amateur Athletic Union's Gold Medal Award for "the citizen of the Metropolitan area who has best served youth and athletics during the year." The National Geographic Society's Hubbard Medal, which has gone to such heroes as Peary, Shackleton, Amundsen, Lindbergh, Byrd and Hillary, runs to fourteen karat. So does the special gold medal which the American Society for the Prevention of Cruelty to Animals conferred in 1960 on Baker, the intrepid Space-monkey—and, posthumously, on Baker's luckless companion Able. The National Geographic Society's Special Gold Medal, however, given to Prince Philip in 1957 for his not-too-perilous world tour, measures four inches across, weighs two pounds four ounces troy, and is of twenty-two karat fineness. Presidents de Gaulle of France, and Lleras of Colombia, also Their Majesties Bhumibol Adulyadej, King of Thailand, and Mahendra Bir Bikram Shah Deva, King of Nepal, have all recently won the fourteen-karat Medal of New York City reserved for kings and heads of state. The Massachusetts Horticultural Society's George Robert White Medal is twenty-two karat.

But the Key of the City of New York, last presented to the Honourable Sir Hugh Stephenson, K.C.M.G., C.I.E., C.U.O., O.B.E., former British Consul-General at New York, is electroplated bronze; like the American Poetry Society's Prince Alexander Droutzkoy's Memorial Award for Services to Poetry. And no gold medals won by the champion skiers who risked life and limb in the Winter Olympics at Squaw Valley were better than "gold-filled"; so a thoughtful California firm copied them in fourteen- and eighteen-karat gold, and put the replicas on sale—for losers as well as winners to frame, if they wished, and hang over their drawing-room grand pianos.*

* In the early winter of 1968 I was awarded the gold medal for Poetry at the Mexican Cultural Olympics; it was silver impregnated with gold. Three weeks later, Queen Elizabeth, at the suggestion of her Poet Laureate, presented me, at a private audience in Buckingham Palace, with her own medal for Poetry. This was eighteen-caret gold and a good deal larger than those ancestral Irish medals hoarded by my family. My mother's ambition for me had at last been realized.

The Word "Báraka"*

The vocabulary of Islam contains an important and powerful word: *BÁRAKA*. It derives from a Semitic root *BRK*, present in the Biblical name *Barak* and in the Phoenician *Barka*. (The city of Barcelona is called after Hamilcar Barca, Hannibal's father.) *Barak* or *barka* or *báraka* means lightning. Since lightning is a phenomenon everywhere attributed to the gods, *báraka* means the sudden divine rapture which overcomes either a prophet or a group of fervent devotees (Dervish dancers, for example, or the primitive Christians at the Feast of Pentecost) whom it unites in a bond of love: it can therefore stand for the blessedness acquired by holy shrines and other places where the spirit of God had been plainly manifested. The word has been adopted into Spanish, and has Hebrew equivalents; but the Jews prefer to derive *báraka* from a root meaning "knee" and therefore devotion to a god whose worshippers kneel.

* This address to the Oxford University Poetry Society had been given in a modified form to the American Academy and Institute of Arts, as the Blashfield Address.

A poem can have *báraka,* inspired by the Muse; and the Moslem *Sufis,* surprisingly enough, own to a female Muse.

This religious metaphor invites lay uses. If a family has settled down peacefully in a house of their own choosing, every room acquires a domestic, rather than an ecstatic, *báraka,* of which the children become conscious and which spells "home." *Báraka* can thus be applied to relics, keepsakes, and other assurances of blessedness.

I always avoid using a foreign word when an English equivalent can be found. But the nearest I know to *báraka* is the Elizabethan "virtue." Tyndale's translation of *Mark* has: "such virtues (i.e. acts of blessedness) as are wrought by his hands." And the Geneva Bible: "in his own virtue (i.e. holy power) Christ rose again," and a solitary instance occurs in the King James Bible: "Jesus knowing that virtue had gone out of him . . ." This sense of "virtue" as spiritual power has become obsolete beyond revival. Virtue is now a moral habit, attributed mainly to the docile and uninspired: and *vertu* is rarity from the collector's point of view: and a *virtuoso* is an expert capable of judging such rarity.

An Arab village woman will prize the dented brass cooking pot that has done service for a generation or more, as having *báraka* and producing far tastier food than the brightest spun-aluminium saucepan in the bazaar. In the United States and England, a pair of blue jeans so often washed that they have faded almost white, or a well-worn gardening jacket, can equally posses *báraka:* and a wife's failure to recognize this while spring-cleaning often causes a deal of trouble.

John Kenneth Galbraith and his fellow-economists in the United States have emphasized that the old American ideal of thrift, which implied producing durable goods and using them with affectionate care until they disintegrated—like the One-Horse Shay of the poem —no longer thrives even in the backwoods. Instead, Expendability is preached: the manufacture and consumption of goods not meant to last for more than a short season. If a new appliance proves to have an uneconomically long life, it must be replaced by a shorter-lived substitute. With care, you may perhaps keep this year's model working for several years; then something will snap, and nobody will offer to repair it. That these practices keep the wheels of industry turning, and salesmen busy, cannot be denied; but when nothing lasts long enough to become an intregral part of a man's life, the principles of artificial obsolescence affect his friendships, loyalties, loves and his tastes in literature and art. The American way of life has now gained a firm foothold in Europe.

Anything made by hand has a certain glow of life. Factory-made objects are born dead—however apt their design, however sound their construction, and must have life breathed into them by affectionate use. A veteran typewriter of which you have grown fond seems to reciprocate your feelings and even encourage the flow of thought. Though at first a lifeless assemblage of parts, it eventually comes alive. And so did an automobile in thriftier days. As for cameras—any good photographer is horror-struck by the loss of a camera that has grown to be part of himself: even if he buys an identical model, there will be a delay of anything from six months to two years before it learns to take his own inimitable sort of picture. Scientists cannot explain such phenomena, and therefore dispute the facts. Let them! *Báraka* will never be a scientific term.

Hand-made things that have been a long time in one household eventually come under the hammer and, if they have any rarity, pass by way of the antique dealer and virtuoso into the hands of the rich collector. The collector does not use them, not even the china and table silver, but displays them, critically labelled, behind glass. Thence they may pass to some museum where their stored-up *báraka* inevitably dies, because what sustains it is the touch of human fingers. A collector at least lets a few friends handle his treasures; but museum visitors are forbidden to touch the exhibits. Nor do museums ever disgorge their exhibits, unless in wartime to drunken looters—however crammed the cellars may be with crates of bequests which they have no room to display. The New York Metropolitan Museum contains no less than three Stradivarius violins: none of them kept alive by playing. And, as a museum curator of silver once told me in a moment of frankness: "museum silver gets the wrong sort of tarnish."

Báraka in literature and the creative arts is of the utmost importance. Remember that it originally meant "divine inspiration" or "blessedness"—a quality which the most daring intellectual experiments, or works most shrewdly designed for the current market, cannot possess. But the new economy, respecting a citizen's inalienable right to buy what he wants (or thinks that he wants), lets the question "Will it sell?" rule commercial production. Writers and artists feel obliged to watch the market, for although a Government may have trouble in disposing of national food surpluses, yet idleness (except among the very rich) still counts as a sin; and public opinion is opposed to the feeding of a parasitic class whose work lacks an assured market value; and *báraka*—the quality of life in poems, or stories, or paintings, or sculptures, or music—is never granted to a man more concerned with selling than with making.

Religious ecstasy and the poetic trance, if one looks at these phenomena subjectively, are both achieved by divine inspiration; or, if looked at objectively, by self-hypnosis. Religious ecstasy is invited by prayers, music, and solemn ritual. Formalities of verse-printing invite the poetic trance: which means, for instance, that a sonnet printed as a prose paragraph will be extremely hard to read as a poem. Prose intelligence operates on one level only; poetic intelligence operates in depth, as if under narcotics, with all its five inner senses alert. I can sharpen my point by mentioning the *báraka* resident in the King James Bible which, though not poetry, is printed in verses and retains the archaic diction and speech-rhythms of its early Tudor translators. In Britain today, this ancient *báraka*, and that of a few unrestored churches and cathedrals, keeps the flickering candle of faith alight. Yet, in the name of progress, various ecclesiastical bodies are now trying to supplant the King James version with *The New English Bible*, a translation carefully purged of all *báraka*. Though this has sold in advance by the million, the verdict of the British countryside is: "We don't like this book. The old one was holier. If I had to swear an oath on this book, I wouldn't feel bound to tell the truth." "Holiness," then, is a near-equivalent of *báraka*, especially if detached from its ecclesiastical setting—as when Coleridge wrote in *Kubla Khan*:

> A savage place, as *holy* and enchanted
> As e'er beneath a waning moon was haunted
> By woman wailing for her demon lover . . .

and again:

> Weave a circle round him thrice
> And close your eyes in *holy* dread . . .

But though the formalities of printing a poem invite readers to fall under its spell, poems so rarely have *báraka* that the eye grows suspicious and seldom succumbs. Myself, I have come to dread the sight of a new book of poems. Too often the spell vanishes after I have read a few lines, and my prose mind reasserts itself. The poem's holy circle has been broken by some extraneous element: whether experimental affectation, or Classical convention, or incoherence, or banality, or didacticism. . . . How to create and preserve the spell must remain a mystery. But one can say, at least, that the words must, as it were, grow together, entranced by the poet's personal rhythm; and that they cannot do so unless unchallengeably his own, the familiar furniture of his mind. All attempts to borrow from the alien languages of science and philosophy will be futile; they have no emotional depth.

Anglo-American poetry of, say, 1911–1929, based on Continental models and psychological theory, provides the text-books with an interesting chapter. Though not commercial in origin, the poems lacked *báraka* because their motive was critical, rather than creative. A poem seems to choose its own colouring, voice, form, gait, character, in the blind moment of inception, just as the human embryo does; these are not predeterminable elements, except perhaps in a test-tube homunculus . . . It had been decided, at any rate, that the yoke of tradition should be broken, as the French were busily breaking theirs. This made poor sense: for French has a remarkably poor vocabulary compared with English, and its severe control by the *Academie Française* tempted anti-academic writers to acts of sabotage. Of English, on the other hand, it could be said in the words of *Ecclesiasticus:* "An ornament of gold is her yoke, and her traces a riband of pure silk." Literature in England and the United States during the first decade of this century was, on the whole, undistinguished to the point of stuffiness—the very riches of our language had scared prominent writers into establishing strict conventions and trying to introduce a Classical impersonality based on Latin practice. Nevertheless, the younger poets did not need to revolt; but only to assert their time-honoured liberties—English, because it is a two-stand language of Anglo-Saxon and Norman-French, permits unlimited rhythmic variations on scores of metrical norms. However, their difficulty lay in this: that to be idiosyncratic without loss of principle, to create a personal poetic style that could be recognized at a glance yet resist parody, demanded too many years of work, too deep a devotion to the language, and too lonely an independence of fashion. Anti-academic experimentalism was far easier. And, paradoxically, their poems have now been accepted by English Faculties in the United States and England and become the most advanced form of academicism. Just how far this tendency has gone was forced on me recently. One of my tasks as holder of the Oxford Chair of Poetry is helping to adjudicate the Newdigate Prize Poem. Twenty-seven out of thirty-one entries were based on modernist technique. Nevertheless, that these candidates chose the modernist formula, rather than the heroic couplet to which they were limited until a few years ago, confirms my feeling that it is already on the way out. The technique that young men choose for a prize poem on a set subject is not one in which they will try to write authentic and original poetry.

The present remarkable public demand for poetry keeps pace with the growing affluence of life throughout the Western world and the gradual shrinking of the work week. Never before have such efforts been made to satisfy the demand, yet never have there been fewer original poets. "This is a critical, not a poetic, age," I am told. "Inspiration is out. Contemporary poems must reflect the prevailing analytic spirit." But I am old-fashioned enough to demand *báraka*, an inspirational gift not yet extinct, which defies critical analysis.

The present economic system is based on expendability. The museum system, which supplements it, is based on what I should call "arrestation of time." The museums emphasize the hopeless distance separating the period pieces exposed behind glass from manufactured goods in current use. A similar distance separates the home vocabulary of most schoolboys and undergraduates from that of their English Literature classes. The thread connecting the two finally snapped thirty years ago. Shakespeare is now a museum exhibit, not for home reading as when I was a boy: so are Wordsworth, Tennyson and Browning. Anyone raised under these conditions faces a difficult dilemma if he tries to write poems: his home vocabulary cannot bear the full weight of thought and emotion he may want to express; yet the museum vocabulary is so little his own that borrowings from it will look artificial.

This is not a problem that has ever worried me: I was born into a bookish family, discovered English poetry for myself at the age of ten, and escaped over thirty years ago to a Spanish village untouched by modern technology—bringing with me my personal possessions and language—which has been my home ever since. If the house seems, to visiting friends, like a museum, that is their mistake: my great-grandfather's silver candlesticks and my great-great-grandfather's spoons, as well as hundred-year-old plates and dishes, are in daily use, and the English poets are ranked around me on book-shelves within easy reach. I feel contemporary with Thomas Hardy, whom I knew well, and through him with Coleridge and Keats, and through them with Shakespeare, Marlowe, Donne, Skelton and Chaucer. Call me a living fossil, if you like.

Expendability is, of course, closely allied to the new phenomenon of haste. Were it not for the immense increase in speed, which makes it possible to transport goods and raw materials in a matter of hours rather than days, we should still be bound by the economy of thrift. The Arabic proverb is to the point here:

> *Háraka Háraka ma fiha báraka.*
> ("Haste, haste, has no virtue.")

I shall leave you to find your own apt instances of *báraka* in art, architecture or music. . . . In poetry, it can cast an immortal spell on the simplest combination of words. The Greeks held a spot struck by lightning so sacred that they built an enclosing wall around it; true poems are equally lightning-struck and equally insulated by their own poetic forms against encroachments of time and fashion. . . . There is also an anti-*báraka*, springing from wilful lovelessness. The atmosphere of houses can be poisoned by years of hatred; the memories of childhood can be made hideous by oppression; lovely jewels can be cursed by greed and envy. Anti-*báraka* in poetry derives, perhaps, from a greater hatred of hypocrisy than an active love of truth. It is critical diabolism challenging the self-assurance of the righteous, and welcome only when a country's leading poets, artists, architects and musicians are ignorant formalists. The Germans call it *Unheimlichkeit*: a sinister unhomeliness.

And let us not undervalue Mother Goose's nusery rhymes, and Edward Lear's nonsense rhymes, and sea-shanties, and occasional so-called minor poems by Herrick, Goldsmith, Crabbe, Southey, Jane Taylor, Poe, Stevenson, Longfellow, Whittier, De la Mare. Though "quaint" and "homely" have become words of polite scorn, "quaintness" is a close English equivalent of this lesser *báraka*, which combines the senses of "skilfully made," "old-fashioned," and "diverting." . . . Most first volumes of verse published today are one-man shows intended for the critics, and wholly lacking in quaintness. . . . Nothing can halt this trend, if only because the publication of expendable books, and of the criticism they provoke, keeps the busy wheels turning. It is worse in the States, where too many of their authors are sponsored by Foundations which, in turn, must find an annual quota of respectable beneficiaries. . . . Is it unrealistic to hanker after an economy of thrift and the restriction of verse to a thin golden trickle?

The Poet's Paradise

We have narrowed our minds by a neglect of the physical senses: relying on reason, we no longer see, hear, taste, smell or feel anything like so acutely as our primitive ancestors did, or as most little children still do before their education hardens. Henry Vaughan's *The Retreat*, imitated by Wordsworth in his better known *Intimations of Immortality*, begins:

> Happy those early days when I
> Shin'd in my angel-infancy,
> Before I understood this place
> Appointed for my second race
> Or taught my soul to fancy aught
> But a white celestial thought,
> When yet I had not walked above
> A mile or two from my first love
> And looking back (at that short space),
> Could see a glimpse of his bright face
> When on some gilded cloud or flower
> My gazing soul would dwell an hour . . .

Civilized man notices a gilded cloud and, at best, mutters "cumulus" or "cirrus" or "mare's tail," speculating on the weather it portends; notices a flower and dismisses it with a casual recognition of the variety. To gaze at a wild rose or buttercup for even a minute and find illumination in the sight, would never occur to him; if only because all his senses are blunted by a persistent disregard of the ugly smells, ugly sounds, ugly sights and unpalatable tastes which the struggle for existence entails. His spirit, also, has lost touch with the ideas of mystery, grace and love that originally informed it: intellect and habit starve out imagination. How to awaken these dormant capacities is a problem seldom raised, except by mystics, who usually suggest a daunting formula of spiritual exercises designed to tame bodily lusts. Some claim to have themselves visited Paradise in a state of trance so induced, and to have found it the seat of true felicity and perfect wisdom. Here is a typical passage from Thomas Traherne's *Centuries of Meditation* (he was a contemporary of Vaughan's):

> The corn was orient and immortal wheat, which never should be reaped nor ever was sown. I thought it had stood from everlasting to everlasting. The dust and stones of the street were as precious gold: the gates were at first the end of the world. The green trees when I first saw them through one of the gates transported and ravished me: their sweetness and unusual beauty made my heart to leap, and almost mad with ecstasy, they were such strange and beautiful things . . . all things abided eternally as they were in their proper places. Eternity was manifest in the light of the day and something infinite behind everything appeared, which talked with my expectation and moved my desire.

Today, the main alleviations for the stress of commercial and industrial life are organized religion, organized entertainment, drink. Organized religion may sober the spirit, but except among the more ecstatic sects, rarely purges it. Organized entertainment distracts, but does not illuminate, the mind. Though some poems, melodies, works of art, love-affairs and fever dreams may give glimpses of a lost magical reality, their spell is short-lasting: it does not create such a permanent nostalgia for the fairyland of childhood as possessed, say, John Clare in Northampton Asylum. The hard, dirty, loveless, synthetic world re-asserts itself as the sole factual truth. Yet a superstitious dream that, somehow, happiness, love, glory, magic lie hidden close at hand, protects the world from the nervous breakdown of which recent wars have been symptomatic: a dream that, when fostered by films and family magazines, becomes optimistically attached to personal success in a career or in marriage and, when fostered by the Church, optimistically attached to a Paradisal afterworld.

In ancient times, "Paradise" was strictly reserved for an illuminated aristocracy, until the Church at last threw open the gates to all converts, however brutish or feeble-minded, who would accept baptism. Priests then preached Heaven's glories (attainable only by a belief in Christ) as the reward of patience and humility after traversing this vale of tears. Yet St. John's Apocalyptic Paradise is borrowed from chapters of the pre-Christian *Book of Enoch*, which are themselves based on the "Eden" chapters of *Ezekiel* and *Genesis*; and these, again, on the Babylonian Paradise described in the Gilgamesh Epic and elsewhere. The Persians knew a similar Paradise; and their name for it; *paridaeza*, yields the Syrian-Greek word *paradeisos* and the Hebrew *pardess*. Those middle-Eastern Paradises, so far back as the Sumerian, are reported as being delightful mountain-top gardens watered by a four-headed crystal river, their fruit-trees laden with flashing jewels; and a wise serpent always haunts them. Rare humans who enter Paradise while in a state of grace are granted "perfect wisdom" by the Serpent—"knowledge of good and evil" means knowledge of "all things that exist"—and only the herb of immortality is denied them. Thus Gilgamesh, having visited the jewelled Babylonian Paradise, dived to the sea-bottom and drew up a herb of immortality; but the Serpent took it from him, and he meekly resigned himself to death. Adam and Eve were driven out of Eden ("pleasure") by God lest they might discover and eat the fruit of immortality; the Cherub, on guard at the gate thereafter with a flaming sword, is the very Serpent who gave them the fruit of knowledge. The King of Tyre, though perfect in beauty and wisdom, is figuratively expelled from Eden (*Ezekiel* xxviii) for claiming to be an immortal god with a seat in the heart of the sea. *Enoch* mentions both the tree of wisdom and the tree of life; and *the Secrets of Enoch* places the latter in the Third Heaven, a paradise to which St. Paul claimed that he had been caught up.

Greek mythographers told of a Paradise on Mount Atlas, the "Garden of the Hesperides," guarded by a hundred-headed Serpent; but made Heracles shoot the Serpent, take away some of the jewelled fruit, and become immortal. This Paradise, like the Sumerian one that antedates Gilgamesh's "Garden of Delights," belonged to a Mother-goddess—it was Hera's before she married Zeus—not to a male god. Christians chose to identify the Serpent in Eden with Satan; they preached that Jesus Christ, a "Second Adam," lives permanently in Paradise, having expelled the Serpent, and is ready there to welcome all believers when it has finally been destroyed on the Day of Judgment.

Why do paradises follow a traditional pattern, widespread and persistent enough to be shared even by Polynesians and pre-Columbian Mexicans? The evidence suggests that, originally, a common drug causes the paradisal visions and provides the remarkable mental illumination described as "perfect wisdom." One such drug, a hallucigenic mushroom, was certainly used in Central America before the Spanish conquest. Professor Roger Heim and R. G. Wasson's massive work, *Les Champignons Hallucigènes de Mexique* (Paris, 1958), contains a coloured reproduction of a fresco from the Aztec city of Tepantitla, dated between 300 and 600 A.D., which shows a soul visiting Paradise. The usual elements are there: a river (stocked with fish), bordered with flowers and bejewelled trees, haunted by bright-coloured butterflies and a spectacular serpent. The soul stands open-mouthed, weeping great tears of joy and wonder, his body connected to the river by a blue thread. This river is shaped like a mushroom and, at its source—the centre of the mushroom head— lurks Tlalóc, God of Mysteries, in toad form, the water issuing from his mouth. Tlalóc, who often wore a serpent head-dress, was a god of lightning. He used a sea-shell as another emblem, and "had his seat in the midst of the seas": at the bottom of the fresco an underwater grotto appears, marked with a cross, the four heads of which are mushrooms. Nobody who has been admitted to the rite thus pictured will find much difficulty in deciphering the symbolism.

R. G. Wasson's ritual experience came as the culmination of a study on which he and his wife had been engaged for years; that of mycophobia. Mycophobia, the unreasoning fear of mushrooms, affects whole populations in Europe, Asia and Africa, being total in some regions, in others modified by certain exceptions (such as the white field mushroom among the English), elsewhere non-existent. Now, a few mushrooms, easily distinguished from edible varieties, do contain a mortal poison; but most are palatable, if not delicious. Why, the Wassons asked, when wholesome fruit and vegetables are eaten freely, with a disregard for the poisonous or the inedible, should this selectivity be denied the mushroom? Why should horrible and obscene names be applied to edible mushrooms? Perhaps mycophobia pointed to an ancient taboo, like that which has given Jews and Moslems a disgust of pork, and Northern Europeans a disgust of horse-flesh—nutritious and tasty meat—both pig and horse having once been holy animals. And, since mushrooms figured alongside toads, snakes and devils in numerous late mediaeval paintings, and still bear popular names connected with toads, snakes and devils, it looked as if they might have been sacred food in a pagan rite, preserved by witches of Western Europe who kept toads and snakes as diabolic "familiars."

A particular variety of mushroom, the *amanita muscaria*, in Britain called "fly-cap," grows under birch-trees in Northern countries, where it is scarlet with white spots; but under conifers to the southward, where its scarlet becomes fox-colour. Fly-cap induces in the Korjaks, a Palaeo-Siberian tribe of Kamchatka, and among the Mongol Hazaras of Afghanistan, a delightful ecstasy which helps them to consult ancestral spirits and utter prophecies. R. G. Wasson guessed that the mushroom had been similarly used in Europe, though reserved for the priesthood; that, for security reasons the taboo had been extended to cover the eating of all mushrooms, on pain of death; and that this taboo hung on long after the rites came to an end— except in countries where famine forced the common people to defy it and become positive mycophiles, as all Slavonic peoples now are. The name "toadstool," particularly applied to fly-cap, is apt; because it contains a poison, *bufotenine*, which is also exuded by toads from their "warts" when frightened.

Moreover, early Spanish archives mentioned Mexican mushroom-oracles that, though officially extinct, were still rumoured to operate in secret far from civilization. A certain mushroom was known as "God's Body" by the Mazateks of Oaxaca Province, because sacramentally eaten. The Wassons, learning of this, visited Oaxaca during the June mushroom season, and were able to attend an oracular meeting at which the *curandero* ("healer") who took charge, ceremoniously ate certain small ill-tasting mushrooms and, speaking for the god, gave an unexpected, surprising and accurate answer to the question they had asked him. Later, when invited by a *curandera* to eat the mushrooms themselves, they understood the solemn local tradition about the feast: "One knows all; one even sees where God dwells." Their visions recalled the heaven shown on the Tepantitla fresco, and it became clear that they had been symbolically eating the body not of Christ, but of the god Tlalóc.

In the different regions of Mexico where the cult survives, certain religious rules are common to all. Devotees, before partaking of a mushroom feast, must fast, abstain from sexual intercourse, and be at peace with the world and themselves. Whoever disregards these rules (the *curanderos* and *curanderas* agreed) may see such demonic visions as to wish they had never been born. The Christian, Jewish, Greek and Babylonian Heavens, it should be recalled, have a Hell which complements Paradise; and the usual vision is of innumerable demon faces grinning from lurid caverns. But those who attend such a feast while in a state of grace, report that the mushrooms not only sharpen their intelligence, so that they seem to possess "perfect wisdom," but shower on them what Christians call "the peace of love that passes all understanding"—a strong, non-erotic sense of spiritual comradeship.

The Roman Catholic Church teaches that Paradise cannot be attained except by repentance; and prepares every sinner for the journey with the *viaticum*, a symbolic consumption of Jesus Christ's body and blood, after asking him to purge his soul by a sincere confession. From what religion, it should be asked, did St. Paul borrow this rite, since it is not attested in the Gospels and is an infringement of the Hebrew law against the drinking of blood? A question that leads to another: in what pre-Christian cult did a god deliver oracles when his flesh was symbolically eaten—as the Mazateks now believe that Tlalóc-Christ does? Tlalóc, we know, was the spirit of lightning-engendered toadstools. More questions arise. What European god claimed this nativity? Or had associations with the serpent or the toad? Or possessed an underwater retreat? Or assisted at mysteries where ineffable visions were witnessed?

The sole European deity known to have matched Tlalóc in these respects was Dionysus. Born as a serpent-crowned child from the Earth-goddess Semele, whom a flash of lightning had impregnated, he went through a variety of transformations, was then torn to shreds and eaten by the Titans, but restored to life by his grandmother, the Goddess Rhea, Creatrix of the world; possessed an underwater retreat in the grottoes of the Sea-goddess Thetis; and assisted at the chief Greek Mysteries, under the protection of goddesses.

The Greek poets tell how when Dionysus' Maenads tore off Orpheus' head, it continued to prophesy. The head of Pentheus, another figure in the Dionysus myth, was torn off by his own mother Agave; both incidents could refer to the practice of tearing the mushroom-head from its stalk—heads alone are used at Mexican oracles. The Eleusinian Mysteries, sacred to the goddesses Demeter and Persephone, and also to Dionysus, were preceded by fasting and a ritual bath in the sea, where devotees transferred their sins to scape-pigs. They then entered a temple, drank mint-water and ate pastries baked in magical shapes and carried in baskets. As a result, they saw celestial visions which could never afterwards be forgotten. The meaning of the Greek word *mysterion* ("mystery") is disputed, but since the mysteries were an autumnal festival complementary to the spring *anthesterion,* and since this means "flower-springing," *mysterion* may well mean *myko-sterion,* or "mushroom-springing."

A distinction should here be drawn between the wild Dionysian orgies of Maenads who went raging over the hills, often in the company of Satyrs (a pre-Hellenic mountain tribe), and the decently conducted temple-mysteries, where no violence occurred. Pliny's remark that an awed hush "descends on people if a toad is placed among them" suggests that Dionysus, like Tlalóc, had a toad epiphany. But the celestial visions of the mysteries are unlikely to have been produced by fly-cap, which loses its toxic quality when cooked, and could not well be introduced raw into food and drink. However, the toxic qualities of *panaeolus papilionaceus,* a hallucigenic toadstool shown on an early Greek vase and now known to have figured in the European witch cult, resist cooking; its liquor may have been mixed in the mint-water, and its flesh baked in the magical pastries. I believe, but cannot prove, that fly-cap, which appears on a carved Etruscan mirror at the feet of the criminal Ixion, was the original mushroom sacred to the universal Toad-god, and that the more tranquil and equally delightful properties of *panaeolus papilionaceus* and *psilocybe,* were discovered by later experiment and also placed under the Toad-god's charge. Fly-cap grows in both hemispheres, and the ancient mushroom-stones of Guatemala show Tlalóc in toad shape, seated underneath a mushroom which appears to be a fly-cap, not a *psilocybe.*

Some of the Eleusinian pastries had phallic shapes and, indeed, *mykes* ("mushroom") also means "phallus" in Greek; others were baked like piglings (a widespread term for mushrooms); some perhaps like toads and serpents. A common name for the toad in European folklore is "the cripple," because of his clumsy feet; and "Dionysus" means "the lame god." One Greek hero who, according to the myths, at first resisted Dionysus, but presently saw the light, was Perseus, King of Argos and founder of Mycenae. Punished for his obduracy with an outbreak of madness among the Argive women—they began eating their own babies raw, as also happened at Thebes when Pentheus resisted the cult—Perseus dedicated a temple to Dionysus at Mycenae. Argos had a toad as its badge, and Perseus is said to have named Mycenae after a mushroom found on the site, "from which proceeded a stream of water." He also made visionary flights through the air, paid a visit to the "Stygian nymphs" on the slopes of Mount Atlas—presumably the Hesperides, who were later kind to his descendant Heracles—and claimed the same sort of nativity as Dionysus, having been engendered by Zeus in a shower of gold. Phryneus, the Toadstool-Dionysus to which these myths point, lay securely hidden behind the Wine-Dionysus and the Grain-Dionysus. Apart from a menacing Greek proverb "Mushrooms are the food of the gods," nobody mentioned the subject. Greek peasants are mycophobes.

Baby-eating, a practice not associated with any Greek cult except that of Dionysus, also figured (according to Catholic missionaries) in the Aztec rain-making rites of Tlalóc. This god's name meant "Pulp of the Earth" (i.e. mushroom?), and he lived at Tlalócan, a mountain paradise, with certain Grain-goddesses and his gentle sister-spouse Chalchiuthlicue, patroness of streams and family-life. Some centuries before the Spanish conquest, matriarchy and clan-totemism had been superseded among the Aztecs by patriarchy and individual totemism. Tlalóc thus officially escaped from the tutelage of goddesses, just as Dionysus did in Classical Greece when he was raised to the Olympic Council of Twelve and took over the Barley-goddess Demeter's winnowing festival, the Haloa. Yet in the Mysteries, Dionysus seems still to have been subservient to Demeter and Persephone. Similarly, the Mazatec *curandera* who initiated the Wassons addressed the Christianized Tlalóc as if he were her wayward son, and she a goddess. It is possible that, alike in Greece and Mexico, the "babies" eaten in sacred pictures were really mushrooms.

The Christian sacrament of bread and wine was a love-feast in Hellenistic style. Initiates of the Lesser Eleusinian Mysteries, who had to undergo a period of probation before being admitted to the Greater Mysteries, saw no celestial visions. Presumably, the mystagogues withheld the sacred hallucigenic agent until sure of a candidate's worthiness; he received bread and wine only, symbols of the Grain-Dionysus and the Wine-Dionysus. The Church has indeed banished the Serpent from Paradise. Her sacramental elements give the communicant no visionary foretaste of the new Jerusalem. The disappointment often felt by Protestant adolescents at their first communion is a natural one—the priest promises more than they are able to experience. I learned only last week, from an Arabic scholar, that the root-word F.T.R. means, in Arabic, first "toadstool," then "divine rapture," then "sacred pellets of bread." This points to a pre-Islamic hallucigenic practice of immense age.

Granted, many Christian mystics and Jewish mystics have undoubtedly seen Paradisal sights, but always after a life of intense spiritual struggle; and these often alternate with terrifying visions of Hell. It is now therefore usual to treat mystics as schizophrenics, arresting them and prescribing electric-shock treatment if their enthusiasm has caused a breach of the peace. The Church herself is apt to discourage a mystic who claims to have seen sights denied to his ecclesiastical superiors; suspecting him, at best, of spiritual pride. This type of schizophrenia is chronic, uncontrollable, and what is called "anti-social." Only when mystics have written poems, or painted pictures, in which the illumination cannot be denied, and only when they have been dead some years—for example St. John of the Cross, El Greco, Blake, van Gogh—are they likely to be valued as great souls.

The use of hallucigenic mushrooms, on the other hand, induces a temporary, controllable schizophrenia within the Mazatek social scheme, and the sole religious demand on participants is that they shall enter the circle fasting, with a clear conscience and a quiet mind. When I ate *psilocybe* on 31 January 1960, a recording of the *curandera's* invocation to Tlalóc as Christ gave the rite a decent solemnity. *Psilocybe* must be eaten in complete darkness—because the least light, even strained through the eyelids, becomes painful as soon as the drug takes effect. The visions last for some four and a half hours. According to the Mazateks, a novice seldom sees persons or historical scenes: he finds it enough to enter the "Garden of Delights." The second and third feast may widen his experiences. Adepts learn to direct their mind wherever they please, visit the past, foretell the future.

Here is the account I wrote of my experience:

That evening, four of us gathered in Gordon Wasson's apartment overlooking the East River, prepared to set out for Paradise under his guidance. He had advised us to fast beforehand, drink no liquor, and try to achieve a state of grace. At seven-thirty he gave us the mushrooms in crystalline form washed down with water and, at eight, began turning out the lights one by one, while we settled down in easy chairs. Soon no sound was heard except the swish-swish of cars passing in an endless stream along the Drive between us and the river: a noise not unlike the sound of waves on a beach.

By eight o'clock I felt a numbness in my arms, and a pricking at the nape of my neck. In the half-light that filtered through the shutters, coloured dots appeared on the ceiling; they shone brighter when I closed my eyes. We all began to shiver, our pulses slowed down, and

Masha Wasson brought in blankets. Since she is a trained nurse and had twice made this journey herself, we welcomed the reassuring pressure of her hand. I remembered a warning quotation: "You are going where God dwells; and will be granted all knowledge. . . . Whoever nurses evil in his heart sees hideous demons and nameless horrors, more proper to Hell than to Paradise, and wishes he had never been born." I anxiously considered my own motives. How honest were they? Would I see demons? Though not a saint, I was at least a dedicated historian and poet; with luck I might be spared punishment.

Since even the half-light had become uncomfortably strong for my eyes, I kept them closed. I knew that the road to Paradise often begins under the sea, or from a lake-bottom; so the greenish water now lapping around me came as no surprise. I entered a marble grotto, passing a pile of massive sunken statuary, and found myself in a high-roofed tunnel lit by brilliantly coloured lamps. The sea lay behind.

This was a perfect schizophrenia. My corporeal self reclined in a chair, fully conscious, exchanging occasional confidences with friends: but another "I" had entered the tunnel—perhaps the same tunnel through which, four thousand years before, the epic hero Gilgamesh made his approach to the Babylonian Paradise?

Still worrying about the demons, I glanced up at the roof. Thousands of pink, green or yellow faces, like carnival masks, grimaced horribly down; but I dismissed them with a wave of my hand, and they obediently vanished. . . . A turn in the tunnel brought me to the domed Treasury, without which no Paradise is complete, whether Hindu, Babylonian, Hebrew, Icelandic, Irish, Greek or Chinese. As the prophet Ezekiel wrote:

Every precious stone was thy covering: the sardius, topaz, and the diamond; the beryl, the onyx and the jasper; the sapphire, the emerald, the carbuncle and gold.

Her Majesty's Crown Jewels at the Tower of London would have looked tawdry by comparison with the fantastic treasure now heaped before me: diadems, tiaras, necklaces, crosses, breast-plates, goblets, ephods, cups, platters, sceptres, blazing or twinkling. But, even richer than these jewels, were the royal silks spread out for my inspection in blue, mulberry and white: vast lengths, miraculously brocaded with birds, beats, flowers. . . . My closest experience to this had been in early childhood when, after waiting endlessly in the cold, dark hall, my sisters and I saw the drawing-room door suddenly flung open, and there blazed the Christmas tree: all its candles lighted, its branches glistening with many-coloured tinsel.

I reached for a notebook and wrote: "9 P.M. Visions of . . ." but got no further: things were happening too fast. Besides, the pen felt strange in my hand, and its scratch on paper sounded offensively loud. I remember saying after awhile: "I have seen enough treasure for a lifetime. Is there no human beauty in Paradise?" At once the diadems, tiaras, necklaces, crosses and sceptres vanished, as the demons had done. Instead, a row of lovely, live, naked Caryatids appeared, lined along the wall, as if supporting the dome. Their faces were shrouded. Yet I hesitated to indulge in erotic fancies, lest the Caryatids turned into filthy, deformed devilkins like the ones in Flemish pictures of St. Anthony's Temptations. Blushing, I dismissed them too, and came out from the tunnel into daylight. What I had been taught at school and in church proved true enough, though the truth enormously transcended the account. Around me lay a mountain-top Eden, with its jewel-bright trees, its flowers and its pellucid streams. And I experienced not only the bliss of innocence, but also the "knowledge of good and evil." Most Christians understand this phrase as meaning the power to distinguish right from wrong; in Hebrew, however, it signifies a universal understanding of all things, whether good or evil. Indeed, my mind suddenly became so agile and unfettered that I felt capable of solving any problem in the world; it was as if I had immediate access to all knowledge everywhere. But the sensation of wisdom sufficed—why should I trouble to exploit it?

Gordon Wasson had switched on the tape-recorder and the *curandera's* voice was now invoking Tlalóc as "Christo." She chanted, scolded, entreated, commanded, coaxed him to do what she required; it might have been the Goddess Aphrodite addressing her froward son Eros. . . . Every now and then she would change her mood and song; would mourn, triumph, or laugh. I fell wholly under her spell, and presently enjoyed the curious experience of *seeing* sound. The song-notes became intricate links of a round golden chain that coiled and looped in serpentine fashion among jade-green bushes: the only serpent I met in Eden. . . . Each song was followed by a pause, and always I waited in a lover's agony for her to begin again, tears pricking at my eyelids. Once the *curandera* seemed to sing off-key. Perhaps this was quarter-tone music; at any rate, my ear was not offended: I knew what she meant when I saw one edge of the golden chain band now formed by the sound spread out into a spectrum; and laughed for pleasure. Towards the end came a quick, breathless, cheerful song of creation and growth. The notes fell to earth but rose once more in green shoots which soared swiftly up, putting on branches, leaves, flowers—until it dominated the sky like the beanstalk in the fairytale.

My spirit followed after into the clear blue air, gazing down on cornfields, fields of poppies, and the spires of a heavenly city, and Thomas Traherne's orient and immortal wheat, "which never should be reaped nor ever was sown."

At last the music ended. The visions were fading now. My corporeal self sighed, stretched luxuriously, and looked around. Most of the company had left the room. Only one friend remained. I asked him: "So the journey seems to be over?"

"Ah, but close your eyes, and you can get back at once," he said. "How do you feel?"

"My mind has never been so clear! Did you hear such music in all your life?"

We joined the others in the kitchen, ate cold turkey sandwiches and compared notes. . . . "I saw huge slow-moving fish in the sea; did you?"—". . . The demons scared me nearly to death! I wept and sobbed; maybe I wasn't in a state of grace. And when I looked at my hand, O God!"—". . . Weren't those buildings *enormous?* But I couldn't place their architectural style."—". . . Me, I'd take the journey all over again—this minute, if I could!"

A curious bond of affection had been established between us: so strong that I felt nothing could ever break it. At two o'clock in the morning we said good-bye. By eight I was on my way to Idlewild, headed for Europe: profoundly refreshed, and (in Wordsworth's phrase) "trailing clouds of glory"—wisps of celestial memory which persisted nearly a month.

Civilized consciences revolt against the abuse of hallucigenic drugs —most of them habit-forming, dangerous, and unobtainable except by prescription, or in the black market. Spirits, tobacco, tranquillizers—all harmful if habitually taken—are however on unrestricted sale and, becuse they provide no visions (apart from the fearful hell of *delirium tremens*), the Churches condone their use; for hard liquor merely depresses the senses, tobacco and tranquillizers merely dull them.

Psilocybin, the active principle of *psilocybe*, is now synthetically made in Switzerland. At present, the medical profession controls the supply, and uses it for the diagnosis of mental illness. But, since the formula has been published, not even severe legislation will prevent the general public from access to the product. It seems likely, therefore, that what was for thousands of years a sacred and secret element, entrusted only to persons chosen for their good conduct and integrity, will soon be snatched at by jaded sensation-seekers. They will be disappointed. The word "drug," originally applied to all ingredients used in chemistry, pharmacy, dyeing and so on, has acquired a particular connotation in modern English, which cannot apply to *psilocybin*: "to drug" is to stupefy, rather than to quicken, the senses. *Psilocybin* provides no welcome semi-death in drunken stupor: though the body is relaxed, the mind is conscious throughout, indeed, supra-conscious. Psychiatrists at the Lexington Addiction Centre, Kentucky, who gave *psilocybin* to alcoholics as a means of discovering why they are trying to escape from reality by drink, find that it intensifies and lays bare mental conflict. Experimentalists are therefore likely to see visions evoked by their own uneasy consciences: weeping for grief, not joy; or even shuddering aghast.

Good and evil alternate in most people's hearts. Few are habitually at peace with themselves; and whoever prepares to eat hallucigenic mushroom should take as careful stock of his mental and moral well-being as initiates took before attending the Eleusinian Mysteries. The friend who ate mushrooms with us while not in a state of peace watched his hand turn corpse-like and slowly disintegrate into a dusty skeleton. This peculiar virtue of *psilocybin*, the power to enhance personal reality, turns "Know thyself!" into a practical precept; and may commend it as the sacramental food of some new religion. *Peyotl*, made from cactus buds, another sacred hallucigenic agent—but, it seems, not in such early religious use among the Mexicans as mushrooms—has already been sanctified by a "Christian church" of two hundred thousand members, extending from Central America to Canada. The Catholic and main Protestant churches can never of course, accept visions that either *peyotl* or *psilocybin* excites as anything but diabolical and illusory. They may even put pressure on public-health authorities to outlaw *psilocybin*, arguing that, although the *psilocybe* mushroom does not make for addiction among the Mazateks, and seems to have no harmful effect on their minds and bodies, this may be due to its short season and a loss of virtue when dried; whereas the virtue is stable in *psilocybin*, and the results of long-term dosing are unknown—a permanent schizophrenia might occur. Liquor and tobacco interests would, no doubt, wholeheartedly support the Churches' plea.

My single experience of *psilocybe* was wholly good: an illumination of the mind, a re-education of sight and hearing, and even of touch, as I handled small objects beside me. The perfect sensory control which I could enjoy, confirmed, by analogy, my lifelong faith in the poetic trance: a world where words come to life and combine, under the poet's supra-conscious guidance, into inevitable and true rhythmic statements. But I find one main difference between the two conditions: a mushroom trance is relatively passive; a poetic trance, active—the pen running briskly across paper.

Research should show how far the similarity of most people's visits to Eden or Tlalócan depends on the mushrooms' toxic properties, and how far on suggestion. I think it unnecessary, here, to cite Jung's theory of the Collective Unconscious, since a common tradition of Paradise may be attributed to ancient cultural contact even between distant civilizations, especially if these experiences can be shown to correspond with the physical action of a common toxin. A distinct lowering of body-temperature occurs an hour after eating *psilocybe*, which would explain both the cool sea-grottoes and Gilgamesh's search for the herb of immortality at the sea bottom; it is also followed by a considerable heightening of colour sensitivity, which would account for the jewels. After all, such writhing and creeping things as torment sufferers from *delirium tremens* are clearly not products of the Collective Unconscious, but due to a characteristic tremor of the optic nerve and an irritation of the skin, caused by alcohol.

Paradise, in fact, seems to be a subjective vision. As Jesus himself said: "The Kingdom of Heaven is within you." He might have added: "So is the Kingdom of Hell." The jewelled "Garden" can be attained by the pure of heart without undergoing so austere a regimen as to become alienated from their friends; many young women have a secret garden which they frequently visit. The love-feast, for all who attend it in a state of grace and with complete mutual trust—by no means a simple condition—strengthens human friendship and at the same time bestows spiritual enlightenment: which are the twin purposes of most religions. Whether the soul visits a non-subjective Paradise or Hell on quitting its body, let theologians dispute.

The natural poetic trance, however, as I have experienced it on different levels—sometimes light, sometimes so deep that the slightest disturbance causes acute distress—means a good deal more to me than any trance induced by artificial means. I understand Coleridge's depreciation of *Kubla Khan,* which he wrote almost automatically after stupefying his mind with laudanum. It was, as it were, a demon's gift; not earned (like his other poems) by active poetic thought. True, I have survived enough operations to know the difference in kind between an opiate dream, where one is the dazed victim, and a mushroom vision that can, I know, be consciously assessed and even controlled. Since I found myself capable of dismissing that vision of Crown Jewels and Caryatids, and since one or two of my companions found it possible to visit particular places when under the influence of *psilocybe,* I hesitate to challenge the claim that Tlalóc's adepts can use their liberation of mental forces for oracular research. Nevertheless, it seems established that Tlalócan, for all its sensory marvels, contains no palace of words presided over by the Living Muse, and no small white-washed cell (furnished with only a table, a chair, pen, ink and paper) to which a poet may retire and actively write poems in her honour—rather than bask sensuously under her spell.*

---

* A year or two later I joined another group of friends at Gordon Wasson's apartment where we tried a new synthetic *poilocybin* produced by the same Swiss firm as first put L.S.D. on the Market. It gave me a fearful hang-over headache and my visionary experiences were not of Tlalócan but of Coney Island. My companions made much the same comment.

Some Instances of Poetic Vulgarity

A French editor invited me the other day to join a symposium in praise of Robert Browning. At the risk of seeming a snob, I excused myself on the ground of his vulgarity, adding: "This does not mean that Browning wrote in a non-academic style for the larger public, as one might call Victor Hugo vulgar, but that he was clearly no gentleman. The Muse has, of course, shown equal favour to poets of every rank and condition: to King Henry VIII; to the Earl of Surrey; to Sir Walter Raleigh; to John Clare, the Northampton-shire peasant; to William Davies, the South Welsh tramp; to John Keats, whose father was a groom; and to William Shakespeare, whose father was a wholesale provision dealer. Therefore to call Browning clearly no gentleman, and seemingly introduce class-bar-riers into a classless society, implies that he was clearly no poet either."

What *is* vulgarity? Ruskin defined it as a "deadness of heart and body resulting from prolonged and especially from inherited, con-ditions of degeneracy." What he calls "vulgar" I should call "banal."

There is a livelier, likeable sort of vulgarity: the strident, active, healthy, uninhibited, generous vulgarity of the Edwardian music-hall, or of New York vaudeville when Teddy Roosevelt was President. But vulgarity as a critical term means, as a rule, someone's swaggering attempt to be at ease in a class or group with different customs and taboos from his own.

Vulgaritas carried no social stigma in ancient Rome, once the power of the aristocratic families had been broken. Gaius Petronius's Trimalchio was rich, insensitive and uneducated; but as a priest of Augustus, he felt thoroughly at ease in bullying and looking down on his better bred and less successful fellow-townsmen. Indeed, I read him as Petronius's satire on the Emperor Nero who, though brought up anyhow under the care of a barber and a Circus dancer, stood high above all social criticism. "Vulgarity," however, in English usage, is historically associated with *vulgus mobile,* "the easily-moved crowd," from which comes the word *mob.* The mob, or "mobility," were, for the three established "Estates," rabble without patrons or clients, without representation, responsibility, or convictions: the objects of either scorn or pity.

Adult suffrage, two world wars, Labour Governments, compulsory education and crippling death-duties have gradually blurred social distinctions in Britain. Sportsmanship is now the one universally recognized moral virtue; all sportsmen rank as gentlemen. The servant class has disappeared; a skilled manual worker often earns more than a university graduate; and the diminished importance given to all but technical accomplishments in education encourages the spread of what used to be called "mob-taste" even among persons of royal blood. The *Daily Sketch* and *Daily Mirror* hail it as "the popular touch."

School anthologies harbour countless examples of vulgar verse, still fed to children as worthy of admiration. Take Browning's *Marching Along,* his ballad of "Kentish Sir Byng," a Cavalier who fought in the Civil War. Browning, the son of a Bank of England clerk, was by birth and environment an enthusiastic crop-headed Ironside. Yet here he casts himself for the part of a great-hearted, long-tressed Cavalier:

Kentish Sir Byng stood for his King,
Bidding the crop-headed Parliament swing:
And, pressing a troop unable to stoop
And see the rogues flourish and honest folk droop,
Marched them along, fifty-score strong,
Great-hearted gentlemen, singing this song.

God for King Charles! Pym and such carles
To the Devil that prompts 'em their treasonable parles!
Cavaliers up! Lips from the cup,
Hands from the pasty, nor bite take nor sup
Till you're—

CHORUS: Marching along, fifty-score strong,
Great-hearted gentlemen, singing this song.

We read that Sir Byng pressed "great-hearted gentlemen" for the King's service. Browning used *pressed* because it had a more urgent sound than "raised," yet "pressing" implies forcibly overcoming their reluctance to serve the King—a trait, however, of which he reports them incapable. *Troop, stoop* and *droop* all seem chosen to rhyme with each other, though *troop* probably occurred to Browning first. Being neither a soldier nor a historian, he did not know what strength a "troop" would have had in King Charles's day; but to glorify Sir Byng (a fictitious character, perhaps short for "Browning," and rhymed with *King*) he put it at 1,000 Cavaliers, or two cavalry regiments. Sir Byng finds them all together by some happy accident, armed and accoutred, at a gigantic wine-and-pasty picnic. Before grace can be said, Sir Byng's apt rhyme about King Charles, Pym's carles, and their treasonable parles, provokes them to rise up, still hungry and thirsty, and march off to battle with no better preparation than a song. Talk of the Pied Piper of Hamelin! As the *Dictionary of National Biography* notes: "Browning's poems everywhere attested unflinching optimism." *Marching Along* is a daydream of glory, doubtless provoked (like the no less unhistorical *How They Brought the Good News from Aix to Ghent*) by the sensuous rhythm of Browning's early-morning horseback constitutional in the Park; and undeniably vulgar.

Here is Browning at sea: a poem worked up from stray diary jottings:

HOME-THOUGHTS, FROM THE SEA

Nobly, nobly Cape Saint Vincent to the North-west died away;
Sunset ran, one glorious blood-red, reeking into Cadiz Bay;
Bluish 'mid the burning water, full in face Trafalgar lay;
In the dimmest North-east distance dawned Gibraltar grand
     and gray;
"Here and here did England help me: how can I help England?"
     —say,
Whoso turns as I, this evening, turns to God to praise and pray,
While Jove's planet rises yonder, silent over Africa.

Nine readers out of ten will identify "this evening" and "the burning water" with the sunset at Cadiz; supposing that Trafalgar lay on the Spanish coast opposite Cadiz Bay, Gibraltar to the North-east where the dawn would presently break, and Cape St. Vincent some miles to the North-west. . . . A glance at the map will surprise them. Cape St. Vincent lies 120 miles almost due west from Cadiz; Trafalgar thirty miles south of Cadiz; and Gibraltar round the corner in the Mediterranean. Sentimental allusions to Nelson's victories at St. Vincent and Trafalgar, and to Lord Heathfield's earlier defence of Gibraltar would, Browning reckoned, make patriotic schoolboys ambitious of joining the Senior Service. The glorious blood-red sunset that reeked into Cadiz Bay is a daringly phrased reminder of Drake's surprise attack—against Royal orders—on the Spanish fleet in 1587. Needing a purple last line, Browning solemnly records that Jove's planet rose silent over Africay—to rhyme with *pray*. Did he expect it to sing *Rule, Britannia?*

Browning's vulgarity is a link between Thomas Campbell's and Rudyard Kipling's. Campbell, the youngest of an impoverished Scottish merchant's eleven children, won verse-prizes at Glasgow University, and was "discovered" by the same Henry Mackenzie who had discovered Burns. *The Battle of Copenhagen, Ye Mariners of England* (not *Scotland*), and other patriotic songs, earned him a

Government pension. Though his hope of political advancement was frustrated by the death of his patron Fox, he lived comfortably from his patriotic verse throughout the Napoleonic Wars; and found it hard to make ends meet only during the long period of peace that followed Waterloo. Then he addressed his trumpet-calls to other nations.

To the Greeks (1822):

> Again to the battle, Achaians,
> Our hearts bid the tyrants' defiance. . . . [sic]

To the Spaniards (1823):

> How rings each sparkling Spanish brand!
>   There's music in its rattle,
> And gay, as for a saraband
>   We gird us for the battle,
>   Follow, follow,
>   To the glorious revelry
>   When the sabres bristle
>   And the death shots whistle.

While encouraging these Spaniards, was Campbell aware that the saraband is a slow, melancholy dance, most unsuitable for the gorgeous revelry of battle—its steps being two forward and three back? Did he even care?

To the Poles (1831):

> And have I lived to see thee, sword in hand
> Uprise again, immortal Polish land?

To the Germans (1832):

> The spirit of Britannia
>   Invokes, across the main,
> Her sister Alemannia
>   To burst the tyrant's chain.

Campbell had served briefly as a volunteer when England's shores were threatened by Bonaparte; "but oh! what fagging work this volunteering is!" he wrote; and having had a grandstand view of real war at Ratisbon—from a monastery garden near the battlefield—felt no inclination to go overseas. He confided to a friend: "I stood with the good monks of St. James to overlook a charge of Kleinau's cavalry upon the French. This proved the most important epoch of my life in point of impressions, but they are so horrible to my memory that I study to banish them." Safe back in London, however, he could write:

> The combat deepens. On, ye brave
> Who rush to glory or the grave!
> Wave, Munich, all thy banners wave
> And charge with all thy chivalry!

Which reminds me of a vulgar old song:

> When the bugle calls we shall march to war
> As we did in days gone by.
> When the bugle calls, we shall march, march, march,
> April, May, June and July.
> When the bugle calls we shall march to war
> And not a man will fear it—
> And I don't care *how* soon the bloody bugle calls,
> So long as I don't hear it.

Campbell's *Wounded Hussar* had swept the country in 1797. A really successful patriotic poem should have a long, rolling metre, assisted by such feminine rhymes as *beaming, streaming; cherished, perished; story, glory;* and be utterly nonsensical in plot:

> Alone to the banks of the dark-rolling Danube
> Fair Adelaide hied when the battle was o'er:
> "O, whither," she cried, "hast thou wandered, my lover?
> Or here dost thou welter and bleed on the shore?"

"What voice did I hear? 'twas my Henry that sighed!"
　　All mournful she hastened; nor wandered she far,
When, bleeding and low, on the heath she descried
　　By the light of the moon her poor wounded Hussar!

From his bosom that heaved the last torrent was streaming,
　　And pale was his visage, deep marked with a scar!
And dim was his eye, once expressively beaming,
　　That melted in love and that kindled in war!

For triumphs like this, Campbell was three times elected Rector of Glasgow University; and buried, on July 3, 1844, in Westminster Abbey, at the very centre of Poets' Corner. Present were Lord Macaulay, Lockhart, Brougham, Sir Robert Peel, the Duke of Argyle, and a guard of grateful Polish nobles, one of whom sprinkled on the coffin a handful of earth from the grave of the patriot Kozciuzcko. . . .

Kipling's uncertainty is explained by his sense of not-belonging—in an Anglo-Indian society where, as a Bombay-born journalist without either a settled English background or a university education, he ranked below the youngest second-lieutenant in the tattiest battalion of the Indian Army. Worse, he was a Methodist, not Church of England. Yet Kipling had a quick journalistic eye and ear. Soon he revenged himself by interpreting British India to the stay-at-homes, with a good deal less sympathy for *pukka sahibs* than for Privates Mulvaney, Orth'ris and company, the regimental water-carrier Gunga Din, and the otherwise under-privileged. At the age of forty-one, he was awarded the Nobel Prize. Kipling claimed to be a no-nonsense poet, a mouthpiece of the common people, who swept away academic humbug. His *Boots, boots, boots, boots!* is now the best-known English poem in the Soviet Union. But when the Establishment beckoned, he followed: at last squarely identifying himself with the Lords and Masters, rather than the "lesser breeds within the Law," and bravely shouldering the White Man's Burden.

Kipling became the unofficial poet-laureate of the British Empire just before its liquidation. He missed the official appointment only because he had earned Queen Victoria's displeasure by alluding to

her as "the Widow of Windsor." Like Browning and Campbell, he
weltered vicariously in gore, as in the climax to his fictional *Ballad of
the Clampherdown:*

> . . . . It was our war-ship *Clampherdown,*
>   Swung round upon the tide,
> Her two dumb guns glared south and north,
> And the blood and the bubbling steam ran forth,
>   And she ground the cruiser's side.
>
> "Captain," they cry, "the fight is done,
>   They bid you send your sword."
> And he answered: "Grapple her, stern and bow.
> They have asked for the steel. They shall have it now;
>   Out cutlasses and board!"
>
> It was our war-ship *Clampherdown*
>   Spewed up four hundred men;
> And the scalded stokers yelped delight
> As they rolled in the waist and heard the fight
>   Stamp o'er their steel-walled pen.
>
> They cleared the cruiser end to end,
>   From conning-tower to hold.
> They fought as they fought in Nelson's fleet;
> They were stripped to the waist, they were bare to the feet,
>   As it was in the days of old.

I could quote nothing from all English literature that transcended
in vulgar bloody-mindedness the third of these stanzas. The stokers,
no doubt ignoble Lascars, unfit to wield a white man's cutlass, are
left below decks; and their screams of pain as salt water reaches the
boilers and steam scalds them, are jovially interpreted as yelps of
delight! "Bubbling," by the way, has been transferred for the sake of
euphony from "blood" to "steam."

A frequent sign of poetic vulgarity is the use of Biblical language
to heighten trivial passages. Kipling specialized not only in grandiose
addresses to the Lord God of Hosts, but also in dewy-eyed quota-

tion from the New Testament. The affected simplicity of *Gethsemane* shows him at his lowest:

> The Garden called Gethsemane
>   In Picardy it was,
> And there the people came to see
>   The English soldiers pass.
>
> We used to pass—we used to pass
>   Or halt, as it might be,
> And ship our masks in case of gas
>   Beyond Gethsemane.
>
> The Garden called Gethsemane,
>   It held a pretty lass,
> But all the time she talked to me
>   I prayed my cup might pass.
>
> The officer sat on the chair,
>   The men lay on the grass,
> And all the time we halted there
>   I prayed my cup might pass.
>
> It didn't pass—it didn't pass—
>   It didn't pass from me.
> I drank it when we met the gas
>   Beyond Gethsemane.

Why, at a period in the First World War subsequent to the issue of gas-masks, as opposed to "respirators" (probably the early summer of 1916), Picardy peasants were still interested in watching the British soldiers pass—"or halt, as it might be"; and why they continued to occupy an area so close to the German lines that gas-masks were habitually shipped there; and why the pretty lass singled out this Christ-like private soldier for her French monologue, when all he could do was lie on the grass in an agony, shut his eyes and pray against gas; and why, for that matter, he *did* get gassed in the end—must remain mysteries. Perhaps the practical Picardaise wanted him to stop praying *un petit moment,* and make sure that his mask had its eye-pieces properly secured. . . .

Non-scholarly pretence at scholarship is another form of poetic vulgarity, used throughout Browning's *Sordello,* though he quotes only the Classics and a little Italian—not Chinese, Sanskrit or Provençal, like his modernist successors.

It is natural for young people to gather in a crowd, play the same games, use the same jargon; and if some physical misfortune or social disadvantage (rather than a rare extra gift of the spirit) differentiates one of them from his fellows, this often tempts him to some sort of megalomaniac over-compensation. Byron knew and regretted the colossal vulgarity which he shrouded by a cloak of aloof grandeur. It was a studious vulgarity: cosmetics and curl-papers tended his elegant beauty; an ingenious, though synthetic, verse technique smoothed his cynical Spenserian stanzas. But he had unexpectedly come into a peerage and an estate while still "wee Georgie Gordon with the feetsies"—whom his hysterical and unladylike mother used to send limping round the corner from her cheap Aberdeen lodgings to buy two-penny-worth of "blue ruin"; and whom, at the age of nine, a nymphomaniac Calvinist housemaid had violently debauched. His unease was prodigious. As he himself confesses in *Childe Harold:*

> His cup was quaff'd too quickly, and he found
> The dregs were wormwood; but he fill'd again,
> And from a purer fount, on holier ground,
> And deem'd its spring perpetual; but in vain!
> Still round him clung invisibly a chain
> Which gall'd for ever, fettering though unseen,
> And heavy though it clank'd not; worn with pain,
> Which pined although it spoke not, and grew keen,
> Entering with every step to look through many a scene.

Shelley noted in a letter to Peacock:

> Lord Byron is an exceedingly interesting person and, as such, is it
> not to be regretted that he is a slave to the vilest and most vulgar
> prejudices, and as mad as a hatter?

Byron adored no Muse, but acted as male Muse to scores of in-
fatuated women who, like Lady Caroline Lamb, knew that he was
"mad, bad, dangerous to know," adding: "His beautiful face is my
fate." I pair Byron and Nero as the two most dangerously talented
bounders of all time.

Swinburne's was an inverted vulgarity. One of his grandfathers
had been an admiral; the other an earl. After a healthy North
Country childhood, he went on to Eton and Oxford. Later, he tried
to edge, not into high society, but into the "fleshly" Bohemian set
of pre-Raphaelite poets and painters. For them he celebrated the
roses and raptures of vice; though, whereas Byron could wearily
boast of having enjoyed over two hundred mistresses and scores of
catamites, the impotent eroticism of Swinburne's verse, even when it
celebrated merely vegetable Nature, leaves a worse taste in the
mouth than *Childe Harold:*

BY THE NORTH SEA

A land that is lonelier than ruin;
    A sea that is stranger than death;
Far fields that a rose never blew in,
    Wan waste where the winds lack breath;
Waste endless and boundless and flowerless
    But of marsh-blossoms fruitless as free;
Where earth lies exhausted, as powerless
    To strive with the sea.

Far flickers the flight of the swallows,
    Far flutters the weft of the grass
Spun dense over desolate hollows
    More pale than the clouds as they pass;
Thick woven as the weft of a witch is
    Round the heart of a thrall that hath sinned,
Whose youth and the wrecks of its riches
    Are waifs on the wind.

Nineteenth-century poetic vulgarity is characterized by over-allit-eration, ingenious rhymes—such as *blew in* and *ruin; riches, which is* —and a reckless disregard of prose sense. In Swinburne's windless, endless, boundless waste, the weft of grass, he says, fluttered far—spun dense over desolate hollows that were paler than the passing clouds, and thick woven as the weft of a witch around the heart of a sinner whose youthful charms had become like waifs in the wind. . . . But did a wind flutter the grass and drive the clouds, or did it not? And how can a waste region of England adjacent to the North Sea be endless and boundless? And how can a weft be *spun*? And if the grass had been spun densely over the desolate hollows, who could tell whether they were as pale as the clouds that passed? And how pale were the clouds anyhow? And how thick a weft does a witch weave around the sinner's heart? And how do fruitless marsh-flowers spread themselves freely across the exhausted earth?

Keats, though no gentleman either by birth or education, had a genuine instinct for poetry and poetic principle; and the close at-tention he paid to craftsmanship made him recognize vulgarity in others and, as a rule, avoid it himself. He particularly lamented the fate of Burns:

> Poor unfortunate fellow—how sad it is when a luxurious imagina-tion is obliged in self-defence to deaden its delicacy in vulgarity, and in things attainable—that it may not have leisure to go mad after things which are not attainable.

Vulgarity in religious dress is insidious; and Keats, who in this letter has been denouncing the hypocritical Kirk, was evidently referring to Burns's *Cottar's Saturday Night*, an "unco-guid" set-piece that contradicted his natural randiness and imitated Robert Fergusson's more authentic *The Farmer's Wife*.

Almost every poet starts to write before finding his own voice, and puffs out his borrowed feathers. Every theatrical impersonation, every political, theological, or philosophical hand-out passed off as his own, is a vulgarity. The writing of true poems happens so un-predictably that the poet is beset by the temptation to write when not in the mood. He may think that this can be induced by withdrawing to a glade or quiet, book-filled study, or by violent adventure among corsairs, alguazils, barmecides, and their modern equivalents. It cannot be.

No poet has yet solved the main problem: how to maintain the gift of certitude. Always to be in love: that is one recommendation. To treat money and fame with equal nonchalance, is another. To remain independent, is a third. To prize personal honour, is a fourth. To make the English language one's constant study, is a fifth. . . . Yet lightning strikes where and when it wills. No one ever knows. It is easy to take up a pen at random and plead: "I'm just keeping my hand in." But nine-tenths of what passes as English poetry is the product of either careerism, or keeping one's hand in: a choice between vulgarity and banality.

Technique in Poetry

God, according to a Hebrew myth, promised our father Adam the helpmate he needed, and invited him to watch while the divine fingers built up a woman's anatomy from primeval sludge. They extemporized bones, tissues, muscles, blood, teeth, brains and glandular secretions, wove them neatly together, co-ordinated their functions, covered the whole ingenious apparatus with the smoothest of cuticles, and embellished it with tufts of hair in selected places. This technical demonstration caused Adam such disgust that, when the First Eve stood up in all her beauty and smiled at him, he turned his back on her. God therefore removed the First Eve and behaved with greater circumspection: He formed the Second Eve from Adam's rib while he slept, then ordered the Archangel Michael to plait her hair and adorn her in bridal array. Adam woke and was enchanted.

I inherit Adam's mistrust of creative technique. It is grammarians, not poets, who lay down the rules of prosody, name metres, list different varieties of poetic licence—deducing them from Greek, Latin, Italian or French practice—as of universal application. English criticism began in Tudor times with the grammarians; and though some, such as George Puttenham, realized that English poetry had its own wayward genius, different from that of the Romance languages, they nevertheless agreed that it must be intellectually disciplined and dedicated to certain social uses. Among these, Puttenham instances the Reporting of the Famous Lives of Princes, the Reproval of Vice, the Treatment of Honest and Profitable Sciences; Solemn Rejoicings at Marriages; Memorials to the Dead. Puttenham links poetic art so securely with the art of rhetoric that, when he has discussed the mathematical rules of metre and proportion, which ensure sweet and tuneful sounds, he next turns to the problem of poetic ornament:

> And as we see in these great Mesdames of honour who, be they never so comely and beautiful, yet if they want their courtly habiliments, or at least such other apparel as custom and civility have ordained to cover their naked bodies, would be half-ashamed or greatly out of countenance to be seen in that sort, and perchance do then think themselves more amiable in every man's eye when they be in their richest attire—suppose of silks or tissues and costly embroideries—than when they go in cloth or in any plain and simple apparel. Even so cannot our Poesie show itself either gallant or gorgeous if any limb be left naked and bare and not clad in his kindly clothes and colours, such as may convey them somewhat out of sight from the common course of ordinary speech and capacity of the vulgar judgement, and yet, being artificially handled, must needs yield it much more beauty and commendation. This Ornament we speak of is given to it by figures and figurative speeches, which be the flowers, as it were, and colours that a Poet setteth upon his language of art, as the embroiderer doth his stones and pearls and passments of gold upon the stuff of a princely garment. . . .

Ornament, as such, should not concern poets, although completely naked poems spring only from extreme passion in love or war. It is true that beautiful women, because of "custom or civility"—not to mention variations of climate—wear clothes as a rule: yet, if truly beautiful and not mere lumps of handsome flesh, they dress for their own pleasure, rather than let fashion-designers (even the

Archangel Michael himself) bedizen them for Adam's gratification. And any jewel a woman wears is not mere ornament but a chosen extension of her inner loveliness.

Grammarians insist that a simple idea may be so ornamented by artifice as to become poetic, and that the reader must applaud the ingenuity of its transformation. Poetical artifice entered our Universities from Rome by way of France; Ovid and Virgil were the masters on whom all students must model themselves. Ovid wrote in the *Fasti*:

> Tres ubi luciferos veniens praemiserit Eos
> Tempora nocturnis aequa diurna feres.
> Inde quater pastor saturos ubi clauserit hoedos
> Canuerint herbae rore recente quater,
> Janus adorandus, cumque hoc Concordia mitis. . . .

When the breaking dawn shall have sent before her three light-bearing days, thou wilt have the hours of day equal to those of night; and when from this the shepherd shall four times have penned his well-fed kids, four times the grass become white with fresh-fallen dew, then Janus and with him Mild Concord will demand adoration. . . .

In simple English: "Three days later comes the vernal equinox; after four more, the feasts of Janus and Concord will be celebrated." Note the superfluousness of the adjectives—*breaking* dawn, *well-fed* kids, *fresh-fallen* dew, *mild* Concord. Every dawn *breaks*: and even if all the shepherd's kids were not *well fed*, their hungry bleatings would not affect the Calendar; dew is always *fresh-fallen*, and Concord always *mild*. In any case, Ovid was writing not for shepherds, but for Augustus' City courtiers—few of whom can ever have seen the inside of a goat pen.

Sir Philip Sidney, in his *Apology for Poetry*, accepts this whole cosmetic parlour of Classical verse-technique as necessary for the production of rich conceits that guide man's soul to moral virtue, courage and erudition; adding, however:

> Certainly I must confess my own barbarousness. I never heard the old song of Percy and Douglas [*Chevy Chase*] that I found not

my heart moved more than by a trumpet; and yet is it sung but by some blind crowder with no rougher voice than rude; which, being so evil apparelled in the dust and cobwebs of that uncivil age, what would it work if trimmed with the gorgeous eloquence of Pindar?

Now, Pindar could never have begun a poem with:

> The stout Earl of Northumberland
> A vow to God did make. . . .

but would have written:

O Queenly Muse, our Mother, come, I beseech thee, on the festal day of the Omnipotent Christchild who bountifully redeemed us from sin: come visiting the spacious halls of our impregnable New Castle that beetles in majesty above the goodly Tynian water. For lo, youthful craftsmen of honey-sweet triumphal songs, skilled also in laments, there attend in long desire for thy voice. Various deeds thirst for various rewards, yet the hunting of high-stepping, lotus-cropping deer that rove the rugged Cheviotian hills, calleth beyond all things for the meed of song, especially when mighty champions contend together in honour, each assuring for himself the certain glory of carrying home in well-wrought horse-drawn wains tasty haunches of unnumbered antlered ones.

It would have taken Pindar a whole page to trim with gorgeous eloquence such stanzas as these:

> It began upon a Monynday
> Ere daylight did appear
> The drivers through the woodës went
> To raise the fallow deer.
>
> The bowmen cleft them to the hearts,
> As down the brae they came,
> And greyhounds through the greves did run—
> To them it was good game.

Two centuries later, Dr. Johnson wrote about *Chevy Chase:*

> Addison descended now and then to lower disquisitions than his praise of Milton. By a serious display of the beauties of *Chevy Chase* he exposed himself to the ridicule of Wagstaff and to the contempt of Dennis who, considering the fundamental position that *Chevy Chase* pleases, and ought to please, because it is natural, observes: "There is a way of deviating from nature by bombast or tumour, which soars above nature and enlarges images beyond their real bulk; by affectation which forsakes nature in quest of something unsuitable; and by imbecility, which degrades nature by faintliness and diminution, by obscuring its appearances and weakening its effects. In *Chevy Chase* there is not much of either bombast or affectation, but there is a chill, lifeless imbecility. The story cannot possibly be told in a manner that shall make less impression in the mind."

The Classicists thus ask us to choose between the "chill and lifeless imbecility" of *Chevy Chase* and such "supreme excellence" as Addison's *Letter from Italy* which, Dr. Johnson says, has "always been praised but never beyond its merit, being more correct with less appearance of labour, and more elegant with less ambition of ornament, than any of his other poems."

A LETTER FROM ITALY
(To the Right Hon. Charles Lord Halifax, 1701)

> While you, my lord, the rural shades admire,
> And from Britannia's public posts retire,
> Nor longer, her ungrateful sons to please,
> For their advantage sacrifice your ease;
> Me into foreign realms my fate conveys
> Through nations fruitful of immortal lays,
> Where the soft season and inviting clime
> Conspire to trouble your repose with rhyme. . . . etc.

I have elsewhere explained the difference between Apollonian poetry and Muse poetry. That Pindar and Addison claim to have the

Muse in their pockets, complicates the situation. Yet the truth is that *Chevy Chase* moved Sir Philip Sidney's heart more than a trumpet because the unknown rude crowder who composed it was himself so moved; and that the Apollonians decry all emotional impulses which have not been modified and ennobled, after a grounding in the humanities, by the acquisition of Classical technique. Technique should not be equated with craftsmanship. Technique is psychological know-how. The technician assumes that poems can be constructed like explosive missiles and aimed at a given target; he despises mere craftsmen for their intellectual sloth. Eliot, Pound, and the later Yeats (still praised by English and American literary journals as the "real masters") have technique; Hardy and Frost have only craftsmanship.

Technique ignores the factor of magic; craftsmanship presupposes it. A journeyman, after seven years as apprentice, will get the feel of his materials and learn what quiet miracles can be done with them. A small part of this knowledge is verbally communicable; the rest is incommunicable—except to fellow-craftsmen who already possess it. The technician's disregard of this inexplicable element, magic, in painting, sculpture, medicine, music and poetry—on the ground that it cannot be demonstrated under laboratory conditions —accounts for the present dismal decline in all arts. A true poem is best regarded as already existing before it has been composed: with composition as the act of deducing its entirety from a single key phrase that swims into the poet's mind.

Here are two well-known pieces of Tennyson's—*The Eagle* and *Move Eastward, Happy Earth*—printed on the same page in his *Collected Poems* and forced on me, when I was seven or eight years old, as works of genius. *The Eagle* is subtitled "A Fragment," suggesting that a longer poem went wrong and that he destroyed all but six sound lines. Whenever this happens to a poet, he should justify by careful craftsmanship the publication of what is salved. But has Tennyson done so?

> He clasps the crag with crooked hands;
> Close to the sun in lonely lands,
> Ring'd with the azure world, he stands.

> The wrinkled sea beneath him crawls;
> He watches from his mountain walls,
> And like a thunderbolt he falls.

My minimum requirement of a poem is that it should make prose sense as well as poetic sense; one main difference between prose and poetry being that prose engages only a small part of the reader's attention. Ideally, a poem should induce in him the same trance of heightened sensibility under which the poet wrote, and make him aware of all the multiple meanings that stretch out in vistas from it. Here, Tennyson's technique has been deliberately impressionistic— he has, in fact, taken no pains to say what he means—and, although his resonant voice with the slight Norfolk burr might have persuaded his hearers that these two stanzas make prose sense (the ear being easily deceived), the reading eye rejects them.

Persistent alliteration pleases children, who enjoy "One old ox opening oysters," and "Two toads, terribly tired, trying to trot to Tilbury." And it pleased simple Anglo-Saxons:

> With Vandals I was and with Vaerns and Vikings;
> With Saxons I was and with Syegs and Swordsmen;
> With Franks I was, with Frisians and Frumtings. . . .

But when, in a Victorian three-line rhyming stanza, four c's appear in a row—*clasp, crag, crooked* and *close*—followed by the two l's of *lonely lands,* we expect the last line to yield an important and equally alliterative statement:

> He clasps the crag with crooked hands
> Close to the sun in lonely lands. . . .

Yet,

> Ring'd with the azure world he stands . . .

disappoints expectation, and adds nothing to the picture. Since the eagle perches on his crag close to the sun, a background of blue sky has already been presumed. Besides, it is not the *world* which is blue, but only the sky. And why "he clasps the crag with crooked *hands*"? Though few men are born with prehensile feet, "hands" might still have passed muster in a portrait of this humanized eagle, had Tennyson not followed it with "he stands." If the eagle stands on his hands, then his wings must necessarily be feet. . . .

Once one thinks along these lines, the poem collapses. *Crooked* is unnecessary: eagles' claws are always crooked. *Lands* is seen to be a rhyme chosen to go with *hands* and *stands*; for the eagle can stand only in one land, not several. To present him as "close to the sun" is hardly fair—what are a few hundred feet, compared with 92,000,000 miles! Nor is he even flying high above the mountain; but grounded on a crag. . . .

Azure is a purely heraldic term for "blue," and if Tennyson thought of the eagle as a heraldic charge—*Azure: below a sun in its splendour or, an eagle of the same, ungled and langed argent*—he should have made this clear. *Ringed with azure* is not the language of heraldry.

> The wrinkled sea beneath him crawls;
> He watches from his mountain walls,
> And like a thunderbolt he falls. . . .

Why is the bird's attention concentrated on the sea? Is he perhaps a sea-eagle, watching for fish? *Crawls* may mean that from a great height waves appear to move slowly; but since *wrinkles* are by definition static, *crawls* must have been put there for the rhyme. And unless we are told exactly what the eagle is watching, his fall may have been as accidental as was, say, Eutychus's when Paul's sermon sent him to sleep and he crashed on to the street from an upper window. . . . Tennyson has a vague sense, perhaps, of the eagle as a royal bird mythologically entitled—like Solar Jove, his master—to a blue nimbus and a thunderbolt. . . . If so, he does not make the point.

He would have done better with:

Jove's Eagle

Charged on an azure field, with claws
Grasping a crag, he overawes
(Like Jove himself) the doves and daws.

Silently watches from his walls
What swims the sea, what flies, what crawls—
Ere like a thunderbolt he falls.

This is still not a poem. I have indulged Tennyson by granting
him his Victorian *daws* and his *Ere;* nor do I much like the similarity
of these two sets of rhymes; but at least the verses now make immediate prose sense and would serve well enough as an anthology
piece.

Now for its companion verse:

Move eastward, happy earth, and leave
    Yon orange sunset waning slow:
From fringes of the faded eve,
    O, happy planet, eastward go;
Till over thy dark shoulder glow
    Thy silver sister-world, and rise
    To glass herself in dewy eyes
That watch me from the glen below.
Ah, bear me with thee, smoothly borne,
    Dip forward under starry light,
And move me to my marriage-morn,
    And round again to happy night.

The gist is: "I shall be so happy when the sunset has ended;
when tonight's moon has come and gone, and morning is here, and
I am married to Maud, and—oh, tomorrow night!"

Nobody can put this poem right. It would have to be re-written
as a popular song:

O tomorrow night,
O tomorrow night,
I'll be so happy when today is done,
And I've said goodbye to the dear old sun. . . .

That an eager lover should implore the weather to remain fine on his wedding day, and the birds to wake him early, and the country-side to rejoice, is understandable. Lovers always take the weather personally. But when Earth is begged to dip forward and carry the poet along with smooth and careful portage for another twenty-four hours or so . . . !

Move eastward, happy earth. . . .

and

O, happy planet, eastward go;

though parallel orders, are far from explicit. "Eastward of what must I dip, Mr. Tennyson?" Mother Earth has a right to ask.

. . . Till over thy dark shoulder glow
    Thy silver sister-world, and rise
    To glass herself in dewy eyes
That watch me from the glen below.
Ah, bear me with thee, smoothly borne,
And move me to my marriage-morn,
    Dip forward under starry light,
    And round again to happy night.

"Thy sister-world" refers to the moon; but just whose dewy eyes are watching Tennyson from the glen below is a puzzle. Perhaps a couple of small lakes? If so, why dewy? Glens may be dewy, but not lakes. And why are they watching? Are they perhaps Maud's eyes? If so, what is she doing down there in the damp glen at this late hour?

Shelley is another culprit:

TO A SKYLARK

Hail to thee, blithe Spirit!
  Bird thou never wert,
That from Heaven, or near it,
  Pourest thy full heart
In profuse strains of unpremeditated art.

Higher still and higher
  From the earth thou springest
Like a cloud of fire;
  The deep blue thou wingest,
And singing still dost soar, and soaring ever singest.

In the golden lightning
  Of the sunken sun,
O'er which clouds are bright'ning,
  Thou dost float and run;
Like an unbodied joy whose race is just begun.

The pale purple even
  Melts around thy flight;
Like a star of Heaven,
  In the broad daylight
Thou art unseen, but yet I hear thy shrill delight,

Like a poet hidden
  In the light of thought,
Singing hymns unbidden,
  Till the world is wrought
To sympathy with hopes and fears it heeded not:

Chorus Hymeneal,
  Or triumphal chant,
Matched with thine would be all
  But an empty vaunt,
A thing wherein we feel there is a hidden want.

> What objects are the fountains
>   Of thy happy strain?
> What fields of waves, or mountains?
>   What shapes of sky or plain?
> What love of thine own kind? what ignorance of pain?

It is a temptation to let Shelley off; but *To A Skylark* ranks among the shoddiest poems ever wished on us as the product of genius! Its metre is difficult, granted. Yet with faith in the power of inspiration to solve all problems of craftsmanship, a poet may commit himself to a metrical scheme that seems cripplingly tight and yet feel free as air within it. Shelley, it seems, snatched idly at an idea that entered his head one afternoon as he tried to locate a lark singing in the sky, and began with:

> Hail to thee, blithe spirit!
>   All unseen thou art,
> That from Heaven, or near it,
>   Pourest thy full heart
> In happy strains of unpremeditated art.
>
> In the golden lightning
>   Of the setting sun,
> Which the clouds is brightening,
>   Thou dost float and run. . . .

Shelley goes home, fetches pencil and notebook, and jots down this much; but then discovers that he has rhymed *thou art* with *unpremeditated art*—which is a "French rhyme" disallowed to English poets since Chaucer's time. One of the two *arts* must be struck out. So, having decided that the metre cannot be managed without recourse to near-rhymes like *wrought* and *not; spirit* and *near it; chant, vaunt* and *want;* he pencils the rhyme scheme in the margin, and changes his original *All unseen thou art* to *Bird thou never wert,* a dramatic statement irreconcilable with his later suggestion that the cock-lark's song is prompted by love for his hen. Nevertheless, he reserves *Unseen thou art* and *happy strain* for a subsequent verse. A second difficulty is the golden light*ning* of the setting sun brighten*ing* the clouds. . . . Too many *ings!* He toys with his pencil, scratches his head, peels a grape, eats it, looks out of the window at the sun, and sees that it has sunk almost below the horizon. So *sunken sun,* instead of *setting sun,* gets rid of one *ing;* but he has forgotten that, unlike nightingales, larks never sing in a darkened sky, and that clouds never brighten, once the sun has disappeared, but turn a dingy red. No matter! The stars are coming out one by one, and it occurs to him that though an hour or two ago the lark was invisible even by broad daylight, neither could he see a single star. So, vaguely remembering the Psalm about the morning stars that sing together, and the Sons of God who shout for joy, he conflates the lark with the star into a single blithe Spirit springing like a fiery cloud higher and higher, while the pale purple evening melts around it, like a poet hidden in the light of thought. . . . This confused image has been much admired; but true poetic ecstasy makes sense, and more than sense.

The rhymes *higher, fire; springest, wingest, singest; Heaven, even; hidden, bidden,* are borrowings from the Hymnal, and not long before his death Shelley thought seriously of becoming an Anglican clergyman. Here he pictures the poet as an amateur hymnologist: singing hymns unbidden. . . . There is something, I own, that endears Shelley to us—a generous-hearted muddle; the patent clumsiness of *To A Skylark* makes us feel for him as for a child of ten who has painted a sunset picture, thinks it wonderful and wants to be praised. We paste it into the family scrap-book and he signs his name to it in large, round characters. "Nice fellow," we say, years later, "good Classic, went to Eton and Oxford, turned out neat translations from the Greek dramatists. Wouldn't hurt a fly; a bit of a radical, of course. Sent down from University for atheism. Pity! Deucedly odd at times—believe it or not, he used to put revolutionary broadsheets into empty wine bottles and throw them into the Bristol Channel, hoping that they might float across to Ireland! Wrote a sonnet about 'em too, beginning:

> Vessels of heavenly medicine, may the breeze
> Auspicious waft your dark green forms to shore
> Safe may ye stem the wide surrounding roar

Of the wild whirlwinds and the raging seas—
And oh, if Liberty e'er deigned to stoop
From yonder lowly throne her crownless brow,
Sure, she will breathe around your emerald group
The fairest breezes of the West that blow. . . .

Sure, he got the colour right: Erin's own emerald. But why did he call for westerly breezes instead of easterly ones? Poetic licence, perhaps. Got drowned sailing in the Mediterranean. Sad, but hardly surprising!"

By way of contrast, a glorious example of how inspiration can make light of severe metrical discipline is Bernard de Cluny's twelfth-century *De Contemptu Mundi*, from which J. M. Neale translated *Jerusalem the Golden with Milk and Honey Blessed:*

Urbs Syon aurea, Patria lactea, cive decora,
Omne cor obruis, omnibus obstruis et cor et ora.
Nescio, nescio, quae jubilatio, lux tibi qualis,
Quam socialia gaudia, gloria quam specialis.
Stant Syon atria conjubilantia, martyre plena,
Cive micantia, Principe stantia, luce serena . . .

Technically, the metre is called *Leonini cristati trilices dactylia,* and Bernard (who was an Englishman, though born in Brittany) has told how, when the Holy Spirit often begged him to write verses, he would not listen until the sudden cry came: "Open the door to thy Beloved!" Then Bernard gave way, praying for heavenly grace that he might worthily sing his Beloved's praises. "Open thy mouth," he heard again, and felt inspiration breathed into him. Bernard writes:

And I say in no wise arrogantly, but with all humility and therefore boldness: that unless the Spirit of wisdom and understanding had been with me, and flowed in upon so difficult a metre, I could never have composed so long a work. . . .

Indeed, the *Contemptu Mundi* runs for some three hundred lines without flagging. We need not question Bernard's testimony that he wrote in an ecstatic love trance. There can be no other explanation. If only Shelley had written *To A Skylark* under the same spell. . . .

The Classical convention in English poetry broke down just before the First World War, and all subsequent attempts to reinstate it failed. Our modernists are still in desperate search for a new convention of equal nonsensicality, yet of international prestige, which will create the impression that they are poets "hidden in the mystic light of thought." But what *objects* are the fountains of their doleful strain? Apparently the sole object is *technique:* which they have made almost a dirty word.

The Poet in a Valley of Dry Bones

Granted a genuine sense of vocation, what technical advice can a young poet be offered? I dislike the word "technique." One hears: "Yes, he (or she) doesn't *move* me in the least, but ah! what dazzling technique!" This implies intellectual achievement in any near-magical art or craft from which the intellect should, I believe, be barred for truth's sake except as an occasional consultant on simple fact. Very well, then: what advice on craftsmanship, even if craftsmanship now means something quaint, laborious and out-of-date? But advice is what everybody gives and nobody takes.

As a young poet, I wrote my first serious poem in the summer of 1906, when I was eleven years old. I had been turned out of the family wagonette by my short-tempered grandfather, for having climbed aboard without my school cap; and so missed a picnic beside the river. I spent the afternoon working out a country-poem in rhymed couplets about a farmer who, so far as I recall, prudently harvested and carted his wheat just before a hailstorm flattened the crops of all his less industrious neighbours. The poem ended:

> The swain gave thanks at daybreak for God's grace;
> At Kirk this morn I saw his smiling face.

I remember thinking that *swain* and *kirk* and *morn* were very elegant words; and that I had scored off my grandfather (to whom, on
his return, I dedicated the poem) by showing how little I cared for
family picnics. This was a false start. Three years later I felt a
genuine afflatus, and wrote one moonlit night in June:

> O, not for me the lute or lyre!
> A knight, I ride my thoughts of fire
> And fly on wings for ever and aye
> Through an unresisting starry sky,
> Where the gleaming aether turns and sings
> Its strange slow song of the birth of things.

There was a difference in kind between these two failures: the first,
an academic exercise, was sadly deficient in technique; the second,
a personal statement, was equally deficient in craftsmanship—but
my hand trembled as I wrote it down; nor did I parade it for public
approval.

One often meets a musical prodigy, but never a poetic prodigy,
of tender age. A long, long experience with language is needed
before words can fully collaborate with one another under the poetic
trance. It seems necessary, too, to have read a great many poems by
other writers, good and bad, before a poet can realize his powers and
limitations. I never have much use for one whose poems I do not
recognize at a glance as inimitably his own; even so, I reject them
if they draw attention to a cultivated eccentricity, to pride in scholarship, or to the mastery of Classical or Modernist technique.

Shakespeare's plays can be arranged in chronological order, and
the development of his verse-craftsmanship studied; but I am not a
play-goer, and the comparatively rare occasions when he included
poems in his theatrical declamations are all that really interest me.
Some plays contain no more than a couple of lines; in others there
are scenes consisting of poem sequences strung together on a thread
of dramatic dialogue. Popular conventions were as strong in Shake-

speare's day as now, and he could not afford to disregard them. No poet ever escapes from the epoch into which he is born; he can only transcend conventions by showing where they do not apply to him. And he should have a sense of belonging to a long line of former free spirits, and decide whether their divergences from contemporary fashion merit his approval; Shakespeare, despite his limited schooling, seems to have been remarkably well read.

The history of English poetry is traced in the text books as a succession of movements or schools—the School of Chaucer, the Allegorical School, the early Tudor Dramatists, the Euphuists, and so on, past the Anti-Jacobins, the Lake School, the mid-Victorian Romantics, etc., until one reaches the Georgians, the Imagists, and the Modernist Movement. But schools and movements are fictions. If a school, meaning the disciples and imitators of a particular verse-craftsman, achieves fashionable renown, this is a grave criticism of his sincerity. A poet should be inimitable. When two genuine poets recognize each other as true to their common vocation, this will only accentuate the difference between them in rhythm, diction and the rest. Any talk of a "school" means that someone is peddling a new technique of verbal conjuring; as in commercial schools that teach writers of advertising copy how to make an easily hypnotizable public buy what they themselves must never believe in.

Craftsmanship is self-taught. A poet lives with his own language, continually instructing himself in the origin, histories, pronunciation, and peculiar usages of words, together with their latent powers, and the exact shades of distinction between what Roget's *Thesaurus* calls "synonyms"—but are there such things? English has no officially approved way of expressing every conceivable thought, as French has; only precedents. A poet may make his own precedents, in disregard of any law of correctness laid down by grammarians—so long as they accord with the natural genius of English. . . . I studied French, Latin and Greek grammar at school, back in the reign of King Edward the Peacemaker, but was told: "Only foreign languages have grammar," and expected to be treated as an imbecile or a yokel if I spoke or wrote bad English. Its proper use was held to be a matter of good manners, not of grammatic law: I still hold this to be so.

Only wide reading, a retentive ear for conversation, and continuous dwelling upon words as disembodied spirits rather than as building materials, can equip a poet for his task. And what does "equip" mean? It comes from the medieval Latin *eschipare*, "to man a ship"; but had become metaphorical even before reaching England —Cardinal Wolsey uses it, first, in the sense of finding soldiers the necessary arms and accoutrements for battle. The poet should be aware, however, that the word *ship* is still latent in *equip*, and so is the sense of making ready for a voyage. In a true poem, produced by the deep trance that integrates all the memories of the mind, the dormant powers of each word awake and combine with those of every other, building up a tremendous head of power. How far the reader is conscious of the inter-related sounds and meanings depends on how much of a poet he, or she, is: for I allow the title of poet to all who think poetically, whether writers or not.

A historical dictionary should always be within a poet's reach: preferably the big *Oxford English Dictionary*—the two-volume edition is insufficient. Over thirty years ago, when I could not afford a set, I remembered the New Testament parable of the pearl, sold all my non-essential books, and bought it. I still consult the O.E.D. at least four or five times a day: never letting a doubtful word go by— I need to know its derivation, its first occurrence, its change of meaning down the centuries, and the sort of people who used it in different contexts.

The Vienna school of psychology presumes a conscious and unconscious mind as two separate and usually warring entities; but a poet cannot accept this. In the poetic trance, he has access not only to the primitive emotions and thoughts which lie stored in his childhood memory, but to all his subsequent experiences—emotional and intellectual; including a wide knowledge of English won by constant critical study. Words are filed away by their hundred thousand, not in alphabetic order but in related groups; and as soon as the trance seizes him, he can single out most of the ones he needs. Moreover, when the first well blotted draft has been copied out fairly before he goes to bed, and laid aside for reconsideration, he will read it the next morning as if it were written by another hand. Yet soon he is back in the trance, finds that his mind has been active, while he was asleep, on the problem of internal relations, and that he can substitute the exact right word for the stand-in with which he had to be content the night before.

One cannot hope to restore the creative processes that supplied certain unusual words in ancient poems. The work-sheets very rarely survive as evidence, and to discuss my own experience in writing poems suggests that I claim poetic merit for them: which no poet can afford to do. All poems are failures in the Muse's eye; and it is this conviction alone that entitles me to discuss the weaknesses in the work of others. One of the Muse's main functions is to abash her poet by making him aware of his stupidities, vanities, and petty dishonesties.

I once wrote a poem called *A Time of Waiting*, the theme of which was a resolve not to prejudice the future by hasty action:

> To take no rash decisions, enter into
> No random friendships, check the run-away tongue
> And fix my mind in a close pattern of doubt. . . .

When reviewing the second or third draft, I saw that *pattern* was too decorative a word.

> And fix my mind in a close *frame* of doubt. . . .

would have been too formal. I tried:

> And fix my mind in a close *net* of doubt. . . .

But a mind can hardly be fixed in a net; besides, *net* has the negative connotations of imprisonment without escape. I had in mind a positive form of quiet doubt, cultivated for the sake of good luck; because the Muse, for whose sake the doubt was assumed, would clearly not hasten to remove it. Finding the exact word seemed of the greatest importance: the poem, when complete, would confirm me in my decision. Poems have an auto-hypnotic function.

When I am writing prose and have a word on the tip of my tongue, or the nib of my pen, which somehow eludes me, I often consult Roget's *Thesaurus*. Reading the list of so-called synonyms in a word-group, I at once recognize the word I need. But I do not use Roget for poems. So, instead, on this occasion I went down to the sea, swam out to a small rocky island, and there the exact right word floated up to me from several fathoms down:

> To take no rash decisions, enter into
> No random friendships, check the run-away tongue
> And fix my mind in a close caul of doubt.

Caul surprised me, because I had not considered the word for at least twenty years; but later, reaching for the "C" volume of the O.E.D., I found that it held all the senses I needed. A caul is, first, a net cap confining the glory of a woman, her hair; then a gossamer web spun by spiders over grass, heavy with dew at dawn. Finally, it is the smooth, cap-like membrane with which a child is sometimes born, a lucky relic of his uterine experiences and, in English superstition, sovereign against death by drowning. A caul is thus the gentlest and happiest of all cerebral restraints. I found three metaphorical uses of *caul*, which set a precedent for mine:

1579—Whoso is blinded with the caul of beauty. . . .

1636—Custom in sin had drawn a caul over my conscience.

1643—A caul drawn on the heart.

That *close call* has a somewhat outmoded slang significance, was an accident that did disturb me. The eye cannot mistake *caul* for *call*, and the eye commands the inner ear. Poetry is read, not listened to, nine times out of ten. And *close* was the right adjective to qualify *caul*; I would have been ungrateful to look for another.

If a poem is lurking at the back of a poet's mind, and he has perfect confidence in bringing it to light under the trance, the keywords sooner or later will always fall into place. Or that is my own long-cherished superstition.

On the sole occasion that I ever discussed poetry with Walter De la Mare, I quoted him the lines from his *All That's Past*:

> —ah, no man knows
> Through what wild centuries
> Roves back the rose. . . .

and asked whether he was satisfied with *roves*. He blushed slightly, and admitted that though *roves* was too close in sound to *rose*, it was the nearest he could get—no, he wasn't satisfied. He needed some word that had the sense of *rambling*—as roses ramble—he had tried *Twines back the rose,* but *wild* and *twines* made an ugly assonance:

> Through what wild centuries
> Twines back the rose. . . .

Gads back the rose had a precedent in Milton's *gadding vine,* but *gad* was too similar in sound to *back* and, since Milton's days, had acquired a vulgar sense from *gad-about.* De la Mare died without finding a satisfactory solution to the problem, perhaps because he was dealing with a conceit, not a poetic thought; and because the technical trick of metathesis—transferring the adjective *wild* from *rose* to *centuries*—had thrown the stanza out of gear. I have no hope of finding the exact right answer myself, because it was never my poem. I once tried ineffectually:

> —ah, no man knows
> From what lost centuries
> Wanders the rose. . . .

or:

> What old, dead centuries
> Bred the wild rose. . . .

But if it has to *wild centuries,* then:

> Through what wild centuries
> Wends back the rose. . . .

is certainly better than *roves back. Wend,* a De-la-Mareish word, is akin to *wander* and *winding,* and makes a neat alliteration with *wild.*

The exact right word is sometimes missing from the dictionary. Thomas Hardy told me, in 1924 or so, that he now made it his practice to confirm doubtful words and that, a few days before, when looking up one such in the *Oxford English Dictionary,* he had found it, to be sure. But the only reference was: "Thomas Hardy: *Far From the Madding Crowd,* 1874."

I have myself hoped to contribute two or three words to the language. In a satire, *Beauty in Trouble,* I had occasion to mention the bat-like wings and cloven hooves of an evil angel. But *bat-like* is a plain, guileless Anglo-Saxon word, and the context demanded a rather grandiloquent Romance one to barb the satire. *Cat-like* and *feline; dog-like* and *canine; horse-like* and *equine:* these pairs, although synonyms in Roget, lie worlds apart. One sees the difference best in the phrase "dog-like devotion." "Canine devotion" is not stubborn personal love but mere animal behaviourism. Very well: *bat-like* needs an equivalent formed from the Latin—as *feline* is from *felis, canine* from *canis, equine* from *equus.* . . . The Latin for *bat* is *vespertilio;* so I coined the word *vespertilian—vespertilionian* seemed too much of a mouthful:

> The fiend who beats, betrays and sponges on her,
>   Persuades her, white is black,
> Flaunts vespertilian wing and cloven hoof
>   And soon will fetch her back. . . .

Among the gaps in the *Oxford English Dictionary* is *garden:* a jeweller's term for the bright cloudiness in certain gems, caused by chemical impurities, but giving them individuality and character. I am told that such a *garden* now proves that it is a genuine stone: such chemists as can artificially produce genuine rubies, emeralds, sapphires and the rest, have not yet got round to making any but flawlessly translucent ones:

> The pale rose-amethyst on her breast
> Has such a garden in it
> Your eye could trespass there for hours
> And wonder, and be lost.

Last year, I addressed the American Academy of Arts and Letters on the Arabic word *báraka*, which means the lively virtue, or blessedness, which a place or object acquires by long use; and deplored the new economic doctrine of built-in obsolescence, which sweeps away out-of-date models into the junk-yard or the garbage can long before they are worn out, and replaces them with others not meant to last for more than a short season. The lively virtue in words is longer-lasting. The doctrine of expendability applies either to semi-scientific terms which go out of date as the theses on which they rest are disproved; or to slang-coinages of novel terms for words like *money, liquor, girl, steal, cheat, policeman, fornicate, get drunk, die,* which add nothing to the simple original concept. A policeman is neither less nor more of a policeman when he is called a peeler, a bobby, an ecilop, a slop, a cop, a copper, a rozzer, a bull, or a fuzz. . . . Slang has been called "poor man's poetry," perhaps because eighteenth-century Classical tradition insisted on a particularized poetic vocabulary; and so did the Romantic Revivalists, though preferring a "Gothic" range of words borrowed from Chaucer, Spenser, Shakespeare, Walpole and Chatterton. Walter De la Mare is said to have started as a poet, while still a clerk with Standard Oil, by compiling lists of mellifluous words, such as *bergamot, chrysoprase, cresset, foredone, besprent,* and introducing them into nostalgic rhymes: his was a deliberate technique of quaintness.

The longer a word lasts in a language before growing obsolete—and one of a poet's moral duties is to rescue and reinstate obsolescent words for which no substitute can be found—the more strength and virtue it acquires. Yet there are well-dressed poems as well as naked ones, and the choice of vocabulary must always be directed by the theme. Donne, for example, specializes in the costumed poem, rather than the naked one. His *Seventh Elegy* alternates between the two different strands of language, Anglo-Saxon and Norman-French, rather than integrating them:

> Nature's lay Ideot, *I taught thee to love*,
> And in that sophistrie, Oh, thou dost prove
> Too subtile: *Foole, thou didst not understand*
> The mystique language *of the eye nor hand*:
> *Nor couldst thou judge* the difference of the aire
> *Of sighes, and say, this lies,* this sounds despaire. . . .

He is working up to the grand close of five splendid Romance words, introduced with eight Anglo-Saxon ones:

> *I had not taught thee then the* Alphabet
> Of flowers, how they devisefully *being set*
> *And bound up, might with speechless* secrecie
> Deliver arrands mutely, *and* mutually.

Donne gets away with a portentous word, *interinanimate*, in *The Ecstasy*, by using only Anglo-Saxon words to introduce it:

> When love with one another so
> Interinanimates two souls. . . .

Shakespeare gets away in *Macbeth* with:

> . . . This hand will rather
> The multitudinous seas incarnadine. . . .

these being enormous, terrifying words suited to Lady Macbeth's guilt and redeemed from bombast by the even more terrifying simplicity of the Anglo-Saxon line that follows:

> Making the green one red. . . .

To incarnadine and *to make red* are not, as is usually thought, tautological; and though *to incarnadine* meant only *to make carna-*

tion-coloured like healthy cheeks, Shakespeare was aware of its ultimate origin in the Latin *caro, carnis,* "flesh," and therefore of its association with words like *carnifex* and *carnivorous.* He so aroused the latent meaning of murder in *incarnadine* that one cannot use it today without thinking of blood.

The lively virtue of words is something of which every poet must be aware. *England* has this virtue, and so has *Scotland;* but not *Britain,* which is an intellectual, not an emotional, concept. Nor has *Britons* much virtue, despite:

> Rule, Britannia! Britannia, rule the waves!
> Britons never, never, never shall be slaves. . . .

The adjective *British,* curiously enough, *has* acquired virtue because of the British Fleet, the British Grenadiers, and so on.

The exact rightness of words can be explained only in the context of a whole poem: each one being related rhythmically, emotionally, and semantically, to every other. This, in effect, rules out any use of the same word in different contexts, unless the two uses are consonant, or parallel. It also rules out any repetition of the same vowel sound, unless for some particular purpose, such as the deliberate stridency of repeated long *a* or *i.* Or as when Keats, who insisted on the need to vary vowel sounds in ordinary contexts, commends Shakespeare for writing of the bees:

> *The* singing *masons* building *cells of wax.* . . .

The four short *i*-sounds in *singing* and *building,* he said, suggested the low buzz of bees.

A poem always chooses its own metre, and any attempt to dress up an idea in a particular metre is, at best, an amusing parlour game; at worst, dreary literature. A poem begins with the usual line-and-a-half that unexpectedly forces itself on the entranced mind and establishes not only the metre, but its rhythmic treatment. . . . The basic English metre is the ten-syllabled iambic line. But the metrical rules, which in Latin poetry were always meticulously maintained, even though the context might be a passionate one, do not apply to

English. A true iambic line in poems of emotional content has been rare since early Tudor times, and appears usually in lulls between gusts. The Earl of Surrey's proud requiem for his friend and companion-in-arms Thomas Clere begins, not in the measured iambic style, but with a drum beat:

> Norfolk sprung thee; Lambeth holds thee dead.
> Clere of the Count of Cleremont thou hight. . . .

before the iambic measure asserts itself:

> Within the womb of Ormond's race thou bred
> And saw'st thy cousin crownèd in thy sight. . . .

Shakespeare, in his indignant sonnet:

> Was it aúght tó mé, to béar the cánopy
> Wíth mý extérn, thíne oútward hónouring. . . .

does much the same thing. The rhythmic variations on this iambic line are infinite; yet, at the back of the mind, the metre still reigns.

The choice made by modernists of the nineteen-twenties to dispense with metre and rhyme altogether, because their Classically-minded predecessors had let these direct the poem, was unnecessary. Granted, a poet whose gentle voice rises and falls regularly in the iambic metre, with the expected rhyme closing each line, cannot hold my attention long. But whoever relies on what he calls "cadence," as opposed to variations in metre, or changes the norm constantly without warning, cannot expect the Muse to approve, or the reader to follow him.

A young poet finds his greatest difficulty in ending a poem. The sudden occurrence of a poetic phrase and an idea are not enough: unless he recognizes that a complete poem is there, let him be patient. He has perhaps not yet learned how to integrate his whole mind in the necessary trance of attention. Donne is an extreme example of impatience: he often begins with splendid candour, and ends in crooked artifice.

When one treats poetry in this sort of way, the notion of technique falls away: all that remains is the poet's service to the Muse, his unwavering love of whom, for all her unpossessibility, assures that his work will be truthful. . . . Every dictionary is a valley of dry bones. The poet is inspired to breathe life into them (as Ezekiel did when he prophesied), and convert them into language. You remember the rattle and shaking, and how the bones came together into skeletons, every bone to its bone, and put on sinews and flesh. That is a metaphor of craftsmanship. Then the four winds blew upon them, and they stood up, in fighting companies; which is how poems come alive. Technique takes one no farther than articulating the skeletons with wire, and plumping them up with plastic limbs and organs.

Itnimations of the Black Goddess

Poets, like prophets and saints, claim to live by certain unshakeable principles. But just as the sole judge of saintless or prophetic truth is God—not popular awe or fallible Church Councils; so the sole judge of poetry for the professed poet, is the Muse-goddess—not textbook critics or auditors of publishers' net-sales. Her inspiration has from time to time been manifested, or presumed, in poems; like that of God in prophecies. But since neither deity ever issues an authentic Royal warrant for any particular servitor, prophets have often prophesied erroneously in God's name; and poets have often misrepresented the Muse.

Though able to prove myself a former soldier by producing a row of tarnished campaign medals, I cannot show that I am a poet merely by displaying a row of well-thumbed verse-volumes. No public honours, no consensus of other poets, no album of press-cuttings, nor even the passage of time itself can give me, or anyone else, more than the courtesy title of poet. The one sure reward for whatever labours we may have undergone is our continued love of the Muse: as prophets count on none other than their continued fear of God. Undeniably a prophet will feel reassured if, in answer to his prayer, he sees the tyrant humiliated, the leper cleansed, the shadow turned back on the sun-dial. Undeniably, too, the poet will feel reassured if, reading what he has written for the Muse's sake, he finds that by some miracle he has said almost exactly what he meant.

The inspired Hebrew prophets were at constant logger-heads not only with the endowed Levitic priesthood, but with the monarchy, of which Samuel had always voiced his disapproval: calling for a pure theocracy. And God, it was agreed, chose prophets by certain signs known only to Himself; not they, God. The prophetic age ended for Israel early in the second century B.C., when her Guild of Prophets was disbanded by the Sanhedrin; as it likewise ended for orthodox Christians at the Crucifixion—when all prophecies were thought to have been fulfilled. Since then, the Jews acknowledge only sages—because prophets answer directly to God, but sages must refer to God's unalterable written Law. And the Church acknowledges only saints—always after strict inquiry into their orthodoxy. Catholic saints (there are, of course, no Protestant saints, with the dubious exception of King Charles the Martyr) live in the Church's shadow, accept her dogma and, because neither married nor forced to earn their livelihood, occupy their entire lives in prayer, preaching, vigils, fasting, and good works. Poets on the other hand, like prophets, reject dogma and patronage as contravening freedom of thought, and take care to live outside the literary establishment in the rough-and-tumble lay world.

Hebrew prophets gave God sole credit for any miracles done through them; a poet gives the Muse sole credit for his poems. But God, for the prophets, was a national deity; the Muse, though originally a tribal goddess, must now be a personal one. Prophets, moreover, being recognized as holy men, could count on hospitality wherever they went, and therefore—as we learn from the story of Elijah and Naaman—refused all payment for their works; but poets cannot count on such generous treatment as they could in ancient Ireland, for times have changed. They view what they have written as the Muse's clarifications of their own confused thought; not as saleable products or passports to fame—lest they incur her deep displeasure. Nevertheless, if their poems receive public acclaim, they need not feel guilty, having meant them, first, for the Muse's eye.

When Shakespeare opened a sonnet with *"Devouring Time, blunt thou the lion's claws,"* and ended it: *"My love shall in my verse ever live young,"* he was thinking of the immortal fame thus conferred on his love, rather than of his own. Some poets affect to despise immediate fame, and address posterity—though with small reason to assume that posterity will be more perspicacious than their own turnip-headed fellow-citizens.

The chaotic ethics of our epoch derive, I believe, from a revolution in early historical times that upset the balance between male and female principles: namely, the supersession of matriarchy by patriarchy. This revolt, and the subsequent patriarchal cult of reason (as opposed to intuitive thought), gave men control over most domestic, agricultural, and other arts. Women became chattels, no longer able even to bestow their love freely or educate their own children.

The poetic trance derives from ecstatic worship of the age-old matriarchal Greek Muse, who ruled Sky, Earth, Underworld in triad, and was worshipped on mountains. Hence her name—the Greek word *mousa* being etymologically connected with the Latin *mons*. Her altars—stone herms, or baetyls, around which women devotees danced counter-sunwise at lunar festivals—stood on the foothills of Parnassus, Olympus and Helicon. A male dance-leader invoked the Muse by improvising hexameter verses to a lyre accompaniment that set an ecstatic round dance in motion. Presently the Muse—like the Love-goddess Erzulie in Haitian *voudoun*—entered into, or "rode," some woman dancer, who now acted, spoke and sang on her mistress's behalf. "Sing, Muse!" had a literal meaning: it was a leader's appeal to the Goddess—"Choose your vessel, and sing to us through her mouth!" I have written elsewhere how at some time before the eighth century B.C., the god Apollo took over Muse-worship and, calling himself "Leader of the Muses," transferred her cult to his own sacred precincts. This meant more than self-identification with the lyre-plucking dance-leader of a nine-woman Maenad company; he was asserting his authority over the Muse herself. The Homeric bards, who based their guild on holy Delos, were Apollo's servitors, itinerant ballad-singers—"ballads" being originally dance songs—and claimed that they could induce the genuine Muse-trance even in a mixed and sedentary audience.

Though, at a later date, ballads were often recited without music, dance measures remained essential to poetic composition: creating a strong hypnotic suggestibility in listeners—and, when written down, in readers. By this stage, however, the Muse's invocation had become a mere formality. Once her worship was separated from the altar rites, she never again spoke through a woman worshipper. Apollo, as Leader of the Muses, henceforth dictated poems. "Metres," originally dance measures, were formalized by the Greek epic and dramatic poets, who applied to them strict Apollonian rules: each variety of metrical foot being assigned its proper emotional use. Yet Apollo, though the patron of formal verse (which included literary epics, odes, hymns and Classical idylls), was incapable of supplying the authentic trance, and discouraged ecstatic utterances except from his own highly tendentious oracles.

The basis of poetry is love, but love between men (apart from rare homosexual pairs) is seldom more than a metaphor—Christians preach on brotherly love, but look how most brothers treat one another! Love between men and women is a fundamental emotion, strong enough to transcend social contracts; and the love bestowed on a poet, however briefly, by a Muse-possessed woman, heightens his creative powers to an unparalleled degree. Poets demand inspiration, rather than tutoring in verse technique by experts of their own sex.

The peculiar strength of the Muse lies in her need to bestow love freely and absolutely, without incurring the least contractual obligation: having chosen a poet, she dismisses him in favour of another, whenever she pleases and without warning. He must never count on her constancy, on her honour, or on her sympathy with his sufferings, but remain faithful beyond reason. And though deep in her heart she may respect nobody more than him, he must not presume on this knowledge nor be deceived by her actions. The prophet's love of his God, a metaphor of filial reverence for a stern father, had this in common with poetic love—that the prophet was unable to rely on God's attention to his prayers.

Poetry is a way of thought—non-intellectual, anti-decorative thought at that,—rather than an art. Would-be poets today experiment in new loveless Apollonian techniques, taking pictorial abstractionism as their model, all working "objectively"—that being for them a term of praise—and unprepared to accept the poetic trance with its fantastic co-ordination of sound, rhythm and meaning. Poets who serve the Muse wait for the inspired lightning flash of two or three words that initiate composition and dictate the rhythmic norm of their verse.

DANCE OF WORDS

To make them move, you should start from lightning
And not forecast the rhythm: rely on chance,
Or so-called chance, for its bright emergence
Once lightning interpenetrates the dance.

Grant them their own traditional steps and postures
But see they dance it out again and again
Until only lightning is left to puzzle over—
The choreography plain, and the theme plain.

There are two distinct, but complementary, orders of women, both of them honoured by poets. First, the ideal woman of patriarchal civilization whom the Greeks deified as the Goddess Hestia, the Latins as Vesta; and who is represented in Christianity by the Virgin Mary—heroine of all old-fashioned songs and stories. Beautiful, tender, true, patient, practical, dependable: the woman whom Solomon described as "more precious than rubies"—the guardian of the sacred hearth, the wife-to-be, dreamt of by romantic soldiers in desert bivouacs.

Then the other woman: the multitudinously named White Goddess, a relic of matriarchal civilization or (who knows?) the harbinger of its return. She scorns any claim on her person, or curb on her desires; rejects male tutelage, hates marriage, and demands utter trust and faithfulness from her lovers—treating love not as a matter of contract, but as a sudden, unforeseeable miracle. She punishes the pride of any suitor who dares hope that he will one day make her his wife. Here is a poem on the subject, cast in seventeenth-century ballad form:

Inkidoo and the Queen of Babel

When I was a callant, born far hence,
You first laid hands on my innocence,
But sent your champion into a boar
That my fair young body a-pieces tore.

When I was a lapwing, crowned with gold,
Your lust and liking for me you told,
But plucked my feathers and broke my wing—
Wherefore all summer for grief I sing.

When I was a lion of tawny fell,
You stroked my mane and you combed it well,
But pitfalls seven you dug for me
That from one or other I might not flee.

When I was a courser, proud and strong,
That like the wind would wallop along,
You bated my pride with spur and bit
And many a rod on my shoulder split.

When I was a shepherd that for your sake
The bread of love at my hearth would bake,
A ravening wolf did you make of me
To be thrust from home by my brothers three.

When I tended your father's orchard close
I brought you plum, pear, apple and rose,
But my lusty manhood away you stole
And changed me into a grovelling mole.

When I was simple, when I was fond,
Thrice and thrice did you wave your wand,
But now you vow to be leal and true
And softly ask, will I wed with you?

The original of these stanzas was written more than four thousand
years ago—the hero Enkidu's address to the Love-goddess Ishtar. I

have translated them word for word from the Babylonian *Gilgamesh Epic,* though omitting to name the "callant born far hence"—in the original, he figured as "Tammuz"; for the Greeks he was Adonis. Enkidu's refusal to trust Ishtar a seventh and last time, earned him the punishment of death without resurrection. It is from this order of wild women that the Muse always emerges. The melancholy strain in traditional poetry records the poet's disappointment that she cannot behave like Vesta.

Odes to the Vestal Virgin Mary have been written by Catholic poets since her sudden rise to power during the Crusades. None ever charges her with unkindness. Poets call on the Blessed Virgin to stand by them even in essentially male occupations. She will guide a battered barque safe to port; bless a young knight's sword after his all-night vigil, and direct it shrewdly when he takes the field; with a twitch of her blue mantle she will draw a murderous bull from the gored matador. . . . But her facial expression never varies, nor do her simple gestures. She offers no surprises, never jokes, teases, hides. Small furry animals gather around her. With lion, fox, lynx, hawk or osprey she has no dealings. She will watch at the sick-bed, drudge in the houses of the poor, wear the plainest clothes, and instruct the men of her household by example only, never by harsh words or deception. The difference between these complementary characters is presented in:

RUBY AND AMETHYST

Two women: one as good as bread,
Bound to a sturdy husband.
Two women: one as rare as myrrh
Bound only to herself.

Two women: one as good as bread,
Faithful to every promise.
Two women: one as rare as myrrh,
Who never pledges faith.

The one a flawless ruby wears
But with such innocent pleasure
A stranger's eye might think it glass
And take no closer look.

Two women: one as good as bread,
The noblest of the city.
Two women: one as rare as myrrh,
Who needs no public praise.

The pale rose-amethyst on her breast
Has such a garden in it
Your eye could trespass there for hours,
And wonder, and be lost.

About her head a swallow wheels
Nor ever breaks the circuit:
Glory and awe of womanhood
Still undeclared to man.

Two women: one as good as bread,
Resistant to all weathers.
Two women: one as rare as myrrh,
Her weather still her own.

The Muse and Vesta rule different worlds. Yet few rubies are unflawed. The sacred hearth fire is often left unattended, and to marry even the Virgin Mary herself did not make a poet of St. Joseph. . . . In fact, more poems spring from a realization that domestic love has cooled or died than from resolute praises of domesticity; and the Muse, the perpetual Other Woman, always inspires them. Nevertheless, there are settled marriages over which the White Goddess has no power. She will smile if the husband writes his faithful wife a well-turned ode on their silver wedding anniversary, and pass on with a disdainful shrug.

Only during the past three years have I ventured to dramatize, truthfully and factually, the vicissitudes of a poet's dealings with the White Goddess. Whatever may be said against her, she at least gives him an honest warning of what to expect—as it were, tying a poison label around her own neck:

LYCEIA

All the wolves of the forest
Howl for Lyceia,
Crowding together
In a close circle,
Tongues a-loll.

A silver serpent
Coiled at her waist
And a quiver at knee,
She combs fine tresses
With a fine comb:

Wolf-like, woman-like,
Gazing about her,
Greeting the wolves;
Partial to many,
Yet masked in pride.

The young wolves snarl,
They snap at one another
Under the moon.
"Beasts, be reasonable,
My beauty is my own!"

Lyceia has a light foot
For a weaving walk.
Her archer muscles
Warn them how tightly
She can stretch the string.

> I question Lyceia,
>   Whom I find posted
>   Under the pine trees
>   One early morning:
> "What do the wolves learn?"
>
> "They learn only envy,"
>   Lyceia answers,
> "Envy and hope,
>   Hope and chagrin.
>   Would you howl too
>   In that wolfish circle?"
> She laughs as she speaks.

The poet listens to her warning:

THE DANGEROUS GIFT

> Were I to cut my hand
>   On the sharp knife you gave me
>   (That dangerous knife, your beauty),
> I should know what to do:
>   Bandage the wound myself
> And hide the blood from you.
>
> A murderous knife it is,
>   As often you have warned me:
>   And if I looked for pity
> Or tried a wheedling note
>   Either I must restore it
> Or turn it on my throat.

The Muse shows a childish delight at being recognized by her poet, and may at first profess grateful love, though never giving him the least assurance of her continuous accessibility:

Seldom, Yet Now

Seldom, yet now: the quality
Of this fierce love between us—
Seldom the encounter,
The presence always,
Free of oath or promise.

And if we were not so,
But birds of similar plumage caged
In the peace of everyday,
Could we still conjure wildfire up
From common earth, as now?

Soon the Muse will multiply her evasions and broken promises, while still demanding the poet's absolute trust; take gifts as her right, rule him with a whim of iron, and subject him to almost insufferable ordeals. . . . If he remains faithful, she will choose a new lover from among his friends; as in the Anatha-Ishtar myth, she always betrayed and murdered him for the sake of his twin, the antipoet:

Horizon

On a clear day how thin the horizon
Drawn between sea and sky,
Between sea-love and sky-love;
And after sunset how debatable
Even for an honest eye.

"Do as you will tonight,"
Said she, and so he did
By moonlight, candlelight,
Candlelight and moonlight,
While pillowed clouds the horizon hid.

Knowing-not-knowing that such deeds must end
In a curse which lovers long past weeping for
Had heaped upon him: she would be gone one night
With his familiar friend,
Granting him leave her beauty to explore
By moonlight, candlelight,
Candlelight and moonlight.

Yet the Muse can exercise no power without her poet, and he is aware of this; but dares not disclose her dependence on his love. *Inkidoo and the Queen of Babel* is to the point here:

When I was a lion of tawny fell,
You stroked my mane and you combed it well,
But pitfalls seven you dug for me
That from one or other I might not flee. . . .

Ishtar, Queen of Babylon, was the original Virgin of the Zodiac, who appears on steles, naked and riding a lion, the poet's zodiacal sign:

LION LOVER

You chose a lion to be your lover—
Me, who in joy such doom greeting
Dared jealously undertake
Cruel ordeals long foreseen and known,
Springing a trap baited with flesh: my own.

Nor would I now exchange this lion heart
For a less furious other,
Though by the Moon possessed
I gnaw at dry bones in a lost lair
And, when clouds cover her, roar my despair.

Gratitude and affection I disdain
As cheap in any market:
Your naked feet upon my scarred shoulders,

Your eyes naked with love,
Are all the gifts my beasthood can approve.

Though the poet's friends may descry his Muse as a vixen, a bitch,
a bird of prey, he is pledged to accept what he would refuse from
any other woman; and suffers most when she uses the light of glory
with which he invests her, to shine in an anti-poetic and even criminal
world. Is she, in truth, his Muse, his love? Or is she acting a part
with sardonic humour? His test will be: which gives the greater pain
—belief or disbelief? Many poets break under the strain:

To Beguile and Betray

To beguile and betray, though pardonable in women,
Slowly quenches the divine need-fire
By true love kindled in them. Have you not watched
The immanent Goddess fade from their brows
When they make private to their mysteries
Some whip-scarred rogue from the hulks, some painted clown
From the pantomime—and afterwards accuse you
Of jealous hankering for the mandalot
Rather than horror and sick foreboding
That she will never return to the same house?

Convinced of her need for his love, the obsessed poet refuses to
break under the strain; though at last realizing that Lyceia meant all
she said at their first encounter: her beauty is her own, and she offers
nothing but envy, hope and chagrin. Unlike Enkidu, he does not
reproach the Goddess with her treacheries, but reads them as just
criticism of his desire to possess her, and continues to love her self-
lessly:

Expect Nothing

Give, ask for nothing, hope for nothing,
Subsist on crumbs, though scattered casually

Not for you (she smiles) but for the birds.
Though only a thief's diet, it staves off
Dire starvation, nor does she grow fat
On the bread she crumbles, while the lonely truth
Of love is honoured, and her pledged word.

Satisfied by this fresh evidence of her power, she softens towards him for awhile; though her eventual function and fate is to betray him, and thus forfeit the glory with which he enshrined her:

IN HER PRAISE

This they know well: the Goddess yet abides.
Though each new lovely woman whom she rides,
Straddling her neck a year or two or three,
Should sink beneath such weight of majesty
And, groping back to humankind, gainsay
The healing power that whitened all her way
With a broad track of trefoil—leaving you,
Her chosen lover, ever again thrust through
With daggers, your purse rifled, your rings gone—
Nevertheless they call you to live on
To parley with the pure, oracular dead,
To hear the wild pack whimpering overhead,
To watch the moon tugging at her cold tides.
Woman is mortal woman. She abides.

Orpheus, in the Greek myth, was taught by the Triple Muse not only to enchant men and wild beasts with his lyre, but to make rocks and trees move and follow him in a dance. According to a later myth, his wife Eurydice (whom he had married after a visit to Egypt) was assaulted by the pastoral god Aristaeus, trod on a serpent as she fled, and died of its venomous bite. Orpheus then boldly harrowed Hell, intent on fetching her back. There, with his lyre, he charmed the Dog Cerberus, the ferry-man Charon and the three Judges of the Dead, temporarily suspended the tortures of the damned, and even persuaded Hades, God of Tartarus, to set Eurydice free. Hades made one condition: that Orpheus must not look behind him until she was safely home under the light of the sun. . . . Eurydice followed him up through the dark passages of Tartarus, guided by his lyre; and it was only on reaching the sunlight that he turned to reassure himself of her presence—and lost her for ever.

This same Orpheus is said, by the mythographers, to have denounced human sacrifice and preached that the Sun was a nobler deity than the Moon—for which blasphemy a group of Moon-worshipping, cannibalistic Maenads tore him in pieces. The Triple Muse collected his mangled limbs and buried them at Leibethra, where nightingales afterwards sang more sweetly than anywhere else in the world. . . . His head, though attacked by a jealous serpent, continued singing and was laid up in a cave at Antissa, sacred to Dionysus, God of Enlightenment. There it prophesied so clearly and constantly that at last Apollo, finding his own oracles at Delphi, Gryneium and Clarus deserted by visitants, stood over the head, crying: "Cease to interfere in my business! I have suffered you long enough." At this, we are told, the head fell silent.

It may well be that, sometime during the second millennium B.C., a Libyo-Thracian (afterwards identified with Orpheus) visited Egypt and brought back a mystic Sun-cult which local Moon-worshippers opposed. Yet there is more to this myth than a kernel of history: Eurydice ("Wide Rule") was, in fact, not Orpheus's wife, but the Triple Muse herself—*Diana in the leavës green, Luna who so bright doth sheen, Proserpina in Hell,* as John Skelton calls her.

Proserpina, or Persephone ("Voice of Destruction"), is the Muse in her most implacable aspect; and we know from the Demeter myth that Persephone, although carried off with a great show of unwillingness by Hades, a Serpent-god, soon broke her hunger strike in Tartarus by eating food of the dead, namely seven pomegranate seeds. As a result, she was ordered by Almighty Zeus to spend seven months of the year (or, some say, three) in Hades's company, but the remainder on earth. This can, of course, be read as a simple nature myth of winter's inclemency—pomegranates being the last fruit to ripen in Greece—and the return of spring, when Persephone's *Anthesterion,* or Flower Festival, was annually celebrated. Yet it yields a different sense when related to the Orpheus story.

Orpheus recognized and glorified the Muse; in gratitude, she lent him her own magical powers, so that he made trees dance—"trees," in ancient Europe, being a widely used metaphor of the poetic craft. Later, in Egypt, he learned a new solar perfectionism, which she rejected as foreign to her nature. How could Orpheus hope to keep her always beside him in the bright upper air of love and truth? Had she not a secret passion for serpents, a delight in murder, a secret craving for corpse flesh, a need to spend seven months of the year consorting with the sly, the barren, the damned? She might cherish Orpheus while still on earth, even calling him beautiful— since his beauty reflected her own—and mourn him when he was murdered. . . . Yet she could not be bound by his hopes for her perfectibility. Eurydice never trod accidentally on a serpent while avoiding Aristaeus's lustful embraces: she surely chose to couple with a serpent—as Mother Eurynome ("Wide Order"), her ancestress, herself had coupled with the world-snake Ophion. Simple-minded Orpheus flattered her pride by challenging death in his descent to Hell, and she pretended to follow him up into the sunlight. . . . but soon retired. He waited awhile at the entrance of the Taenaran Cave, keeping his back to it; then turned about and saw himself deceived once more:

FOOD OF THE DEAD

Blush as you stroke the curves—chin, lips and brow—
Of your scarred face, Prince Orpheus: for she has called it
Beautiful, nor would she stoop to flattery.
Yet are you patient still, when again she has eaten
Food of the dead, seven red pomegranate seeds,
And once more warmed the serpent at her thighs
For a new progress through new wards of hell?

Arabs, when down-trodden, robbed or cheated, often refrain from curses, since these are apt to boomerang back. They merely cry instead: "*Maslum, Maslum, Maslum!*", which means "I am oppressed, I am oppressed, I am oppressed!" and leave the avenging of their

injury, if undeserved, to God or Fate. So should the poet refrain
from cursing Eurydice, however ill she has used him:

EURYDICE

"I am oppressed, I am oppressed, I am oppressed"—
Once I utter the curse, how can she rest:
No longer able, weeping, to placate me
With renewed auguries of celestial beauty?

Speak, fly in her amber ring; speak, horse of gold!
What gift did I ever grudge her, or help withhold?
In a mirror I watch blood trickling down the wall—
Is it mine? Yet still I stand here proud and tall.

Look where she shines with a borrowed blaze of light
Among the cowardly, faceless, lost, unright,
Clasping a naked imp to either breast—
Am I not oppressed, oppressed, three times oppressed?

She has gnawn at corpse-flesh till her breath stank,
Paired with a jackal, grown distraught and lank,
Crept home, accepted solace, but then again
Flown off to chain truth back with an iron chain.

My own dear heart, dare you so war on me
As to strangle love in a mad perversity?
Is ours a fate that can ever be forsworn
Though my lopped head sing to the yet unborn?

Orpheus was torn in pieces: the fate of all Muse-worshipping
poets. But his head continued to sing; and even the cynical Serpent
(who asks: "Why deceive yourself? She will always need corpse
flesh and the charm of my subtle tongue") could not silence it.
Neither could Apollo, God of Reason, make Orpheus hold his
peace for ever. In the Palestinian myth of the rival twins, Aleyan
and Mot, the Goddess Anatha lured first one, then the other, to her
bed—murdering each in turn. Mot was the demi-god of drought,

lack and evil. The Muse, in fact, alternates between the worlds of good and evil, plenty and lack; and her poet will have his head torn off and his limbs gnawn by greedy teeth if he attempts to change her. Yet still he believes that, one day, Eurydice must mount into the everlasting Garden of Paradise which she planted, and there make him her sole lover:

A LAST POEM

A last poem, and a very last, and yet another—
O, when can I give over?
Must I drive the pen until blood bursts from my nails
And my breath fails and I shake with fever,
Or sit well wrapped in a many-coloured cloak
Where the moon shines new through Castle Crystal?
Shall I never hear her whisper softly:
"But this is truth written by you only,
And for me only; therefore, love, have done?"

A poet who elects to worship Ishtar-Anatha-Eurydice, concentrates in himself the emotional struggle which has torn mankind apart: that futile war for dominance waged between men and women on battle-fields of the patriarchal marriage bed. He rejects the crude, self-sufficient male intelligence, yet finds the mild, complaisant Vesta insufficient for his spiritual needs. Renascent primitive woman, the White Goddess, to whom he swears allegiance, treats him no less contemptuously than she does anyone else in this man-ruled world; as in a race riot the colour of one's face is all that counts. . . . There can be no kindness between Ishtar and Enkidu, between Muse and poet, despite their perverse need for each other. Nor does a return to Vesta's gentle embraces—though he may never have denied her his affection—solve his problem. Marriage does not satisfy the physiological and emotional needs of more than one couple in ten.

Nevertheless Ishtar, though the most powerful deity of her day, did not rule alone. At Hierapolis, Jerusalem and Rome she acknowledged a mysterious sister, the Goddess of Wisdom, whose temple was small and unthronged. Call her the Black Goddess: Provençal and Sicilian "Black Virgins" are so named because they derive from an ancient tradition of Wisdom as Blackness. This Black Goddess, who represents a miraculous certitude in love, ordained that the poet who seeks her must pass uncomplaining through all the passionate ordeals to which the White Goddess may subject him.

The *Orphic Fragments* tell how Night mothered a Love-god named Phanes, who set the Universe in motion. Night, for the Orphics, appeared in triad as Blackness (namely, Wisdom), Order and Justice. Before her cave sat the inescapable Rhea—the White Goddess—beating a brazen drum and compelling man's attention to Night's oracles. Throughout the Orient, Night was regarded as a positive power, not as a mere absence of daylight; and Black as a prime colour, not as absence of colour, was prized for capturing the Sun's virtue more than any other.

This myth surely needs no gloss? The Provençal and Sicilian Black Virgins are Sufic in origin—Perso-Arabic applications to Christian doctrine of the same ancient myth. The Virginal St. Sophia —that is, Wisdom—mothers the creative Love-god:

That Other World

Fatedly alone with you once more
As before Time first creaked:
Sole woman and sole man.

Others admire us as we walk this world:
We show them kindliness and mercy,
So be it none grow jealous
Of the truth that echoes between us two,
Or of that other world, in the world's cradle,
Child of your love for me.

In the Jewish Wisdom-cult, also apparently of Orphic origin, seven pillars are set up to support Wisdom's shrine: namely, the seven planetary powers of the seven-branched Candlestick. And when the Shunemite bride, whom Solomon in his wisdom adored, says in the *Canticles:* "I am black, but comely," her meaning is: "Though comely, I am as wise as any crone." She adds, half-humorously: "The Sun has looked upon me." And the Orphics, seekers after Wisdom like Hebrews and Sufis, chose the Sun as their metaphor of illumination.

Night had a dove's head, and Phanes, God of Love, was hatched from a silver egg that she laid. There is no more ancient emblem of love than the turtle-dove; or of spiritual re-birth than the phoenix. Shakespeare's strange prophetic line *The Phoenix and the turtle fled in a mutual flame from hence,* carries a world of meaning. The phoenix, according to the Egyptians, was born as a worm from the ashes of its self-consumed predecessor and, after four years, grew to a chick:

THE HEARTH

Here it begins: the worm of love breeding
Among red embers of a hearth-fire,
Turns to a chick, is slowly fledged,
And will hop from lap to lap in a ring
Of eager children basking at the blaze.

But the luckless man who never sat there,
Nor borrowed live coals from the sacred source
To warm a hearth of his own making,
Nor bedded lay under pearl-grey wings
In dutiful content,

How shall he watch at the stroke of midnight
Dove become phoenix, plumed with green and gold?
Or be caught up by jewelled talons
And haled away to a fastness of the hills
Where an unveiled woman, black as Mother Night,
Teaches him a new degree of love
And the tongues and songs of birds?

Poetry, it may be said, passes through three distinct stages: first, the poet's introduction, by Vesta, to love in its old-fashioned forms of affection and companionship; next, his experience of death and recreation at the White Goddess's hand; and lastly a certitude in love, given him by the Black Goddess, his more-than-Muse.

The Black Goddess is so far hardly more than a word of hope whispered among the few who have served their apprenticeship to the White Goddess. She promises a new pacific bond between men and women, corresponding to a final reality of love, in which the patriarchal marriage bond will fade away. Unlike Vesta, the Black Goddess has experienced good and evil, love and hate, truth and falsehood in the person of her sister; but chooses what is good: rejecting serpent-love and corpse flesh. Faithful as Vesta, gay and adventurous as the White Goddess, she will lead man back to that sure instinct of love which he long ago forfeited by intellectual pride.

It is idle to speculate what poets will then become, or whether the same woman can, in fact, by a sudden spectacular change in her nature, play two diverse parts in one lifetime. Everything is possible. The Black Goddess may prefer to keep her maidenhead unbroken. Or appear disembodied rather than incarnate. . . . Does it matter? Poets, at any rate, will no longer be bullied into false complacency by the submissive sweetness of Vesta, or be dependent on the unpredictable vagaries of Anatha-Ishtar-Eurydice.

Standards of Craftsmanship

Since it is mainly undergraduates, perhaps only half of you from the English School, who come to these lectures, I have been wondering just how far I can count on you to follow my far from academic views on poetry, or even on poetry's homely half-sister verse. How much poetry have you read?

Most of you have, it seems, been exposed at one time or another to Sir Arthur Quiller-Couch's *Oxford Book of English Verse*—first published in 1900, enlarged by him at the outbreak of the Second World War, and not since re-edited, though still in great demand. Hundreds of other anthologies are published in England and America yearly, but the *Oxford Book* remains entrenched as the Establishment's first choice for well-educated men and women. Over half a million copies have, it is claimed, been sold. Arthur Quiller-Couch, originally an Oxonian (Trinity College), went to the Other Place as head of the English School; a gracious action which, enhanced by the popularity of his robust novels, gave him an unimpeachable critical standing.

He prefaced his first edition adroitly with rhetoric:

For this anthology I have tried to range over the whole field of English Verse from the beginning, or from the Thirteenth Century to this closing year of the Nineteenth, and to choose the best. Nor have I sought in these Islands only, but wheresoever the Muse has followed the tongue which, among living tongues, she most delights to honour. To bring home and render so great a spoil compendiously has been my capital difficulty. It is for the reader to judge if I have so managed it as to serve those who already love poetry, and to implant that love in those young minds not yet initiated. . . . Care has been taken with the texts. But I have sometimes thought it consistent with the aim of the book to prefer the more beautiful to the better attested reading. I have often excised weak or superfluous stanzas when sure that excision would improve; and have not hesitated to extract a few stanzas from a long poem when persuaded that they could stand alone as a lyric. The apology for such experiments can only lie in their success: but the risk is one which, in my judgement, the anthologist ought to take. A few small corrections have been made, but only when they were quite obvious.

The numbers chosen are either lyrical or epigrammatic. Indeed I am mistaken if a single epigram included fails to preserve at least some faint thrill of the emotion through which it had to pass before the Muse's lips let it fall, with however exquisite deliberation. But the lyrical spirit is volatile and notoriously hard to bind with definitions; and seems to grow wilder with the years. . . .

Having set my heart on choosing the best, I resolved not to be perturbed if my judgement should often agree with that of good critics. The best is the best, though a hundred judges have declared it so; nor had it been any feat to search out and insert the second-rate merely because it happened to be recondite.

In 1939, he added a hundred pages of what he calls "numbers" by recent poets of genius, and wrote:

. . . I shrank, or course, from making the book unwieldy; but in fact also I felt my judgement insecure amid post-War poetry. Although I cannot dispute against Time, this is not to admit a charge of crabbèd age: since it has been my good fortune to spend the most part of these later years with the young and to share—even in some measure to encourage—their zest for experiment. The Muses' house has many mansions: their hospitality has outlived many policies of State, more than a few religions, countless heresies—*tamen usque recurret Apollo*—and it were profane to misdoubt the Nine as having forsaken these so long favoured islands. Of experiment I still hold myself fairly competent to judge. But, writing in 1939, I am at a loss what to do with a fashion of morose disparagement; of sneering at things long by catholic consent accounted beautiful; of scorning at "Man's unconquerable mind" and hanging up (without benefit of laundry) our common humanity as a rag on a clothes line.

The word "number," by the way, has two meanings. From 1878 onwards, it was used for identifying numbered pieces in a collection of songs, or poems, or in a concert. But as used by Milton, Scott, Pope, Wordsworth and the rest, "numbers" meant metrical periods. Pope, who himself "lisped in numbers," rightly disparaged those

> Who must by numbers judge a poet's song;
> And smooth or rough, with them is right or wrong.

Quiller-Couch uses "number" in lieu of "poem" to forestall criticism, as he also names his anthology the *Oxford Book of English Verse;* though with the hint that every piece must obey established rules of scansion.

For the sake of convenience I shall use this anthology as a text-book; questioning how far the various "numbers" included fall short of the natural standards of verse-craftsmanship; and distinguishing occasional poems from non-poems. This is an even more invidious task than compiling an anthology, since one can more easily show what is wrong with a set of verses—as the Classical master blue-pencils faults in grammar, or quantity, or metre, in the Latin verse compositions offered him—than what makes a poem good. I have somewhere compared a real poem to a round tower built of stone, with the blocks so carefully cut and fitted that they leave no least handhold or foothold, and seem all of a piece. Also to a magic circle, from which all temporal irrelevancy has been excluded. A real poem has instant and permanent durability, however impermanent the world in which it first appears; and indeed however impermanent the emotional crisis which evoked it.

Two pages were missing from our nursery copy of *Alice Through the Looking Glass,* and some fifty years passed before I read them for the first time in a *Lewis Carroll Omnibus.* . . . They struck me as both dull and badly written. Yet reason told me that they were no better and no worse than the rest of the book, to which I had been devoted by long familiarity. So it is with a great many pieces included in the *Oxford Book of English Verse;* if you knew them before your critical judgement had formed, you will forgive me if I ask you to take a closer look at them.

John Hayward, introducing the new *Oxford Book of Nineteenth-Century Verse,* writes sensibly enough:

> . . . In so far as the present collection represents within the compass of a single volume the poetic achievement of the 19th century, it does so in the light of the taste and critical opinion of a later age. . . . If standards of appreciation were not subject to periodical revision it would contain little, for example, of Blake and Clare, of Meredith and Hardy, and a great deal, for example, of Southey and Campbell, or Mrs. Browning and Bailey. What was once acclaimed as poetically valuable is subsequently devalued and rejected. Who now reads *The Curse of Kehama, Gertrude of Wyoming, Aurora Leigh,* or *Festus?*
>
> . . . Of course, many poems in this collection have stood the test of time. Their selection presents little difficulty. But there are also many whose right to a place must depend upon balancing the conflicting claims to representation of poets who appear to have been over-valued in their day and of those who appear to have been undervalued or even, like Darley, scarcely recognized. . . . This gives rise to curious speculation on the influence of the *Zeitgeist,* the nature of poetic sensibility, and the validity of Dr. Johnson's dictum that "by the common sense of readers uncorrupted with literary prejudice must be finally decided all claim to poetical honours." Why was Wordsworth's *The Prelude* or Bailey's *Festus* a best-seller in Victorian England? And who knows whether the future will not judge *The Testament of Beauty* to have been underrated and Pound's *Cantos* overrated (or *vice versa*) in their time? How much space will the *Oxford Book of Twentieth-Century English Verse* allot a hundred years hence to Dylan Thomas and Betjeman?

Yet Mr. Hayward has begged the question whether certain constant principles may exist of which the few dedicated poets of every age become increasingly conscious, and which it is their task to refine. No true poet of my acquaintance would deny this; all of them consider themselves the friends and contemporaries of their equally dedicated predecessors. What standards of verse may commend themselves to the Palgraves and Quiller-Couches—old-clothesmen of literature, rather than poets—of a hundred years hence is a matter of supreme indifference to poets.

Verse is a craft; poetry is a way of life, a vocation or profession. As such it is not operationally organized like the professions of medicine, law, architecture, pedagogy, the Civil Service—all of which, of course, include certain members fanatically devoted to principle. Indeed, though verse has long been used as a vehicle of prophetic or poetic utterance, one may be a poet, in a sense, without ever writing a line. The craft of English verse can be taught, but no better than that of academic Latin verse: the craftsman, that is to say, chooses a stock theme which he learns to work out with cool intelligence from a memory well-stocked with Classical examples. In poetry, contrariwise, the theme is always new and chooses the poet: allowing him no rest until its demands have been satisfied by lines of ungainsayable originality.

It is perhaps easier to distinguish between a monumental mason and a free sculptor. The monumental mason has learned how to handle a chisel, distinguish different kinds of stone, and carve a few stock emblems: weeping willows, clasped hands, cherubs and the like, as headings for his obituary legends. The sculptor, using a similar chisel, begins where the monumental mason leaves off. But consider what has happened to sculpture in the last generation. Because it became so highly academicized during our Victorian period, which hung over into the Edwardian and the Georgian; and because popular reaction to the profitable war-memorial art was so long delayed; and because the eventual rebels, Henry Moore, Barbara Hepworth, and Reg Butler, won such high-level acclaim that the revolution had to be taken still further—therefore the basic crafts of stone-cutting and casting in bronze are no longer in fashion. The present sculptural trend is to work with an oxyacetylene torch: welding together random dingbats of interestingly corroded metal salved from junkyard or car-cemetery. You can make an analogy here, if you wish, with modernist "beat" poems, which originated in America as excusable protests against academic neo-Victorianism.

I find the standards of verse-craftsmanship offered by the *Oxford Book of English Verse* deplorably low, compared with those demanded from you undergraduates in, say, mathematics, physics and biology. Real poems have a rhythmic pattern: the variation of emotional intensity from line to line, or stanza to stanza, can be drawn in the air with one's finger. The end usually provides the climax; though sometimes the climax comes earlier, and the end is what the Elizabethans called "a dying fall." Occasionally a calm level is sustained throughout, with only minor troughs and valleys. Donne was peculiar in often beginning with his climax, and letting the whole poem die away: like a Lenten sermon preached too long or on too stirring a text. Competent verse must also have a pattern of varying emphasis, skilfully maintained by the rhythmic control of words. Quiller-Couch seems to have been more interested in the "beauties" of verse, meaning incidental phrases that catch the eye, than in the patterns.

Here, for example, is his version of the *Lyke-Wake Dirge;* which happens to be a real poem, so that what he has done to it cannot easily be pardoned:

A LYKE-WAKE DIRGE

This ae nighte, this ae nighte,
　—Every nighte and alle,
Fire and fleet and candle-lighte,
　And Christe receive thy saule.

When thou from hence away art past,
　—Every nighte and alle,
To Whinny-muir thou com'st at last;
　—And Christe receive thy saule.

If ever thou gavest hosen and shoon,
—Every nighte and alle,
Sit thee down and put them on;
And Christe receive thy saule.

If hosen and shoon thou ne'er gav'st nane
—Every nighte and alle,
The whinnes sall prick thee to the bare bane;
And Christe receive thy saule.

From Brig o' Dread when thou may'st pass,
—Every nighte and alle,
To purgatory fire thou com'st at last;
And Christe receive thy saule.

If ever thou gavest meat and drink,
—Every nighte and alle,
The fire sall never make thee shrink;
And Christe receive thy saule.

If meat or drink thou ne'er gav'st nane,
—Every nighte and alle,
The fire sall burn thee to the bare bane;
And Christe receive thy saule.

This ae nighte, this ae nighte,
—Every nighte and alle,
Fire and fleet and candle-lighte,
And Christe receive thy saule.

I wonder how much sense you have got from this poem? Quiller-Couch has not even allowed you to realize that the soul of the *lyke*, or corpse, is being ritually mourned at a "wake" with fire, salt and candlelight. He has also fallen into the common error of printing *fleet* instead of "selte" (salt)—the old-fashioned *s* of *selte* having been mistaken for an *f* by the broadside ballad's printer; and the *l* and first *e* interchanged. Quiller-Couch glosses *fleet* as "house-room"; a meaning, however, not sustained by the *Oxford English Dictionary*, or any other of standing.

He also leaves out part of the title: *The Cleveland Lyke-Wake Dirge*. This dirge used to be sung over corpses at Cleveland in Yorkshire until the beginning of the eighteenth century. A platter of *selte* was always placed on the corpse's breast to keep away the Devil—as when one throws spilt salt over one's shoulder at table. Three candles were lighted in honour of the Trinity, and as a reminder of three ordeals that the soul must face in its passage-ritual to Paradise. First, Whinny-muir, a wide gorse scrub which lay close to Cleveland town:

> If hosen or shoon thou ne'er gav'st nane,
> The whinnes sall prick thee to the bare bane. . . .

The last ordeal was Purgatory Fire:

> If meat or drink thou ne'er gav'st nane,
> The fire sall burn thee to the bare bane. . . .

But what of the intermediate ordeal, the Brig (or Bridge) o' Dread, which is here merely mentioned but not described? That part of the dirge must be included, as surely as there must be fourteen lines to every sonnet.

The omitted verses run:

> If ever thou gavest of silver and gold,
> —Every nighte and alle,
> At Brig o' Dread thou'lt find foothold,
> And Christe receive thy saule!

> If silver or gold thou never gavest nane,
> —Every nighte and alle,
> Thou'lt tumble down intil hell's flame,
> And Christe receive thy saule!

Anthologists and others have every right to print what version they prefer of an anonymous ballad, or to take the best of a worse version and patch a better one with it. Quiller-Couch has often availed himself of this right, but in his version of *The Queen's Maries*, he has again spoiled the poetic pattern by omitting several essential stanzas, and including others irrelevant to it.

This is how the ballad should, in my judgement, go:

> Marie Hamilton's to the kirk gane
> Wi' ribbons on her breast;
> The King thought mair o' Marie Hamilton
> Than he listen'd to the priest.
>
> Marie Hamilton's to the kirk gane,
> Wi' gloves upon her hands;
> The King thought mair o' Marie Hamilton
> Than the Queen and a' her lands.
>
> Now, word's come till the kitchen
> And word's gone to the ha'
> That Mary Hamilton gangs wi' child
> To the highest Stewart of a'.
>
> The King's gane to the Abbey close
> And pulled the Abbey tree,
> That burden frae her heart to scale—
> But the thing it wad na ne.
>
> Now word's come till the kitchen
> And word's come to the ha'
> That Mary Hamilton's brought to bed,
> But the bonny babe's awa'.
>
> O' she's rowed it in a pinerpeg,
> And she's set it on the sea—
> "Gae sink or swim ye, bonny babe,
> Ye's get nae mair o' me."
>
> Mary Hamilton's back to bed,
> And stretchéd on her sheet,

When by there comes the Queen hersel'
And stands at her bed feet,
Says "Mary Hamilton, whar's your babe?
Fu' sair I heard it greet."

"There's ne'er a babe intil my room
As little designs to be,
It was but a stitch in my ain fair side
And sair it troublet me."

"Rise up, put o' your robes o' black
Or else your robes o' brown,
For ye maun gang wi' me this morn
To ride thro' Edinburgh town."

"I will na put on my robes o' black
Nor yet my robes o' brown
But I'll put on the glistering gold
To ride thro' Edinburgh town."

When she rade down the Cannongate
The Cannongate sae free,
The bailie's wife and the provost's wife
Cried: "Och and alas for thee!"

"Why weep ye sae, ye burgess wives,
Sae sore ye weep for me?
For I am come intil your town
A rich wedding to see."

When she clomb up the Tolbooth stair,
The stair it was so hee
The cork flew off from baith her heels
And condemned she was to dee.

Then by there came the King himsel',
Looked up wi' a pitiful ee:
"Come down, come down, Mary Hamilton:
Tonight thou's dine wi' me."

"Nay haud your tongue, my sovereign liege,
    Nay let your folly be,
An ye had a mind to save my life,
    Wad ye sae ha' shaméd me?

"Last nicht your Queen had four Maries,
    The nicht she'll hae but three:
She had Mary Seaton, and Mary Beaton,
    Mary Carmichael and me. . . .

"Come hangman bring me a cup, a cup,
    But and a can o' wine,
That I may drink to my well-wishérs
    And to the days lang syne.

"O, here's your health, ye travelling men,
    And ye sailors on the sea,
But let na my father nor mother ken
    The dog's death I must dee.

"For did word come to my father's ha'
    Where brethren I have three,
It's far wad flow the gude red bloud
    The same wad spill for me.

"Yestreen I washéd the Queen's feet
    And bore her to her bed,
This day I've gotten for my reward
    The gallows-tree to tread.

"Cast off, cast off my gowden gown,
    But let my pettycoat be,
And tie a napkin about my face
    That the gallows I may nae see."

Though Quiller-Couch has enlarged this ballad by four verses, he has contrived to omit Mary's bold defiance of the Queen in the matter of the dress; her refusal to be pitied by the burgesses' wives; her satiric mention of the wedding (in Quiller-Couch's version she

has been foolishly deceived by the Queen into thinking that they
are invited to attend one). Omitted also are the tardy arrival of the
King at the Tolbooth, and Mary's proud refusal to be pardoned by
him; her turning away to ask the hangman for the can of wine;
her desire to be hanged decently, though not in the glistering
golden gown—doubtless a gift from the King himself.

I should prefer "Mary Fleming" to the usual "Mary Carmichael,"
for that was the original name, and it scans better; but Mary Hamilton was really Mary Livingston, and it seems a pity to change that
too. "Hamilton" got transferred to this ballad from a similar, but far
later, scandal at the Romanov court in St. Petersburg. In the cases
of widely dispersed ballads an editor is free to choose his texts, and
it is impossible to tell how much of any version was part of the
original. *The Three Maries* is such a one. But . . .

If a poet has printed more than one version of his own poem, an
editor again has liberty of choice. Sometimes the first is preferable.
Wordsworth, in old age, usually spoiled his earlier poems. But when
an irrepressible editor rewrites a poem, as Tottel of *The Miscellany*
rewrote Sir Thomas Wyatt, and as the prison doctor of Northampton
Lunatic Asylum rewrote John Clare, one should obviously reprint
the original.

As long ago as 1927, I protested that Quiller-Couch used Tottel's
miserable, and even unmetrical, revision of Wyatt's *They Flee From
Me, That Sometime Did Me Seek;* but he unrepentantly reprinted
it in 1939 and it is still there. The original runs:

> It was no dream; for I lay broad awaking:
>   But all is turned, thorough my gentleness,
> Into a strangë fashion of forsaking;
>   And I have leave to go of her goodnéss,
>   And she also to use new-fangleness:
> But since that I so kindly am servéd:
> I would fain know what she hath déservéd?

Tottel changed this to:

> It was no dream; I lay broad waking:
>   But all is turned, thorough my gentleness,

Into a strange fashion of forsaking;
  And I have leave to go, of her goodness;
  And she also to use new-fangleness.
But since that I unkindly so am served,
"How like you this?"—what hath she now deserved?

And though similarly warned, about the same time, by Edmund
Blunden's reprint of Clare's *I Am, But What I Am Who Cares Or
Knows?*, Quiller-Couch persisted in using the prison doctor's version,
as follows:

I am! yet what I am who cares, or knows?
  My friends forsake me like a memory lost.
I am the self-consumer of my woes;
  They rise and vanish, an oblivious host,
Shadows of life, whose very soul is lost.
And yet I am—I live—though I am toss'd

Into the nothingness of scorn and noise,
  Into the living sea of waking dream,
Where there is neither sense of life, nor joys,
  But the huge shipwreck of my own esteem
And all that's dear. Even those I loved the best
Are strange—nay, they are stranger than the rest.

I long for scenes where man has never trod—
  For scenes where woman never smiled or wept—
There to abide with my Creator, God,
  And sleep as I in childhood sweetly slept,
Full of high thoughts, unborn. So let me lie—
The grass below; above, the vaulted sky.

The original was:

I am: yet what I am none cares or knows,
  My friends forsake me like a memory lost;
I am the self-consumer of my woes,
  They rise and vanish in oblivious host,
Like shades in love and death's oblivion lost;
And yet I am, and live with shadows tost

> Into the nothingness of scorn and noise,
>   Into the living sea of waking dreams,
> Where there is neither sense of life nor joys,
>   But the vast shipwreck of my life's esteems;
> And e'en the dearest—that I loved the best—
> Are strange—nay, rather stranger than the rest.
>
> I long for scenes where man has never trod,
>   A place where woman never smiled nor wept;
> There to abide with my Creator, God,
>   And sleep as I in childhood sweetly slept:
> Untroubling and untroubled where I lie,
> The grass below—above, the vaulted sky.

The hero of the *Oxford Book of English Verse* is Matthew Arnold, my predecessor in this Chair exactly a century ago, and venerated by Quiller-Couch. Arnold won the poetry prize at Rugby School with a well-written number, *Alaric at Rome*; and the New-digate Prize here at Oxford with an equally competent *Cromwell*. He was so capable, honest and humourless a monumental mason that he deserves more honour than most of his energetic and vain-glorious contemporaries—the Brownings, Tennysons and Rossettis. Here are three very well-managed stanzas of his from *The Scholar-Gipsy*:

> Go, for they call you, Shepherd, from the hill;
>   Go, Shepherd, and untie the wattled cotes;
>   No longer leave the wistful flock unfed,
> Nor let thy bawling fellows rack their throats,
>   Nor the cropp'd grasses shoot another head.
>   But when the fields are still,
> And the tired men and dogs all gone to rest,
>   And only the white sheep are sometimes seen
> Cross and recross the strips of moon-blanch'd green;
> Come, Shepherd, and again begin the quest. . . .
>
> O born in days when wits were fresh and clear,
>   And life ran gaily as the sparkling Thames;
>   Before this strange disease of modern life,

With its sick hurry, its divided aims,
　　Its heads o'er tax'd, its palsied hearts, was rife—
　　Fly hence, our contact fear!
Still fly, plunge deeper in the bowering wood!
　　Averse, as Dido did with gesture stern
From her false friend's approach in Hades turn,
Wave us away, and keep thy solitude.

Still nursing the unconquerable hope,
　　Still clutching the inviolable shade,
　　　With a free onward impulse brushing through,
　　By night, the silver'd branches of the glade—
　　　Far on the forest-skirts, where none pursue,
　　　　On some mild pastoral slope
Emerge, and resting on the moonlit pales,
　　Freshen thy flowers, as in former years,
With dew, or listen with enchanted ears,
From the dark dingles, to the nightingales. . . .

But for whom are poems like this written? They belong to an old, old realm of poetic artificiality which starts with Virgil's mannered Latin borrowings from the Greek *Idylls* of Theocritus who, though an Alexandrian, had a genuine feeling for the Sicilian countryside; and continues with mannered Italian borrowings from Virgil by the fifteenth-century Italian Baptista Mantuanus, and from Mantuanus by Sannazaro the Neopolitan; and further English borrowings from Sannazaro by the Elizabethan University wits—Greene, Peele, Lodge, Sidney—and by Spenser in his *Shephards Calendar*. Shakespeare, indeed, who missed a University education, satirized the Arcadian pastoral in his *Love's Labour's Lost,* contrasting the false countryfolk with the true. Milton capitulated to it, though he followed Spenser's example in lending the scene English trees and flowers. The tradition is an insincere pretence of the dilettante city man that he wishes himself a simple yokel; and the construction of a pasteboard theatre for Arcadian dreams of lost poetic truth.

Readers accept the imposture, out of politeness to the schoolmasters who descant on its Classical beauty and who judge each new pastoral piece solely by its tunefulness and correctness. Matthew

Arnold, the last capable performer in this style, was more sincere than most of his predecessors. Though continuously engrossed with his post as Inspector of Schools for the Board of Education, he hankered for the countryside:

Too rare, too rare, grow now my visits here!
  But once I knew each field, each flower, each stick;
    And with the country-folk acquaintance made
  By barn in threshing-time, by new-built rick.
    Here, too, our shepherd pipes we first assay'd.
      Ah me! this many a year
  My pipe is lost, my shepherd's-holiday!
    Needs must I lose them, needs with heavy heart
    Into the world and wave of men depart;
  But Thyrsis of his own will went away.

It irk'd him to be here, he could not rest.
  He loved each simple joy the country yields,
    He loved his mates; but yet he could not keep
  For that a shadow lower'd on the fields,
    Here with the shepherds and the silly sheep.
      Some life of men unblest
  He knew, which made him droop, and fill'd his head.
    He went; his piping took a troubled sound
    Of storms that rage outside our happy ground;
  He could not wait their passing, he is dead!

Arnold chose his dear companion, A. H. Clough, to represent the Shepherd Thyrsis; and fixed Arcadia in the still unspoiled country around Oxford, where they had wandered about as undergraduates. Naturally he left out the Railways, and the Police, and the new Telegraph as unpoetical; and seldom goofed, as here, by introducing too modern a note:

But hush! the upland hath a sudden loss
  Of quiet;—Look! adown the dusk hill-side,
    A troop of Oxford hunters going home,
    As in old days, jovial and talking, ride!

From hunting with the Berkshire hounds they come—
Quick, let me fly, and cross
Into yon further field! . . .

The pastoral is now dead. So are Classical references to amaranth, acanthus, asphodel, and other poetic Greek flowers that not one reader in a million would recognize growing—and this is an exaggeration because the amaranth was a wholly unbotanical bloom, and moly is wrongly described by Homer himself. Conceits are also out. I haven't seen an old-fashioned Classical conceit published since at least the reign of Edward VII. The *Oxford Book of English Verse* contains some fantastical nonsensical ones from the early seventeenth century. Here is one by William Browne, with a misplaced "only," banning song-birds and flowers in May because a girl friend of his died in that month:

> May! Be thou never graced with birds that sing,
>   Nor Flora's pride!
> In thee all flowers and roses spring,
>   Mine only died.

and another, also by Browne, on the death of the Dowager Countess of Pembroke:

> Underneath this sable herse
> Lies the subject of all verse:
> Sidney's sister, Pembroke's mother:
> Death, ere thou hast slain another
> Fair and learn'd and good as she,
> Time shall throw a dart at thee.

In a sillier vein, here is Browne's contemporary, William Strode, writing about Chloris:

> I saw fair Chloris walk alone,
> When feather'd rain came softly down,
> As Jove descending from his Tower
> To court her in a silver shower:

> The wanton snow flew to her breast,
> Like pretty birds into their nest,
> But, overcome with whiteness there,
> For grief it thaw'd into a tear:
> Thence falling on her garments' hem,
> To deck her, froze into a gem.

The popular view of poetry as beautiful nonsense which has to be interpreted by literary *cognoscenti*, has survived the Classical Age and still haunts the present. American high-school students write to me: "Dear Professor Graves, we have been asked by our prof to write a thesis on the meaning of your poem [such and such] and are writing to invite your kind assistance . . ." To which I reply: "It says exactly what it means, and if you can tell me where it stops being comprehensible, I shall be sincerely grateful." That silences them.

Reaction against the conceit is simplicity reduced to utter vapidity. Samuel Rogers is represented here by a poem called *The Wish*:

> Mine be a cot beside the hill;
> A bee-hive's hum shall soothe my ear;
> A willowy brook, that turns a mill,
> With many a fall shall linger near . . .

A typical poem of escape; but escape from what? Turn Samuel Rogers up in the encyclopedia, and you will find that his father was a rich banker, but that Samuel, while continuing the business after his father's death, preferred to be known as an art-connoisseur and man of letters, bought works of art cheap in Paris during the French Revolution, wrote for *The Gentleman's Magazine*, published a fragmentary epic about Columbus, became the literary dictator of London, a patron of needy men of letters; was offered but refused the laureateship on the death of Wordsworth (for whom he had obtained the famous sinecure as distributor of stamps). Byron praised Rogers's *Pleasures of Memory* with: "There is not a vulgar line in the poem," and he is credited with being the last verse-practitioner who "could elevate and refine familiar themes in eighteenth-century style by abstract treatment and lofty imagery." To make any sense of *The Wish*, we should introduce it with some honest introduction of this sort:

> My father's business at Cornhill
>   Came to me at his death, but I
> Devoted more of heart and will
>   To the pursuit of poetry.
>
> In gilded parlours of the great
>   And rich, my youthful years were spent;
> And while I dared not underrate
>   Such luscious comfort as they lent,
>
> Often I wished myself obscure,
>   A simple-minded country clown
> With healthful frame and morals pure,
>   And thus I wrote these wishes down:
>
> Mine be a cot beside the hill;
>   A bee-hive's hum shall soothe my ear;
> A willowy brook, that turns a mill,
>   With many a fall shall linger near.
>
> The swallow oft beneath my thatch
>   Shall twitter from her clay-built nest;
> Oft shall the pilgrim lift the latch
>   And share my meal, a welcome guest.
>
> Around my ivied porch shall spring
>   Each fragrant flower that drinks the dew;
> And Lucy at her wheel shall sing
>   In russet gown and apron blue.
>
> The village church among the trees,
>   Where first our marriage vows were given,
> With merry peals shall swell the breeze
>   And point with taper spire to Heaven.

Poetry is the profession of private truth, supported by craftsmanship in the use of words; I prefer not to call it an art, because the art of Classical Verse from the time of Virgil onwards allied itself to the art of Rhetoric, and became the art of cozenage, not of truth.

Milton's *Hymn on the Morning of Christ's Nativity* is a perfect example of cozenage:

It was the Winter wilde,
While the Heav'n-born childe,
    All meanly wrapt in the rude manger lies;
Nature in aw to him
Had doff't her gaudy trim,
    With her great Master so to sympathize:
It was no season then for her
To wanton with the Sun her lusty Paramour.

Only with speeches fair
She woo's the gentle Air
    To hide her guilty front with innocent Snow,
And on her naked shame,
Pollute with sinful blame,
    The Saintly Vail of Maiden white to throw,
Confounded, that her Makers eyes
Should look so neer her foul deformities.

But he her fears to cease,
Sent down the meek-ey'd Peace,
    She crown'd with Olive green, came softly sliding
Down through the turning sphear
His ready Harbinger,
    With Turtle wing the amorous clouds dividing,
And waving wide her mirtle wand,
She strikes a universall Peace through Sea and Land.

No War, or Battails sound
Was heard the World around,
    The idle spear and shield were high up hung;
The hookéd Chariot stood

Unstain'd with hostile blood,
   The Trumpet spake not to the arméd throng,
And Kings sate still with awfull eye,
As if they surely knew their sovran Lord was by. . . .

The conceits are gross and insincere. The Goddess Nature, instead of continuing to indulge in amorous frolics with her lover the Sun, puts on a garment of snow to hide her lascivious body from God's eyes. But God reassures her by sending down the dove of peace, and thereupon ensues universal peace throughout the world. As a good Classical scholar and historian, Milton knew well enough that Jesus was not born in the week following the Winter Solstice (a date chosen by the early Fathers to disguise their celebration, protected by a Mithraic feast honouring the Unconquered Sun) but probably in August. He knew too that the whole world was not at peace, and that the fifth-century Christian historian Orosius invented the story of Augustus' shutting the doors of Janus' temple in Jesus' honour. Furthermore that, according to the Gospel, Jesus himself declared: "I have come not to bring peace but a sword!"

Milton continues:

But peacefull was the night
Wherein the Prince of light
   His raign of peace upon the earth began:
The Windes with wonder whist,
Smoothly the waters kist,
   Whispering new joyes to the milde Ocean,
Who now hath quite forgot to rave,
While Birds of Calm sit brooding on the charméd wave.

The Stars with deep amaze
Stand fixt in stedfast gaze,
   Bending one way their pretious influence,
And will not take their flight,
For all the morning light,
   Or Lucifer that often warn'd them thence;
But in their glimmering Orbs did glow,
Untill their Lord himself bespake, and bid them go.

And though the shady gloom
Had given day her room,
 The Sun himself with-held his wonted speed,
And his his head for shame,
As his inferior flame,
 The new enlightn'd world no more should need;
He saw a greater Sun appear
Than his bright Throne, or burning Axletree could bear.

The first stanza Classically connects the "halcyon" days of Mediterranean calm with Jesus's nativity; and, indeed, the middle of December is usually calm enough; but when Milton speaks of the stars waiting until the Child should dismiss them, and of the Sun halting his usual speed in the Child's honour, we know, and he knows we know, that this is "a lie of genius," as Adolf Hitler later called it.

The *Oxford Book of English Verse* contains few real poems; and, of course, everyone should make his own private collection of real poems, rather than rely on public anthologists. But it is a useful museum of fashion. "How pretty, how quaint, how vulgar, how neat, how monstrous," we should say as we read.

Let me venture a view which has forced itself on me more and more strongly in the last few years. It is that both in England and the Commonwealth, and the United States, standards of versecraftsmanship *seem* to have risen appreciably as the result of modern poems being included in school and college curricula. But is it not rather that far more attention is now paid to the standards of versecraftsmanship deduced by academic critics from certain fashionable modern poets? The rudiments of craftsmanship can be best learned, not by imitation but by personal experience in writing, after varied acquaintance with poems of different ages and styles; and by a gradual discovery of the need—which is my main insistence in these three lectures—to question every word and sound and implication in a poem either read or written.

Poetry is another matter altogether. The present trend in politics, economics and ethics seems wholly inimical to the appearance of new poets, or the honourable survival of those who may have already appeared; but this perhaps means that the occasional exception, the poet born with a light in his head, will be more surely tempered than before against departure from poetic principle; which is a simple, obstinate belief in miracle: an asseveration of personal independence against all collective codifications of thought and behaviour.

A Favourite Cat Drowned

One of the most popular poems in the *Oxford Book of English Verse*, particularly welcome because it enlivens a long dull stretch between the Restoration poets and the Romantics, is Thomas Gray's *On A Favourite Cat, Drowned In A Tub of Gold Fishes*. It used to be a favourite of mine, too, until I re-read it carefully the other day for the first time in forty years, and realized how scandalously less trouble Gray had taken with it than with, for instance, his *Elegy in a Country Churchyard*:

> 'Twas on a lofty vase's side,
> Where China's gayest art had dyed
>   The azure flowers that blow;
> Demurest of the tabby kind,
> The pensive Selima reclined,
>   Gazed on the lake below.
>
> Her conscious tail her joy declared;
> The fair round face, the snowy beard,
>   The velvet of her paws,

Her coat, that with the tortoise vies,
Her ears of jet, and emerald eyes,
    She saw; and purr'd applause.

Still had she gazed; but 'midst the tide
Two angel forms were seen to glide,
    The Genii of the stream:
Their scaly armour's Tyrian hue
    Betray'd a golden gleam.

The hapless Nymph with wonder saw:
A whisker first and then a claw,
    With many an ardent wish,
She stretch'd in vain to reach the prize.
What female heart can gold despise?
    What Cat's averse to fish?

Presumptuous Maid! with looks intent
Again she stretch'd, again she bent,
    Nor knew the gulf between.
(Malignant Fate sat by, and smiled.)
The slipp'ry verge her feet beguiled,
    She tumbled headlong in.

Eight times emerging from the flood
She mew'd to ev'ry wat'ry god,
    Some speedy aid to send.
No Dolphin came, no Nereid stirr'd:
Nor cruel *Tom*, nor *Susan* heard.
    A Fav'rite has no friend!

From hence, ye Beauties undeceived,
Know, one false step is ne'er retrieved,
    And be with caution bold.
Not all that tempts your wand'ring eyes
And heedless hearts, is lawful prize;
    Nor all that glisters, gold.

The poem began, I surmise, with the lines:

> Demurest of the tabby kind,
> The pensive Selima reclined,
>   Hard by the Gold Fish tub. . . .

But Gray could not find a satisfactory rhyme to *tub* ("rub," "shrub," "scrub", "sillabub"?) and started again, changing the tub to a large decorated Chinese vase, or wine-cooler—an unlikely container for goldfish; one would have expected a glass jar—and making the cat recline on the vase's shoulder. But "vase's shoulder" would not scan, so he had to use *side*:

> 'Twas on a lofty vase's side,
> Where China's curious art had dyed
>   The gayest flowers that blow,
> Demurest of the tabby kind . . .

He rightly disliked two superlatives—*gayest* and *demurest*—so close to each other, and therefore changed *curious* to *gayest*, and *gayest* to *azure*:

> Where China's gayest art had dyed
>   The azure flowers that blow . . .

though cereamic art does not, of course, dye flowers that blow. Gray cannot have noticed that, though a poem of this sort demands a constant variation of vowel sounds to lend it richness, he had used the words *China, side, dyed, kind, reclined:* all long *i*'s. Worse, he had not as yet considered the end of the poem, which proved to be a moral warning: "Young women, never risk your reputation by greed of money or of sensual pleasure." So a pensive, demure Selima was inappropriate. If she had been an amiable sort of cat, not a pampered favourite, the servants Tom and Susan would have kept a sharper lookout and listened to her agonizing appeals for help. Gray should have established her as plump and vain:

> 'Twas on a lofty vase's side,
> Where China's gayest art had dyed
>   The azure flowers that blow;
> Demurest of the tabby kind,
> The pensive Selima reclined,
>   Gazed on the lake below.

He should also have made it immediately clear that Selima saw her image mirrored in the water (which was doubtless why he preferred a China vase to a glass tub that would not have provided the necessary reflection) and should have left the twitching tail for later:

> Her conscious tail her joy declared;
> The fair round face, the snowy beard,
>   The velvet of her paws,
> Her coat, that with the tortoise vies,
> Her ears of jet, and emerald eyes,
>   She saw; and purr'd applause.

Declared and *beard* are not close enough rhymes for such neat drawing-room verse; and to secure a rhyme for *eyes,* he has awkwardly changed the tense in *vies* from past to present (although Selima is already dead before the poem ends). But to change *vies* to *vied* and rhyme it with *pride* meant repeating the *ide*-rhyme of the first stanza. And *coat with tortoise shell that vies* is an awkward inversion. Moreover, *saw and purred applause* is an unmusical line.

At this point Gray adopted the then popular mock-heroic style:

> Still had she gazed; but 'midst the tide
> Two angel forms were seen to glide,
>   The Genii of the stream:
> Their scaly armour's Tyrian hue
> Thro' richest purple to the view
>   Betray'd a golden gleam.

This is shocking! Either the water is lakelike and unmoving or else it is a stream. Gray cannot make up his mind.

Still had she gazed; but 'midst the tide. . . .

He is back again in the *ide*-rhyme but, having avoided them in the last stanza, he doesn't care so much. Nevertheless his ear was, I believe, offended by all the long *i*'s of his first draft:

> . . . 'midst the tide
> Two forms divine were seen to glide,
> The Genii of the stream . . .

and he therefore substituted *angel forms* for *forms divine*. An unhappy decision, because angels fly; they never wet their wings, and they always bring messages, as these do not.

> Their scaly armour's Tyrian hue
> Thro' richest purple to the view
> Betray'd a golden gleam. . . .

Thro' richest purple to the view is shameless padding for the sake of the rhyme; nor do goldfish have a Tyrian purple aspect when seen in a China vase. I should like to believe that Gray was thinking of the golden Mediterranean amber which (unlike Baltic amber) has a distinct purple gleam, and which the Tyrian merchants prized; but this is most unlikely.

> The hapless Nymph with wonder saw:
> A whisker first and then a claw,
>   With many an ardent wish,
> She stretch'd in vain to reach the prize.
> What female heart can gold despise?
>   What Cat's averse to fish?

Here we have even shoddier verse. The second line reads like the object of *saw*. *With many an ardent wish* is peculiarly feeble, and one knows from a mile away that the rhyme *fish* is coming. Selima did not stretch a whisker or a claw; she will have stretched her neck and paw. Gray could have combined these last two stanzas into one, and lost nothing but mere length:

> Presumptuous Maid! with looks intent
> Again she stretch'd, again she bent,
>   Nor knew the gulf between.
> (Malignant Fate sat by, and smiled.)
> The slipp'ry verge her feet beguiled,
>   She tumbled headlong in.

The hapless Nymph with wonder saw . . . comes too close after *Presumptuous Maid! with looks intent.* . . . Both are unnecessary to the argument. *Nor knew the gulf between* . . . is unclear. Did this gulf lie between herself and the fish, or between the fish and the surface? And *between* rhymes badly with *in.*

> (Malignant Fate sat *by,* and *smiled.*)

More long *i*'s; and *her* refers grammatically not to Selima but to Fate, whom he should have put in the plural.

> Eight times emerging from the flood
> She mew'd to ev'ry wat'ry god,
>   Some speedy aid to send.
> No Dolphin came, no Nereid stirr'd:
> Nor cruel Tom, nor Susan heard.
>   A fav'rite has no friend!

The water, hitherto described as a lake, a stream with genii, and a tide, now appears as a flood: to rhyme, more or less, with *wat'ry god.* Dolphins, though sacred to Apollo, are not gods; nor would a dolphin fit easily into even the largest-sized Chinese vase. "Triton" should match *Nereid.*

> From hence, ye Beauties undeceived,
> Know, one false step is ne'er retrieved,
>   And be with caution bold.

> Not all that tempts your wand'ring eyes
> And heedless hearts is lawful prize;
> Nor all that glisters, gold.

Beauties undeceived should mean that they see through shams; but what Gray evidently intends is "not yet undeceived by disaster." And *heedless hearts* is wrong. He means "greedy hearts"—*heedless* should go with ears. *And be with caution bold* is too elliptic a phrase.

Now, although all this may be negative criticism, you can hardly challenge me to rewrite a poem which is not mine, and which I could never have been tempted to write. I can guess how unpopular I already am for having spoiled your early love of this playful piece—which, at any rate, did not bore you, as for example Gray himself did, with his *Pindaric Ode, The Progress of Poesy*:

> Awake, Aeolian lyre, awake,
> And give to rapture all thy trembling strings.
> From Helicon's harmonious springs
> A thousand rills their mazy progress take:
> The laughing flowers, that round them blow,
> Drink life and fragrance as they flow.
> Now the rich stream of music winds along
> Deep, majestic, smooth and strong,
> Thro' verdant vales, and Ceres' golden reign:
> Now rolling down the steep amain,
> Headlong, impetuous see it pour;
> The rocks and nodding groves rebellow to the roar.

Nevertheless, I am prepared to be more unpopular still by accepting the challenge and suggesting improvements to the Cat poem:

> On a tall vase's curving side
> By Pekin's potters beautified
> With flowers of azure hue,
> Most pampered of her tabby sort
> Plump Selima reclined in sport
> The lake beneath to view.

As in a looking-glass appeared
Her fair round face and snowy beard,
    The velvet of her paws,
Her coat, which vied with tortoiseshell,
Black ears and emerald eyes; "'tis well,"
    Thought she, and purred applause.

Her long tail twitched; for, ah, behold
Athwart the image, scaled with gold
    Two creatures swam in sight!
What young heart goes not pit-a-pat
At sight of specie? For what cat
    Are fishes no delight?

Fond creature! On the prize intent
She dipped a paw and forward bent
    To hook some tail or fin;
Malignant Fates, observing, smiled,
The slippery verge her feet beguiled,
    She tumbled headlong in.

Eight times from death she drowning rose
And mewed a piteous prayer to those
    Who aid divine could send.
No Triton came, no Nereid stirred—
Though maybe Tom or Susan heard,
    A favourite has no friend.

Learn, maids by fraud yet undeceived,
That one false move is ne'er retrieved.
    Then cautious be, though bold.
Not all that tempts your greedy eyes
And wandering thoughts is lawful prize,
    Nor all that glisters, gold.

An important rule of craftsmanship in English Verse is that a
poet should never tell his readers how romantic, pathetic, awe-
inspiring, tragic, mystic or wondrous a scene has been. He must
describe the details himself in such powerful but restrained language

(nouns and verbs always outnumbering the adjectives), that it will be the reader who catches his breath, looks up from the page and says: "How romantic, how pathetic, how awe-inspiring, how . . . !"

Longfellow, a sweet, simple, loving but poetically ineffective New Englander, often breaks this rule:

> Ah! what pleasant visions haunt me
>   As I gaze upon the sea!
> All the old romantic legends,
>   All my dreams come back to me.
>
> Sails of silk and ropes of sandal,
>   Such as gleam in ancient lore;
> And the singing of the sailors,
>   And the answer from the shore!
>
> Most of all, the Spanish ballad
>   Haunts me oft, and tarries long,
> Of the noble Count Arnaldos
>   And the sailor's mystic song.
>
> Telling how the Count Arnaldos,
>   With his hawk upon his hand,
> Saw a fair and stately galley,
>   Steering onward to the land;—
>
> How he heard the ancient helmsman
>   Chant a song so wild and clear,
> That the sailing sea-bird slowly
>   Poised upon the mast to hear.
>
> Till his soul was full of longing,
>   And he cried, with impulse strong,—
> "Helmsman! for the love of heaven,
>   Teach me, too, that wondrous song!"
>
> "Wouldst thou,"—so the helmsman answered,—
>   "Learn the secret of the sea?
> Only those who brave its dangers
>   Comprehend its mystery!"

What a second-hand way of telling the story! Pleasant visions haunt Longfellow sometimes as he gazes on the Atlantic Ocean from Casco Bay, Massachusetts; literary reminiscences, especially of a Spanish ballad—he spent a few months in Spain in the late 1820s—echo in his ears. But he records only a sentimental gist of the ballad, not the ballad itself.

> Ropes of sandal such as gleam in ancient lore . . .
> Haunts me oft and tarries long . . .

The pay-off: *Only those who brave its dangers Comprehend its mystery!* is in the pure style of *Hymns, Ancient and Modern*. The reader doesn't care a button for Longfellow's feelings; he wants to hear the original ballad or, if he can't read Spanish, its equivalent in English.

I have taken the trouble to look up the ballad, which was originally written in twelfth-century Catalan—*Cancó del Compte l'Arnau*; but the version Longfellow recalled was a Castilian one, published in the 1550 edition of the *Cancionero de Romances*. If Longfellow had contrived to curb his New England corniness, and written a translation of the ballad closer to the traditional English style than his famous *Schooner Hesperus*, it would have run something like this:

> O the bold Lord Arnold, what did he hear
> That midsummer day in the morning clear?
>
> Lord Arnold rode with hawk upon hand
> As down he coursed to the salt sea strand.
>
> He saw a galley—I tell no lies—
> Was making the beach before his eyes!
>
> Her sails were silk, of sandal her gear,
> And a practised mariner took the steer.
>
> He trolled so wild and he trolled so well
> He fetched all nature under a spell,

The winds were bated and no more blew
That calm as a mere the salt sea grew.

O, the fish schooled up, it was thick and fast,
And sea-cobs perched on the galley's mast.

"O mariner good who has ta'en the steer
And trollest a song that I love to hear,

"Do but teach me to sing that same, pardie,
And a chest of treasure thou's earn in fee."

"Nay, songs there are that a helmsman sings
May never be boughten with bright shillings,

"And mine's a ditty of worth, pardie,
Taught only to who dare sail with me."

You will observe that Longfellow's memories of the *Conde de Arnau* ballad have played him false. In the original there are no sailors but only a helmsman; and not a single gull perches on the mast, but flocks of them; also the winds and seas are calmed, and the fish swim up in shoals. The helmsman is not ancient, nor does he make any moralistic remarks about the mystery of the sea; and the ship appears—this is most important—on St. John's Day, namely Midsummer Day, when one should expect magical apparitions. The helmsman will have been Herne the Hunter, whose oak occurs in Shakespeare's *A Midsummer Night's Dream*—or Herne's Spanish equivalent; and he was tempting Arnaldos the hunter with melodies of a pagan fairyland. Herne and Hermes Trismegistos, who conveyed souls to the paradise of the mystics, are the same divine character.

While I am on the subject: Longfellow's line, *He cried with impulse strong*, reminds me that, while still an undergraduate here in 1922, I published a book called *On English Poetry*, from which I will quote a paragraph:

An old Italian portrait-painter, coming to the end of his life, gathered his friends and pupils together and revealed to them a

great discovery he had made, as follows: "The art of portrait painting consists in putting the High Lights at exactly the right place in
the eyes." When I come to my death bed, I have a similarly important
message to deliver: "The art of poetry consists in knowing exactly
how to manipulate the letter S."

Of all well-known poets of the nineteenth century, Shelley was
perhaps the most deficient in his control of sibilants. His *Ode to the
West Wind* contains such lines as:

> All overgrown with azure moss and flowers
> So sweet the sense faints picturing them . . .

and:

> When to outstrip thy skiey speed
> Scarce seemed a vision . . .

> Thou on whose streams mid the steep sky's commotion,
> Loose clouds like earth's decaying leaves are shed. . . .

Quiller-Couch admitted Longfellow and Poe into the *Oxford Book
of English Verse* to prove he was no more snobbish about English
poems written in America, than about those written in Scotland or
Ireland, so long as they accepted the verse-standards set at Oxford,
Cambridge and London. This rule excluded Robert Frost and e. e.
cummings, although both came into his period. He granted Longfellow another poem, *Chaucer,* which recalls the Poet Laureate's
recent *Homage to Shakespeare* and seems to have been written in
perfect idleness of spirit:

> An old man in a lodge within a park;
>   The chamber walls depicted all around
>   With portraitures of huntsman, hawk, and hound,
> And the hurt deer. He listeneth to the lark,
> Whose song comes with the sunshine through the dark
>   Of painted glass in leaden lattice bound;
> He listeneth and he laugheth at the sound,

Then writeth in a book like any clerk.
He is the poet of the dawn, who wrote
 The Canterbury Tales, and his old age
  Made beautiful with song; and as I read
I hear the crowing cock, I hear the note
 Of lark and linnet, and from every page
  Rise odours of plough'd field or flowery mead.

An old man in a lodge within a park—at a lodge within a park would have been neater—perhaps North Petterton Park, Somerset, of which Chaucer was appointed Forester in late middle age but which is unlikely to have been his residence; its chamber walls depicted with portraitures of animals. . . . We wait for the main verb, but are disappointed. Animals, by the way, in English, can be depicted *on* a wall; but a wall cannot be depicted *with* pictures. If he means "hung with an arras," why not say so? The animals include a hurt deer—*hurt* is used rather of injured feelings than of physical injuries—perhaps Longfellow remembers the sequester'd stag in *As You Like It* that from the hunters' aim had ta'en a hurt and wept big round tears into the swift brook. "Stricken" or "wounded" is what was meant, but he has not left himself enough room for it in the line. "He *listeneth* to the lark, Whose song *comes*" (why not "cometh"?) with the sunshine through the dark of painted glass. . . . *Dark* is used for the sake of the rhyme and misdirects the reader into recalling St. Paul's "as through a glass, darkly." "In leaden lattice *bound*" has also been used for the sake of the rhyme, which should never be allowed to obscure or divert the sense.

He listeneth to the lark, and he laugheth, then he writeth like any clerk. . . . What does *like any clerk* mean? In Chaucer's time it could have meant that, though an uneducated man, he had somehow surreptitiously learned to read and write. Chaucer, however, was very much of a clerk: being Royal Comptroller of Customs and often sent abroad on diplomatic missions.

He is the poet of the dawn. . . . What dawn? Real or metaphorical? And, yes, everyone knows that he wrote *The Canterbury Tales.*

And as I read, I hear the crowing cock. . . . Is this metaphorical of the dawn? And is Longfellow himself reading at an early hour?

Or is he referring to Chauntecler in *The Nun-Priest's Tale?* He also hears *the note of lark and linnet.* . . . We can grant Chaucer knowledge of larks, though he used them only in the plural—*flocks of laverockes and turtles* occur in the *Romaunt of the Rose*—but "linnet" enters English literature only a century and a half later. In Longfellow's time, because of its rhyming facility—"linnet," "minute," "begin it," "in it," "win it," and so on—the linnet ousted from anthologies the chaffinch, bullfinch, redstart and all other small passerine birds. "Red-poll," the linnet's proper name when wearing summer-plumage, hardly ever appears. . . . No amount of repair work could make a prize poem of this sonnet.

Edgar Allan Poe's verses entranced the late Victorian English. The English always take pity on drunken, ill-living and unbalanced poets as soon as they are dead. Here is Poe's famous *To Helen:*

> Helen, thy beauty is to me
> Like those Nicean barks of yore
> That gently, o'er a perfumed sea,
> The weary way-worn wanderer bore
> To his own native shore.
>
> On desperate seas long wont to roam,
> Thy hyacinth hair, thy classic face,
> Thy Naiad airs have brought me home
> To the glory that was Greece,
> And the grandeur that was Rome.
>
> Lo, in yon brilliant window-niche
> How statue-like I see thee stand,
> The agate lamp within thy hand,
> Ah! Psyche, from the regions which
> Are holy land!

He addresses Helen, whose name is evocative of ships, though the real Helen sent over a thousand ships away and brought few back. The Nicean barks are unclassical. The most important Nicaea, a Hellenistic city in Bithynia, lay inland on a lake; the second was built by Alexander the Great on the banks of the Jelum in India; the third, now Nice, was of no importance at all in Graeco-Roman times. Which is intended? Probably Poe knew of the Nicaean Creed, and used the word because it sounded nice.

The argument of the poem is that the Classical beauty of a girl named Helen has brought Poe home over a perfumed sea—which? Black Sea, Mediterranean or Indian Ocean?—though long wont to roam in desperate ones—which, again?—to the glory that was Greece and the grandeur that was Rome.

The craftsmanship of the poem is shoddy. In the first stanza, *weary, wayworn, wanderer bore* gives excessive alliteration; and *worn* and *bore* are too similar in sound. The second stanza is clumsily inverted:

> On desperate seas long wont to roam,
> Thy hyacinth hair, thy classic face,
> Thy Naiad airs have brought me home
> To the glory that was Greece,
> And the grandeur that was Rome . . .

so that it seems that Helen's hyacinth hair and classic face are long wont to roam on desperate seas. The explanation seems to be that Poe has attempted to hide the false rhyme of *Rome . . . roam* by keeping them as far away from each other as possible. In English, *hyacinth* hair means blue hair; but here it apparently stands for "hyacinthine," an adjective borrowed by English poets from "locks like the hyacinth flower"—a metaphor coined by Homer to whom, some grammarians say, it meant black; and some, gold.

In the third stanza Poe switches from Helen to the Psyche of Apuleius' *Golden Ass* as portrayed by a Royal Academician. It does not keep up the rich variation of vowel sounds that he has used hitherto:

> Lo, in yon brilliant window-niche
> How statue-like I see thee stand,
> The agate lamp within thy hand,
> Ah! Psyche, from the regions which
> Are holy land!

He gives us three short *i*'s in a row—*brilliant, window, niche*—then five short *a*'s—*statue, stand, agate, lamp, hand.* The subject of the phrase *from the regions which Are holy land!* is hard to discover. Since it cannot be Psyche herself—one can't *stand* from regions —it may be the agate lamp. . . . But what Poe means is anyone's guess. The lamp in Apuleius' allegory served only to burn Cupid with its drop of scalding oil, and get Psyche into desperate trouble.

Quiller-Couch claims to have included in his anthology no single epigram which "failed to preserve some thrill of the emotion through which it had to pass before the Muse's lips let it fall, with however exquisite deliberation." Let us take a look at a couple of pieces by Walter Savage Landor, who was renowned as an epigrammatist:

> Ah, what avails the sceptred race!
>   Ah, what the form divine!
> What every virtue, every grace!
>   Rose Aylmer, all were thine.
>
> Rose Aylmer, whom these wakeful eyes
>   May weep, but never see,
> A night of memories and sighs
>   I consecrate to thee.

This is a private poem; the poet has deliberately suppressed every clue to its meaning and instead given us a false clue, calling the woman whom he celebrates, by a false name. The sentences beginning with *Ah, what* end in "notes of admiration"—as they were called in Landor's day—rather than notes of interrogation. Yet they cannot be spoken except as questions, and seem to mean: "What is the good of having royal blood, or being divinely beautiful, or possessing every grace and virtue? None of all this helped poor Rose Aylmer." The second stanza:

> Rose Aylmer, whom these wakeful eyes
>   May weep, but never see,
> A night of memories and sighs
>   I consecrate to thee . . .

explains that he may never see Rose, though he may perhaps weep for her; and will dedicate a whole night of memories and sighs to thinking about her.

Well, what happened? Did she die? But, if so, why "may never see?" *May* can imply either possibility or permission. If possibility, perhaps she went into a nunnery where royal blood and graceful social virtues were at a discount, and the poet felt it unlikely that he would be allowed to see her, even through a grille. Or perhaps he had gone blind? Or, since he does not say "may never see you again," does *may* simply mean that God had not permitted a meeting, by separating them in time? Is she a historical character, or even a fictional character, with whom he has fallen in love? If Rose Aylmer were a surrogate, say, for Lady Jane Grey, who had every virtue and grace and came of royal blood, but was executed for high treason because someone had injudiciously proclaimed her Queen of England—that would make sense. A sensitive Victorian, falling in love with her portrait, might easily dedicate a night of tears and sighs to historical memories of her fate. But why choose "Rose Aylmer,"* a name lacking in the true genealogical bouquet? Is it perhaps an accident that Jane's tutor was John Aylmer, afterwards Bishop of London? Try it this way:

ON ADMIRING A MINIATURE OF LADY JANE GREY

Ah, what availed the sceptred race?
Ah, what the form divine?
What every virtue, every grace?
Sweet Lady, all were thine!

By Aylmer tutored in the arts
To be a very sage;
Yet smiling sovereign of all hearts,
And Rose of her rude age.

* She is said to have been a young noblewoman who died in Calcutta at the age of twenty; but I doubt it.

> Ah, Jane, whom my adoring eyes
> Weep, but may never see,
> A night of retrospective sighs
> I'll consecrate to thee.

No epigram stands up unless, like most of those in the *Greek Anthology*, or those Latin ones quoted by Suetonius, it is absolutely succinct. How much of Landor's *Proud Word You Never Spoke* could be omitted without damage to the sense?

> Proud word you never spoke, but you will speak
> Four not exempt from pride some future day.
> Resting on one white hand a warm wet cheek,
> Over my open volume you will say,
> "This man loved *me*"—then rise and trip away.

Four not exempt from pride is too succinct. He means "*exempt from a charge of pride.*" But why not:

> Proud word you never spoke, but you will speak
> Four, some future day?

And why *future*? *Will speak* is in the future tense. Why not: "Four, some day"?

> Resting on one white hand a warm wet cheek. . . .

All that matters is that she has been crying; the whiteness and warmness are irrelevant. Both cheeks will have been equally warm and wet, and all ladies in those days kept their hands out of the sun. "Tearfully, your head propped on one elbow" is the required sense. But why prophesy her posture?

You will speak, followed by *you will say*, is clumsy. And which *open volume*? It may have been a volume of sermons, or a travel book, or a scientific monograph. . . . The reader must realize that it is a book of poems written to the girl with the warm, wet cheek, under the Landorian *nom de plume* of "Ianthe," "Dirce" or "Clementina."

Then rise and trip away is unnecessary; and *trip* seems too jaunty a gait in the circumstances. She will surely have stumbled away to her bedroom—this was before the time of bathrooms—and washed her face in cold water? But perhaps Landor wishes to think of her as still young and beautiful after his death: hence *trip*. Also the reader should not be asked to count four words. Three is better; one does not count numbers up to three. To convert this into a Classical epigram, the lines must be shortened and reduced to a four-line stanza:

> You are not proud, yet I can hear you speak
>   Three words of pride, one day,
> Over this book: tears dewing either cheek,
>   "He loved me," you will say.

Landor's epigram *Verse* cannot be remedied, since no real emotion underlies it:

> Past ruin'd Ilion Helen lives,
>   Alcestis rises from the shades;
> Verse calls them forth; 'tis verse that gives
>   Immortal youth to mortal maids.
>
> Soon shall Oblivion's deepening veil
>   Hide all the peopled hills you see,
> The gay, the proud, while lovers hail
>   These many summers you and me.

Landor misdirects his readers throughout this poem. *Past ruin'd Ilion Helen lives.* . . . To begin with, even if they recognize "Ilium" as a poetic synonym for "Troy," used by Marlowe and others, *Ilion*, the Greek form, will puzzle them. Next, *past* is ambiguous. If I were to tell you casually: "Helen is living past the ruined church," your natural conclusion would be that my friend Helen had a house on the road past the ruined church. But *past* here apparently means that Helen—Queen Helen, not just any Helen—has survived the sack of Troy. Having got at least so far, one says: "Yes, that's right. Helen did survive for many years, and eventually settled down happily with Menelaus at Sparta."

Alcestis rises from the shades. . . . "Yes," one says again. "That's right. Although Alcestis had consented to die for her husband Admetus's sake, Heracles reduced her from Death's clutches and brought her safe home again. So she and Helen had something in common: both arrived safely home after a lot of trouble."

Then comes the line *Verse calls them forth* . . . and with it the realization that we have been misdirected. Neither Helen nor Alcestis was rescued from trouble by Orpheus's charmed singing. Landor comments:

> 'tis verse that gives
> Immortal youth to mortal maids. . . .

So Helen and Alcestis have, after all, been chosen at random as Greek heroines—they might just as well have been Nausicaa or Iphigeneia or Ariadne—and Landor is merely reminding us that Greek poets have perpetuated the youth of long dead women! Or does *gives immortal youth to mortal maids* mean that Apollo as a beardless youth, ever fair and young, charms mortal girls when his poets are inspired by him?

The second stanza is a real mess;

> Soon shall Oblivion's deepening veil
> Hide all the peopled hills you see,
> The gay, the proud, while lovers hail
> These many summers you and me . . .

Landor says that *you*—whoever this *you* may be—will soon forget all about the peopled hills you see. Can he mean the seven hills of Rome?—for hills are not usually peopled. His next four words, *The gay, the proud,* can hardly refer to the hills, and grammatically go with the *you* contemplating them; if so, the proud and gay are being contrasted with the lovers who hail *you and me,* and who must therefore be conceived as humbly, gloomily, but memorably alive in a valley or on a plain. This *you* can hardly be the same *you*, and we are led to guess, but cannot be sure, that the lovers are hailing Landor as the poet, and Ianthe as the young woman to whom he has given immortal youth in his verse.

Charles Lamb's *Old Familiar Faces* is included by Quiller-Couch. The recurrent line, *All, all are gone, the old familiar faces*, is thought to justify by its pathos the rambling incompetence of the argument:

> I have had playmates, I have had companions,
> In my days of childhood, in my joyful school-days—
> All, all are gone, the old familiar faces.
>
> I have been laughing, I have been carousing,
> Drinking late, sitting late, with bosom cronies—
> All, all are gone, the old familiar faces.
>
> I loved a Love once, fairest among women:
> Closed are her doors on me, I must not see her—
> All, all are gone, the old familiar faces.
>
> I have a friend, a kinder friend has no man:
> Like an ingrate, I left my friend abruptly;
> Left him, to muse on the old familiar faces.
>
> Ghost-like I paced round the haunts of my childhood,
> Earth seemed a desert I was bound to traverse,
> Seeking to find the old familiar faces.
>
> Friend of my bosom, thou more than a brother,
> Why wert not thou born in my father's dwelling?
> So might we talk of the old familiar faces—
>
> How some they have died, and some they have left me,
> And some are taken from me; all are departed—
> All, all are gone, the old familiar faces.

The companions are childhood playmates who all in turn have disappeared. Eventually Lamb makes a friend, the kindest in the world, more than a brother, but leaves him abruptly and revisits the haunts of his childhood where he moons about like a ghost. The friend, not having been born in Lamb's own dwelling, falls short of perfection; he is unable to appreciate Lamb's sorrow for those who have died, or deserted, or been removed from him. Unfortunately for the reader, Lamb has not kept the story straight. The old familiar faces are here enlarged to include grown-up cronies with whom he used to drink and sit up late, and a beautiful woman who, for some unexplained reason, has closed her doors on him.

Lamb certainly could not complain of having been deserted by all his childhood friends: his sister Mary, and Coleridge who had been at school with him at Christ's Hospital, remained very close to him until his death. There was a childhood playmate, Ann Simmons, met when he went on holidays to Widmore, for whom he later wrote sonnets. It is even suggested that because she would not marry him, his mind became temporarily unhinged and he was briefly committed to an asylum. But that the poem is modelled on Horace's *Odes* suggests the bosom-cronies to have been fellow-scholars from his beloved Christ's Hospital—Wordsworth? Leigh Hunt?—whereas the beloved friend had unfortunately not studied there with him.

> I have had playmates, I have had companions,
> In my days of childhood, in my joyful school-days—
> All, all are gone, the old familiar faces . . .

should surely read:

> Once I had playmates, once I had companions

And:

> So we might talk of the old familiar faces
> How some they have died, and some they have left me,
> And some are taken from me . . .

could easily be improved by half a minute's care. Thus:

> How this one is dead, and that one has left me,
> A third taken from me.

And *Why wert thou not born in my father's dwelling?* is extravagant. For the friend to have been born merely "in the self-same village" would surely suffice. A simple omission of the stanzas about the bosom cronies and the beautiful woman would make sense of the poem: though only as a macabre account of what would now be called "a regressive infantile fixation."

The Reverend Robert Herrick is an endearing character: the jolly anti-Puritan parson who encouraged his parishioners to keep England merry, who would give a favourite sow ale from a silver tankard and who, when rudely extruded from his cure, never wrote again; even on his return at the glorious Restoration. But Herrick's verse shows little care. His most famous song *Gather Ye Rosebuds While Ye May* fails to satisfy even casual scrutiny, and no melody however bewitching could blind us to the demerits of at least one of its four stanzas:

> Gather ye rosebuds while ye may,
>   Old Time is still a-flying:
> And this same flower that smiles to-day
>   To-morrow will be dying.
>
> The Glorious lamp of heaven, the sun,
>   The higher he's a-getting,
> The sooner will his race be run,
>   And nearer he's to setting.
>
> That age is best that is the first,
>   When youth and blood are warmer;
> But being spent, the worse, and worst
>   Times still succeed the former.
>
> Then be not coy, but use your time,
>   And while ye may, go marry:
> For having lost but once your prime,
>   You may for ever tarry.

Old Time is still a-flying? Why *old*? *Old Time* conjures up an image of Father Time with scythe and hourglass, who creeps rather than flies. Herrick means, in fact, that the time of youth, not Old Time, is flying. The words *Old Time*, moreover, are hard to sing. And Herrick's near-contemporary Milton would have frowned at *Time, flying, smiles; rose, old; same, to-day*, which sadly reduce the variation of vowels called for by so pretty a start.

Here, for comparison, are a few lines from Milton's *Arcades*, to show how verse should be written:

> O're the smooth enameld green
> Where no print of step hath been,
> Follow me as I sing,
> And touch the warbléd string.
> Under the shady roof
> Of branching Elm Star-proof,
>   Follow me,
> I will bring you where she sits
> Clad in splendor as befits
>   Her deity.
> Such a rural Queen
> All Arcadia hath not seen.

One can't fault Milton in sound—he was a musician *manqué*—though, as I have observed elsewhere, when his sound and sense are in conflict, the sense always loses. *Touch the warbléd string*, for example, is indefensible.

In *Gather Ye Rosebuds* the sense as well as the sound is ill-used. *This same flower*, presumably a rosebud, does not die within twenty-four hours of its first opening—unless in exceptionally severe weather; though roses already in full bloom have a shorter life, and the word *to-morrow* would fit their case.

The second stanza is simple to the point of fatuousness; contains too many *the*'s; and is syntactically unbalanced at the close:

The Glorious lamp of heaven, the sun,
The higher he's a-getting,
The sooner will his race be run,
And nearer he's to setting. . . .

The third stanza is on the same pattern, but more carelessly written:

That age is best which is the first,
When youth and blood are warmer;
But being spent, the worse, and worst
Times still succeed the former. . . .

That age is best which is the first, should refer to the first of the Seven Ages of Man, or Woman. The construction of the third and fourth lines raises difficulties for the singer, who must pause an awkwardly long time between *But being spent* and *the worse*, to keep them from combining in a wrong sense. And *worst times still* is the sort of syzygy (meaning the connection between the end of one word and the start of the next, as one speaks them) which cannot be admitted in any song.

The final stanza runs:

Then be not coy, but use your time,
And while ye may, go marry;
For having lost but once your prime,
You may for ever tarry. . . .

This adds nothing to the first stanza, and has other weaknesses. *Your time* and *Old Time* are unrelated in sense. Nor are the two *may*'s parallel. *While you may* means "while ye still can," whereas *you may for ever tarry* means "it is possible that you will tarry." As a Spaniard answered me once when I asked: "Can visitors go into that convent?", "They can, but they don't may." Again, *For having lost but once your prime*, is difficult to sing; and *but once* is introduced solely to pad out the metre. "Having lost your prime" would

be quite enough. And why does *ye* turn into *you?* The convention
that *ye* is nominative, and *you* accusative, has been broken.

Most of these points are negligible by themselves, but in mass
they detract from the poem's value. If Herrick had taken more trouble,
he would have written something like this; but better, of course, because it was his poem, not mine:

> Gather ye rosebuds while ye may—
> Their time is fast a-flying
> And many a bloom that's blown today
> Tomorrow will be dying.

> That glorious Lamp of Heaven, the Sun,
> The nearer noon he's getting,
> The earlier will his race be run
> And swifter fall the setting.

> Then seize the forelock of Old Time
> And while ye may, go marry:
> Lest, having missed your lovesome prime,
> Ye should for ever tarry.

Fortunately several songs included in the anthology are written
by poets with a sensitive ear for music. James VI of Scotland's
courtier Alexander Montgomerie, for example, in his *The Night Is
Near Gone:*

> Hey! now the day dawis;
> The jolly cock crawis;
> Now shroudis the shawis
>   Thro' Nature anon.
> The thissel-cock cryis
> On lovers wha lyis:
> Now skaillis the skyis;
>   The nicht is neir gone.

The fieldis ouerflowis
With gowans that growis,
Quhair lilies like low is
    As red as the rone.
The turtle that true is,
With notes that renewis,
Her pairty pursuis:
    The nicht is neir gone.

Now hairtis with hindis
Conform to their kindis,
Hie tursis their tyndis
    On ground quhair they grone.
Now hurchonis, with hairis,
Aye passis in pairis;
Quhilk duly declaris
    The nicht is neir gone. . . .

It is the neatest, prettiest, rightest, most varied in sound of any
Tudor song I know.

Thomas Campion, Montgomerie's English contemporary, made
sure of his words by writing their music himself. Though not nearly
so lively as Montgomerie's, because the music seems to have dictated
them, they do read sensibly, at least:

Now Winter nights enlarge
    The number of their hours,
And clouds their storms discharge
    Upon the airy towers.
Let now the chimneys blaze
    And cups o'erflow with wine;
Let well-tunéd words amaze
    With harmony divine.
Now yellow waxen lights
    Shall wait on honey love,
While youthful revels, masques, and courtly sights
    Sleep's leaden spells remove.

This time doth well dispense
  With lovers' long discourse;
Much speech hath some defence,
  Though beauty no remorse.
All do not all things well;
  Some measures comely tread,
Some knotted riddles tell,
  Some poems smoothly read.
The summer hath his joys,
  And winter his delights;
Though love and all his pleasures are but toys,
  They shorten tedious nights.

A Pretty Kettle of Fish

I never considered the arts of Latin and Greek Verse taught me at my public school as bearing any relation to poetry. Nor, I think, did any master or fellow-pupil. To the Oxford University awards for verse-competitions in these dead languages the Newdigate Prize has been added which, as I noted in my first lecture, Matthew Arnold won with a poem about Cromwell. It seems to have been Sir Roger Newdigate's hope to encourage proficiency in the writing of English heroic couplets, Miltonic blank verse, or Pindaric Odes; and as an *ex officio* judge of the Prize, I should feel bound to respect his wishes, if the candidates did likewise. In the last three years, however, the only compositions submitted in the old-fashioned style have fallen so far short even of early nineteenth-century standards, that my fellow-judges and I have either withheld the prize or crowned a candidate who showed a certain sincerity and an understanding of the proper use of English; and whose poem would neither bore nor shock the Heads of Houses, doctors and graduates assembled in the Sheldonian at the Encaenia.

For Sir Roger, a liberal-minded colliery owner, and for others like him, what is actually said has always seemed less important than the decorous formality of its expression. As soon as Jacobinism and the Romantic Revival invited English poets to break the verse conventions borrowed from France at the Restoration, everyone went a different way. Some adopted the precepts of Ben Jonson, our first and best Poet Laureate, who chose his words carefully for their emotional force, history, exact connotation, sound, texture, and weight; and who taught young poets this essential craft. Wordsworth and Coleridge, at their best, followed Jonson. Others, such as Keats, compromised by building up a more ornate verse convention, largely based on Spenser and the later Milton. Still others, like Shelley, felt sanctioned to write whatever they pleased in any metre that occurred to them. All of them, however, were sufficiently traditional to write set pieces: Odes to Melancholy, Autumn, Duty, the West Wind, the Departing Year, Solitude, the Mediterranean Sea, and so forth.

I despise odes, myself, as wholly unilateral. Neither Melancholy, Autumn, Duty, the West Wind, the Departing Year, Solitude, nor the Mediterranean Sea itself, can answer or even acknowledge these addresses. And odes or sonnets to the dead are ruled by the consideration of *De mortuis nil nisi bonum*—or, as Hilaire Belloc once rewrote the tag: *De mortuis, cui bono?*

The *Oxford Book of English Verse* contains Wordsworth's *Sonnet to Milton*:

> Milton! thou shouldst be living at this hour:
> England hath need of thee: she is a fen
> Of stagnant waters: altar, sword, and pen,
> Fireside, the heroic wealth of hall and bower,
> Have forfeited their ancient English dower
> Of inward happiness. We are selfish men;
> O raise us up, return to us again,
> And give us manners, virtue, freedom, power!
> Thy soul was like a Star, and dwelt apart;
> Thou hadst a voice whose sound was like the sea:
> Pure as the naked heavens, majestic, free,
> So didst thou travel on life's common way,
> In cheerful godliness; and yet thy heart
> The lowliest duties on herself did lay.

Did Wordsworth really mean this? Or did he plume himself on having succeeded Milton as poetic Mentor to the English nation, and write this in vindication of his claim? Surely he is congratulating himself because he also has a soul like a Star, and dwells apart in the Lake District? Yet Milton did not have a soul like a Star; nor did he give England manners, virtue, freedom, power; nor did he even dwell apart—until forced to do so by blindness and the Restoration. Either Wordsworth is most ill-read in history, or he is advocating what would now be called "undisguised Fascism." During the Civil War, Milton had written his famous *Areopagitica* (a plea for the freedom of the Press) but afterwards became Assistant Press Censor for the Council of State and helped to enforce a most repressive Censorship Law. This Council of State, you will remember, was the executive branch of a minority government set up by the mutinous New Model Army, after they had suppressed the House of Lords, and forcibly reduced the Commons by a purge of the conservative majority to a small group of Independents—the Rump—who would co-operate in the execution of the King and the abolition of the monarchy.

Milton's married life was ugly. He did not "travel on life's common way in cheerful godliness," not did his hall or bower keep their ancient English dower of inward happiness. . . . "Many of his choicest years of life," it is recorded by his nephew, "were employed in wrangling and raquetting back conjugal reproach, accusation and sarcasm." When his first wife left him, he tried unsuccessfully to commit bigamy. After her death he bullied his three daughters, stinted them of pocket money, and condemned them to the "reading aloud and exact pronouncing of all the languages of whatever book he should think fit to peruse: the Hebrew (and, I think, the Syriac), the Greek, the Latin, the Italian, the Spanish, the French—of which they understood not one word. . . ." And he cut them out of his will on the ground that their mother's marriage portion had never been paid him. He had also defrauded their maternal grandmother of her "widow's thirds."

It is clear, however, that Wordsworth admired Milton's versecraft, and envied him his political power under the Commonwealth, though keeping far away from Whitehall himself: he had badly blotted his copybook during the first years of the French Revolution. Take, from the *Oxford Book English Verse*, Wordsworth's *Valedictory Sonnet to the River Duddon*, and see what its sonorous majesty disguises:

> I thought of Thee, my partner and my guide,
>   As being pass'd away.—Vain sympathies!
>   For, backward, Duddon! as I cast my eyes,
> I see what was, and is, and will abide;
> Still glides the Stream, and shall for ever glide;
>   The Form remains, the Function never dies;
>   While we, the brave, the mighty, and the wise,
> We Men, who in our morn of youth defied
> The elements, must vanish;—be it so!
>   Enough, if something from our hands have power
>   To live, and act, and serve the future hour;
> And if, as toward the silent tomb we go,
>   Through love, through hope, and faith's transcendent dower,
> We feel that we are greater than we know.

Translated into prose this means: "Once I wrote poems about the River Duddon, because it happened to flow near my house in Cumberland; and, on moving from the neighbourhood, considered it dead without me. I realize now that this was, in part, a mistake. It still, of course, flowed in the same bed and will continue to do so, outlasting even brave, renowned, wise men like myself—who, when young, would think nothing of going for a walk in a thunderstorm. No, I cannot compete in longevity with this stream; it will be enough if my poems poetically inspire future generations; and if, as I die full of faith, hope and charity, I feel that I have perhaps underrated my enormous poetic powers."

Matthew Arnold had a pretty secure command of verse-craft and as little humour as either Milton or Wordsworth, but an honest and humble heart. A friend has complained to me that it was hardly fair to underline the essential dullness of the *Thyrsis* stanzas which I read in my first lecture—entries for Apollo's annual Newdigate Prize

—when Arnold had at least written *Dover Beach*. This poem does not occur in the *Oxford Book of English Verse,* but he has asked me to present it for your judgement:

> The Sea is calm tonight.
> The tide is full, the moon lies fair
> Upon the straits;—on the French coast the light
> Gleams and is gone; the cliffs of England stand,
> Glimmering and vast, out in the tranquil bay.
> Come to the window, sweet is the night-air!
> Only, from the long line of spray
> Where the sea meets the moon-blanch'd land,
> Listen! you hear the grating roar
> Of pebbles which the waves draw back, and fling,
> At their return, up the high strand,
> Begin, and cease, and then again begin,
> With tremulous cadence slow, and bring
> The eternal note of sadness in.
>
> Sophocles long ago
> Heard it on the Aegean, and it brought
> Into his mind the turbid ebb and flow
> Of human misery; we
> Find also in the sound a thought,
> Hearing it by this distant northern sea.
>
> The Sea of Faith
> Was once, too, at the full, and round earth's shore
> Lay like the folds of a bright girdle furl'd.
> But now I only hear
> Its melancholy, long, withdrawing roar,
> Retreating, to the breath
> Of the night-wind, down the vast edges drear
> And naked shingles of the world.
>
> Ah, love, let us be true
> To one another! for the world, which seems
> To lie before us like a land of dreams,
> So various, so beautiful, so new,

Hath really neither joy, nor love, nor light,
Nor certitude, nor peace, nor help for pain;
And we are here as on a darkling plain
Swept with confused alarms of struggle and flight,
Where ignorant armies clash by night.

I agreed with my friend that this was a poem of genuine feeling, however miserably muddled in expression.

The moon lies fair upon the strait. The sea is calm, the tide is full: which should mean that the full moon was reflected in the water, seen from a cliff top, not from the beach, where all Arnold could have observed was its broken track on the crests of the waves. The light gleams on the French coast, and is gone. Not *a* light, but *the* light. He does not specify which. Surely, not the light of the moon? What light then? At Dover, one cannot see lights on the French coast except with a telescope from the cliff top; so Arnold's window seems certainly to be up there. Is he staying at a coast-guard's cottage? Does the gleam come from Cap Gris Nez lighthouse? So far, so good. The subject of the poem is *Dover Cliffs*, not *Dover Beach*. But the cliffs are said to stand in the tranquil bay. Surely, only ships and jetties stand *in* Brighton Bay? The cliffs enclose it. If the sea is calm, whence comes the line of spray? Does Arnold mean "foam" and use *spray* for the rhyme?

He has heard in the distance the grating roar of pebbles begin a tremulous cadence slow. How? A grating roar can't logically begin a tremulous *cadence*, musicians assure me, even in very modern music.

Now, for Classical reassurance, in comes Sophocles posted on another, Aegean, cliff. He too is said to have heard the tide. Sophocles must have had good ears; there are no observable tides in the Aegean. According to Arnold, he likened the turbid ebb and flow of the tide to human misery. Did he? No, he did not. He likened the beating of a storm against the coast, with its dark tangling weed-wrack, to the troubles experienced by mankind—which was a different matter altogether. Arnold extends this illegitimate metaphor to the Sea of Christian Faith, once at full tide, but now universally at low ebb. He gets into further trouble here by confusing the ebb and flow of particular waves, which one can hear, with the gradual ebb and flow of a whole tide—the sound effects of which can be distinguished only by standing at the window for several hours.

The folds of a bright girdle furl'd . . .

is not only ugly in sound, and too obviously waiting for the *world* rhyme, but inaccurate. One doesn't furl one's girdle, like a sail or a flag, but coils it. And does *I only hear* mean "Only *I* hear" or "I only *hear*, but do not time or count"? One can never be too careful with the word *only*. Thoughts of naked shingle make Arnold clutch at his wife in passionate despair:

Ah, love, let us be true
To one another. . . .

He means "to each other," not to *one another*—unless both of them are schizophrenes.

The next few lines appear to mean that, although Christianity is at a low ebb, he and she must never forget their marriage vows. He complains that the world, which seems to lie before them like a land of beautiful dreams, is really a very bad place indeed. *Seems* is here used only for the rhyme; or else *dreams* is. Either the land *seems* to be a beautiful land, but isn't; or else it lies before them *like* a land of dreams. The two ideas, if run together, cancel each other out. Arnold's hysterical castigation of the world as really containing no joy, love, light, certitude, peace, or help from pain, has an almost comic ring. Are his wife and himself alone in their seemingly precarious possession of all these beautiful human abstractions?

I have never liked the pseudo-poetic *darkling*, an adverb borrowed from Milton's thrush that *sings darkling* (meaning "in the dark") as if it were the participle from a verb "darkle," the opposite of "sparkle." And even if Arnold were justified in changing the scene, at the last moment, from a moon-blanched shore to a darkling plain, armies cannot clash ignorantly by day on a darkling plain unless during an eclipse; so *darkling* is unnecessary. I wonder what battle Arnold had in mind? Perhaps it was Inkerman, the Soldiers' Battle, fought only a few years before the poem appeared, beginning at dawn on 15 November 1855, and continued murderously, though purposefully, all day by the Russians and ourselves in a haze of gunpowder smoke, both the commanding generals having lost all control of their troops.

Arnold should have known better than write a poem about Dover. Keats had advised his fellow-poets against this many years before, giving as a warning example the euphoric sonnet (1802) which Wordsworth had written there after visiting Calais during a brief lull in the Napoleonic Wars. Wordsworth sailed across to settle matters with Annette Vallon on whom, ten years before, he had fathered an illegitimate daughter, Caroline; and whom he had then heartlessly deserted in terror of having his allowance stopped by two guardian uncles. Theirs must have been an awkward encounter, because he had since been faithless not merely to her but to his revolutionary principles. However, a nice, solid, English Protestant girl, Mary Hutchinson, to whom he was now betrothed, was waiting on Dover beach to forgive his former peccadilloes and fix their marriage for October.

> Here, on our native soil, we breathe once more.
> The cock that crows, the smoke that curls, that sound
> Of bells;—those boys who in yon meadow-ground
> In white-sleeved shirts are playing; and the roar
> Of the waves breaking on the chalky shore;—
> All, all are English. Oft have I looked round
> With joy on Kent's green vales; but never found
> Myself so satisfied in heart before.
> Europe is yet in bonds; but let that pass,
> Thought for another moment. Thou art free,
> My Country! and 'tis joy enough and pride
> For one hour's perfect bliss, to tread the grass
> Of England once again, and hear and see,
> With such a dear Companion at my side.

Keats, unaware of Wordsworth's immense relief at getting safe home without forfeiting Mary's affection—which is the emotional core of the sonnet—parodied it with a random list of dislikes, to caricature Wordsworth's oversmug likes:

> The House of Mourning written by Mr. Scott—
> A sermon at the Magdalen,—a tear
> Dropt on a greasy novel,—want of cheer
> After a walk uphill to a friend's cot,—
> Tea with a maiden lady,—a curs'd lot
> Of worthy poems with the author near,—
> A patron lord,—a drunkenness from beer,—
> Haydon's great picture,—a cold coffee pot
> At midnight when the Muse is ripe for labour,—
> The voice of Mr. Coleridge,—a french bonnet,
> Before you in the pit,—a pipe and tabour,—
> A damn'd inseparable flute and neighbour,—
> All these are vile,—but viler Wordsworth's sonnet
> On Dover: Dover! who could write upon it?

Yes, Arnold should have been warned. Wordsworth had later written an even more psychopathic sonnet at Dover, aghast at the close proximity of that vile country, France, from which God protected England (because she was so virtuous and wise) by a narrow but sufficient span of water. . . . And two others, some fifteen years after Keats's death.

As for Keats—Quiller-Couch omits the human Keats who wrote, for instance, the There Was A Naughty Boy doggerel in a letter to his sister Fanny—as distinct from the ambitious young author of Endymion and Hyperion:

(1)
There was a naughty Boy,
  A naughty boy was he,
He would not stop at home,
  He could not quiet be—

(2)
There was a naughty boy
  And a naughty boy was he
For nothing would he do
  But scribble poetry—

He took
In his Knapsack
A Book
Full of vowels
And a shirt
With some towels—
A slight cap
For night cap—
A hair brush,
Comb ditto,
New stockings
For old ones
Would split O!
This Knapsack
Tight at's back
He rivetted close
And followed his Nose
　　To the North,
　　To the North,
　And follow'd his nose
　　To the North.

He took
An ink stand
In his hand
And a pen
Big as ten
In the other,
And away
In a Pother
He ran
To the mountains
And fountains
And ghostes
And postes
And witches
And ditches,
And wrote
In his coat
When the weather
Was cool,
Fear of gout,
And without
When the weather
Was warm—
Och the charm
When we choose
To follow one's nose
　　To the north,
　　To the north,
　To follow one's nose
　　To the north!

(3)
There was a naughty boy
　And a naughty boy was he,
He kept little fishes
　In washing tubs three
　　In spite
　　Of the might
　　Of the Maid
　　Nor afraid

Of his Granny-good—
He often would
Hurly burly
Get up early
And go
By hook or crook
To the brook
And bring home
Miller's thumb,
Tittlebat
Not over fat,
Minnows small
As the stall
Of a glove,
Not above
The size
Of a nice
Little Baby's
Little fingers—
O he made,
'Twas his trade,
Of Fish a pretty Kettle
A Kettle—
A Kettle
Of Fish a pretty Kettle
A Kettle!

(4)

There was a naughty Boy,
    And a naughty Boy was he
He ran away to Scotland
    The people for to see—
        Then he found
        That the ground
        Was as hard,
        That a yard
        Was as long,
        That a song
        Was as merry,
        That a cherry
        Was as red—
        That lead
        Was as weighty,
        That fourscore
        Was as eighty,
        That a door
        Was as wooden
        As in England—
    So he stood in his shoes
        And he wonder'd,
        He wonder'd,
    He stood in his shoes
        And he wonder'd.

Instead we are given several of Keats's fashionable Odes, and the following "number"—which I find a useful example of sheer bad craftsmanship:

In a drear-nighted December,
    Too happy, happy tree,
Thy branches ne'er remember
    Their green felicity:
The north cannot undo them,
With a sleety whistle through them;
Nor frozen thawings glue them
    From budding at the prime.

> In a drear-nighted December,
> Too happy, happy brook,
> Thy bubblings ne'er remember
> Apollo's summer look;
> But with a sweet forgetting,
> They stay their crystal fretting,
> Never, never petting
> About the frozen time.
>
> Ah! would 'twere so with many
> A gentle girl and boy!
> But were there ever any
> Writhed not at passèd joy?
> To know the change and feel it,
> When there is none to heal it,
> Nor numbèd sense to steal it,
> Was never said in rhyme.

The trouble begins at once:

> In a drear-nighted December,
> Too happy, happy tree,
> Thy branches ne'er remember
> Their green felicity . . .

which ninety-nine readers out of a hundred will take as referring
to the Christmas Tree in Hans Andersen's story, made the happiest
tree in the world by its decorations and the cries of joy with which
the children acclaim it. And they will read the next four lines:

> The north cannot undo them,
> With a sleety whistle through them;
> Nor frozen thawings glue them
> From budding at the prime . . .

as meaning that the tree is protected against the north wind by
being placed in the parlour.

Now, this misdirection is not altogether Keats's fault; because

Christmas trees, though common in Germany and Denmark, were not popularized in England until long after his death. Yet he should have stated clearly that he had in mind the bare boughs of a deciduous tree—a birch, or oak out on Hampstead Heath—which was happy for some other reason than the proximity of Christmas. And if a tree can be credited with memory (and why not?), it must certainly recall its green felicity; otherwise it could not repeat the annual process of successful leafing in the spring.

> In a drear-nighted December,
>   Too happy, happy brook,
> Thy bubblings ne'er remember
>   Apollo's summer look. . . .

How the bubblings of a brook can be charged with a failure of memory for what happened last summer, when new water is perpetually coursing along its channel, will puzzle the reader. And when he reaches the end of the stanza he will be further misdirected:

> But with a sweet forgetting,
> They stay their crystal fretting,
> Never, never petting
>   About the frozen time,

He will take *stay their crystal fretting* to mean "stop worrying about being iced over," when what Keats really intended was "they will stop trying to wear away the banks (another meaning of *fret*) with their clear waters." The reader's eye will also be confused by the word *petting*, which here stands for "being petulant" rather than, as now, "treating with endearments." So he will naturally translate the *would 'twere so with many a gentle girl and boy* as Keats's wish that they would abstain from petting parties about the frozen time; namely, the first half of January. And he will then continue in the same sense: "But as it is, they all writhe at the thought of the illicit pleasures they enjoyed in summertime, when Apollo the Sun-god enabled them to pet in comfort beside the unfrozen brook."

Keats really meant, I suppose: "If only girls and boys could forget the joys of summer, instead of regretting them with such agony when winter comes!"

The last four lines are baffling:

> To know the change and feel it,
> When there is none to heal it,
> Nor numbèd sense to steal it,
>   Was never said in rhyme. . . .

How anyone can heal a change, or how any numbed sense can steal a change, I honestly do not know. . . . *Was never said in rhyme* is perfectly true: this stanza is a unique muddle.

Keats applies *happy* to tree and brook because they go along with Nature, and accept winter as a necessary lull; but why *too happy*, a suggestion that they will be overtaken by misery in Spring? Perhaps he means that gentle girls and boys are unnecessarily miserable because they fail to imitate tree and brook and, growing jealous of their power for forgetting, call them *too happy*? But this is not clearly stated; he has got tangled up with his rhyme sequence and fails to preserve the sense. The poem cannot, I fear, be repaired. Even if Keats had started:

> This drear-nighted December,
> O naked chestnut tree,
> Thy twigs will scarce remember
>   Their green felicity . . .

he would have got into the same mess as before—the fact being that girls and boys are just as amorous in December as during the summer, and can always look forward, as the tree does, to the next springtime. The question of old age and waning passions is not touched upon here.

Quiller-Couch omits *The Eve of St. Agnes*, and all the poems inspired by Isabella Jones, Keats's first Muse, except the so-called "Last Sonnet"—*Bright Star, Would I Were Steadfast As Thou Art*—

which he had addressed to Isabella before he ever met Fanny Brawne. You can read about Isabella in Robert Gittings's recently published *Keats: The Living Year*. Most of you will recall that ecstatic midnight picnic in *The Eve of St. Agnes*:

> Then by the bed-side, where the faded moon
> Made a dim, silver twilight, soft he set
> A table, and, half anguish'd, threw thereon
> A cloth of woven crimson, gold and jet:—
> O for some drowsy Morphean amulet!
> The boisterous, midnight, festive clarion,
> The kettle-drum, and far-heard clarinet,
> Affray his ears, though but in dying tone:—
> The hall door shuts again, and all the noise is gone.
>
> And still she slept an azure-lidded sleep,
> In blanched linen, smooth, and lavender'd,
> While he from forth the closet brought a heap
> Of candied apple, quince, and plum, and gourd;
> With jellies soother than the creamy curd,
> And lucent syrops, tinct with cinnamon;
> Manna and dates, in argosy transferr'd
> From Fez; and spicèd dainties every one,
> From silken Samarkand to cedar'd Lebanon.
>
> These delicates he heap'd with glowing hand
> On golden dishes and in baskets bright
> Of wreathèd silver: sumptuous they stand
> In the retired quiet of the night,
> Filling the chilly room with perfume light.—
> "And now, my love, my seraph fair, awake!
> Thou art my heaven, and I thine eremite:
>   Open thine eyes, for meek St. Agnes' sake,
> Or I shall drowse beside thee, so my soul doth ache."

This, as Robert Gittings shows, records Keats's midnight escapade with Isabella on St. Agnes' Eve, January 20, 1819. The anachronistic long carpets rising along the gusty floor were laid in the love-nest lined for her at 34 Gloucester Street, Holborn, by the old bald-pate Donough O'Callaghan, M.P., her rich septuagenarian Whig protector. Isabella, later credited by Charles Woodhouse, Keats's friend, with having suggested the theme of the poem, was about Keats's own age. Her beauty, character, judgement and taste included her in the same remarkable company of *hetairai* as Harriet Wilson of the *Memoirs*—my favourite early nineteenth-century auto-biographer—though, indeed, Harriet restricted her favours strictly to the nobility.

> Hush, hush! tread softly! hush, hush my dear!
>   All the house is asleep, but we know very well
> That the jealous, the jealous old bald-pate may hear,
>   Tho' you've padded his night-cap—O sweet Isabel!
>   Tho' your feet are more light than a Fairy's feet,
>   Who dances on bubbles where brooklets meet,—
> Hush, hush! soft tiptoe! hush, hush my dear!
> For less than a nothing the jealous can hear.
>
> No leaf doth tremble, no ripple is there
>   On the river.—all's still, and the night's sleepy eye
> Closes up, and forgets all its Lethean care,
>   Charm'd to death by the drone of the humming Mayfly;
>   And the Moon, whether prudish or complaisánt,
>   Has fled to her bower, well knowing I want
> No light in the dusk, no torch in the gloom,
> But my Isabel's eyes, and her lips pulp'd with bloom.
>
> Lift the latch! ah gently! ah tenderly—sweet!
>   We are dead if that latchet gives one little clink!
> Well done—now those lips, and a flowery seat—
>   The old man may sleep, and the planets may wink;
>   The shut rose shall dream of our loves, and awake
>   Full blown, and such warmth for the morning's take,
> The stock-dove shall hatch her soft brace and shall coo,
> While I kiss to the melody, aching all through!

Isabella had indeed padded O'Callaghan's night-cap: that is to say, had given him an overdose of what we now know was

Ferintosh's famous Scotch Whisky; but the lovers would have been ruined had the latchet of the door given a single clink. The situation was an impossible one. Isabella, I think, loved Keats as whole-heartedly as she ever loved anyone: and he, her. But while she lived under the old bald-pate's protection, they could come together only on terms morally difficult for both. Marriage was out of the question; even if he had enjoyed better health. He had no money and no talents that could be harnessed to money-making. She was accustomed to a life of luxury and indolence, and had nothing to sell but her charms. Yet *The Eve of St. Agnes* and *Bright Star* somehow insulate and make durable their true sense of each other, in a way that his subsequent infatuation with Fanny Brawne never did. Isabella was wise and generous. Fanny was a coquettish *Belle Dame Sans Merci*, who gave him little but pain.

Verse-craft, as practised in monumental masonic style, cannot admit the least "fie-fie," as it was once called, or breach of convention. Thus Burns's stickily sentimental version of *John Anderson My Jo John* has long usurped the wonderfully vigorous original, printed at last in a collection called *The Merry Muse;* where the faithful wife deplores her husband's declining virility.

Burns comes off badly in the *Oxford Book of English Verse.* His was a difficult case. As an authentic ploughman and ribald satirist of low life, he had a wonderful sense of language. Take, for example, *The Holy Fair,* meaning the administration of the Sacrament, in a rowdy Scots parish:

> . . . Here farmers gash, in ridin' graith,
>   Gaed hoddin' by their cottars;
> There, swankies young, in braw braid-claith,
>   Are springin' owre the gutters.
> The lasses, skelpin' barefit, thrang,
>   In silks and scarlets glitter;
> Wi' sweet-milk cheese, in mony a whang,
>   An' farlis bak'd wi' butter,
>   Fu' crump that day.

... Here stands a shed to fend the show'rs
 An' screen our country gentry,
There, racer Jess, an' two-three whores,
 Are blinkin' at the entry.
Here sits a raw of tittlin' jauds,
 Wi' heaving breast and bare neck,
An' there a batch o' wabster lads,
 Blackguarding frae Kilmarnock
   For fun this day.

Here some are thinkin' on their sins,
 An' some upo' their claes;
Ane curses feet that fyl'd his shins,
 Anither sighs and prays:
On this hand sits a chosen swatch,
 Wi' screw'd-up grace-proud faces;
On that a set o' chaps at watch,
 Thrang winkin' on the lasses
   To chairs that day.

... Now a' the congregation o'er
 Is silent expectation:
For Moodie speels the holy door,
 Wi' tidings o' damnation.
Should Hornie, as in ancient days,
 'Mang songs o' God present him,
The vera sight o' Moodie's face,
 To's ain het hame had sent him
   Wi' fright that day.

Hear how he clears the points o' faith
 Wi' rattlin' an' wi' thumpin'!
Now meekly calm, now wild in wrath,
 He's stampin' an' he's jumpin'!
His lengthen'd chin, his turn'd-up snout,
 His eldritch squeal and gestures,
Oh, how they fire the heart devout,
 Like cantharidian plaisters,
 On sic a day!

Unfortunately, Quiller-Couch drew the line at dialect, and instead fobbed his readers off with the genteel Burns who had been taken up by carefully English-speaking Edinburgh society and who, as the new national bard-designate, was cannily giving them what they thought they wanted:

> O were my Love yon lilac fair,
> Wi' purple blossoms to the spring,
> And I a bird to shelter there,
> When wearied on my little wing;
> How I wad mourn when it was torn
> By autumn wild and winter rude!
> But I wad sing on wanton wing
> When youthfu' May its bloom renew'd.
>
> O gin my Love were yon red rose
> That grows upon the castle wa',
> And I mysel' a drap o' dew,
> Into her bonnie breast to fa';
> O there, beyond expression blest,
> I'd feast on beauty a' the night;
> Seal'd on her silk-saft faulds to rest,
> Till fley'd awa' by Phoebus' light.

A song of this kind demands perfection in sound, form and sense; Burns has taken no trouble over it. The first lines of the two stanzas should be parallel:

> O were my Love yon lilac fair . . .

should be matched by:

> O were my Love yon red, red rose. . . .

Alternatively:

> O gin my Love were yon red rose . . .

should be matched by:

O gin my Love yon lilac were. . . .

Moreover, Burns changes his rhyme scheme in the two stanzas: with eleven rhymes in the first, and only eight in the second. Nor are the lilac and the rose parallel. One is a whole bush; the other a single flower. The rose grows upon the castle wa'; but why on such an unlikely spot, we are not told—perhaps Burns is seated on a well-stuffed drawing-room sofa in Castle Street, Edinburgh, and pointing up through the braw window-panes to the Castle high aboon? Where the lilac grows, we are not told. The fourth line of the first stanza ends in *little wing*; the eighth, in *wanton wing*. Perhaps he meant to contrast *weary wing* with *wanton wing*, but could not quite manage it. . . . The notion that a bird could mourn the damage caused to the bare lilac branches by autumn gales is ridiculous, as Burns knows well. But the ladies sitting around him may well swoon at the conceit.

The first half of the second stanza is in irreproachable Scots style, but the second half has become fashionably romantic:

O there, beyond expression blest . . .

two ugly *esses* that he would have been ashamed to admit into *The Holy Fair*.

I'd feast on beauty a' the night
Seal'd on her silk-saft faulds to rest . . .

a line that drags altogether too sensuously for a song.

Till fley'd awa' by Phoebus' light. . . .

On consulting Burns's original, I find not only that Quiller-Couch has officiously reversed the order of the stanzas, but that the lines:

O gin my Love were yon red rose
That grows upon the castle wa',

> And I mysel' a drap o' dew,
> Into her bonnie breast to fa' . . .

are not Burns's own. The genuine ballad from which he borrowed them concerned, it seems, the beautiful heiress of some Scottish earl, to whose hand the poet dangerously aspired—a meaning which has been smothered by Burns's introduction of the lilac; lilac being a fashionable shrub not yet imported into Scotland when the rose of love still grew on that castle wa'.

Till fley'd awa' by Phoebus' light—but with *morning* instead of the Apollonian *Phoebus*—belongs to the original.

On climbing from ordinary verse into the region of poetry, we sometimes come upon incoherences seemingly due to haste and lack of poetic control, as in Blake's *The Tyger*. Angels were thick on Blake's staircase: some divinely eloquent, some mouthing nonsense. *The Tyger* makes a tremendous impact on the reader of the *Oxford Book of English Verse*, especially after his tedious progress through the earlier "numbers" of the eighteenth century.

> Tiger, tiger, burning bright
> In the forests of the night,
> What immortal hand or eye
> Could frame thy fearful symmetry?
>
> In what distant deeps or skies
> Burnt the fire of thine eyes?
> On what wings dare he aspire?
> What the hand dare seize the fire?
>
> And what shoulder and what art
> Could twist the sinews of thy heart?
> And, when thy heart began to beat,
> What dread hand and what dread feet?
>
> What the hammer? What the chain?
> In what furnace was thy brain?
> What the anvil? What dread grasp
> Dare its deadly terrors clasp?

> When the stars threw down their spears,
> And water'd heaven with their tears,
> Did He smile His work to see?
> Did He who made the lamb make thee?

> Tiger, tiger, burning bright
> In the forests of the night,
> What immortal hand or eye
> Dare frame thy fearful symmetry?

But all is not well here. The lines:

> On what wings dare he aspire?
> What the hand dare seize the fire?

make a sudden change in tense from the past tense, *Burnt the fire of thine eyes*, to the present. "He dare" was good eighteenth-century English for "he dares"; but not for "he durst," nor for "he dared." And the tenses are confused again in the next stanza:

> In what furnace was thy brain?
>   . . . What dread grasp
> Dare its deadly terrors clasp?

Also, the third stanza makes no obvious sense:

> And what shoulder and what art
> Could twist the sinews of thy heart?
> And, when thy heart began to beat,
> What dread hand and what dread feet?

This last question is incomplete. Blake may be thinking of the building-up of the tiger's remaining anatomy, but does not say so. Instead he switches to the metaphor of the smith working with hammer and anvil, and we suspect that *feet* has come into the poem for the sake of the rhyme, when we read:

> What the hammer? What the chain?
> In what furnace was thy brain?
> What the anvil?

For the chain also seems introduced for the sake of the rhyme. Chains are used in measurement, but not in smithcraft.

> What dread grasp
> Dare its deadly terrors clasp?

The antecedent to *its* is *anvil;* but who has ever seen a smith clasp his anvil? And if Blake is referring to the brain in the furnace, smiths who use hammer and anvil also use tongs to remove their artifacts from the fire.

One can seldom trace exactly the origin of any poetic muddle. This happens to be an exception, since the *Rossetti Manuscript* supplies early drafts of several of Blake's poems, including *The Tyger.* We find that the question

> What dread hand and what dread feet?

is incomplete simply because Blake has struck out the following rather turgid lines:

> Could fetch it from the furnace deep
> And in thy horrid ribs dare steep—
> In the well of sanguine woe?
> In what clay and in what mould
> Have thy eyes of fury rolled?

This last question shows, at least, that Blake had a potter's craft in mind and suggests that he let *what dread feet* stand as a reference to the potter's habit of puddling clay with his toes; perhaps also to the smith's use of his feet for working the bellows.

> When the stars threw down their spears,
> And water'd heaven with their tears . . .

The stars are, I suppose, angels (as sometimes in the Scriptures), but Blake has not made it clear whether they throw down their spears in bellicose mood, or whether they merely let them fall from their grasp in grief.

We have a right to know what he means, but suspend our doubts because of the clarity with which he asks:

> Did He smile His work to see?
> Did He who made the lamb make thee?

A simple omission of the middle part of the poem would repair the damage:

> Tiger, tiger, burning bright
> In the forests of the night,
> What immortal hand or eye
> Could frame thy fearful symmetry?
>
> In what distant deeps or skies
> Burnt the fire of thine eyes?
> On what wings dared he aspire?
> What the hand dared seize the fire?
>
> And what shoulder and what art
> Could twist the sinews of thy heart?
> Did He smile His work to see?
> Did He who made the lamb make thee?
>
> Tiger, tiger, burning bright
> In the forests of the night,
> What immortal hand or eye
> Dared frame thy fearful symmetry?

The truth is that Blake could not reconcile poetic creation, whether human or divine, with planned intellectual creation, or inspired human behaviour with moral laws; and it may be argued that the very confusion of his mind, when he considers the problem of how an All-loving God could have created both lamb and tiger, lends the poem this needed agonizing element. I cannot agree. If a poet believes wholly in what he says, the right words—however distraught they seem—will leap up to their exact place in the poem; and these are clearly not the right ones.

Coleridge's *The Ancient Mariner* is printed here at full length. It was first published in *Lyrical Ballads*, Coleridge's collaboration with Wordsworth; who persuaded him that any supernatural incidents of which he wrote should be put under the discipline of the natural emotions that they excited. This accounts for the extraordinary alternation of pure poetry and pathetic twaddle in *The Ancient Mariner*. The poem begins pseudo-dramatically with a wedding. The bridegroom's next-of-kin and, apparently, "best man" is stopped at the church door by an old sailor who insists on telling him a long, irrelevant story—though why no one sends the rascal about his business, we are not told. And the poem ends moralistically with:

"Farewell, farewell! but this I tell
To thee, thou Wedding-Guest!
He prayeth well, who loveth well
Both man and bird and beast.

He prayeth best, who loveth best
All things both great and small;
For the dear God who loveth us,
He made and loveth all."

The Mariner, whose eye is bright,
Whose beard with age is hoar,
Is gone: and now the Wedding-Guest
Turn'd from the bridegroom's door.

He went like one that hath been stunn'd,
And is of sense forlorn:
A sadder and a wiser man
He rose the morrow morn.

In the middle of the poem we are subjected to an implausibly banal dialogue between two spirits, which begins:

> "But tell me, tell me! speak again,
> Thy soft response renewing—
> What makes that ship drive on so fast?
> What *is* the Ocean doing?"

And we are introduced to an unnecessary Hermit good who lives in a wood, Which slopes down to the sea; He loves to talk with mariners, Who come from a far countree. . . . But the rest of the poem is extraordinary, from a wholly other region; and though clumsy in places, beyond all textual criticism. As when the small sail-boat comes close up to the ship:

> And straight the Sun was fleck'd with bars
> (Heaven's Mother send us grace!)
> As if through a dungeon-grate he peer'd
> With broad and burning face.
>
> Alas (thought I, and my heart beat loud)
> How fast she nears and nears!
> Are those her sails that glance in the Sun,
> Like restless gossameres?
>
> Are those her ribs through which the Sun
> Did peer, as through a grate?
> And is that Woman all her crew?
> Is that a Death? and are there two?
> Is Death that Woman's mate?
>
> Her lips were red, her locks were free,
> Her locks were yellow as gold:
> Her skin was white as leprosy,
> The Nightmare Life-in-Death was she,
> Who thicks man's blood with cold.
>
> The naked hulk alongside came,
> And the twain were casting dice;

> "The game is done! I've won! I've won!"
> Quoth she, and whistled thrice. . . .

Soon after which, we are asked to welcome a contrastive return to the pietistic sanity of the kirk on the hill and the villagers flocking there in Sunday attire.

By the way: an obscure British officer in the early eighteenth-century Merchant Navy, by name Simon Hatry, had the extraordinary fortune to enter twice into English literature: first as the mate of the vessel that rescued Alexander Selkirk (Robinson Crusoe) from the island of Juan Fernandez; and then as Coleridge's Ancient Mariner. Hatry seems to have died in a Spanish prison. He shot the albatross with a musket, not a crossbow; and, curiously enough, was thereby trying to placate his crew, who thought the bird unlucky—because it was black instead of white.

Coleridge has plunged down deep into his own hell, and though the false antiqueness of the ballad style in which he writes may offend an ear attuned to the real Border Ballads, the story somehow rings true. The ancient mariner reminds Coleridge of the gigantic powers which a poet can command under the true poetic trance, and of their destructiveness when not directed by love. Yet the vision was so frightening that Coleridge could not face its implications in terms of creative love between man and woman—as he again shirked them in *Christabel*—but turned instead to a love of simple uncommitted creatures, the water-snakes:

> Beyond the shadow of the ship,
> I watch'd the water-snakes!
> They moved in tracks of shining white,
> And when they rear'd, the elfish light
> Fell off in hoary flakes.

> Within the shadow of the ship
> I watch'd their rich attire:
> Blue, glossy green, and velvet black,
> They coil'd and swam; and every track
> Was a flash of golden fire.

> O happy living things! no tongue
> Their beauty might declare:
> A spring of love gush'd from my heart,
> And I bless'd them unaware:
> Sure my kind saint took pity on me,
> And I bless'd them unaware.

And from the water-snakes he slid down to the petty idealism of Christian neighbourliness, and of *Brown bread, white bread, And a cottage well thatched with straw.*

Christabel was a demoness, not his own true love; and his poem about her grows shoddier and shoddier as it proceeds. But at least Coleridge understood the poetic problem, even if he could not live with it and had, instead, to seek the dubious consolations of Hegelian philosophy.

Heaven help all poets who try to live with the problem! The curse that falls on them is that they are continually forced by their poetic demon into ecstatic regions which they fatally seek to identify with their own domestic life, though forming part of a different world altogether. Such experience, if recorded with absolute truth, is what survives, what blossoms, what becomes themselves when the poets are dead—whether or not they have subsequently reneged and settled for every-day reality. All but a very few have reneged, earlier or later in life—though continuing to practise the banausic craft of verse; which has been the subject of these three lectures.

The Duende

Throughout my lectures of the past four years I have dwelt on the difference between Muse Poetry and Apollonian poetry: a difference between the non-ecstatic and the ecstatic—*ecstasy* meaning in Greek a "standing outside." Outside what? I suppose outside the reality of our normal circumstances: so that any practical "because" of a poem seems irrelevant to its nature.

In Muse poetry, the "because" of a poem must be the poet's personal obsession with the Muse. Apollonian poetry is an arrangement of reasonable opinions in a memorizable verse form, with carefully chosen semi-archaic diction lending them authority: in fact, a form of rhetoric, which meets society's demand for the god of rational enlightenment rather than for the impractical Muse.

My views on the Muse Goddess are deduced from the multilingual corpus of love-poetry. I regard her as the primitive female who has separated herself from whatever laws have hitherto governed society, and whom man consistently fails to discipline. She is guardian of the love magic which all religious leaders, philosophers, and legalists in turn officiously attempt to define for her but which always eludes them. Only poets are convinced that a watchful trust in the undisciplined Muse Goddess will eventually teach them poetic wisdom and make them welcome to her secret paradise. Muse poetry is a distillation of love in its most unsocial, unphilosophical, unlegalistic, unliterary sense; written occasionally by those few women poets whom the Goddess possesses but, far more often, by men who have been granted access to her love-magic.

History begins with patriarchal annals:

> And each new year would recapitulate
> The unkind sloughings and renewals
> Of the death-serpent's chequered coat.

Poetic love is uncalendared, and a woman's capacity for Musedom cannot be measured by her ethical virtues, or by her intellectual powers, or by any of the qualities that make a good wife, mistress, secretary. The sole proof will be that the poet has responded to a magic of her own without which his poems would have remained sterile. He may be reproached for celebrating someone without constancy of direction, tenderness of conscience or recognized social background, rather than standing by a nobler, more predictable, other woman whose fixed devotion to duty should earn her the highest eulogies. But solid virtues, tempered by intellect and loyalty to social convention, yield no poetic inspiration; and who would reproach a metallurgist for showing only vague interest in a huge lump of forty-per-cent copper ore, or even in a gold nugget, when what he really needed was rock containing minute but recoverable traces of uranium or titanium? The chemistry of poetic magic cannot be explained; it can only be observed. Magic originates with women, but is extended as a love-gift to man. The concealed purpose of modern university education for women is to drain off the magic. On the whole it is successful: but some women resist. Not many; just a few.

Traditionally, the Goddess Bau, or the God Marduk, or Prometheus, or some other deity, created man from clay.* Palaeontologists

---

* Which was true in the poetic sense that all clay is detritus of primitive life.

dismiss this view as erroneous, arguing from fossilized bones that human beings have evolved from earlier creatures and that, though we have been men or hominoids in the physical sense for some six million years or so, yet lizards and even lower forms of life must be acknowledged among our ancestors. Physically this is true; we are primates, close cousins of the ape, sloth, tarsier, lemur and loris. Yet we are separated even from the ape, our nearest-in-kin, by an immense gulf not so much of intelligence as of magic. Apes can be taught to roller-skate, smoke cigarettes and not disgrace themselves at a tea party; but little more.

At some point in prehistory, perhaps not more than a couple of hundred thousand years ago, perhaps even less, a man and a girl—as I conceive the scene—looked at each other in wonder under the full moon and signalled: "We are we." This birth of magic incidentally encouraged the fine arts of flint chipping, singing, weaving and tattooing; but must have meant to these first real ancestors of ours far more than an expanded use of tools. It will have implied the discovery of such supernatural faculties as prophecy, healing, close communing at a distance, disembodied travel, and especially the magical extension of sexual understanding between man and woman into an all-powerful interchange of souls, for which lovers' gifts are the metaphor. These can be judged neither by their price nor by their utility, nor need they commemorate a particular anniversary. It is the surprise of their exact rightness and timing that distinguishes them from ordinary gifts. A shell, leaf, feather or curious stone carries an unspoken message clarifying the choice. As the author of the Elizabethan lutanist song *Fine Knacks for Ladies* wrote:

> Great gifts are guiles and look for gifts again;
>   My trifles come as treasures from the mind.
> It is a precious jewel to be plain:
>   Sometimes in shell the Orient's pearl we find.

The truth of love is proved by a constant change of such slight gifts, and imperilled by the greater ones—especially, of course, money, however useful in practical life.

Not improbably, however, the love-token custom was borrowed from the bower-bird and penguin, and love was lent a more domestic sense by observation of doves, ravens and storks, whose marital faithfulness as pairs had hitherto been unknown among primates. Wings have long emblemized freedom and exaltation; and the sensation of having the heart sprout feathers is a common phenomenon among lovers. On the other hand, the organization of clans and tribes for mutual defence or food-sharing seems likely to have been borrowed from ants, bees and other insect communities, where individual love-pairing is unusual. The basic present dilemma of mankind is, indeed, whether we should go for wisdom to the ant, or to the dove. Flying dreams are perhaps prophetically indicative of the latter choice.

The bitter nineteenth-century conflict between priests and scientists as to the origin of man can be resolved by agreeing that Adam and Eve (or Deucalion and Pyrrha) were the first true man and woman, moulded suddenly by a divine impulse. A mother's natural control over her children until they fend for themselves sanctified matriarchy, a later stage in human development: the control being now extended into adult life. Male totem-clans gave their allegiance to a Queen Mother, who claimed not only descent from the Moon as a visible emblem and source of magic, but the magical monopoly of agriculture and arboriculture, in trust for her female kin. Matriarchy, however, put man in such awe of woman that it falsified the original love-union between Adam and Eve. Magic ceased to be a secret shared between lovers and become a royal female attribute used for tribal ends; and, finding monogamy irksome, matriarchal women took lovers only for as long as it suited them.

The "heroic" age followed, poetic in part but cut short by a patriarchal revolution. Kings usurped power, claiming to be of solar descent; woman's mysteries were profaned, and women gradually degraded to drudges. The patriarchs ruled by force, reason and sorcery—sorcery being the male employment of magic for private ends—and by glorifying man as the superior sex. Judaism, Christianity and Islam set religious seals on this new dispensation.

Where are we now? Patriarchy still rules in theory; but the father no longer plays the domestic tyrant as he did throughout Old Testament times and still does in the Middle East. The Western world has accepted a mechanarchy which collectivizes human life—women's as much as men's. Financiers, politicians and scientists, relying on the people's traditional subservience to Queen-Mothers and Kings, have used the figment of democracy to seize power. In mythological terms it is another Palace Revolution of the Gods Hermes, Pluto and Apollo against Father Zeus; and except in old-fashioned monarchies and backward faiths allows no sacrosanct man or woman to prolong the illusion of divine magic. Allegiance to the State, a political machine with financial and scientific buttresses, is required instead. Everywhere the trend is towards a scientific and financial *élite* working closely with a political *élite,* to control and administer all human necessities, to reduce superstition—"superstition" meaning what is "left over" from old habits of thought—and eradicate or suppress all individualistic being. This is done either by censorship and imprisonment, as beyond the Iron Curtain; or by an increasingly close State control of education, industry and communication, as in the Western world.

William Whyte, a contemporary American scientist employed as a mouthpiece of business corporations, explains their final object as social unanimity brought about by reducing haphazard custom to terms rational:

> The conditions which determine human happiness are discoverable scientific methods and largely capable of realization. The world's greatest need is a science of human relationship and an art of human engineering based on its laws. These relationships are extremely complex, but science is gradually reducing them to fundamentals that respond to direct and simple treatment.

William Whyte is claiming that one can eventually fool not only half the people all the time, nor all the people half the time, but all the people all the time. And Elton Mayo, founder of the Harvard School of Business and the "human relations" school of industrial psychology, envisages a happy collectivism on the lines of the Australian aboriginal societies:

. . . an almost perfect collaboration drilled into members of a tribe in such a fashion that a kinship relation, a social ceremony, or an economic duty, become signals or commands to act or respond in a certain manner—each member knows his place and part, although he cannot explain it. A century of scientific development and the effects of education have led us to forget how necessary this type of non-logical social action is to satisfactory achievement in living.

It is true that the few aboriginal tribes still not wholly contaminated by missionaries or traders live an almost insectival life—in automatic obedience to tribal custom even where the individual seems penalized because the due rewards of his skill are denied him. But at least they use their bodies and senses to the full, in their successful survival of climatic hardships which would destroy any unequipped modern man within a week. What Elton Mayo demands is instinctive obedience to a political machine, controlled by logical experts who will gladly employ direct or indirect brainwashing techniques to secure non-logical allegiance.

We are still living in the Late Christian Age among superstitious relics of even earlier cultures, but there can be no doubt what is being planned for us. We are to be insects, not birds. The new mechanarchic ideal is to free peoples not only from the need to think for themselves, but from the temptation to form habits inconsistent with the smooth development of rational life. The justificatory excuse is that no violence must imperil the mechanarchic ant-heap, and that reduced working hours should allow ants as much leisure time as possible for private amusement. Yet the financial and political importance of this leisure time, which already amounts to three-quarters of every human week, has been carefully assessed. Our would-be rulers are set on so controlling leisure-time that the mainly mechanized entertainment provided will hypnotize us into also accepting their inescapably mechanized employment. Modern finance has become a careful card-castle of organized endless debt, in which workers are involved by the hire-purchase system, by compulsory insurance, by inflation of currency, by taxation that discourages savings, and by constant temptations to spend the last penny they owe.

The countryside is industrialized. Horses are supplanted by

tractors, the soil is poisoned by chemicals and wild life exterminated; farmers are told what to plant and how much; farm labourers, directed into industry, bequeath their cottages as week-end pleasances for the richer townsfolk. Picturesque villages become holiday centres with urban business controlling all rustic amenities: village bakeries are disappearing; village breweries have long disappeared; little of the food locally eaten originates locally; saddlers, thatchers, smiths, carpenters and even masons grow rare.

Since few except the aged take religion seriously, the parish priest has become a welfare officer rather than a saver of souls. Unless professing himself a modernist—or even in extreme cases an agnostic —and adapting himself to the mechanarchic process, he can exercise almost no ethical authority. Yet, since business encourages a religious façade, births, marriages and deaths are still largely solemnized under ecclesiastic authority—as business also converts the trappings of constitutional monarchy into a tourist attraction, and protects the ancient sanctity of gold by keeping the gold-standard alive while withdrawing gold coin from circulation.

Oliver Goldsmith wrote nostalgically in 1769:

> How often have I bless'd the coming day,
> When toil, remitting, lent its turn to play,
> And all the village train, from labour free,
> Led up their sports beneath the spreading tree.

Sport has long left the village green and become professionalized. Intensive training for particular events breaks new athletic records every year; modern football, scientifically played, is watched by enormous crowds, few of whom have ever played themselves, and has become the roulette table for vast betting schemes. This limited development of individuals fails to remedy the general physical inertia; for although stuffy and crowded dancehalls may limber up a good number of restless teenagers there is little demand for new playing-fields.

Has mankind ceased to think creatively and abdicated in favour of a self-perpetuating mechanical process, automatically geared to public education? Fifty years ago only one American citizen in twenty went to college; now fourteen do so. The proportion is also rising steeply in the United Kingdom; universities are proliferating. Everyone seems much happier because everyone shares the same worries. Most businessmen, scientists, educationalists and executives claim to have clean consciences besides occasional ulcers and cardiac weaknesses. They prefer to assume that the mechanarchic system is under control, with careful economic and scientific safeguards against collapse. All ugly phenomena are swept under the rug every morning. The fact is that no dictator with an anthropological bent has yet been summoned to take even nominal charge of the mechanarchic process. Indeed, nobody at all is in charge, and individual experts in this science or that have very poor liaison with one another. Even worse liaison exists between national blocs, despite international conferences and the boasted advance of scientific reasoning.

What has become of magic? Does its denial by the mechanarchs imply its reversion to the first discoverers of love-miracle: to a reborn Eve and Adam? Since all social virtues are now associated with complicity in the antimagical State, Eve is likely to have had "a difficult home background" where patriarchal control has broken down. She will be passionately proud of her womanhood and of her latent powers: ready to bestow love, but unwilling to risk humiliation at the hands of any would-be husband, and wildly shying away from the least threat of male possessiveness. *"Adam, Adam, ubi es?"* she cries, and is seldom answered except by Samael the subtle serpent.

Adam is equally disappointed in his search for Eve. Catullus' "Lesbia"—if Apuleius was right in identifying her with Clodia, second daughter of Publius Claudius Pulcher, Cicero's enemy— came from one of the most difficult home backgrounds in Rome, a family notorious for incest and sacrilege. Catullus may have read her wildness not as viciousness (which it seems to have been) but as wholesome criticism of a social morality no longer based on faith in the divine. Living in spirit outside the dead world which such wild women also reject, a poet trusts them to use their magic for poetic, curative and creative ends. He looks both backwards and forwards to the appearance of miracle in regions exempt from contumacious male philosophy. Wild women do indeed recognize the part which they are thus expected to play, and the creation of poetic magic can be a prospect that entrances them. Yet, even when the bond of physical love is transcended by magical experience, they still suspect its threat to their freedom of action. Too often they dismiss their poets, resenting that love-magic cannot be wholly divorced from the physical love, not in itself sacramental, which Adam and Eve enjoyed in Eden. Zoologically, poets and wild women are still primates.

> Desire first, by a natural miracle
> United bodies, united hearts, blazed beauty;
> Transcended bodies, transcended hearts.
>
> Two souls, now unalterably one
> In whole love always and for ever,
> Soar out of twilight, through upper air,
> Let fall their sensuous burden.
>
> Is it kind, though, is it honest, even,
> To consort with none but spirits—
> Leaving true-wedded hearts like ours
> In enforced night-long separation
> Each to its random bodily inclination,
> The thread of miracle snapped.

The question of faith kept between a poet and his incarnate Muse is legally unresolvable. Catullus wrote bitterly:

> Caeli, Lesbia nostra, Lesbia illa,
> illa Lesbia, quam Catullus unam
> plusquam se atque suos amavit omnes,
> nunc in quadriviis et angiportis
> glubit magnanimi Remi nepotes.

And when the thread snaps, poems alone, for what they are worth, survive to record its suprahuman moments.

Now that contraceptive devices provide one main mechanarchic solution of the leisure-time problems, and now that the publishing of sexological literature has been approved by our courts of Justice, few young women still feel bound to hoard their virginity for future

husbands. The prevailing custom is, as among Polynesians, to experiment with a sequence of lovers. Yet it goes against a poet's
nature to sleep with anyone but the women with whom he is in
love: mere physical congress spells for him a loss of virtue—virtue
in the sense of power. The New Testament Greek word for what
Jesus felt stolen from him when secretly touched by a woman patient
is *dynamis,* power; and though in that case the loss of virtue was
ritual rather than poetic—the woman suffered from vaginal hæmor-
rhage and her touch would have made him unclean for some hours
—the principle remains the same. A poet feels unclean when his body
has betrayed him, and finds *sex* a dirty word: it implies an adulter-
ated public view of a private ritual between two individuals. A Muse-
woman feels the same: although her sense of honour is not a male
one, she never plays her body false. While gratified by a poet's
attachment and humorously jealous of rivals, she may well become
irked by his intensity and prefer another man's undemanding casual-
ness; for monogamy is a patriarchal, not a matriarchal, invention.
If a Muse-woman should feel a natural need for children, her poet
may well seem the most unsuitable possible choice as a husband:
his physical faithfulness threatening her emotional independence.
Even while admitting herself inevitably bound to him as the one
man who has fully recognized her powers, she may argue that his
passionately declared love is essentially self-esteem, that his tears are
tears of self-pity, and that the poems which she inspires and for
which he gets the credit are in a sense stolen from her. Why not
choose a simple, uncomplicated, wholly unpoetic husband? How
could the poet deny her that pleasure?

The mythical role allotted to the White Goddess reflects much
the same situation. She is represented as making alternate love first
with the creative, impassioned demi-God of the Waxing Year, and
then in pity with his murderer, the luckless demi-God of the Waning
year, named Lack, Drought and Envy.

A poet cannot afford to identify himself with any organization
formed for political, financial or ecclesiastic ends. There is no fixed
rule for his social behaviour except to be himself and live in the
company of those like-minded. At the outbreak of the First World
War I volunteered for the regular infantry and found myself

among men whom detestable trench conditions and persistent danger either destroyed or ennobled. Although we were caught in a demonic machine, officially sanctified by a corps of regular padres; although the war's final result would be worse than the power-politics that had caused it, ordinary civilized virtues had given place to heroic ones. We remained free because we were volunteers and bound to one another by a suicidal sacrament. Holding a trench to the last round of ammunition and the last man, taking a one-in-three chance of life when rescuing a badly wounded comrade from no-man's-land, keeping up a defiant pride in our soldierly appearance: these were poetic virtues. Our reward lay in their practice, with possible survival as a small bright light seen at the end of a long tunnel. We despised all civilians; wounds were nothing by comparison with the grief of losing new-found friends in the periodic massacres. Yet after only a few weeks of trench life in a dangerous sector we grew sick, poisoned by our own adrenal glands, our memories became impaired and the sense of crisis grew less intense; it took some of us as long as ten years to recover our health.*

Though most of my comrades were content, after the War, to relax, find a safe job, marry "the only girl in the world," and become respectable members of the British Legion, I swore a poetic oath never again to be anyone's servant but my own; and gradually grew more and more obsessed by poetic principle. Its sorrows and distresses proved in their way as acute as my war-time ones.

The pride of "bearing it out even to the edge of doom" that sustains a soldier in the field, governs a poet's service to the Muse. It is not masochism, or even stupidity, but a determination that the story shall end gloriously: a willingness to risk all wounds and hardships, to die weapon in hand. For a poet this defiance is, of course, metaphorical: death means giving in to dead forces, dead routines of action and thought. The Muse represents eternal life and the sudden lightning-flash of wisdom.

* Two of my biographers, neither of whom can claim to be my friend, have written that I had gone for psychiatric treatment to Professor W. H. R. Rivers, who cared for Wilfred Owen and Siegfried Sassoon. This is wholly untrue. I have never in all my life gone to any psychiatrist for treatment.

The walking dead surround the poetic obsessionist, trying to interest him in universal topicality, and at the same time to drain his life-force. "The world must go on," they tell him. "Why not join us? Support the machine that we have created, and give it an appearance of human meaning. Join our guild of united morticians. We will pay you well and shower honours on you—you may even be elected an honorary vice-president."

"You smell like the dead," he answers. "Give me the faintest proof that you still have any spark of life left in you, and I will listen."

No answer.

He is tempted to use violence on them, in the hope of awakening some faint living response. But it is unlucky to strike the dead; and if he does so, the worst they can do is to send him a lawyer's letter of complaint. And a poet cannot live always at the pinnacle of his power, among the similarly entranced: he needs simple, virtuous, lively neighbours with whom he can watch the clouds go by.

Richard Korn, an American poet, enlarges bitterly on those ugly phenomena swept under the rug every morning: especially by organizations which the State sponsors for keeping its underprivileged, sick or delinquent citizens in order. He writes that the novice who chooses to work in one of these "Human Service bureaucracies" brings with him little more than his training qualifications, his enthusiasm and a reflected faith that the Human Service can redeem the lost, sick or needy committed to its charge; but his passage from the stage of novice to that of professional is chequered by shocks and disillusions. Only his poker-faced acceptance of these will mark him in his colleagues' eyes as fully matured. The earliest and bitterest disillusion is the discovery that his particular Human Service cannot possibly fulfil the mission assigned to it: that crime, mental disease or poverty need national solutions. If he enquires why his colleagues have not yet forced these problems on the public, he meets with a second major disillusion. They are all, he finds, aware of their own ineffectuality but unanimous on the need for public confidence in Human Services. He learns the great unwritten law of bureaucracy: "Do Nothing to Embarrass Us." Every bureaucracy lives in a perpetual state of fear that public knowledge of its inadequacies may lead to disenfranchisement; so that an inordinate amount of effort is wasted in dishonestly maintaining a favourable public image. Staff-members aware of organizational felonies must be silenced, and the best technique is to involve them in complicity; thus no member can be promoted until he has demonstrated his readiness to betray the community on behalf of the organization.

The novice's third shock is the discovery that no bureaucracy can survive except by shelving the very responsibilities that it was created to accept. The policeman must live with a guilty awareness that the largest single class of persons systematically and daily violating the law are his fellow-policemen. The mental-health worker must accept the fact that the largest single class of persons engaged in the mistreatment of the mentally sick are his fellow-workers at the hospital. And so on. If he is willing to sacrifice his personal scruples for the upkeep of the organization he will even perhaps be decorated as a public benefactor. If he chooses to serve the community in disregard of the organization's *amour propre*, he will be defined as a traitor and probably expelled from his profession. If he elects to remain, avoiding what complicity he can in official misdemeanours, he may be tolerated so long as his good works do not obstruct the organization's most pressing business: that of self-aggrandizement. But, in such cases, he must content himself with permanent low status under constant threat of expulsion. If he fights the system and denounces it, he will die in good company—with philosopher Alexander Herzen who thus diagnosed his intellectual generation: "We are not the doctors. We are the disease."

Richard Korn's picture may be overdrawn, and he is writing about his own country, not ours. But the bureaucratic spirit is international. My own decision to remain free after leaving the Army was caused in part by having found myself forced into complicity with military misdemeanour, as an officer of sufficient rank to sit on courts-martial. Once when ordered by the Divisional General to pronounce sentence of death on a deserter, in aid of military morale, I did wrong. Instead of attending the court-martial and boldly protesting against this iniquitous order I made an exchange with the only other competent officer available: he attended the court-martial while I took over his command in the trenches.

Some would-be poets expect the State to support them. So do

artists. I sympathize more with the artists, because they get a far rougher deal: from the art-dealers who decide on trends, prices and personality cults. An artist who fails to do what his Gallery expects of him may have no means of paying for his rent and materials. But the sort of artist whom a bureaucracy would choose to hire is rarely one whose pictures I should choose for my own walls. The poet needs no materials except pen and ink, and his task is, or should be, to remove himself from the State's line of vision. He knows his powerlessness to effect any immediate betterment of society; but he can at least keep the flame of magic alight among his few intimates.

Until a hundred years ago, a small liberal-minded section of the community, sponsored by some eccentric millionaire, could produce a local working-model for a better world. That time has passed. "It just won't work, Mac," as I heard early this year at the Green Hornet Bar in Greenwich Village, New York, where a wild Boston Irishman edged up to me and began talking about millions of poor devils starving in India and Africa and China and such places; and about the thousands of gangsters and delinquents in the big cities; and about the hundreds of Federal ships tied up empty in the Hudson, waiting for God only knew what.

"I'm a stranger here," I said cautiously. "A Limey. But you may be right. There's always marginal tonnage lying around except in wartime. When the freight rates rise, it can amount to a lot."

He went on about the huge farm surpluses that Americans either hoard or destroy, because nobody there can eat it all, and because the poor starving devils abroad can't pay for it all: and about the vast criminal waste in New York and the other big cities—enough to feed and clothe millions! And about all those philanthropic Christian and Jewish do-gooders and Peace Corps characters who want to prevent crime, starvation, idleness.

The barman said: "What the hell, Mac? All this don't hurt *you* none, surely?"

Mac said: "Sure, it hurts me as a human being. I ask myself: why can't we put the Christian and Jewish do-gooders in charge of the delinquent no-gooders? Why not give the no-gooders a grand job which would be to load those idle boats (or 'marginal tonnage,' as the Prof. calls them) with surplus food and clothing and send them sailing over the wide ocean with gifts for the poor starving devils abroad? Sure then everyone would feel good. What's wrong with that for a solution?"

"No, Mac," said the barman. "It just wouldn't work. The Longshoremen's Union and the Seamen's Union and the Teamsters Union would raise hell. And you've got to respect Big Business. Big Business wouldn't stand for any of that, not even to save the world from Communism—no more than the Unions wouldn't. Free gifts destroy markets, don't you see?"

Mac pointed out that there was no market there, anyway. He said: "Those poor devils have no cash, so they have to starve. Only plump them up with cash and they'll start producing again and have money to throw around."

"And put us Americans out of jobs by undercutting prices?" sneered the barman. "No, Mac, it just wouldn't work. Forget it."

I agreed that nothing sensible and simple ever works: just because no organizations *think* sensibly or simply. In the end, of course, something snaps and then you have a recession, or a war, which changes the problem.

What the Spaniards call a *duende* (short for *duen de la casa*—"master of the house") was originally a goblin or genie or, at the worst, a poltergeist that had taken possession of a home. It then came to mean the spirit that possesses dancers or singers at a house of entertainment and makes them exceed their normal powers. The *duende* is caused by an exchange of love between performer and audience, unhindered by any inimical presence. Yet the word *duende* can be extended to the possession that makes poets, painters, and composers surpass themselves when working alone, animated by this magical love. This *duende* implies two complementary love-principles; one concerned with doing, the other with being: neither of which deserves separate credit for the product. Love is catching, like fire, wherever there is tinder. At a house of entertainment, although the *duende* seems to be born from a sudden recognition of complementary love between the main performer and a single member of the audience, it affects everyone present. One can readily distinguish the gasp of wonder when this sort of *duende* appears, from the loud applause that a footlight favourite can count upon, night after night, so long as the house is full, expectation high, and the seats expensive enough.

Garcia Lorca wrote about the *duende*:

"The great artists of Southern Spain, gypsies and flamenco people, sing, dance, play the guitar but know that no real emotion can come without the *duende*. They deceive their audiences by their ability to create an impression of a *duende* without its presence, as you are daily deceived by writers or painters or followers of literary fashion who also lack *duende*; but it is enough to think about it for a moment and not allow yourselves to be misled by a lack of attention. You will soon discover the truth and dismiss the impostors with their artificial utterances. . . . It is the mysterious power which everyone feels but no philosopher explains."

Manne Torres once said:

"Everything that has black* sounds has—*duende*. No truth is greater than this. Nobody finds pleasurable diversion in either flamenco or the bullfight when the *duende* appears; and the *duende* never repeats itself anymore than do the patterns on the sea when the gale ruffles it."

The miracle of true love—the *duende* that heals and enlightens any company into which a fortunate pair of lovers strays—is not rare. Yet few adults still recall those mystical visions of early childhood, first noted by the poet Vaughan, which correspond with their later intimations of love. The remainder either suppress them under pressure of practical logic; or surrender to comfortable routines of affection that keep love at a low simmer; or forfeit their powers by deliberate acts of cruelty, perversion or greed; or reject love as a social impossibility, choosing a second-best or third-best to fill the gap.

* Black in the sense of a pigment concentrating every colour.

Ideally women *are*, meaning that they possess innate magic; sometimes they also *do*, but theirs is not doing in the male sense. Whenever men achieve something magically apt and right and surprising, their *duende* has always, it seems, been inspired by women. Whatever they attempt in male pride, by the ingenious use of intellect or fancy, is sorcery rather than magic.

> Woman with her forests, moons, flowers, waters,
> And watchful fingers:
> We claim no magic comparable to hers—
> At best, poets; at worst, sorcerers.

Right doing by men is achievement. Right doing by woman is a simple by-product of being; quiet, unemphatic, non-competitive, but breathtaking.

Most ordinary couples are ripe for constant bickering even before their honeymoon has ended, with concealed jealousies and resentments leading to open fights, and open fights leading to passionate reconciliations. They argue that since marriage limits sexual freedom, any violent marital quarrel with its happy ending of renewed mutual embraces will prove that love is still alive—and not merely in the domestic sense which implies a common purse, routine planning, shared meals, regular hygienic love-making and the careful maintenance of children. But bickering can grow ugly. The time comes when quarrels find no passionate sequel of forgiveness, but only sullen brooding on vengeance or escape. Granted, in most bourgeois societies, amicable agreements allow both parties equal freedom of sexual unfaithfulness, though with careful safeguards to protect the social sanctity of marriage. Yet this implies affection and no longer love. True love may be presumed even after years of marriage; but how can a *duende* appear once a home has become a mere machine for living? It must at least be a centre where other lovers come calling with their excitements, troubles, and discoveries. And if the married pair can, by some miracle, preserve each other's freedom of action, avoiding any drudgery of planned routine, neither face need fail to light up at the sight of the other's after the briefest absence. But how many such pairs exist?

The obvious advantages of a home are that it allows the exercise of unstinted hospitality, and the right to shut the front door fast against all that is idle, weak, sick, greedy or unreal. A single man or woman finds it harder to keep these elements away, because of loneliness. And yet most homes are prisons. Light a fire with the logs laid on a heap of kindling, the ends pointing into the room. It burns well; but the heap of kindling, namely shared meals and a shared double-bed, is soon consumed. Children grow up and lose close contact with their parents; and the fire of love goes out if the logs are placed either so closely together that no draught can pass between them, or so far apart that the space cannot be filled with the flame of truth.

A young man finds it difficult to realize that a woman is subject to two severe climactic changes from which he is exempt; motherhood and the menopause. He may even be unaware of her emotional rhythm while she is still subject to her monthly courses. And she finds it difficult to accept his inability to change as she changes. The case is complicated by the newly discovered male rhythm of emotional intensity, which does not coincide with the month and appears to be considerably longer than a woman's. And the man who experiences no dramatic change of life but, apart from a gradual slowing down of physical energies and a weakening of his vision, should remain substantially the same from the age of fifteen to seventy-five or longer. Usual mistakes on the woman's part are expecting him either to grow old gracefully before his time, or to remain young beyond his time—for many men are played out by forty.

Love is the main theme and origin of true poems. I have myself conceived it in quiet, elegiac terms: as of a golden wedding already celebrated in two hearts thrust through by the same golden dart; a life seasonally punctured by the feasts of Candlemas, when the country year begins; Midsummer, when nights are shortest; Martinmas, when Autumn reaches its peak; Christmas, the family feast. Yet I found myself writing, very many years ago during my first marriage:

> Be assured, the Dragon is not dead
> But once more from the pools of peace
> Shall rear his fabulous green head.

The flowers of innocence shall cease
And like a harp the wind shall roar
And the clouds shake an angry fleece.

"Here, here is certitude," you swore,
"Below this lightning-blasted tree.
Where once it struck, it strikes no more.

"Two lovers in one house agree.
The roof is tight, the walls unshaken.
As now, so must it always be."

Such prophecies of joy awaken
The toad who dreams away the past
Under your hearth-stone, light forsaken,

Who knows that certitude at last
Must melt away in vanity—
No gate is fast, no door is fast—

That thunder bursts from the blue sky,
That gardens of the mind fall waste,
That fountains of the heart run dry.

Despite the elegiac "true love" concept of domesticity, to which my poems have returned time after time, I am drawn to the conclusion that though a poet must experience this before understanding the full perils of his profession, there can be no solution in time, to the problem of love; only in timelessness.

Blake speaks of "the marriage-hearse," but it need be no hearse unless a poet expects from his wife more than tenderness, loyalty and affection. To marry the woman in whom the Muse is resident negates poetic principle; if only because the outward view of marriage implies wifely subservience to a husband. Recognition of magic on the poetic level is irreconcilable with the routine of domesticity; and once a woman's single love for a man has been distracted by love for her children, the magic tie between them breaks, however proud he may be of his fatherhood; if only because she must accept her social

548 ON POETRY: COLLECTED TALKS AND ESSAYS

dependence on him. For me, poetry implies a courtship of the Muse prolonged into a magical principle of living. There is no domestic poetry.

Occasional married pairs come so close together in their shared routine as to enjoy only the same foods, drinks, music, pictures and plays; even their handwriting becomes almost identical. The Greeks knew them as "Baucis and Philemon"; the English say "Darby and Joan." The one who dies first is not long survived by the other. Such identical love justified the institution of marriage for those worthy of it; their occasional bickering is playful, and for the most part used to assure the outside world that each retains personal liberty. Most ordinary married pairs air their painful disagreements only in private.

Complementary love, as distinct from the identical love of Darby and Joan, is the most difficult sort. Darby and Joan send each other such simple telepathic messages as: "We must get the washing in; it will soon rain," whereas those exchanged by complementary lovers are surprising to both.

> Lovers in time of absence need not signal
> With call and answering call:
> By sleight of providence each sends the other
> A clear more than coincidental answer
> To every still unformulated puzzle,
> Or a smile at a joke harboured, not yet made,
> Or power to be already wise and unafraid.

The theme of complementary love does not occur in Classical literature, even by Homer. Although the Siege of Troy is provoked by Helen's fateful elopement with Paris, the physical attraction between this pair is all that we are allowed to see, and she calls herself a bitch for having deserted her husband Menelaus and caused so many deaths. The domestic affection between Hector and his wife Andromache is endangered only by the sense of male honour which sends him to his death at Achilles' hands; but the blind overwhelming power which took Helen to Troy has been sanctified in poetry at the expense of all other emotions, despite the eventual defeat of both lovers.

> What if Prince Paris, after taking thought,
> Had not adjudged the apple to Aphrodite
> But, instead, had favoured buxom Hera,
> Divine defendress of the marriage couch?
> What if Queen Helen had been left to squander
> Her beauty upon the thralls of Menelaus,
> Hector to die unhonoured in his bed,
> Penthesileia to hunt a poorer quarry
> The bards to celebrate a meaner siege?
> Could we still have found the courage, you and I,
> To embark together for Cranaë
> And consummate our no less fateful love?

Apart from certain passages in the Song of Solomon which Pharisee editors included in the Biblical canon because of its traditional use at weddings, and because the love of Solomon for the Shunemite could be used as a metaphor of God's love for Israel, no word about complementary love is to be found in the Bible. Jacob's readiness to serve seven years for Rachel, Laban's younger daughter, after already serving seven for Leah, should be read as a mythical anecdote explaining the predominance of the three Rachel tribes in Israel, although they were junior in origin to the Leah tribes. Even the attempt on Joseph by Potiphar's wife is not a love story; Joseph had no yearning for her and the Hebrew text makes it clear that Potiphar was a eunuch and that Zuleika, which was her name, would have dared anything to get herself with child.

Nevertheless the prime ancient legend concerned with poetic love is of Biblical origin: that of Solomon and the Queen of Sheba. Jewish, Arabic, Christian and Ethiopian sources show that its strength lay in the complementary nature of their bond; each having a crown to wear and neither being able to relinquish it for the other's sake.

A hundred questions about love stem from their story. The Queen of Sheba, it appears, came from a matriarchal, or at least a matrilineal, people, and will have had no husband, but only a subservient stud of lovers, representatives of the tribes owing her allegiance. The concept of a man living independently of his mother and grandmother, or of the woman who had chosen him as a semi-permanent lover, must have been bizarre to her. Solomon, on the other hand, was a patriarch who inherited his father David's harem and added to it by marriage with princesses from the twelve tribes of Israel and from neighbouring royal houses; hence the matriarchal way of thinking, natural to the Queen of Sheba, must have astounded him.

They fell in complementary love; he never having met a real woman before, nor she a real man. No solution seemed possible: Solomon could not sail off for Sheba and there humble himself by becoming one more lover to the Queen; nor could she stay in Israel and humble herself by becoming merely one more of Solomon's wives or concubines. Nevertheless, she had a child by him, and according to some accounts they jointly conquered a new Ethiopian territory lying between their own countries, and placed the child, by name Menelik, on its throne; both would then visit its capital at the same time each year, and so renew their acquaintance.

True love is often discovered after one of the lovers, or both, has become involved in marriage, or taken a religious vow, or become otherwise inaccessible. Each is tempted to accuse the other of not sacrificing everything in their single cause. The *duende* instead of assisting their efforts to time a concerted flight in each other's company, becomes a dangerous poltergeist that causes physical sickness and accidents. It is better not to dwell on this, but rather on the wisdom that Solomon learned from his Queen.

Muntu, Mammon, Marxism

A poet's life is ruled by the principle of avoiding loveless circum-stance, or of passing through it as speedily and uninvolvedly as possible. "Loveless circumstance" means the full impress of mechan-archy, functionalism, routine: methods invented by scientists and financiers to dehumanize and control life. One can now, if it pleases, live entirely alone in a crowded city without speaking to a soul for weeks: mechanized transport, self-service supermarkets, self-service restaurants, built-in television entertainment, all-electric domestic service—(if one has the money)—and at the same time manage without any hand-made utensil, appliance or decoration whatsoever. This is the way of death, against which the Beat poets inarticulately howl, while at the same time using language as a self-service con-trivance to which they give a despairing twist or kick to show their disrespect for tradition. It never occurs to them that they can simply quit, walk away and go on walking until they come to a place where people are still dependent on one another for exchange of human warmth and services.

"Functionalism" is used by architects and industrial designers as a word of praise for the simplest and most economical design possible that will serve a single limited purpose. My late son-in-law, an atomic engineer from New Zealand, once teased me for spending a lot of money on eighteenth-century silver spoons made by Hester Bateman, and on early nineteenth-century flint-glass tumblers—when I could have bought perfectly good functional table ware from Woolworth's at a twentieth of the price. Why pay for art and age? he asked. Had he been a simple financier I should have explained that both the glass and silver would enhance their value at least 800% in the course of the next twenty years, if I took good care of them. But since he was a scientist I explained that he had forgotten a principle function of tableware: not only must it be of convenient size, weight and design for eating or drinking purposes, but it must encourage the appetite and create no fatigue-reaction. Polished silver and fine glass, whatever their contents, stimulate the gastric juices; and the subtle differences in shape between each of a dozen hand-forged spoons or a dozen hand-blown tumblers, give every place at table an individual look. Which (I added) is partly why restaurant meals seldom taste so good as those served in a well-furnished home, and why diners-out constantly try new places. Manufactured tableware is *dead*, like the interior decoration of most restaurants.

Functionalism in prose is a Latin concept, adapted by the French to their less rigid vernacular: the theory that ideas are inacceptable unless cast in certain set grammatic and vocabularistic forms. Neither Latin nor French has, of course, a purely mechanical flow; some words are more charged with emotion than others, and a stylist takes care to vary the rhythm of his paragraphs. Nevertheless, a grammarian in either language has the right to blue-pencil any sentence as incorrect. English prose, on the other hand, reserves for itself perfect choice of idiosyncratic usage, and so while still able to convey subtle shades of meaning untranslatable into French or even Humanistic Latin need never weary the reader's eye. English-speaking scientists fall between two stools. They should never have discarded Humanistic Latin but, having done so, ought now to learn a live English that causes the reader no fatigue reactions.

My friend the late Norbert Wiener, Professor of Mathematics at the Massachusetts Institute of Technology, and an outstanding scientist, prefaces his famous book on Cybernetics with the following two paragraphs. He is trying to write simply in justification of the book's title: *The Human Use of Human Beings*. But although an electronic scientist, he has failed to respect the human brain as an electronic receiving apparatus which must be fed information in clear, accurate and unrepetitive style, never interrupted by atmospherics, "fading effect," interference from other transmitters, or short circuits.

The beginning of the twentieth century marked more than the end of a hundred-year period and the start of another. There was a real change of point of view even before we made the political transition from the century on the whole dominated by peace, to the half century of war through which we have just been living. This was perhaps first apparent in science, although it is quite possible that whatever has affected science led independently to the marked break which we find between the arts and literature of the nineteenth and those of the twentieth centuries.

Newtonian physics, which had ruled from the end of the seventeenth century to the end of the nineteenth with scarcely an opposing voice, described a universe in which everything happened precisely according to law, a compact, tightly organized universe in which the whole future depends strictly upon the whole past. Such a picture can never be either fully justified or fully rejected experimentally and belongs in large measure to a conception of the world which is supplementary to experiment but in some ways more universal than anything that can be experimentally verified. We can never test by our imperfect experiments whether one set of physical laws or another can be verified down to the last decimal. The Newtonian view, however, was compelled to state and formulate physics as if it were, in fact, subject to such laws. This is now no longer the dominating attitude of physics, and the men who contributed most to its downfall were Bolzmann in Germany and Gibbs in the United States.

What he meant to write was, I think, something like this:

When the warlike twentieth century succeeded the pacific late-nineteenth, Western art, literature and politics were swiftly transformed; which seemed to justify the popular superstition that new centuries inaugurate new epochs of thought and sentiment. Perhaps the most striking change occurred in physics: Bolzmann in Germany and Gibbs in the United States together prompted a general rejection of Sir Isaac Newton's still dominant theory that the Universe is ruled by temporal causality. Though he had admitted his concept to be unverifiable by detailed experiment, because scientists can have only a limited view of the Universe—as we now admit it undisprovable for the same reason—Newton nevertheless framed what these two physicists considered altogether arbitrary laws for its presentation.

By omitting the suggestion in the first sentence of a popular century-superstition, on the general truth of which he fails to comment, and which is therefore irrelevant to his argument, Wiener could have reduced three hundred words to just over one hundred, and guarded his readers still further against fatigue. The principles of prose-writing underlie those of writing poetry, though the poet must pay infinitely closer attention to the interacting sound, texture, rhythm, history and emotional force of all the words he uses.

The present cult of functional deadness in science, industry, religion and administration, as well as in prose writing, is perhaps mankind's reflex action taken with the object of reducing itself to a more manageable size by catastrophe, and of never again attempting to think in cosmic, as opposed to terrestrial, terms. Yet when the eventual warning comes, sufficient people should still be found to enter Noah's ark, as it were, and sail beatifically away; namely, the few people who have continued to think in magical terms. One mystical Moslem view is that there are always 4,000 people around, no less, no more, however large the statistical number of births. Why 4,000?—I suppose because forty is used in the East to denote any fairly large unascertainable figure, which one multiplies a hundred times for generosity. The number of true poets, painters, composers alive at a given time seems to vary little despite the increase in population. There never seem to be more of any one sort than can be counted on the fingers of a single hand. Perhaps the 4,000 include also mystics, saints, and all others who are more concerned with being than doing; which means a high proportion of women.

A friend of mine once rescued a battery hen from its battery pen and wanted to put it with free-ranging fowls to scratch for its own food; but decided that it would be at once pecked to death—so gave it in charge of a single free instructress. The bird did not at first respond to the change and many months passed before it acted in the least like a hen. Now Purity is managing well enough in a flock of Rhode Island Reds, and may soon be a real mother. Ordinary citizens are becoming more and more like battery hens—or battery capons—and even those who try to escape from their environment may find themselves helplessly at a loss. How to go anywhere without a car, how to go up and down flights of stairs without a lift, how to cook without electricity, how to make soup without a soup-packet, how to wash clothes without a clothes-washer, how to support life without a refrigerator, a radio and a record-machine, how to write a letter without a typewriter! Which is, I suppose, why Beat poets stay miserably where they are. Ordinary citizens use the end-products of agriculture, yet would not recognize an apricot if they saw it hanging green from a tree, or even hops if they saw them hanging from poles; or an unhusked walnut; or a tobacco flower, or a marijuana plant in blossom. Yet they are interested in space-travel and in the scarred surface of the moon, and in abstract art and computers and ocean bed exploration and in the development of plastics, and in erotic literature and psychodelic drugs and electric guitars and the performances of racing cars. They have got further away from humanity and the magic of love and the simple joy of being alive than any people anywhere ever before. Being truly alive, for a poet, implies three things: affectionate understanding between friends; an intense love-life with a particular person; and the occasional luxury of being alone. To be dead is to have acquaintances, not friends; to enter on occasional sexual experiences with whoever is available, rather than to fall in love; and to hate solitude.

"A man must swallow a peck of dirt in his life-time." But a peck is a few pounds only. Enlarged to a bushel it still remains a small amount. Most people in the Western world, however, make dirt their main diet. How many of them really enjoy their work as such? And are on affectionate, or intimate, terms with their fellow-workers? And are genuinely interested in the quality of the goods that they help to manufacture or sell, or in the services that they supply? A man may be satisfied to have made a success of his job—to have reached, for example, high executive rank in an advertising agency, where he can point to a steady rise in the sales of a particular product handled by himself, or in a new technique of salesmanship, or in the acquisition of additional accounts. But it seldom matters a row of pins to him whether the product is any better than any other of the same commercial sort, or whether he may be defrauding the public by asking them to pay three times the value of the product because of advertising costs. Yet it is part of his work to brainwash his underlings, especially travelling salesmen, into believing that the product *is* in fact as unique as it is valuable.

Schoolmasters beyond the most elementary teaching stages are, as a rule, discouraged from imparting any knowledge that they themselves believe strange or useful: dull and tendentious text books for their use are decided upon by central committees, against whose choice they have no recourse if they want their pupils to pass the set examinations. Although the acceptance of academic values and the power of memorizing irrelevant facts are no proof of intellectual sensibility, the students who can pass these examinations without feelings of disgust fit better into the mechanarchy than those who cannot.

In 1945 the Reverend Father Placide Tempels, a Dutch missionary, published his *La Philosophie Bantoue* at Elizabethville in the Congo. Originally written in Dutch, it has now been translated into English by the Reverend Colin King. The Bantus' reaction to European mechanarchic culture is a mixed one. They admire material inventions such as well-made tools, fabrics, medicines, motorcars, pocket-torches, shot-guns, plastic buckets and the like, only because these promise to develop and fortify the one possession that they prize beyond all others: their vital force. Otherwise they shrink from them as diabolic. Vital force, which they call *muntu*, is in theory bequeathed them by their ancestors—as Western scientists talk of genes and inherited constitutions—and demands continuous care for its preservation. A man's *muntu* can increase or decrease according to the terms on which he lives with others: it will depend on his use of this power, for good or evil, while associating with his superiors in rank, his equals, his inferiors and foreigners; and on what returns of vital force are made. The greatest praise to a benefactor is: "You give me life." If envy, hatred, jealousy, insincerity or scorn are evident in another's deeds or bearing, this is regarded as a sort of witchcraft: as in the Hebrew Decalogue the command, "thou shalt not covet," meant "thou shalt not bewitch." He asks: "Are you trying to kill me?" In a native court of law, the damage to a wronged man's vital force cannot be assessed only in terms of money. The judge's task is to decide who was at fault, and thereupon insist on a public avowal of guilt and a ritual cleansing. Every illness, wound, disappointment, suffering, depression, fatigue, or failure counts as a diminution of a man's vital force, and the Bantus guard against these by building-up a reserve of energy through natural magic. An autopsy on a corpse proving that a man died of an infectious illness does not nullify the relatives' plea that he died because an evil person underminded his *muntu;* in most cases the accused will plead guilty and make all ritual amends in his power.

Bantus go at times into trances and claim to be reborn with renewed magic powers; nor, like the ancient Greeks, do they undertake any creative task without appealing to a spiritual force which will enable them to dominate the material. The European traders' first conversion of young Africans to the view that money will buy anything, that money alone has moral value, and that the machine-gun is a power beyond human argument, caused such a shock in many tribes that thousands of old people went into deep depression and the population noticeably dwindled. To this youthful repudiation of love, truth, and respect for tradition there could be no adequate reply but: "My sons, you have killed us."

European infiltration into African life has set the Bantus hopelessly at odds among themselves: a confusion increased by the often unselfseeking missionary work of rival Christian and Moslem sects. It is difficult to see how the original Bantu principles can survive

under native governments educated, administered and armed in
Western fashion. Yet these are the very same principles that provide
the *muntu* for Western poets who look hopefully beyond the universal mechanistic catastrophe to their restoration.

Shakespeare's parallel, drawn by Theseus in *A Midsummer Night's
Dream,* between the lunatic, the lover, and the poet is not fanciful
if the words are all used in their purest sense.

> Lovers and madmen have such seething brains
> Such shaping fantasies, that apprehend
> More than cool reason ever comprehends.
> The Lunatic, the lover and the poet
> Are of imagination all compact.
> One sees more devils than vast hell can hold;
> That is the madman. The lover, all as frantic,
> Sees Helen's beauty in a brow of Egypt.
> The poet's eye, in a fine frenzy rolling,
> Doth glance from heaven to earth, from earth to heaven,
> And as imagination bodies forth
> The forms of things unknown, the poet's pen
> Turns them to shapes and gives to airy nothings
> A local habitation and a name.
> Such tricks hath strong imagination
> That, if it would but apprehend some joy,
> It comprehends some bringer of that joy;
> Or in the night, imagining some fear,
> How easy is a bush supposed a bear.

"Lunatic" originally means someone whose emotional life is affected by phases of the moon. There are many such, not only
gipsies, whose lives seem to hinge on these phases. A new moon
implies holiness and promise; a full moon, intoxication of the senses;
a waning moon, reflection. I myself try never to make an important
decision except under a new moon. A "lover" is one whose whole
mind focuses on the object of his love, and who cannot be distracted
from it by any outside influence or rational argument. The poet is
lunatic in the sense that the poets' Muse is traditionally a Moon

Goddess, and that her love-mysteries were always celebrated under a full moon. But he is even more conscious than the lunatic of the hyperphysical influence which the moon exercises, and even more conscious than the lover of the hyperphysical influence of love.

A fellow-poet wrote on my seventieth birthday to ask whether I knew what poetry was all about; he was still in the dark. I answered that I knew a little more about it than once: such as that the problem of writing poems was like that of reconciling the solar with the lunar calendar. Every few generations or so, a full moon almost exactly coincides with the moment of the summer solstice—yet this is a phenomenon not even visually experienced. Rare and hidden correspondences between the souls of a poet and a Muse-woman are what matter in poetry; they give him courage not to die while still alive, nor to fudge and cheat in any work he undertakes, nor to pity himself because the coincidence of souls cannot be prolonged or repeated. Marvell's poem makes good sense up to a point:

> My love is of a birth as rare
>   As 'tis by nature strange and high:
> It was begotten by despair
>   Upon impossibility.

The word *despair* seems to have been dictated by the rhyme *rare*, but even so the statement is partial. What about the woman concerned? I should have written it otherwise:

> Our love is of as pure a breed
>   As 'tis by nature strange and high,
> Engendered by the lover's need
>   Upon impossibility.

The subject of poetry is the certitude that, despite all possible doubts and difficulties, true lovers will one day reconcile lunar with solar time, imagination with reason, intuition with planning, honour with freedom; the male with the female mind. This happens only in a timeless *now*, which must not, however, be dismissed as a fanciful *then* by its participants: it is the *now* of wisdom, the poetic *now*, the *now* of the Black Goddess—of Wisdom as Night.

As Hippolyta says, in answer to Theseus's reflections upon lovers and madmen and poets:

> But all the story of the night told over,
> And all their minds transfigured so together
> More witnesses than fancy's images
> And grows to something of great constancy
> But, howsoever, strange and admirable.

The poet is not a schizophrene—with his mind torn in two parts —but a *deuteropotmos*: a "second-fated" one who has, as it were, already died and conversed with the cracular dead, thus being gifted with the spirit of prophecy. At Athens anyone who had been paid funeral rites but afterwards returned alive to his family was a *deuteropotmos*, and thereafter forbidden to visit any temple of the Infernal Deities. It is active death to have been in love with a woman for ever, *meaning* for ever, and to have been afterwards betrayed, murdered and left by the wayside. And anyone who, like myself, has officially died of wounds will agree that active hyperphysical death is far more painful, and takes one far deeper down into the land of the dead than the ordinary physical sort.

THE SECOND-FATED

My stutter, my cough, my unfinished sentences,
Denote an inveterate physical reluctance
To use the metaphysical idiom.
Forgive me: what I am saying is, perhaps, this:—
Your accepted universe, by Jove's naked hand
Or Esmun's or Odomankoma's or Marduk's—
Choose which name jibes—formed scientifically
From whatever there was before Time was,
And begging the question of perfect consequence,
May satisfy the general run of men

(If "run" be an apt term for patent paralytics)
That blue-prints destine all they suffer here—
But does not satisfy certain few else.

Fortune enrolled me among the second-fated
Who have read their own obituaries in *The Times*,
Have heard "Where, death thy sting? Where, grave thy
    victory?"
Intoned with unction over their still clay,
Have seen two parallel red-ink lines drawn
Under their manic-depressive bank accounts,
And are therefore strictly forbidden to walk in graveyards
Lest they scandalize the sexton and his bride.

We, to be plain with you, taking advantage
Of a brief demise, visited first the Pit,
A library of shades, completed characters;
And next the silver-bright Hyperborean Queendom,
Basking under the sceptre of Guess Whom?
Where pure souls matrilineally foregather.
We were then shot through by merciful lunar shafts
Until hearts tingled, heads sang, and praises flowed;
And learned to scorn your factitious universe
Ruled by the death which we had flouted;
Acknowledging only that from the Dove's egg hatched
Before aught was, but wind—unpredictable
As our second birth would be, or our second love:
A moon-warmed world of discontinuance.

I have told the following story before. One fine summer evening, at the age of twelve, I was sitting on an iron roller behind the school cricket pavilion, with nothing much in my head, when I received a sudden celestial illumination: it occurred to me that *I knew everything*. I remember letting my mind range rapidly over all its familiar subjects of knowledge; only to find that this was no foolish fancy. I *did* know everything. To be plain: though conscious of having come less than a third of the way along the path of formal education, and being weak in mathematics, shaky in French grammar, and hazy about English history, I nevertheless held the key of truth in my hand, and could use it to open any lock of any door. Mine was no religious or philosophical theory, but a simple method of looking sideways at disorderly facts so as to make perfect sense of them.

I slid down from the roller, wondering what to do with my embarrassing gift. Whom could I take into my confidence? Nobody. Even my best friends would say "You're mad," and either send me to Coventry or organize my general scragging, or both. It occurred to me that perhaps I had better embody the formula in a brief world-message, circulated anonymously to the leading newspapers. In that case I should have to work under the bedclothes after dark, by the light of a flash-lamp, and use the cypher I had recently perfected. But I remembered my broken torch-light bulb, and the difficulty of replacing it until the next day. No: there was no immediate hurry. I had everything securely in my head. Again I experimented; and again the doors opened smoothly. Then the school-bell rang from a distance, calling me to preparation and prayers.

Early next day I awoke to find that I still had a fairly tight grasp of my secret; but a morning's lessons intervened, and when I then locked myself into the privy, and tried to record my formula on the back of an old exercise book, my mind went too fast for my pen, and I began to cross out—a fatal mistake—and presently crumpled up the page and pulled the chain on it. That night I tried again under the bedclothes, but the magic had evaporated and I could get no further than the introductory sentence.

My vision of truth did not recur, though I went back a couple of times to sit hopefully on the roller; and, before long, doubts tormented me—gloomy doubts about a great many hitherto stable concepts, such as the authenticity of the Gospels, the prefectibility of man, and the absoluteness of the Protestant moral code. All that survived was an after-glow of the bright light in my head, and the certainty that it had been no delusion. This is still with me, for I now realize that what overcame me that evening was a sudden awareness of the power of intuition, the supra-logic that cuts out all routine processes of thought and leaps straight from problem to answer. I did not in fact know everything, but became aware that in moments of real emergency the mind can weigh an infinite mass of imponderables and make immediate sense of them. This is how poems get written.

I have since found that this mystic experience is not at all an uncommon one. Something like one person in twenty has enjoyed it and I am convinced that the original moment, when Adam and Eve first looked at each other in wonder under the moon and signalled "We are We," was an experience of the same sort, complementarily enjoyed by both: their foretaste of ultimate wisdom.

> How often have I said before
> That no soft "if," no "either-or,"
> Can keep my obdurate male mind
> From loving true and flying blind?
>
> Which, though deranged beyond all cure
> Of temporal reason, knows for sure
> That timeless magic first began
> When woman bared her soul to man.

I have been looking at the poems of Yevgeny Yevtushenko, as translated by George Reavey. Since I cannot read Russian which, everyone agrees, is—next to English of course, and some say Demotic Greek—the best living language for poems, because of its extraordinary shades and graduations of meaning, I can judge Yevtushenko's general attitude to poetic principles only as evidenced by the translations. It is an attitude noticeably deformed by a Marxist education and Yevtushenko's dependence for a living (and indeed for avoidance of gaol) on the vagaries of the political censorship. His preoccupation with the perennial danger of being a Russian poet—as George Reavey says, "one need only mention the tragic fates that befell Pushkin, Lermontov, Blok, Gumilev, Yesenin, Mayekovsky, Mandelshtam and Tsvetayeva"—makes him advance with forced assurance, very carefully *not* looking over his shoulder. And although demanding the freedom to be a poet and an individual he insists on his "hard, proud faith in the Revolution" and on his hatred of those who have betrayed it—especially of Stalin, because Yevtushenko's poetic life began after Stalin's death and posthumous disgrace and the stigma thereupon attached to the personality cult. He also proclaims his nationalistic pride in Russian space travel, and attacks his fellow-citizens for not reaching above mediocrity in the true spirit of the Revolution.

Here is a seemingly dangerous poem:

> The twentieth century has often fooled us.
> We've been squeezed in by falsehood as by taxes.
> The breath of life has denuded our ideas
> As quickly as it strips a dandelion.
>
> As boys fall back on biting sarcasm,
> So we rely for our trusty armour
> On an irony not too unobtrusive,
> Not too naked either.
>
> It has served as a wall or dam
> To shield us against a flood of lies,
> And hands have laughed as they applauded,
> And feet sniggered as they marched.
>
> They could write about us, and we've allowed them
> To make movies of this scribbled trash,
> But we have reserved the right
> To treat all this with quiet irony.
>
> In our contempt we felt superior,
> All this is so, but probing deeper,
> Irony, instead of acting as our saviour,
> You have become our murderer.
>
> We're cautious, hypocritical in love.
> Our friendships are lukewarm, not brave,
> And our present seems no different from
> Our past, so cunningly disguised.
>
> Through life we scurry. In history,
> Like any Faust, we've been pre-judged.
> With Mephistophelian smile, irony,
> Like a shadow, dogs our every step.

In vain we try to dodge the shadow,
The paths in front, behind, are blocked.
Irony, to you we've sold our soul,
Receiving no Gretchen in return.

You have buried us alive.
Bitter knowledge has made us powerless,
And our weary irony
Has turned against ourselves.

However, be not deceived! This poem is written not about himself
and his contemporaries in Moscow but about the *littérateurs* of New
York City; and purports to prove that he has not been fooled by the
crude materialistic comforts of Capitalism. Here is another poem:

THE AMERICAN NIGHTINGALE

In the land of perlon and dacron
And of science that has become a fetish,
I suddenly heard a kindred, kindred sound—
A sound quite inimitable and pure.
A branch can easily bear a bird,
And on one of those branches
This American nightingale was perched,
Singing just like a Russian nightingale.
Mournfully he sang, and happily,
And someone stormily unleashed
Flashes of lilac clusters in reply—
This earth's awakening joy.
This was in Harvard in the spring.
There everything was topsy-turvy—
In laughing Harvard's merry-go-round,
Swaying drunkenly after the exams,
The students sang, out on a spree
And to their foundations all things
Seemed mixed in a rainbow cocktail
Of students, birds and flowers.
Proudly, unfailingly, that nightingale—

That so kindred nightingale—thundered
Above the half-truths and the lies,
Above all the restless chatter,
Above all the black deeds,
Above the millions of questionnaires
And the shark-like bodies
Waiting for rockets to spring into action.
And somewhere in the heart of Russia
The same sort of little scamp,
Restively opening his small beak,
His little Russian brother sang
In Tambov, Harvard, and Miami,
For the delight of villages and cities
The branches in all the gardens bent
Beneath the nightingales in ecstasy.
The music, like a blizzard, lashed
One continent and then another . . .
All nightingales will understand each other,
Everywhere they speak one language.
In their tremulous union,
They sing ever higher, more tenderly.
But we men, shall we never
Understand each other?

My contention has long been that facts are not truth, though facts may challenge truth. To assert that the Sheldonian Theatre lies opposite St. John's College in the Cornmarket, and to base some mystical argument on this geographical affinity, would be untruthful. It detracts from my pleasure in Keats's sonnet "On First looking into Chapman's Homer," not that Homer had been denied to Keats in the original Greek, but that he used a metaphor of stout Cortés gazing on the Pacific Ocean, silent upon a peak in Darien—when Pisarro's lieutenant Balboa, not Cortés, was the first European to see the Pacific. Does it matter? It does to me, because the original very humorous account of this occasion should have fixed the name in Keats's mind: he is using secondary, not primary, sources. So with Yevtushenko's ornithology. It is true that the Eastern European nightingale sings as far north as Tambov; whereas the Virginia nightingale (it only winters in Virginia), never reaches Massachusetts, except as a cage bird. Anyhow, this Virginia nightingale is a grosbeak, not a nightingale, as can be observed from its entirely different plumage and song. There are in fact *no* true American nightingales, nor do grosbeaks and nightingales confabulate amicably. Moreover, true nightingales are choosy birds: the West European variety avoids Ireland and Brittany, though visiting all other parts of France and the British Isles.

A nightingale does not naturally seek out other nightingales: its song, like the robin's, being a claim to rule a certain territory. Nor is Yevtushenko's "Nightingales of the World Unite" cry a poetic one. Nor are poets members of a football team—Yevtushenko made a great reputation on the football field—to address as "brothers" and urge goalwards under the coloured jerseys of Walt Whitman or Pushkin. He is puzzled by his fellow-poets, the angry young men of America, who rebel against the twentieth century, the great age of the sputnik. What they want, he says, he doesn't understand. He speaks to them bluntly, a fellow-poet just arrived from Moscow, as man to man, harbouring no wretched disbelief but loud in love for his country, battling in her ranks. *Their* eyes, he says, shine with contempt for the age, they despise political parties, governments and philosophizing seers. The twentieth century is not a father to them, but a mere stepfather.

It is true enough that most run-of-the-mill poets in America feel obliged to choose between academicism and revolt; but when Yevtushenko summons the great Twentieth Century with its triumphal sputnik to pluck them out of their dark confusions, he is speaking as a politican, not a poet. Russian academicism is the direct result of the Russian Revolution and out-academicizes any Western academicism because more carefully controlled by the Party. There can be no revolt in Russia because the Revolution was the revolt to end all revolts; and Yevtushenko does not feel entitled to criticize his country except by saying that it has not lived up to the standards it has set itself; he cannot openly quarrel with the standards.

One of his first errors was to write a poem called *Babi-Yar* about the wartime massacre by Germans, in Russia, of ninety-six thousand Jews. It made Yevtushenko suspect of accusing the Party of anti-

Semitism: he had singled out the massacred Jews and it was complained that this would create the impression of their having been the sole victims of Fascist oppression. He was eventually forced, by the embarrassing interruption of his reading with enthusiastic cries of "Babi-Yar, Babi-Yar," to insert a few lines telling how a Ukranian woman had lost her life in trying to save a Jewish child. That put him right with the Party, but it was a warning which he has ever since been obliged to regard.

The most politically dangerous side to Yevtushenko's poem-writing and dramatic readings is that it encourages a personality cult of poets—something that has always set the democratic Russians against them—a danger that a football team, or a local soviet, or an orchestra, or a *corps-de-ballet* can disregard because their leading performers are dependent on others for their success. That a poem is a single poet's work, and recognizable as his alone, has its obvious disadvantages. In theory all men should be equally talented, especially the proletariat, without any nonsense about genetics. Yet the poet cannot remain anonymous unless the poem is composed on ballad lines for communal singing among close friends and constantly added to, or altered, by these and their successors.

Yevtushenko can best be understood from a record of his recitations, which are theatrical triumphs. All the organ-stops, growls, yells, groans, whispers, sneers are used with what used to be called "rabble-raising eloquence." Either the listener must allow himself to be enchanted, or he must fight the enchantment; the Illinois poet Vachel Lindsay used much the same technique; so did Dylan Thomas the Welshman.

Trained actors read poems in the style taught them by elocution teachers. Not a syllable is lost. Every word is made to tell. . . . Personally, I cannot stand it. I suppose because I know that the truer the poem, the more it loses from being recited in a trained voice to a large audience. As with a folk-song, or an Elizabethan love-song played on a lute, the smaller and more intimate its audience the better.

Recently in New York I recorded poems for a long-playing disc. The other four or five records I had made elsewhere sounded all wrong, as if I were reciting the poems to an auditorium of ten thousand listeners; the theatrical falseness was obvious. So now I went to the studios without a collar or tie, kicked off my shoes, called for a Scotch-and-soda, and shooed everyone out of the studio except my three closest New York friends—two painters and a composer, whom I had brought with me. I talked the poems to them in the ordinary voice I use when something really interests me, having asked them to raise a finger whenever a wrong note crept in—so that I could at once say "Cut!" and read the poem again. The studio officials were behind glass; I paid no attention to them. As a result the poems sounded very much as they had sounded in my head while I was composing them.

The principle is important. In ancient days a group-spirit created by common interests of work, defence, kinship, habitat, and sharing of natural resources allowed one to declaim a poem to a gathering of two or three hundred people and be accepted by every heart. It may still be possible to do this in a few anthropological backwaters of Africa and Oceania. Everywhere else, except for rare cases of common disaster or danger, the natural group-spirit has disappeared, and a false one has been created as a convenience for government either by a despot or by a cult priesthood.

Such priesthoods are not necessarily religious: indeed, Marxism, although patriarchal in spirit, is avowedly atheistical. And the dominant Western Mammon cult which is equally patriarchal but has tried to absorb religion in its system, wars against the Marxist priesthood with the utmost bitterness. Both have enlisted mechanarchic help to further their control of the masses and to break down all local attachments of a superstitious nature. For Marxists, what really matters in theory is that workers should work in unison for their common benefit; for the Mammonists, all that matters in theory is that the consumer should consume more and more, and the producer should produce more and more. In both cases, the priesthood, like the tribe of Levi in Israel, are financially supported by the masses, and claim rights of ideological decision denied to them. This is a closer analogy than appears at first sight: the Levite priesthood under the Alexandrian-Greek House of Boethus, which had collaborated with the Romans to keep the Palestinian Jews quiet and hard at work, contained a group of millionaires.

There is, however, a certain difference between Marxists and Mammonists in their attitude to poetry, music and the arts. Marxism has got tied up with social realism, which means that because the arch-enemy Mammon exploits the workers and grinds their faces, one must concentrate attention in art and literature exclusively on this simple phenomenon; whereas Mammon has got tied up with religion, which means that the glories of this world must be despised in favour of those promised in the world to come—so long as the producer produces whatever the consumer can be persuaded to consume, and so long as the market remains scientifically controlled. Nevertheless a producer who can sell his poetry, paintings, sculpture or music to the consumer, whatever their quality or ideology, is not discouraged. That some of these goods are not only irreligious but unscientifically produced, mostly by hand, and show a marked difference from the products of factories, makes their value a variable element which few financial experts can assess. The very rich get fun from forcing up the price of these products, and inviting the producer to their salons.

A poet is often tempted to become a "do-gooder" by organizing political interference with the mechanarchy, rather than by giving a personal example of how to be oneself and not a conditioned human machine. He can have a certain foreknowledge of eventual miracle; and, for a poet, what will be, is.

Concentration on force of circumstances has distracted me, for the last few minutes, from talking about poetry. I should have kept off the subject of literary concerts and Marx and Mammon and dwelt, rather, on poetic love. It happens in country places, and even in towns, that a boy and his girl have never had eyes for any but each other; they court and marry and are one for the rest of their lives. It is different with poets, who fall wholeheartedly in love, suffer every agony by love's souring, find themselves alone again, catch at partial love, throw it off, and again give their whole hearts—this time, they swear, for ever. What went before was doubtless true love, and though it has been superseded in time, they still have fragrant memories of it, or a sad sense of having been at fault, and still treasure tokens of its nobility. If it had not been for these earlier loves they would not be their new, informed, wide-eyed, still innocent, still passionate selves, constantly enlarged in sensibility. And unless this is understood by both partners in a final love bond, with unjealousy shared and then viewed as growing pains of an understanding so close that it illuminates the whole world . . .

But there is no "unless" for poets.

Circumstances oppress and threaten, but lack poetic reality. Lovers should never plan, which means to consider the result if a conjectural course is taken; for conjecture has no part in love. Every practical question should be settled by instinctive action when the time comes. Talk between lovers should be signals of common awareness; with an implied blessing of all the loves that each has had before, leading to this culmination.

A Lost World

"Dear love, why should you weep
    For time's remorseless way?
Though today die in sleep
    And be called yesterday,
    We love, we stay."

"I weep for days that died
    With former love that shone
On a world true and wide
    Before this newer one
    Which yours shines on."

"Is this world not as true
    As that one ever was
Which now has fled from you
    Like shadows from the grass
    When the clouds pass?"

"Yet for that would I weep
    Kindly, before we kiss:
Love has a faith to keep
    With past felicities
    That weep for this."

It is usual to talk of the male and female principles as being present together with varying proportions in most people. I find this physiologically confusing, though indeed natural *baeddels* (from which Anglo-Saxon noun the adjective "bad" is derived) are often born: effeminate men, mannish women, cocks in hen's plumage, hermaphrodites. It is easier to think of the situation in terms of Sun and Moon. The Sun in the Western world has been for some three millennia associated with man as the King, from whom the Moon, his Queen, borrows a dim and secretive light. The White Goddess about whom I have so often written rules the Underworld and the Sea, but is also a Moon Goddess; and in this context the poet has been a Sun Hero ever since the Heroic Age. Yet Eastern, and even Western, mythology also allows for love between a Sun Goddess and a Moon hero. It may be that the great mechanarchic catastrophe for which we are waiting, now that all moral values and religious concepts are being turned upside down, will involve a poetic change from Woman as Moon—you will remember the famous Egyptian stele of Akhenaton as the transcendental Sun-God and Nefertiti as his Moon Goddess—to woman as Sun. In extreme cases of poetic love, even where the poet is Sun-like in his maleness and heroic pride, while the Muse-woman appears to be wholly ruled by the Moon, an interchange of planetary influences may be observed. The incarnate Muse will borrow the poet's Sun; the poet will borrow her Moon. When the Unicorn (who began as a metaphor of the Sun's course through the five 72-day Egyptian seasons) lays his horned head on the lap of the pure Moon-Virgin, their spirits are united. I have mentioned the impossibility of reconciling Solar and Lunar time; yet it is mythologically recorded that the Sun-Goddess Grainne and her lover the Moon-hero Diarmuid bedded together every evening of the year during their flight across Ireland.

THE BEDS OF GRAINNE AND DIARMUID

How many secret nooks in copse or glen
We sained for ever with our pure embraces,

No man shall know; though indeed master poets
Reckon one such for every eve of the year,
To sain their calendar.
                   But this much is true:
That children stumbling on our lairs by chance
In quest of hazel-nuts or whortleberries
Will recognize an impress of twin bodies
On the blue-green turf starred with diversity
Of alien flowers, and shout astonishment.
Yet should some amorous country pair, presuming
To bask in joy on any bed of ours,
Offend against the love by us exampled,
Long ivy roots will writhe up from beneath
And bitterly fetter ankle, wrist and throat.

Ecstasy

With this lecture I complete the active duties of my five-year Professorship here. I shall never know whether the University has regretted its vote; but at least I have not regretted it. You may be unaware that the salary, once irrecoverable income tax and forced benevolences to the University Chest have been deducted at source, and my return fare from Mallorca and a term's living expenses have been paid, amounts to an impressive minus figure, each lecture costing me around £150.

I am grateful for being thus acquitted of having mercenary ends; and even more grateful for the licence to say whatever comes into my mind so long as I avoid obscenity, blasphemy or provocations to breaches of the peace. I have been responsible to each successive Vice-Chancellor alone—of whom none was ever ungentlemanly enough to utter a word of reproof.* I would always rather be a Court Fool than a Laureate.

* "Graves delivered a lecture on Virgil that outraged even people who didn't know anything about Virgil"—*Observer*, 6 February 1966. This comment on a 1961 lecture is not quite fair; when I submitted it to a couple of Classical dons for historical inaccuracies they gave it a clean bill of health.

One or two general comments. The historical study of Art enfeebles art. The historical study of Economics destroys the intimate magic of money. The historical study of Science confirms its degradation from an original Humanity, compatible with painting, poetry and medicine, into a mechanarchic process. It has suffered a series of apoplectic strokes: the first in Hellenistic times, the second stroke in the thirteenth century, the final stroke at the close of the nineteenth. There may be a few starry-eyed young scientists still around who belong anachronistically to earlier human epochs; just as there are still a few starry-eyed soldiers, despite similar degradations of honourable warfare at these same turning-points.

As for the historical study of poetry—the first volume of Warton's *History of English Poetry,* based on a scribbled programme of Alexander Pope's, was published in 1774. Pope had arranged his design in "eras," each era marked by new subsections beginning "School of. . . ." Warton's book and its successors, culminating in Courthope's *History of English Poetry,* first published in 1895, one sinister chapter of which is headed "Development of the Ethical School of Pope," have all but brought about the end of Poetry. There can, of course, be no real History of Poetry, as there can be no real schools of poetry; there are only occasional poets and poems, with swarms of imitators. Even the official *Lives and Letters* of individual poets, as distinct from the history of fashions in prosody, diction and subject, tell us little about poetry itself. The present dearth of poets throughout the Western World, but especially in the United States, is due in part to the notion that poetry can be the object of academic study and thus to the inclusion even of contemporary poems in University curricula.

Last year I discussed craftsmanship in poems; because poetry presupposes, at the very least, an intuitive understanding of how to control the reader's attention and direct his inner ear and inner eye along an intended route. This power of direction is a craft which can be learned only by writing. Poetry itself begins where craftsmanship ends; and while trying, last year, to persuade you just how certain well-known anthology pieces broke down in craftsmanship I observed that it was always easier to say why a poem is *no good* than why it is *good.*

I lived in a so-called war-zone in Devonshire throughout the Second World War, and spent a lot of my time looking at Red Devon cows on a country neighbour's farm; because there wasn't much else on the move except soldiers. I got the knack of judging a good milker and confirmed it on a visit to an Exeter cattle show, with an expert beside me. Not that I ever milked a cow in my life, but I had observed the sort of Red Devon that proved a good milker and learned to recognize something about the shape and gait and build that all Red Devon good milkers had in common. I put this knowledge to no commercial use; but it fascinated me. The same with soldiers. I had rented a farmhouse near Dartmouth and one day I called excitedly to my wife who was busy in the nursery: "Darling, look, *soldiers!*" She said rather crossly: "What do you mean *soldiers?*—they go past all the time."

I repeated: "Look, *soldiers!*"

I had learned in World War One to recognize real soldiers. And here real soldiers were marching past the house. A whole platoon of the first Commando Battalion—picked men from different regiments, three or four of them, I was glad to note, wearing the flash and grenade of my own regiment, the Royal Welch Fusiliers. No mistaking them. Real soldiers!

So with real poets. . . . What I have been telling you for the last five years amounts to this: that poetry—even *Beowulf*—is not a department of literature as studied in the English School, but a way of being and thinking: as it were the power of walking down a familiar corridor and suddenly disappearing through a stone wall at the end. A power given to few; and sceptically viewed by the academic intellectual mass, whose experts say in an off-hand way: "Yes, of course, it is all done with mirrors. . . ."

In a way they are right. About a year ago my friend James Metcalfe, the sculptor, happened to be turning over the pages of a scientific book on mirrors: he wanted to find out whether the concentrated rays of sun from large curved mirrors could have been used by ancient metallurgists for fusing obdurate metals. Suddenly his eyes opened wide at a small diagram and he gasped: "My God, it was all done with mirrors!"

"What was?" we asked.

"All those fantastically complicated Celtic mirror-back designs. About forty of them from the first century B.C. to the first century A.D. All from the British Isles except a single, rather earlier one, from Paris. Art-historians try to explain them away as an imaginative development of the acanthus motif. . . ."

He hurried off to an observatory, where he borrowed a set of small convex steel mirrors for experimental purposes, and later had a few more forged and polished. The intricate pattern on those Celtic mirror-backs, every one of which he succeeded in reproducing, proved to be interlinked images of several round mirrors set at different angles to one another, as reflected on the last of the series.

This is a close enough metaphor for Poetry. The source of light strikes the first mirror, which is that of immediate sensuous perception; the image is reflected in a second mirror, a more epicritic one: and if one accepts the view that every person has various degrees of consciousness, corresponding to the Classical seven degrees of hypnosis, into which the poet's mind descends during the composition of a Muse poem, it is fair to say that the extraordinary complex patterns of such a poem are eventually derived from the first pure illumination of the poet's mirror. It is the *angle* at which the mirrors are set that determines the final result.

My own ineradicable view of poets, as opposed to dramatic or literary show artists, is that one cannot separate them from their work: a flaw in character will always reveal itself as a flaw in poetic craft. And the self-satisfaction derived from joining any society, cult or movement, whose laws they consent to adopt, will prevent them from insulating their work against the corrosion of dogma or convention—against deadness of soul. A poet need not be a rebel. . . . He must admit his place in the society into which he was born, while tacitly criticizing it by unrebellious but self-assured abstention from routine thinking or acting; and he must keep all his seven mirrors brightly polished.

What I like most about this University is the extraordinary freedom it allows anyone who does not abuse the right to be himself or herself, and think accordingly—so long as he or she reads the set books and causes no breach of the peace. I cannot think that the least blame attaches to University College for having sent Percy Bysshe Shelley down. The charge was not atheism but bad manners. Shelley had every right to be an atheist; and he had every right to send his *Necessity of Atheism* pamphlet around to bishops and others, so long as he kept Oxford out of his personal quarrel with the Church. But he had no right, once his authorship and University status became known, to treat the Master and Fellows or University College with contumacity, declining again and again to admit authorship.

I have been suspected, by some, of academic bad manners in suggesting that Virgil, Milton, and Wordsworth, despite the enormous respect still paid them by traditionalists, frequently departed from poetic principle. This accusation has never been brought home: I suppose because I took the advice given me in 1921 by Colonel T. E. Lawrence when he was a fellow of All Souls' and I an undergraduate of St. John's; I used to visit his rooms almost daily. He reminded me that resounding invectives by young men against sacrosanct literary idols are always construed as jealousy or spite. The only effective way to rock their pedestals, he said, was by quoting pejorative textual and domestic details—the smaller and more particular the better—which would suggest that, though idols, they were not the sort of men whom one would invite to breakfast in one's rooms or trust with one's cat while away on holiday. By the way: I regret the desuetude which has overtaken that ancient Oxford breakfast ceremony. In my undergraduate days we felt no tension of time and routine, and came to Oxford for education by private talk, and by games—mostly by talk. Examination schools had to be respected eventually, but one learned more wisdom at College breakfast in one's rooms than on any other occasion. At St. John's, and most other colleges, it is no longer allowed. As I was saying, T. E. Lawrence held that, for instance, the best way to break a general's military reputation was to observe and comment on his behaviour in the hunting field. So with Shelley and Pope: I have pointed out that neither could control his s's—which is a critical *meiosis* of mine.

It is commonplace of criticism to deny that a poet can exist without an audience. The word "audience"—and a poet must always be extremely sensitive to the original meaning, or meanings, of the words he uses—implies a reading aloud. And although every poem should be suited for reading aloud, with full value given to every sound, pause and rhythmic idiosyncrasy—as prose need not be, because the *inner ear* to which poems are addressed is quasi-dormant in prose—a poem read silently in private yields far more of its magic truth than a poem read in a concert hall.

Perhaps the most startling difference between the world into which I was born and the world developed by the Welfare State, is that private living has been slowly put out of fashion by public, or pop, living. In modern pop living, everyone streams through everyone else's house without formal invitation, borrows what he needs and does not return it; and nobody seems to mind—I suppose because all property is now considered expendable, and solitude is identified with lonesomeness. The silent reading of poetry, which requires a high degree of private insulation, forms no part of pop life.

In the first quarter of this century, our half-starved under-privileged classes were fighting under the Socialist banner for freedom to enjoy a full life—released from the wicked Tory landlord and the wicked Capitalist. They won that fight, with the help of concessions forced from Parliament by their services in two World Wars; and most young English poets identified themselves with the cause. That fight need never, perhaps, be fought again. The laurels of victory are pop living and Telly land; and pop art and pop music and pop poetry; and "Boy, you have never had it so good."

The connection between pop art and pop poetry is a close one. In modern art-schools, one observes little lack of talent among the students, only lack of purpose. No one, or practically no one, has any fixed beliefs: except that all traditions must be broken because they hamper freedom of expression, and that what is brand-new must necessarily be good while it lasts. The whole corpus of art from Aurignacian cave-painting to Picasso is now finally "out" (or perhaps Picasso is finally "in" again, for non-artistic reasons—I must ask my contacts) and thrown into the trash-bucket or refuse bin. There are no standards left: standards collapsed when non-figurative expressionism helped the art dealers to impose fictitious values on whatever wares they could buy cheaply, sell dearly, and the output of which they could control. In my young days, painting standards were fixed: a trained ability to handle one's brushes competently and produce a picture that reflected visible nature. By the Forties,

Nature had gone out; the inner recesses of the soul took her place. Revelations of these tended to be dull, one soul recess being very much like another—as you may also say about coal-cellars—and soon a non-figurative academicism appeared: it became unnecessary to judge between soul recesses. To brisk things up, however, painters resorted to shocking the public with stark sexual imagery, or making them laugh with *trompe-l'oeil* tricks and irrelevant juxtapositions of irrelevant objects. A further stage was reached when psychodelic drugs provided all the intricate patterns and convolutions of negative ecstasy, and still another was reached when the long-standing artistic protest against commercial art carried to a fine point of sales-persuasion, was dropped; and everyone said: "Why be snobs? Commercial art has pop appeal. We are people too. Why not use commercial techniques and play the fool with them?"

This they did. But that all the different new movements were equally academic could be judged by the way that students dressed. If a couple of seniors chose to wear white canvas shoes enlivened by bright yellow soles and heels, everyone else wore the same before the week was out; and similarly with hair-styles, scarves and waistcoats. Lectures on perspective ceased to be compulsory.

To be in the gaudy forefront of fashion, to *out-zeitgeist* the *zeitgeist* is the pop artist's whole intent, to express himself in terms of the latest possible movement, to bicker with rivals and allies. Never to find out what he really is—individualism has become a snobbery— or what are his capacities and limitations and personal illusions; but to throw reckless parties and excite a communal spirit with which to identify himself. Often lonely figures teach themselves a craft, to beat out something that excites admiration and imitation and can be used as a pointer for still another movement. The saddest cases are artists who begin with a small genuine individual craft, but, enraged by imitators, decide to start a new, theatrical gimmicky style, instead of perfecting the genuine one by an inclusion of all deeper or darker sides of their nature, hitherto concealed, to the point at which it can no longer be imitated.

The same phenomenon appears among poets. W. B. Yeats, a careful craftsman, who began with strong poetic principles, was later seduced into a period of grandiose literary showmanship. I find the later, strutting Senator Yeats a pathetic, rather than a commanding, figure.

Poetry readings to mass audiences, as popularized in Russia, are now being imitated in the Western world. The pop poetry-reading, or "literary concert," has even reached England, where the Albert Hall was recently hired for a performance of Beat poets, and filled by the same sort of audience that goes hysterical over the Beatles, the Rolling Stones, the Animals and other pop singing groups.

The poems declaimed at the Albert Hall were, I am told, deliberate acts of rebellion against the rules or principles that control written verse. A great deal of their emotional force lay in the microphonic explosion of banned four-letter words to shock the Squares, and in the exploitation of "significant sound," namely the confused tense battling noises of the street, bar and brothel. A modern pop poet is an actor before anything else, and the character of his performances cannot possibly be conveyed in print. Even a tape-recording is inadequate; a small live manikin is needed, to posture and shout and be sold with every copy. In short, ultra-modern poetry is either trailed at the chariot-tail of art and philosophy, or becomes an accessory of pop music. Few pop poets think beyond the immediate demand for kicks—and the wilder and less coherent the improvisation, the easier it is to put over. Much of it is written under the influence of marihuana, alias "pot."

I have nothing much to say against "pot," except that, having been made illegal in nearly every country in the world, it gives the police a splendid chance of winning promotion by planting packets of it on people they dislike for other reasons. It is far less harmful than hard liquor—here in England we have reached the point where, it is claimed, certified alcoholics and mental cases with an alcoholic history, outnumber regular Church communicants. In fact, doctors have so far been unable to prove that "pot" causes either addiction or the lung cancer attributed to cigarette-smoking. Nevertheless, its sale is illegal. "Pot" has therefore to be steered clear of, although the passing of a reefer around a group of friends is almost invariably soothing and harmonious in its effects: whereas one cannot say the same about a bottle of gin. Too often the bottle of gin is used to enhance the effects of pot-sodality—a nice

Irish word, "sodality"—and, often, more than a single bottle. More-over, though occasionally beneficial in its effects—and I suspect that the famous pipe of peace smoked at tribal and inter-tribal meetings by North American indians was not merely leaf-tobacco but con-tained "pot" or some similar weed, in addition to tobacco stalk—"pot" is not creative; in fact, it is the very opposite. A friend of mine had the curiosity once to tape-record his apparently inspired declamations during a "pot" session after the reefer had gone around several times and the gin bottle had been emptied. Played back, they sounded almost as nonsensical as the seemingly won-derful poems that one composes in dream. He decided never to get high again. But the most cogent argument against pot is that it makes the smoker vulnerable to suggestion, and that not only lecherous wolves but pushers of "hard" addiction drugs, such as heroin, use it to further their nefarious ends.

The effects of such mild psychodelic drugs as psilocybin are dif-ferent. My own view is that a single "trip" under psilocybin, the toxic derivation of a Mexican mushroom, can under proper medical control be most informative. It provides an extraordinary interrela-tion of the senses of sound, colour and form; and reveals in pictorial imagery the hidden terrors and aspirations of the patient's mind. Yet such drugs should be taken not only after careful assurance of their chemical purity—which is always doubtful unless they come from a licensed physician—but in a state of grace, which is a state of love; otherwise the mind may find itself left naked and lost, out of touch with native circumstances, and frequently suicidal.

An American Protestant priest decided last year to choose a group of young ordinands from a theological seminary, and divide them into two groups, for control purposes, one of these being given L.S.D. early on Good Friday, when they should be in the necessary state of grace for such an experience; and the other given merely a sugar *placebo*. The idea was that the L.S.D. group should get mystical visions, which might be denied to the others, and so understand the language of the great Christian mystics. I never heard what the results were. But L.S.D. has a base of ergot, the enemy of mankind, and can cause lasting damage to the brain and also genetic malfunctions.

Yet the Sufi sages are right: though an ecstatic trance may be induced by purging the mind of all worldly preoccupations through the controlled whirling of the traditional Dervish dances, and by other quieter means, such as over-breathing, they attach no particular value to ecstasy. What matters is the use made of the mind thus purged. They give more importance to active love of one's fellow-creatures than to mystical union with God—a principle anticipated by the Jewish sage Hillel, an elder contemporary of Jesus, who said that "Thou shalt love thy neighbour as thyself" was a more important Torah text than: "Thou shalt love the Lord thy God with all thy heart and soul and strength."

Ecstasy, whether produced by austere religious self-discipline or by psychodelic intoxication, immobilizes the mind; the perceptive senses of eye, ear and touch take over and the spirit detachedly examines a self displayed in complex coloured images. If one is in a state of grace, which means bound by a poetic vow of love, to whoever or whatever it may be, the spirit will enter into the clarity of its destined paradise. But an ecstasy of horror awaits spirits not integrated, spirits not vowed to love, where all is pure confusion: the patient may be utterly appalled by the experience and even seem to be dying.

> What if my Cerberus, the mind, should be
> Flung to earth by the very opiate
> That frees my senses for undared adventure,
> Waving them wild-eyed past me to explore
> Limitless hells of disintegrity—
> Jumbled, undifferentiable fate
> Scrolled out beyond the utter rim of nowhere,
> Scrolled out. . . .
>   who on return fail to surrender
> Their memory-trophies: random wisps of horror
> Trailed from my shins or tangled in my hair?

Ecstasy's sole justification is a journey to a larger, unsuspected region of perception: from which the mind returns informed and able to act.

When the immense drugged universe explodes
In a cascade of unendurable colour
And leaves us gasping naked,
This is no more than ecstasy of chaos:
Hold fast, with both hands, to the royal vow
Which alone, as we know truly, can restore
Fragmentation into true being.

So we come to love ecstasy. At its purely physical level, one expects no more than a sense of ease, euphoria, steady affection; but when the physical attraction between lovers has reached its secondary and tertiary stages, so that ecstasy is attained by a mere interlocking of fingers, or even by sitting opposite each other in the same room, the result is a miraculous conjunction of souls, a foretaste of wisdom, a power communicable to all who become aware of this bond. Donne has written about this is his *Ecstasie*.

Where, like a pillow on a bed,
    A pregnant banke swel'd up, to rest
The violets reclining head,
    Sat we two, one another's best.
Our hands were firmly cimented
    With a fast balme, which thence did spring,
Our eye-beames twisted, and did thred
    Our eyes, upon one double string;
So t'entergraft our hands, as yet
    Was all the meanes to make us one,
And pictures in our eyes to get
    Was all our propagation.
As 'twixt two equall Armies, Fate
    Suspends uncertaine victorie,
Our soules, (which to advance their state,
    Were gone out,) hung 'twixt her, and mee.
And whil'st our soules negotiate there,
    Wee like sepulchrall statues lay;
All day, the same our postures were,
    And wee said nothing, all the day.
If any, so by love refin'd

That he Soule's language understood,
And by good love were grown all mine,
    Within convenient distance stood,
He (though he knew not which soul spake,
    Because both meant, both spake the same)
Might thence a new concoction take,
    And part farre purer than he came.
This Extasie doth unperplex,
    We said, and tell us what we love,
Wee see by this, it was not sexe,
    Wee see, wee saw not what did move:
But as all severall soules containe
    Mixture of things, they know not what,
Love, these mixt soules, doth mixe againe,
    And makes both one, each this and that.
A single violet transplant,
    The strength, the colour and the size,
(All which before was poore, and scant,)
    Redoubles still, and multiplies.
When love with one another so
    Interinanimates two soules,
That abler soule, which thence doth flow,
    Defects of lonelinesse controules.
Wee then, who are this new soule, know
    Of what we are composed and made
For, th'Atomies of which we grow,
    Are soules, whom no change can invade.
But aye alas, so long, so farre
    Our bodies why doe wee forbeare?
They are ours, though they are not wee, Wee are
    The intelligences, they the spheares.
We owe them thankes, because they thus,
    Did us, to us, at first convay,
Yielded their forces, sense, to us,
    Nor are drosse to us, but allay.
On man, heaven's influence workes not so,
    But that it first imprints the ayre,
Soe soule into the soule may flow,
    Though it to body first repaire.

As our blood labours to beget
   Spirits, as like soules as it can,
Because such fingers need to knit
   That subtile knot, which makes us man:
So must pure lovers' soules descend
   T'affection, and to faculties,
Which sense may reach and apprehend,
   Else a great Prince in prison lies.
To our bodies turne wee then, that so
   Weake men on love reveal'd may looke,
Love's mysteries in soules doe grow,
   But yet the body is his booke.
And if some lover, such as wee,
   Have heard this dialogue of one,
Let him still marke us, he shall see
   Small change, when we're to bodies gone.

And Rumi, the Persian poet, has reached a stranger condition when the presence of his beloved is physically felt despite a hundred miles separation.

Happy the moment when we are seated in the palace, thou
   and I,
With two forms and with two bodies but with one soul, thou
   and I.
The colours of the grove and the voice of the birds will bestow
   immortality.
At the time when we come into the garden, thou and I.

The stars of heaven will come to gaze upon us;
We shall show them the moon itself, thou and I.
Thou and I, single no more, shall be conjoined in ecstasy,
Felicitous and secure from foolish converse, thou and I.
All the bright-plumed birds of heaven will devour their hearts
   with envy.
There, where we laugh in such a fashion, thou and I.
This is the greatest wonder, that thou and I, seated together
   here in the same nook . . .
Are at this moment both in Irak and Khorosan, thou and I.

But, as Donne suggests, what matters is the curative use to which the lovers put their minds and hearts that have been purged by ecstasy.

I have not yet mentioned jealousy. Lovers assure each other:

> I'd die for you and you for me,
> So furious is our jealousy,
> And if you doubt this to be true
> Kill me outright, lest I kill you.

Yet jealousy must not be confused with envy. To be jealous is, originally, to be zealous: "The Zeal of Thy House has eaten me up." The Biblical Lord God is a jealous god: he is jealous, or zealous, for the righteousness and wisdom of his people, not envious of demons and false deities. In Spanish, *celoso* still has both senses. Both the poet and his incarnate Muse are jealous or zealous for the maintenance of the miraculous love they share; and on finding that anyone has intervened to cloud that love, either of them will grow murderously jealous for its natural brightness. I do not deny that lovers grow jealous, in the bad sense, of friendships from which they seem excluded; which is an unfortunate inheritance of patrilineal marriage. In matrilineal societies men are not jealous of their wives' friendships with other men of noble character. The celebrated fourteenth-century Moslem traveller, Ibn Batuta of Tangier, visiting the Western Sudan was shocked to discover his host's wife, sitting unveiled on a divan in earnest talk with a male visitor, while the host, one Yandakan, sat on a carpet. Ibn Batuta asked, much scandalized: "And are you, who have lived in Tangier and know our sacred law, content with this?"

Yandakan rebuked Ibn Batuta for his interference, explaining: "The free association of women with men is a good custom when decently carried out. Here it arouses no suspicion, our women not being like those of your country."

Ibn Batuta, deeply offended, never visited the house again. Yandakan's people were matrilineal Berbers; a man's heirs were his sister's sons, not his own. A woman could divorce at will, and always remained undisputed mistress of her property, keeping her own camel brand. A husband was absolutely forbidden to treat his

wife violently, whatever the provocation, and expected to bear humorously with all her caprices: though never tolerating the least
injury or discourtesy from a man. Many of these customs still prevail
among the Berbers on both sides of the Sudan; and seem curiously
apt in the poet-Muse relation.

*

European poets from Ennius onwards have hankered for posthumous fame; a weakness excusable at least in pre-Christian poets
who, unless they belonged to some mystery religion, had no hopes
of a glorious after-world. Few men can imagine the world going
on without them, and most serious ones would therefore like to
achieve something memorable, such as breeding a new rose, building
an almost indestructible castle, beating the world's record for the
quarter-mile, or founding an art museum.

The convenient belief in an afterworld can be so forced on
children that it survives to comfort their old age. Unluckily the
ecclesiastical Christian-Jewish heaven was "frozen" as a dogma at
a time when supreme magnificence and awe were to be found only
in Eastern courts under a supreme monarchy. Angels, messengers,
jewels, harpists; more jewels, more angels, more harpists. No sea,
no streams, no trees, no grass, no beautiful women presiding over
the mead-vat as in the Celtic heaven. Hardly a place to sigh for,
even when peopled mainly by saints, apostles, virgins, prophets,
martyrs—especially if one is a Republican citizen, as most Christians
now are, or subject to a Queen. Not even organ music is allowed
in Heaven; the organ having originally been a secular instrument—
first made famous by that popular virtuoso, the Emperor Nero, and
introduced into churches very late, after much righteous opposition
and scandal.

When any ordinary person exclaims "This is Heaven!", he does
not mean the ecclesiastical Heaven where nothing occurs except
endless harping, endless prostrations before the Throne, and endless
choral singing. He means the garden Paradise of which we are
given a glimpse in Genesis. All Paradises are much the same the
world over, doubtless because induced by the same chemical action
on the brain: a withholding of oxygen encourages the play of

fantasy in coloured images. Paradise can be visited by saints who wear out their bodies through prayer and fasting; by drowning people; by schizophrenes whose corporeal chemistry is not working as it should; or by takers of natural hallucinogenic drugs. I am neither a saint nor a schizophrene, but I have visited Paradise twice. First, when I officially died in battle—though I made no record of the experience apart from a fragmentary reference in a jocose early poem:

> Above me on my stretcher swinging by
> I saw new stars in the subterrene sky:
> A Cross, a Rose in bloom, a Cage with Bars,
> And a barbed arrow feathered in fine stars . . .
> It was Proserpina who sent me back
> Breathless, with leaping heart, along the track.

On the second occasion, which I have described elsewhere, I had taken *psilocybe*; and was afterwards startled to find that the deities in charge of the Paradise that I visited—the appearances of which is authenticated by Mexican legends and words of art—namely Tlalóc and Chalciolithicue, correspond exactly with the Greek God Dionysus and his mother Semele (another name for Proserpine or Persephone). It seems that the ritual eating of the Mexican mushroom had its Greek counterpart in the eating of the divine food *ambrosia* ("not for mortals"), and that the autumnal *Ambrosia*, sacred to Dionysus, were sacramental feasts in which the divine flesh of the bitter mushroom was eaten. Dionysus and Tlalóc—to whom the toad is sacred—were both born from a flash of lightning and their divine characteristics are identical—the alleged eating of infant boys ascribed to both apparently refers to the *hombrecitos* ("little men") as the mushrooms are called in Mexico.

THE AMBROSIA OF DIONYSUS AND SEMELE

> Little slender lad, toad-headed,
> For whom ages and leagues are dice to throw with,

Smile back to where entranced I wander
Gorged with your bitter flesh,
Drunk with your Virgin Mother's lullaby.

Little slender lad, lightning-engendered,
Grand master of magicians:
When pirates stole you at Icaria
Wild ivy gripped their rigging, every oar
Changed to a serpent, panthers held the poop,
A giant vine sprouted from the mast crotch
And overboard they plunged, the whey-faced crew!

Lead us with your song, tall queen of earth!
Twinned to the god, I follow comradely
Through a first rainbow-limbo, webbed in white,
Through chill Tyrrhenian grottoes, under water,
Where dolphins wallow between marble rocks,
Through sword-bright jungles, tangles of unease,
Through halls of fear ceilinged with incubi,
Through blazing treasure-chambers walled with garnet,
Through domes pillared with naked caryatids—
Then mount at last on wings into pure air,
Peering down with regal eye upon
Five-fruited orchards of Elysium,
In perfect knowledge of all knowledges.

And still she drowsily chants
From her invisible bower of stars.
Gentle her voice, her notes come linked together
In intricate golden chains paid out
Slowly across brocaded cramoisy,
Or unfold like leaves from the jade-green shoot
Of a rising bush whose blossoms are her tears . . .
O, whenever she pauses, my heart quails
Until the sound renews.

Little slender lad, little secret god,
Pledge her your faith in me
Who have ambrosia eaten and yet live.

I was never saved from drowning, but many of those who have been saved record that their forcible resuscitation was far more painful than the experience. The result of the lungs being filled with water is that the brain becomes deoxygenated. Sailors have a name for the drowners' paradise, from which few return to tell the tale. It is Fiddler's Green, sometimes called merely "The Green," where they find perpetual dancing, drinking and jollity. According to the *Folk Lore Record* 1881, Cornish sailors describe it as an Isle of the Blest. Kirkby's dictionary of West Yorkshire dialect words places it "ten miles 'tother side of Hell Square"—and I suppose this quotation reflects the difference between a sailor who drowns in a state of grace and one who drowns with a sin-laden conscience. I have written on this subject in a poem:

> Whoever had drowned and awhile entered
> The adamantine gates of afterwards,
> Stands privileged to reject heavenly joy
> (Though without disrespect for God's archangels)
> With "never again"—no moon, no herbs, no sea,
> No singular love of women.
> True joy, believe us, is to groan and wake
> From the merrymakers' rout on Fiddler's Green,
> The lungs now emptied of salt water,
> With gradual heat returning to clammed veins
> In the first flicker of reanimation,
> Repossession of now, awareness
> Of her live hands and lips, her playful voice,
> Her smooth and wingless shoulders.

The phenomenon of Fiddler's Green should interest all atheists across the Iron Curtain who secretly envy Christian priests their power to mould people's characters by persuading them that righteous action in this world earns rewards in Heaven. To offer rewards only in this world has proved insufficient; under organized atheism the absence of any hell-fire threat puts a great burden on the police and their force of spies and stool-pigeons. Atheists ought to adopt the view that except in rare cases, such as a disintegrating explosion, a human being dies slowly by the stoppage of his heart; and that

ECSTASY   593

since the one eternity acceptable to the brain is the very last moment
of consciousness—because the mind cannot consciously put an end
to it—inevitably this same last moment, which one either dreads
or longs for, is the sole endless Heaven or Hell logically conceivable.
And if it be true that, on the point of death (as survivors attest)
a man's past life swims before him, then the total sense of either
triumph or guilt will be then recorded. Therefore, if the dying man
has lived an honest, industrious and co-operative life in the best
interests of his family, community and country, he will experience
Heaven; if not, it will be either a Purgatory or a real Hell.

This sort of eternity has no relation to the eternity with which
some poets credit their poems. Shakespeare writes:

> Devouring Time, blunt thou the lion's paws,
> And make the earth devour her own sweet brood,
> Pluck the keen teeth from the fierce tiger's jaws
> And burn the long-liv'd phoenix in her blood;
> Make glad and sorry seasons as thou fleets,
> And do whate'er thou wilt, swift-footed Time,
> To the wide world and all her fading sweets;
> But I forbid thee one most heinous crime,
> O carve not with thy hours my love's fair brow,
> Now draw no lines there with thine antique pen.
> Him in thy course untainted do allow,
> For beauty's pattern to succeeding men.
>   Yet do thy worst, old Time; despite thy wrong,
>   My love shall in my verse ever live young.

Although this is not a temporal eternity, since English is unlikely
to last many centuries more as a spoken language, the *Sonnets*
are still very much alive. Their main defect is that they give us no
clear picture of the beloved, but only of the lover.

All true poems have, I repeat, a durable quality. Durability need
not be the antonym of temporality. The sole draft of a durable
poem may be burned in an accidental blaze or torn up by mistake;
and although the *Sonnets* happen to have survived, so also has
The Lover's Complaint, which was bound up with them and is

surely one of the least durable of minor Elizabethan poems, though
written by Shakespeare. It begins:

> From off a hill whose concave womb re-worded
> A plaintive story from a sistering vale,
> My spirits t'attend this double voice accorded,
> And down I laid to list the sad tun'd tale;
> Ere long espied a fickle maid full pale,
> Tearing of papers, breaking rings atwain,
> Storming her world with sorrow's wind and rain.

I use "durable" in the sense that one may buy a durable pair
of gardening boots, or a pair of whipcord trousers, or plant a yew
tree. A durable poem is like a durable picture. When one buys
or is given a picture to hang in the living room, one gradually
grows to dislike or despise it for some obtrusive alien quality, at
first unnoticed, which at last becomes unbearable, and the picture
has to be taken down. Or else it gradually fades away as a picture
until one ceases to be aware of its colour or subject, and only a
sudden unfaded patch on the wall-paper will recall its former existence. Or else it lives and lasts and welcomes one with the smile
of a friend, and becomes a central fact of domestic life.

The qualities that make a poem durable are no mystery. If a
practising poet revives the canon of his poem every few years,
passages of time will help him to recognize the derivative, the
over-clever, the flawed, the repetitious, the didactic, the irrelevant.
Durability implies that a poem was written for the right reasons, at
the right time, and in the right state of mind. I mean that a poem
had been forming unprompted in his imagination; that the time
came when its nucleus suddenly appeared—the nucleus that pre-
determines the whole; and that he then fell into a trance that
gave him full control on his faculties: that he did not view the
poem as literature or as a saleable commodity, but as self-illumination.
The poet alone knows how far any particular poem has obeyed
these creative principles; indeed, the sole limitation he can put on
the rejection of old work is the awareness that no perfect poem
has ever been, or ever will be, written. To suppress his whole
canon would mean inviting the old-clothes-men of literature to re-

publish the bad along with the good, the durable with the impermanent, in ignorant selections of their own.

It is an act of social politeness to make one's will, because of the family's trouble in dealing with certain sentimental relics. It is equally polite for a poet to cut his canon down to a reasonable size. If all his predecessors had shown decent testamentary politeness, the required reading-list of the Oxford English School would be wholesomely curtailed. After all, what the student should know about is the poems themselves, not movements or fashions in style.

I cannot honestly deny an interest in the survival of my poems, but this does not imply a quasi-continuance of my life. I reject the state-supported Judaeo-Christian afterworld and even the humaner paradise in which the Irish Master-poets so firmly believed that they would lend money, without interest, for repayment when debtor and borrower met again beside the heavenly mead-vat. Or did they believe? Was this perhaps merely a courteous way of giving a colleague what he could not hope to repay, while saving him from embarrassment? If I die in a state of grace, my timeless paradise will be the secret garden of the woman I love best.

At all events, cosmic science has done us the service of suggesting that time is no more than a useful terrestrial convention. Instead we are offered a time-space continuum in which the moment of miracle not only has its place but can be endlessly observed from endless points of vantage. In fact, cosmically speaking, to demand an after-life is to count on occupying two places at once in the time-space continuum—which is as greedy as plural voting.

Since we are able by miracle to forsee the future and re-create the past, even in our own lifetimes, what more can we ask? If we have lived our life amiss, and hope to do better next time, even a late repentance and renascence seem better than another try. If we have led poor miserable lives, there must always have been compensations, else we should have simply died; my own conviction is that rewards and punishments are neatly balanced in this world. My old nurse used to sing:

> Count your blessings, count them one by one
> And it will surprise you what the Lord hath done.

Granted, a continuous sense of gratitude at being alive, and in love, and having no grudge against practical circumstances—if only because of having obstinately avoided being enslaved by them— may imply that the dedicated poet has been constantly wounded and bruised by attempting the impossible. Will his poems then figure as durable records of blessedness, or will they do no more than convey, truthfully, the darkness of his self-deception? This seems to me a philosophical, and therefore irrelevant, question. A poet's destiny is to love.

A few years ago, after an emotional crisis, I wrote a poem advising myself to be content with the mild pleasures of old age and in-action:

> Into your outstretched hands come pouring
> Gifts by the cornucopiaful—
> > What else is lacking?
> Come, enjoy your Sunday
> While yet you may!
>
> Cease from unnecessary labours,
> Saunter into the green world stretching far,
> > Light a long cigar,
> Come, enjoy your Sunday
> While yet you may!
>
> What more, what more? You fended off disaster
> In a long war, never acknowledging
> > Any man as master;
> Come, enjoy your Sunday
> While yet you may!
>
> Are you afraid of death? But death is nothing:
> The leaden seal set on a filled flask.
> > If it be life you ask,
> Come, enjoy your Sunday
> While yet you may!

On a warm sand-dune now, sprawling at ease
With little in mind, learn to despise the sea's
   Unhuman restlessness:
Come, enjoy your Sunday
While yet you may!

But it was already another Monday morning; the Moon being in-
sistent in her demands:

In the last sad watches of night
Hardly a sliver of light will remain
To edge the guilty shadow of a waned moon
That dawn must soon devour.
                   Thereafter, another
Crescent queen shall arise with power—
So wise a beauty never yet seen, say I:
A true creature of moon, though not the same
In nature, name or feature—
Her innocent eye rebuking inconstancy
As if Time itself should die and disappear.

So was it ever. "She is here again," I sigh.